CHEESE:
CHEMISTRY, PHYSICS AND MICROBIOLOGY

Volume 1

General Aspects

CHEESE: CHEMISTRY, PHYSICS AND MICROBIOLOGY

Volume 1
General Aspects

Edited by

P. F. FOX

*Department of Dairy and Food Chemistry, University College,
Cork, Ireland*

ELSEVIER APPLIED SCIENCE
LONDON and NEW YORK

ELSEVIER APPLIED SCIENCE PUBLISHERS LTD
Crown House, Linton Road, Barking, Essex IG11 8JU, England

Sole Distributor in the USA and Canada
ELSEVIER SCIENCE PUBLISHING CO., INC.
52 Vanderbilt Avenue, New York, NY 10017, USA

WITH 30 TABLES AND 84 ILLUSTRATIONS

© ELSEVIER APPLIED SCIENCE PUBLISHERS LTD 1987

British Library Cataloguing in Publication Data

Cheese: chemistry, physics and microbiology.
1. Cheese
I. Fox, P. F.
637'.3   SF271

Library of Congress Cataloging-in-Publication Data

Cheese: chemistry, physics, and microbiology.

Bibliography: p.
Includes index.
Contents: v. 1. General aspects—v. 2. Major cheese
groups.
1. Cheese. 2. Cheese—Varieties. I. Fox, P. F.
SF271.C43 1987   637'.3   86-24288

ISBN 1-85166-052-6 (v. 1)
ISBN 1-85166-053-4 (v. 2)
ISBN 1-85166-054-2 (set)

The selection and presentation of material and the opinions expressed are the sole responsibility of the author(s) concerned.

Printed in Great Britain by Galliard (Printers) Ltd, Great Yarmouth

Preface

Cheese manufacture is one of the classical examples of food preservation, dating from 6000–7000 BC. Preservation of the most important constituents of milk (i.e. fat and protein) as cheese exploits two of the classical principles of food preservation, i.e.: lactic acid fermentation, and reduction of water activity through removal of water and addition of NaCl. Establishment of a low redox potential and secretion of antibiotics by starter micro-organisms contribute to the storage stability of cheese.

About 500 varieties of cheese are now produced throughout the world; present production is $\sim 10^7$ tonnes per annum and is increasing at a rate of $\sim 4\%$ per annum. Cheese manufacture essentially involves gelation of the casein via isoelectric (acid) or enzymatic (rennet) coagulation; a few cheeses are produced by a combination of heat and acid and still fewer by thermal evaporation. Developments in ultrafiltration facilitate the production of a new family of cheeses. Cheeses produced by acid or heat/acid coagulation are usually consumed fresh, and hence their production is relatively simple and they are not particularly interesting from the biochemical viewpoint although they may have interesting physico-chemical features. Rennet cheeses are almost always ripened (matured) before consumption through the action of a complex battery of enzymes. Consequently they are in a dynamic state and provide fascinating subjects for enzymologists and microbiologists, as well as physical chemists.

Researchers on cheese have created a very substantial literature, including several texts dealing mainly with the technological aspects of

v

cheese production. Although certain chemical, physical and microbiological aspects of cheese have been reviewed extensively, this is probably the first attempt to review comprehensively the scientific aspects of cheese manufacture and ripening. The topics applicable to most cheese varieties, i.e. rennets, starters, primary and secondary phases of rennet coagulation, gel formation, gel syneresis, salting, proteolysis, rheology and nutrition, are reviewed in Volume 1. Volume 2 is devoted to the more specific aspects of the nine major cheese families: Cheddar, Dutch, Swiss, Iberian, Italian, Balkan, Middle Eastern, Mould Ripened and Smear Ripened. A chapter is devoted to non-European cheeses, many of which are ill-defined; it is hoped that the review will stimulate scientific interest in these minor, but locally important, varieties. The final chapter is devoted to processed cheeses.

It is hoped that the book will provide an up-to-date reference on the scientific aspects of this fascinating group of ancient, yet ultramodern, foods; each chapter is extensively referenced. It will be clear that a considerable body of scientific knowledge on the manufacture and ripening of cheese is currently available but it will be apparent also that many major gaps exist in our knowledge; it is hoped that this book will serve to stimulate scientists to fill these gaps.

I wish to thank sincerely the other 26 authors who contributed to the text and whose co-operation made my task as editor a pleasure.

P. F. Fox

Contents

List of Contributors

T. M. COGAN
The Agricultural Institute, Moorepark Research Centre, Fermoy, Co. Cork, Ireland

D. G. DALGLEISH
Hannah Research Institute, Ayr, Scotland KA6 5HL, UK

C. DALY
Department of Food Microbiology, University College, Cork, Ireland

H. J. M. VAN DIJK
Central Laboratory, Melkunie-Holland, Woerden, The Netherlands

BENT FOLTMANN
Institute of Biochemical Genetics, University of Copenhagen, 2A Øster Farimagsgade, DK-1353 Copenhagen K, Denmark

P. F. FOX
Department of Dairy and Food Chemistry, University College, Cork, Ireland

T. J. GEURTS
Department of Food Science, Agricultural University, De Dreijen 12, 6703 BC Wageningen, The Netherlands

ALISTAIR S. GRANDISON
AFRC Institute of Food Research (University of Reading), Shinfield, Reading RG2 9AT, UK

ix

MARGARET L. GREEN
AFRC Institute of Food Research (University of Reading), Shinfield, Reading RG2 9AT, UK

T. P. GUINEE
Department of Dairy and Food Chemistry, University College, Cork, Ireland

BARRY A. LAW
AFRC Institute of Food Research (University of Reading), Shinfield, Reading RG2 9AT, UK

J. H. PRENTICE
Formerly Food Research Institute, Shinfield, Reading RG2 9AT, UK. Present address: Rivendell, 3 Millbrook Dale, Axminster, Devon EX13 7TF, UK

E. RENNER
Justus-Liebig-Universität, Bismarckstrasse 16, D-6300 Giessen, Federal Republic of Germany

P. WALSTRA
Department of Food Science, Agricultural University, De Dreijen 12, 6703 BC Wageningen, The Netherlands

Chapter 1

Cheese: An Overview

P. F. Fox

*Department of Dairy and Food Chemistry,
University College, Cork, Ireland*

1. HISTORICAL

Cheese is the generic name for a group of fermented milk-based food products produced in at least 500 varieties throughout the world. From humble beginnings, simply as a means of conserving milk constituents, cheese has evolved to become a food of *haute cuisine* with epicurean qualities, as well as being highly nutritious. Sandine and Elliker[1] suggest that there are more than 1000 cheese varieties. Walter and Hargrove[2] describe more than 400 varieties and list the names of a further 400, while Burkhalter[3] classified 510 varieties (although some varieties are listed more than once).

It is commonly believed that cheese originated in the 'Fertile Crescent' between the Tigris and Euphrates, in what is now Iraq, some 8000 years ago. Cheese is just one of many major items of food and agricultural practice that originated in this area, frequently referred to as the cradle of civilization. It is very likely that cheese originated accidentally; at some stage in pre-history, Man realized the nutritive value of milk produced by his domesticated animals (domestication of dairy animals, initially sheep and goats and later cattle, occurred 8–10 000 years BC), and contrived to share the mother's milk with her offspring. Unfortunately, milk is also a rich source of nutrients for bacteria, some species of which utilize milk sugar, lactose, as a source of energy, producing lactic acid as a by-product. Such growth might have occurred during storage or during attempts to dry milk in the prevailing warm, dry atmosphere to produce a more stable product—air-drying of meat and probably fruit and vegetables appears to

1

have been practised as a primitive form of food preservation at this period in Man's evolution. When sufficient acid has been produced, the milk protein coagulates, i.e. at the isoelectric point of casein, to form a gel entrapping the fat; the world's first fermented dairy foods were probably produced thus and similar products are still popular in the Middle-East and in other parts of the world.

If the milk gel is broken, e.g. accidentally by movement of the storage vessels or intentionally by breaking or cutting, it separates into curds and whey. It would have been realized quickly that the whey made a pleasant, refreshing drink for immediate consumption while the curd could be consumed fresh or stored for future use. It was probably soon realized that the shelf-life of the curd could be greatly extended by dehydration and/or by addition of salt; heavily-salted cheese varieties (e.g. Feta and Domiati) are still widespread throughout the Middle-East.

This is the presumed origin of one group of cheeses—the acid cheeses—modern members of which include Cottage cheese, cream cheese, Quarg and Queso Blanco. While lactic acid, produced *in situ*, is believed to have been the original milk coagulant, an alternative mechanism was also recognized from an early date. Many proteolytic enzymes can modify the milk protein system, causing it to coagulate under certain circumstances. Enzymes capable of causing this transformation are widespread in nature, e.g. bacteria, moulds, plants and animal tissues but the most obvious source would have been animal stomachs. It would have been observed that the stomachs of slaughtered young animals frequently contained curd, especially if the animals had suckled shortly before slaughter; curd would also have been observed in the vomit of human infants. Storage of milk in bags made from stomach was probably common (as it still is in many countries); under such circumstances milk would extract coagulating enzymes from the stomach tissue, leading to coagulation during storage.

The properties of rennet curds are very different from those produced by isoelectric (acid) precipitation, e.g. they have better syneresis properties which make it possible to produce low-moisture cheese curd without hardening. Rennet curd can therefore be converted to a more stable product than acid curds and rennet coagulation has become predominant in cheese manufacture, being responsible for the vast majority of modern cheese varieties. Although animal rennets were probably the first enzyme coagulants used, rennets produced from a range of plant species appear to have been common in the period BC. However, plant rennets are not suitable for the manufacture of long-ripened cheese varieties and rennets from young animals were the standard rennets for several thousand years. They are still regarded as the best rennets but shortage of supply has made it necessary to introduce 'rennet substitutes', as will be discussed later.

Cheese manufacture obviously accompanied the spread of civilization throughout the Middle-East, Egypt, Greece and Rome. There are several references in the Old Testament to cheese, e.g. Job (1520 BC), and Samuel (1170–1017 BC) and in classical Greek literature, e.g. Homer (1184 BC), Herodotus (484–408 BC), Aristotle (384–322 BC). Apparently, cheese was prescribed for the diet of Spartan wrestlers in training. Cheese manufacture was well established by the time of the Roman empire and was a standard item in the rations issued to Roman soldiers. Cheese must have been popular with Roman civilians also and demand must have exceeded supply because the Emperor Diocletian (AD 284–305) fixed a maximum price for cheese. Many Roman writers, e.g. Varro (116 BC), Columella (AD 50), Pliny (AD 23–89), wrote at some length on cheese manufacture and quality; Columella, in particular, gave a detailed account of cheese manufacture in his treatise on agriculture, *De Re Rustica*.

Movements of Roman armies and administrators would have spread the use of cheese throughout the then known world. Although archaeological evidence suggests that cheese may have been manufactured in pre-Roman Britain, the first unequivocal evidence credits the Romans with the establishment of cheesemaking in Britain. Palladius wrote a treatise on Roman-British farming in the 4th century AD, including a description of and advice on cheesemaking. Cheesemaking practice appears to have changed little from the time of Columella and Palladius until the 19th century.

The great migrations of peoples throughout Europe after the fall of the Roman Empire must have promoted the further spread of cheese manufacture, as must the Crusaders and other pilgrims of the Middle Ages. However, possibly the most important agents contributing to the development of cheese 'technology' and to the evolution of cheese varieties were the monasteries and the feudal estates. In addition to their roles in the spread of Christianity and to the preservation and expansion of knowledge during the Dark Ages, the monasteries made a considerable contribution to the advancement of agriculture in Europe and to the development and improvement of food commodities, notably wines and cheeses. Many of our current well-known cheese varieties were developed in monasteries, e.g. Wensleydale (Rievaulx Abbey, Yorkshire), Port du Salut or Saint Paulin (Monastery de Notre Dame du Port du Salut, Laval, France), Fromage de Tamie (Abbey of Tamie Lac d'Annecy, Geneva),

Maroilles (Abbey Maroilles, Avesnes, France); Trappist (Maria Stern Monastery, Banja Luka, Bosnia). The inter-monastery movement of monks would have contributed to the spread of cheese varieties and probably to the development of hybrid varieties. The great feudal estates of the Middle Ages were self-contained communities. The conservation of surplus summer food for winter use was a major activity on such estates and undoubtedly cheese represented one of the more important of these conserved products, along with cereals, dried and salted meats, beer and wine. Cheese probably represented an item of trade when amounts surplus to local requirements were available. Within these estates, individuals acquired special skills which were passed on to succeeding generations. The feudal estates evolved into villages and some, later, into larger communities.

Because monasteries and feudal estates were essentially self-contained communities, it is readily apparent how several hundred distinct varieties of cheese could have evolved from essentially the same raw material, milk or rennet curd. Almost certainly, these varieties arose by accident because of a particular set of local circumstances, e.g. a peculiarity of the local milk supply, either with respect to chemical composition or microflora, an 'accident' during storage of the cheese, e.g. growth of mould or other micro-organisms. Presumably, those accidents that led to desirable changes in the quality of the cheese would have been incorporated into the manufacturing protocol; each variety would thus have undergone a series of evolutionary changes and refinements.

Cheesemaking remained an art rather than a science until relatively recently. With the gradual acquisition of knowledge on the chemistry and microbiology of milk and cheese, it became possible to direct the changes involved in cheesemaking in a more controlled fashion. Although few new varieties have evolved as a result of this improved knowledge, the existing varieties have become better defined and their quality more consistent. Considering the long history of cheesemaking, we might be inclined to the idea that what we have come to regard as standard varieties have been so for a long time. However, although the names of many modern varieties appeared several hundred years ago (Table I) these cheeses were not standardized; for example, the first attempts to standardize the well-known English varieties, Cheddar and Cheshire, were made by John Harding and his family in the mid-19th century. Prior to that, 'Cheddar cheese' was that produced in a particular area in England around the village of Cheddar, Somerset, and probably varied considerably depending on the manufacturer and other factors. It must also be

TABLE I
First recorded date for some major varieties[a]

Gorgonzola	879	Cheddar	1 500
Schabzieger	1 000	Parmesan	1 579
Roquefort	1 070	Gouda	1 697
Maroilles	1 174	Gloucester	1 783
Schwangenkäse	1 178	Stilton	1 785
Grana	1 200	Camembert	1 791
Taleggio	1 282	St. Paulin	1 816

[a] From Scott.[4]

remembered that cheese manufacture was a farmstead enterprise until the mid-19th century—the first cheese factory in the US was established near Rome, New York, in 1851 and the first in Britain at Longford, Derbyshire, in 1870. Thus, there were thousands of cheese manufacturers and there must have been great variation within any one general type. When one considers the very considerable inter-factory, and indeed intra-factory, variation in quality and characteristics which still occur today in well-defined varieties such as Cheddar, in spite of the very considerable scientific and technological advances, one can readily appreciate the variation that must have existed in earlier times.

A major source of variation in the characteristics of cheese resides in the species from which the milk was produced. Although milks from several species are used in cheese manufacture, the cow is by far the most important; sheep, goat and buffalo are commercially important in certain areas. There are very significant interspecies differences in the composition of milk which are reflected in the characteristics of the cheeses produced from them. There are also significant differences in milk composition between breeds of cattle and these also influence cheese quality, as do variations due to seasonal, lactational, nutritional and manufacturing factors.

The final chapter in the spread of cheese throughout the world resulted from the colonization of North and South America, Oceania and Africa by European settlers who carried their cheesemaking skills with them. Cheese has become an item of major economic importance in some of these 'new' countries, notably the US, Canada, Australia and New Zealand, but the varieties produced are mainly of European origin, modified in some cases to meet local requirements. It is not certain whether or not cheeses were manufactured in these regions before colonization by Europeans but in most cases, probably not. For further information on the history of cheese, the reader is referred to Refs 4–7.

2. CHEESE PRODUCTION AND CONSUMPTION

World cheese production was $\sim 12 \times 10^6$ tonnes in 1982 and has increased at an average annual rate of $\sim 4\%$ over the past 20 years.[8,9] Europe, with a production of $\sim 6 \times 10^6$ tonnes p.a., is by far the largest producing block; North America and USSR, with populations approximately similar to Europe, produce approximately 50% and 25% of European production, respectively (Table II).

TABLE II
Regional world production of cheese, 1982[a]

	Tonnes $\times 10^3$	*% of Total*
Africa	389	3·25
North and Central America	2 687	22·43
South America	457	3·82
Asia	758	6·33
Europe	5 899	49·24
USSR	1 525	12·73
Oceania	264	2·20

[a] From Ref. 8.

Cheese consumption varies widely between countries, even within Europe; it is noteworthy that with the exception of Israel, no Asian, African or South American country is listed among the top 25 cheese-consuming countries (Table III).[10] Cheese consumption in most reporting countries has increased considerably since 1970.[9]

Thus, while cheese manufacture is practised worldwide, it is apparent from Tables II and III that cheese is primarily a product of European countries and those populated by European emigrants. With a few exceptions, notably Egypt, cheese is of relatively little importance in Asia, Africa and Latin America where diets are based much more strongly on plant than on animal products and where no tradition of dairying exists. However, cheese in some form is produced in most countries throughout the world and some interesting minor varieties are produced in 'non-dairying' countries (cf. Chapter 10, Volume 2).

TABLE III
Cheese consumption (kg per head) per annum, in the leading countries (1981)[a]

Rank	Country	Ripened cheeses	Fresh cheeses	Total
1	Greece	20·7	0·9	21·6
2	France	14·2	4·7	18·9
3	Iceland	7·3	7·1	14·4
4	Italy			14·3
5	FRG	7·9	6·2	14·1
6	Sweden	13·3	0·6	13·9
7	Israel	3·2	10·6	13·8
8	Belgium	11·2	2·4	13·6
9	The Netherlands	12·5	0·9	13·4
10	Switzerland	12·7	0·5	13·2
11	Norway	12·1	0·4	12·5
12	Poland	2·6	9·7	12·3
13	Denmark	10·5	0·4	10·9
14	Czechoslovakia	5·1	5·1	10·2
15	Luxembourg			10·2
16	USA	7·9	1·9	9·8
17	Canada	7·9	1·3	9·2
18	Austria	5·5	3·2	8·7
19	Finland	7·5	1·1	8·6
20	New Zealand			8·5
21	Australia			6·6
22	Hungary	3·0	3·6	6·6
23	United Kingdom	6·3	0·1	6·4
24	USSR			4·6
25	Spain			3·8
26	Ireland			3·6
27	Chile	1·8	0·3	2·1
28	South Africa	1·3		1·3
29	Japan			0·7

[a] From Ref. 10.

3. CHEESE SCIENCE AND TECHNOLOGY

Cheese is the most diverse group of dairy products and is arguably the most academically interesting and challenging. While many dairy products, if properly manufactured and stored, are, biologically and biochemically, very stable products, cheeses are, in contrast, biologically dynamic materials. Throughout manufacture and ripening, cheese production represents a finely orchestrated series of successive and concomitant biochemical events which, if in tune, lead to products with highly desirable aromas and flavours but if out of balance, off-flavours and odours result. Considering that, in general terms, a basically similar raw material (milks of a very limited number of species) is subjected to a manufacturing protocol, the general principles of which are common to most cheese varieties, it is fascinating that such a diverse range of products can be produced. No two batches, indeed no two cheeses, are identical.

A further important facet of cheese is the range of scientific disciplines involved: study of cheese manufacture and ripening involves the chemistry of milk constituents, microbiology, enzymology, flavour chemistry, rheology and chemical engineering.

It is not surprising, therefore, that many scientists have become involved in the study of cheese manufacture and ripening. A voluminous scientific and technological literature has accumulated, incuding several text-books[4−7,11−21] and chapters in many others. However, these textbooks deal mainly with cheese technology; this book will concentrate on the more scientific aspects of cheese.

The more general aspects of cheese manufacture, i.e. molecular properties of rennets, coagulation mechanism, curd syneresis, starters, salting, rheology, pre-concentration by ultrafiltration, proteolysis and nutritional aspects, which apply, more or less, to most cheese varieties, are considered in the first volume of this text. The second volume deals with specific aspects of the principal families of ripened cheeses.

The principal objective of this introductory chapter is to provide an integrated overview of cheese manufacture and ripening against which the more detailed later chapters may be highlighted. A second objective is to provide some recognition of non-rennet cheeses since the rest of the text concentrates exclusively on the rennet cheeses.

4. OUTLINE OF CHEESE MANUFACTURE

Although some soft cheese varieties are consumed fresh, i.e. without a ripening period, production of the vast majority of cheese varieties can be sub-divided into two well-defined phases, manufacture and ripening:

$$\text{Milk} \xrightarrow{\text{Manufacture}} \text{Fresh} \xrightarrow{\text{Ripening}} \text{Mature}$$

$$\begin{array}{ccc} & \text{'green'} & \text{cheese} \\ & \text{cheese} & \\ & \text{curd} & \end{array}$$

The manufacturing phase might be defined as those operations performed during the first 24 h, although some of these operations, e.g. salting and dehydration, may continue over a longer period. Although the manufacturing protocols for individual varieties differ in detail, the basic steps are common to most varieties; these are:

acidification,
coagulation,
dehydration (cutting the coagulum, cooking, stirring, pressing, salting
    and any other operation that promotes gel syneresis),
shaping (moulding and pressing),
salting.

Cheese manufacture is essentially a dehydration process in which the fat and casein in milk are concentrated between six- and twelvefold, depending on the variety. The degree of hydration is regulated by the extent and combination of the above five operations, in addition to the chemical composition of the milk. In turn, the level of moisture in the cheese, the salt content and the cheese microflora regulate the biochemical changes that occur during ripening and hence determine the flavour, aroma and texture of the finished cheese. Thus, the nature and quality of the finished cheese are determined in very large measure by the manufacturing steps. However, it is during the ripening phase that the characteristic flavour and texture of the individual cheese varieties develop.

4.1 Selection and Pre-treatment of Cheese Milk

Cheese manufacture commences with the selection of milk of high microbiological and chemical quality. The importance of microbiological quality will not be considered here; suffice it to say that milk of the highest quality should be used with particular attention being paid to *Clostridium tyrobutyricum* in milk to be used for Dutch and Swiss cheese varieties. Obviously, cheese milk must be free of antibiotics. The importance of the chemical quality of cheese milk can best be treated in the chapters dealing with the rennet coagulation of milk and subsequent chapters on curd tension, gel syneresis and cheese texture.

In modern commercial practice, cheese milk is normally cooled to 4°C immediately after milking and may be held at about this temperature for several days on the farm and at the factory. Apart from the development of an undesirable psychrotrophic microflora, cold-storage causes physico-chemical changes (changes in calcium phosphate equilibrium and dissociation of some micellar caseins) which have undesirable effects on the cheesemaking properties of the milk; these changes will be discussed at some length in several subsequent chapters.

Although raw milk is still used in both commercial and farm-house cheesemaking operations, most cheese milk is now pasteurized, usually immediately prior to use. Pasteurization alters the indigenous microflora and facilitates the manufacture of cheese of more uniform quality, but unless due care is exercised, it may damage the rennet coagulation and curd-forming properties of the milk, as will be discussed in later chapters.

4.2 Acidification

The first and one of the basic operations in the manufacture of most, if not all, cheese varieties is a progressive development of acidity throughout the manufacturing stage, i.e. up to 24 h, and for some varieties during the early stages of ripening also, i.e. acidification commences before and transcends the other manufacturing operations. Acidification occurs via *in situ* production of lactic acid. Until relatively recently, the indigenous microflora was relied upon for acid production. Since this was probably a mixed microflora, the rate of acid production was unpredictable and the growth of desirable lactic acid-producing bacteria was usually parallelled by the growth of undesirable bacteria leading to the production of gas and off-flavours. It is now almost universal practice to add a culture (a starter) of selected lactic acid-producing bacteria to the pasteurized cheese milk to achieve a uniform and predictable rate of acid production. For cheese varieties that are cooked to not more than 40°C, a starter consisting of *Streptococcus lactis* and/or *Str. cremoris* is normally used while a mixed culture of *Str. thermophilus* and *Lactobacillus* spp (*L. bulgaricus, L. helviticus, L. casei*) or a *Lactobacillus* culture alone is used for varieties that are 'cooked' to higher temperatures, e.g. Swiss and hard Italian varieties.

Originally, and in many countries still, mixed-strain mesophilic starters were used. Because the bacterial strains in these starters may be phage-related (i.e. subject to infection by a single strain of bacteriophage) and also because the strains in the mixture may be incompatible, thereby leading to the dominance of one or a few strains, the rate of acid production by mixed-strain starters is variable and unpredictable, even when utmost care in their selection and handling is exercised. To overcome these problems, single-strain starters were introduced in New Zealand about 1935. Unfortunately, many of the fast acid-producing, single-strain starters produced bitter cheese, the cause(s) of which will be discussed in later chapters. This problem was resolved by using selected pairs of fast and slow acid producers. The current practice in many countries is to use a mixture (cocktail) of 3–6 selected, phage-unrelated strains which give very reproducible rates of acid production if properly selected and maintained.

The science and technology of starters have become highly developed and specialized; Chapter 6, Volume 1, is devoted to these developments. Other reviews on starters include Refs 22–30.

Acid production at the appropriate rate and time is the key step in the manufacture of good quality cheese (excluding the enzymatic coagulation of the milk, which is a *sine qua non* for rennet cheese varieties). Acid production affects several aspects of cheese manufacture, many of which will be discussed in more detail in later chapters, i.e.:

1. Coagulant activity during coagulation.
2. Denaturation and retention of the coagulant in the curd during manufacture and hence the level of residual coagulant in the curd and thus the rate of proteolysis, with its various consequences, during ripening.
3. Curd strength, which influences cheese yield.
4. Gel syneresis, which controls cheese moisture and hence regulates the growth of bacteria and the activity of enzymes in the cheese; it thus strongly influences the rate and pattern of ripening and the quality of the finished cheese.
5. The rate of pH decline determines the extent of dissolution of colloidal calcium phosphate which modifies the susceptibility of the caseins to proteolysis during manufacture and influences the rheological properties of the cheese, e.g. compare the texture of Gouda, Cheddar and Cheshire cheese.
6. Acidification controls the growth of many species of non-starter bacteria in cheese, especially pathogens, food poisoning and gas-producing micro-organisms—in fact properly-made cheese is a very safe product from the public health viewpoint. In addition to acid production, many starter bacteria produce antibiotics that also check the growth of non-starter micro-organisms.

Mesophilic *Streptococci* are capable of reducing the pH of cheese to 4·9–5·0 and *Lactobacilli* to somewhat lower values, perhaps 4·6. Thus, the natural ultimate pH of cheese curd falls within the range 4·6–5·1. However, the period required to attain the ultimate pH varies from ~5 h for Cheddar to 6–12 h for Blue, Dutch and Swiss varieties. The differences arise from the amount of starter added to the cheese milk (0·2–5%) and the cooking schedule which may check the growth of the starter micro-organisms. The pH of Blue cheese curd is 6·1 at draining and decreases in a smooth curve to 5·1 within 6 h. The pH of Gouda curd also decreases smoothly whereas that of the Cheddar is irregular; this is due to the higher cooking temperature used in the latter which retards the rate of acid development during cooking.

Acidification is more complex in Emmental and Gruyère cheeses which are cooked to high temperatures (53–56°C) and in which the starters (*L. helveticus* and *Str. thermophilus*) grow mainly after pressing. The curd is placed in the press at 50°C and cools during pressing at markedly different rates at the periphery and centre; hence the rate of starter growth and the extent of acid development vary throughout a cheese (cf. Ref. 31). This results in a lactic acid gradient from the outer to the centre zones of the cheese which approaches equilibrium, due to diffusion, as the cheese ages. The concentration of lactic acid and pH influence the development of *Propionibacteria shermanii* and hence the amount of CO_2 development. Variations in pH probably also influence the functional properties of the cheese proteins and hence the cheese texture. Both the rate of production and the volume of CO_2 and the rheological properties of the protein matrix control eye development, number and distribution, which is an essential feature of these cheese varieties.

The level and method of salting have a major influence on pH changes in cheese. The level of NaCl in cheese (commonly 0·7–4%, i.e. 2–10% salt in the moisture phase) is sufficient to halt the growth of starter bacteria. Some varieties, mostly of British origin, are salted by mixing dry salt with the curd toward the end of manufacture and hence the pH of curd for these varieties must be close to the ultimate value (pH 5·1) at salting. However, most varieties are salted by immersion in brine or by surface application of dry salt: as will be discussed in Chapter 7 (Volume 1), salt diffusion in cheese moisture is a slow process and thus there is ample time for the pH to decrease to ~5·0 before the salt concentration becomes inhibitory. The pH of the curd for most cheese varieties, e.g. Swiss, Dutch, Tilsit, Blue, etc., is 6·2–6·5 at the stage of moulding and pressing but decreases to 5 during or shortly after pressing and before salting. The significance of various aspects of the level and distribution of NaCl in cheese will be discussed in Chapter 7 (Volume 1).

In a few special cases, e.g. Domiati, a high level of NaCl (10–12%) is added to cheese milk, traditionally to control the growth of the indigenous microflora. This level of NaCl has a major influence, not only on acid development, but also on rennet coagulation, gel strength and syneresis (cf. Chapter 9, Volume 2).

4.3 Coagulation

The essential characteristic step in the manufacture of all cheese varieties involves coagulation of the casein component of the milk protein system to form a gel which entraps the fat, if present. Coagulation may be achieved by:

1. Limited proteolysis by selected proteinases.
2. Acidification to $\sim$pH 4·6.
3. Acidification to pH values $> 4·6$ (perhaps 5·2) in combination with heating.

The vast majority of cheeses are produced by enzymatic (rennet) coagulation. With a few exceptions (e.g. Sierra cheese (Portugal) in which a plant proteinase, from species of the genus *Cynara*, is used), acid (aspartate) proteinases of animal or fungal origin are used. Chymosin from the stomachs of young animals (calves, kids, lambs, buffalo) were traditionally used as rennets but decreased supplies of such rennets (due to the increasing trend in many countries to slaughter calves at an older age than previously), concomitant with a worldwide increase in cheese production has led to a shortage of calf rennet and consequently rennet substitutes (usually bovine and porcine pepsins and less frequently chicken pepsin, and the acid proteinases from *Mucor miehei* and less frequently *M. pusillus* and *Endothia parasitica*) are now used widely for cheese manufacture in many countries with more or less satisfactory results. Reviews on rennet substitutes include Refs 32–39.

The molecular and enzymatic properties of calf chymosin and other acid proteinases used as rennets are reviewed in detail in Chapter 2 (Volume 1).

Although it appears to have been recognized since 1917 (cf. Ref. 40) that milk is not clotted by rennet at temperatures $< \sim 15°C$, even though the enzyme alters the protein at low temperatures, Berridge[40] is usually credited with clearly demonstrating that the rennet coagulation process occurs in two phases: a primary enzymatic phase and a secondary non-enzymatic phase. The primary phase has a temperature coefficient ($Q_{10^\circ C}$) of ~ 2 and occurs down to $0^\circ C$ while the secondary phase has a $Q_{10^\circ C}$ of ~ 16 and occurs very slowly or not at all at low temperatures ($< \sim 15^\circ C$). The two phases can thus be readily separated by performing the primary phase at $< 15^\circ C$; if renneted milk is warmed, coagulation occurs very quickly. Cold renneting, followed by rapid warming, forms the basis of attempts to develop methods for the continuous coagulation of milk. In normal commercial rennet coagulation, the two phases overlap to some extent, the magnitude of overlap being quite high at low pH, high temperatures and in milks concentrated by ultrafiltration (cf. Ref. 41).

The primary phase of rennet action appears to have been recognized, in general terms, by Hammersten (1880–90) who observed the formation of small peptides. Views on rennet coagulation were extended by Linderstrom-Lang in the 1920s but a full explanation of the process had to await the isolation of the casein micelle-protective protein, κ-casein, by Waugh and von Hipple.[42] These workers showed that the protective capacity of κ-casein was destroyed on renneting and Wake[43] demonstrated that κ-casein is the only milk protein hydrolysed during the primary phase of rennet action. Only one peptide bond, Phe (105)–Met (106), is hydrolysed[44] resulting in the release of the hydrophilic C-terminal segment of κ-casein (the (caseino) macropeptides, some of which are glycosylated). The unique sensitivity of the Phe–Met bond of κ-casein, hydrolysis of which occurs optimally at pH $5 \cdot 1$–$5 \cdot 5$ (Ref. 45) has been the subject of extensive study since 1965 and this work is reviewed in Chapter 3 (Volume 1).

Since κ-casein is the principal factor stabilizing the casein micelles (cf. Refs 46, 47), its hydrolysis causes destabilization of the 'residual' (para-casein) micelles in the presence of a critical concentration of Ca^{2+} at temperatures $> \sim 18^\circ C$ in the secondary, non-enzymatic phase of rennet coagulation. Although the precise mechanism has not yet been described, the kinetics of the process can be described by the theory of Smoluchkovski for the slow aggregation of hydrophobic colloids. It has been known for some time that hydrolysis of κ-casein in the primary phase of rennet action reduces the zeta potential of the residual micelles to about 50% of that of the native micelles and presumably this is a major contributor to coagulation, although a critical concentration of Ca^{2+} and a minimum temperature are required for coagulation. It is also well known that reduction of the colloidal calcium phosphate (CCP) content of the casein micelles prevents coagulation unless the $[Ca^{2+}]$ is increased.[48] This is perhaps unexpected since CCP-free milk is unstable to Ca^{2+}; to our knowledge, the Ca-sensitivity of renneted CCP-free milk has not been investigated. Perhaps disruption of the micellar structure by removal of CCP alters the 'conformation' of the micelles such that a protein gel network cannot be formed.

Recent work on the secondary phase of rennet coagulation is reviewed in Chapters 3 and 4 (Volume 1).

The visual coagulation of milk is really only the start of the gelation process which continues for a considerable period thereafter. Although it is these post-coagulation changes which determine many of the critical cheesemaking properties of the gel, e.g. curd tension (with its influence on cheese yield) and syneresis properties (which determine the moisture content and hence the ripening profile of the cheese), it is perhaps the least-well understood phase of the cheesemaking process. The recent literature on aspects of the post-visual coagulation phase is reviewed in Chapters 4 and 5 (Volume 1).

4.4 Post-coagulation Operations

A rennet gel is quite stable if maintained under quiescent conditions but if it is cut or broken, it synereses rapidly, expelling whey. The rate and extent of syneresis are influenced, *inter alia*, by milk composition, especially $[Ca^{2+}]$ and [casein], pH of the whey, cooking temperature, rate of stirring of the curd–whey mixture and of course, time. The composition of the finished cheese is to a very large degree determined by the extent of syneresis, and since this is readily under the control of the cheesemaker, it is here that the differentiation of the individual cheese varieties really begins although the composition of cheese milk, the amount and type of starter and the amount and type of rennet are also significant in this regard. The unique manufacturing schedules for the specific varieties are not considered in this text and the interested reader should consult appropriate texts (Refs 2, 4, 11–21). Some chemical and physico-chemical aspects of the manufacture of the major cheese families are discussed in Volume 2.

The last manufacturing operation is salting. While salting contributes to syneresis, it should not be relied upon as a means of controlling the moisture content of cheese. Salt has several functions in cheese which are described in Chapter 7 (Volume 1). Although salting should be a very simple operation, quite frequently it is not performed properly with consequent adverse effects on cheese quality.

As indicated previously, cheese manufacture is essentially a dehydration process. With the development of ultrafiltration as a concentration process it was obvious that this process would have applications in cheese manufacture not only for standardization of cheese milk with respect to fat and casein but more importantly for the preparation of a concentrate with the composition of the finished cheese, commonly referred to as 'pre-cheese'. Standardization of cheese milk by adding UF concentrate (retentate) is now common in some countries but the manufacture of pre-cheese has to date been successful commercially only for certain cheese varieties, most notably Feta and Quarg. Undoubtedly, the use of ultrafiltration will become much more widespread in cheese manufacture.

5. RIPENING

Some cheeses are consumed fresh and as indicated in Table III, fresh cheeses constitute a major proportion of the cheese consumed in some countries; some fresh cheeses are discussed briefly below. However, most cheese varieties are not ready for consumption at the end of manufacture but undergo a period of ripening (curing, maturation) which varies from ~ 4 weeks to > 2 years, the duration of ripening being generally inversely related to the moisture content of the cheese, although many varieties may be consumed at any of several stages of maturity depending on the flavour preferences of consumers.

Although curds for different cheese varieties are recognizably different at the end of manufacture (mainly as a result of compositional and textural differences which in turn arise from both milk compositional and processing factors), the unique characteristics of the individual cheeses develop during ripening although in most cases the biochemical changes that will occur during ripening, and hence the flavour, aroma and texture of the mature cheese, are pre-determined largely by the manufacturing process, i.e. by composition, especially moisture, NaCl, pH, by type of starter and in many cases by secondary inocula added to the cheese milk or curd.

During ripening an extremely complex set of biochemical changes occur through the catalytic action of the following agencies:

1.   Coagulant.
2.   Starter bacteria and their enzymes.

3. Secondary microflora and their enzymes. These microflora may arise from the indigenous microflora of milk that survive pasteurization or gain entry to the milk after pasteurization, e.g. *Lactobacilli, Pediococci,* or they may arise through the use of a secondary starter, e.g. *Propionibacteria* in Swiss cheese, *Penicillium roqueforti* in Blue varieties, *P. caseicolum* in Camembert or Brie or the cheese may acquire surface microflora from the environment during ripening, e.g. *Brevibacterium linens* in Tilsit, Limburger, Munster, etc. The characteristics of the finished cheeses are dominated by the metabolism of these micro-organisms in many cases.

4. Indigenous milk enzymes, especially proteinase and lipase, which are particularly important in cheese made from raw milk.

The primary biochemical changes involve glycolysis, lipolysis and proteolysis but these primary changes are followed and overlapped by a host of secondary catabolic changes, including deamination, decarboxylation, desulphurization, β-oxidation and even some synthetic changes, e.g. esterification.

It is impossible to review the biochemistry involved in the ripening of all individual cheese varieties. Instead proteolysis, which is considered by many researchers to be the principal ripening reaction in many cheese varieties, in general, and the rheological properties of cheese are reviewed in Chapters 8 and 10 (Volume 1). More detailed discussions of specific aspects of the ripening of the principal families of cheese, Cheddar, Dutch, Swiss, Iberian, Italian, Balkan, mould-ripened, bacterial surface-ripened, high-salt varieties and processed cheeses are given in Volume 2. An attempt has been made in Chapter 10 (Volume 2) to collate information on a number of minor but interesting non-European cheese varieties. In most cases, these varieties have not been well studied, microbiologically, biochemically or physically, and consequently the treatments are very superficial in comparison with those for the major varieties. Nevertheless, it was considered that some of these minor varieties warranted some mention; perhaps some interest will be generated in the study of these cheeses as a result.

While most of us consume cheese principally for its organoleptic qualities, it must be remembered that cheese is a very valuable source of nutrients, especially protein, calcium and phosphorus. The nutritional aspects of cheese are considered in Chapter 9 (Volume 1).

6. FRESH CHEESES

Most, if not all, of the cheeses coagulated by acid or a combination of heat and acid are unripened varieties. Coagulation occurs at the isoelectric point, $\sim$ pH 4·6, or at somewhat higher values when higher temperatures are used. Fresh acid cheeses are produced throughout the world and predominate in some countries (cf. Table III); they are quite important in underdeveloped countries (see Chapter 10, Volume 2). It is not possible to consider the numerous varieties of fresh cheeses here and only a few of the major varieties are considered briefly as examples.

6.1 Cottage

The name 'cottage' is applied to many fresh cheeses, produced originally on farms in Europe, but the name is now generally taken to refer to acid cheese developed in the USA and now quite popular in many other countries. The manufacture of this variety is described in some detail by Emmons,[49] Emmons and Tuckey[50] and Kosikowski.[19] The curd is normally prepared by the *in situ* production of lactic acid by starters consisting of *Str. lactis, Str. cremoris* and *Leuc. citrovorum* (for flavour production). The milk may also be acidified by direct acidification with preformed acid, acidogen or acid whey.[51–53] Direct acidification has obvious technological advantages, e.g. the manufacturing process may be completed in $\sim$ 35 min.[52] The body and texture of direct-acidified Cottage cheese is considered to be slightly inferior to that of the biologically cultured product but may be improved by 'pre-culturing' the milk to $\sim$ pH 6·0;[52] the beneficial effect is presumably due to proteinases secreted by the culture micro-organisms.

A continuous fermentation (CF) system for Cottage cheese manufacture was described by White and Ray[54] and the product therefrom compared with Cottage cheese made by the conventional process or by direct acidification (DA). Cheese made either by CF or DA had cutting times $\sim$ 33% those of conventionally-made cheese; the DA method required cooking times of only 40% those used in the conventional method. Cheese made by conventional or CF methods received higher flavour and texture scores than that made by DA.

The milk supply for Cottage cheese may be fresh, pasteurized (72°C for 15 s) skim milk or reconstituted skim milk powder; a more severely heated milk (90°C for 2–3 min) may also be used, in which case, the denatured whey proteins are included in the curd. Although not originally used, it is now normal practice to add a low level of rennet (1 ml per 500 litres) to the cheese milk to give a more firm coagulum with better syneresis characteristics. The desired pH is ~ 4.6, which may be reached in 5–16 h depending on the level (0.5–5%) of starter addition and the set temperature (22–32°C).

Perhaps the most distinctive feature of American Cottage cheese compared with other fresh acid cheese is that it is prepared in granular form. The coagulum is cut and cooked to 50–55°C over a 1.5 h period during which considerable syneresis occurs and the curd assumes a firm, meaty texture (the curd may also be held at the final temperature for 30–60 min). The whey is then removed and the curd washed 3 times with water at decreasing temperature: 30, 16 and 4°C. The purpose of washing is to remove residual lactose from the curd and thus stabilize the pH and extend its shelf-life.

The washed curd is normally salted ($\sim 1\%$ NaCl) and mixed with a creaming mix to give a level of $\sim 4\%$ fat in the finished cheese. The creaming mix may also contain any of a range of flavourings. A good quality product has a shelf-life of 1–2 weeks which may be extended by packaging in an atmosphere of CO_2, by freezing or freeze-drying. Several variants of Cottage cheese are described by Kosikowski.[19]

For nutritional reasons, there is interest in reducing the level of sodium in cheeses, including Cottage. Demott *et al.*,[55] who found the average Na content of Cottage cheese in Tennessee to be 4.57 mg/g, reported the production of satisfactory low-Na Cottage cheese by replacing up to 50% of the NaCl by KCl.

Based on the results of a survey of Cottage cheese manufacture in 6 large factories,[56,57] Dunkley and Patterson[57] identify the following areas as meriting further research: optimizing cooking conditions, influence of washing procedures on composition and properties of the curd, draining characteristics of the curd, increasing uniformity of cream absorbing properties of curd and consumer acceptance studies. The influence of cooking procedure on the properties of Cottage cheese curd was later studied by Chua and Dunkley[58] in laboratory-scale cheesemaking. The total solids in unwashed curd increased linearly with heating time (20–140 min) and temperature (42–64°C) and with heating rate (0.18–0.50°C/min) at a given temperature. Higher heating rates yielded a firmer curd but 'healing' time (5–40 min) and the duration of holding the curd in whey (0–40 min) did not influence the solids content of unwashed curd. Increasing the rate of agitation increased the solids content of the curd, the extent of curd breakage and hence the level of curd losses in the whey. The influence of pH (and the effects of gas-producing cultures thereon) at cutting on the yield and quality of Cottage cheese were investigated by Emmons and Beckett.[59,60] Studies on the manufacture of Cottage cheese from milk concentrated by ultrafiltration or dialfiltration to 25% protein were described by Covacevich and Kosikowski.[61] The product had a gelatin-like quality and absorbed cream dressing very poorly; retentate prepared by diafiltration with simultaneous fermentation gave the best but still an unsatisfactory product. Satisfactory Cottage cheese could be made from retentate diluted in water or permeate.[62]

An alternative approach to increasing cheese yield by incorporating whey proteins into the curd using sodium hexametaphosphate (and possibly other polyelectrolytes) was reported by Dybing *et al.*;[63] a slight increase in cheese yield was recorded without significant incorporation of whey proteins.

As with other cheeses, there is concern about the growth of psychro-trophs in milk used for Cottage cheese. The activity of extracellular pro-teinases secreted by these micro-organisms interferes with milk coagulation (perhaps causing complete failure), decreases yields (due to loss of casein peptides in the whey) and impairs quality and shelf-life.[64,65]

Electron microscopic studies on the microstructure of Cottage cheese[66] have shown that Cottage cheese is a uniform porous mass without a skin at the curd surface, as had been postulated previously.

6.2 Quarg (Quark, Tvarog (in Eastern Europe))

Quarg might be regarded as the German equivalent of Cottage cheese; 300 000 tonnes of Quarg per annum are produced in Germany with considerable quantities also in neighbouring countries. The product, which is enjoying a considerable increase in popularity in many European countries, is a very flexible food ingredient which may be consumed as such in natural or flavoured forms or may be included in several food recipes.

Quarg is normally made from pasteurized (72°C for 15 s) skim milk by acidification with a *Str. lactis/Str. cremoris* starter, usually including *Str. diacetylactis* for flavour development. The amount of starter may be varied from 1 to 5% to give a pH of ~4·7 in 6–16 h, as required, at 22–23°C. A low level of rennet (1–2 ml/100 litre) is usually added to give a more firm curd. Efforts to increase cheese yield have focussed on incorporating the whey proteins into the curd; this may be accomplished by (1) heating the cheese milk at 90–95°C for 1–5 min, (2) adding heat-denatured whey proteins to cheese milk, i.e. the Centri whey process, (3) mixing heat-denatured whey protein with regular Quarg, i.e. the Lactal process, (4) ultrafiltration. The flavour of the product is altered by ultrafiltration due to the higher calcium content but this may be resolved by ultrafiltering (at 35–40°C) the milk after partial or full acidification when the colloidal calcium has been solubilized and is removed on ultrafiltration.

After setting, the coagulum is broken and the whey removed from the uncooked curd/whey mixture, traditionally by filtration through cheesecloth bags or tables and more recently by centrifugation in special Quarg separators, which make large-scale production units feasible.

Quarg may also be produced from whole or partly skimmed milk, or skim milk Quarg may be mixed with cream to yield a range of products.

Obviously, the principles of manufacture for Quarg and Cottage cheese are very similar; they differ mainly in that Quarg has a smooth consistency, whereas Cottage is particulate, coagulum for Quarg is not cooked or washed and hence has a significant lactose content (Table IV).

Korolczuk *et al.*[67] have described a method for extending the shelf-life of Quarg: milk is acidified to pH 3·1–3·7 by a *L. acidophilus* starter (43°C for 16–18 h). The acidified milk is pasteurized at 65°C for 20 min, cooled to 25–30°C and then mixed with unacidified milk until the pH reaches 4·5–4·6 (usually 1 part of acidified milk to 1–2 parts of unacidified milk). Butter starter may be added to the mixture or the unacidified milk to impart flavour to the product.

Reviews on Quarg manufacture include Refs 68–73.

TABLE IV
Typical composition of some fresh acid cheeses

	Bakers[a]	Neufchatel[a]	Cream[a]	Petit Suisse[b]	Quarg[c,d]
Water	74	64	54	54·6	82
Fat	0·2	20·5	33·5	35	trace
Protein	19	12	9·8	7·3	12
Salt	0	0·75	0·75	—	—
Lactose	—	—	—	—	2·8
Ash	—	—	—	—	0·95

[a] From Kosikowski.[19]
[b] From Walter and Hargrove.[2]
[c] From Winwood.[71]
[d] Value for skim milk Quarg; may also be made from whole milk or cream may be added to skim milk Quarg.

6.3 Bakers', Neufchatel, Cream and Petit Suisse Cheeses

The principles and method of manufacture of these cheese varieties are very similar to that for Quarg. They are produced by *in situ* production of acid (or by direct acidification) of skim milk (Bakers'), whole milk (Neufchatel) or cream (Cream or Petit Suisse). The coagulated milk or cream ($\sim$pH 4·5) can be separated into curds and whey by filtration through cheesecloth bags or more recently by centrifugation. They may also be produced from pre-cheese prepared by ultrafiltration. The typical compositions of these cheeses are shown in Table IV.

Gums may be added to Neufchatel and Cream cheeses to improve texture and consistency and both may be heat-treated (74°C for 30 min) and homogenized (2500 psi) to produce a product with a longer shelf-life.[19]

6.4 Queso Blanco

Queso Blanco is the genetic name applied to a number of cheese varieties produced in Latin America (cf. Chapter 10, Volume 2) but a version of such cheese is now produced in the USA and is included here as a fresh cheese. It is produced in the USA by a combined heat–acid process which has been fairly extensively studied in recent years.

Siapantas and Kosikowski[74-76] used glacial acetic acid at 82°C as precipitant, while Chandan *et al.*[77] found that citric acid (pH 4·6–4·7, 82°C) gave best results. Torres and Chandan,[78] who reviewed the literature on Queso Blanco, described many of the variants and the various uses for the product. One of the interesting properties of the cheese is that it can be fried without melting and thus may be used in the preparation of various snack foods, e.g. breaded products. If a rennet curd rather than an acid curd is prepared it may be used as a base for a pasta filata-type cheese. It may be used as grating cheese for various applications including a mixture with tomato sauce called 'chorreada' to be used with potatoes or meat dishes. It may be mixed with various spices including chili sauce to yield a product called Queso Enchilado. It may also be made into a processed cheese.

Queso Blanco type cheeses are usually consumed fresh although they may be ripened for various periods. Torres and Chandan[79] investigated the possibility of improving the flavour and texture of Queso Blanco by addition of thermophilic (yoghurt) or mesophilic cultures or lipases (pregastric esterase) to the drained curd and ripening for up to 12 weeks. The impact of any of these treatments on the organoleptic qualities of the cheese depended on the age of the cheese and the improvement, if any, was slight.

Some textural characteristics of Queso Blanco were investigated by Parnell-Clunies et al.[80] Cheese hardness increased linearly with time over the 17 day test period and decreased significantly with increasing moisture content over the range 50–54%. Salting temperature had little effect on hardness but cheese salted at lower temperatures exhibited significantly more stress decay under constant strain.

6.5 Ricotta, Ricottone, Impastata

These soft Italian cheeses, also produced in the USA, are also coagulated by a combination of acid and heat. Ricotta is made from whole or partly skimmed milk or whey/skim milk mixtures.[19] The milk is acidified to pH 5·9–6·0 by addition of starter (which is used simply as an acidifying agent), acetic acid, citric acid (or other food grade acid) or acid whey. The mixture is heated at ~85°C for 15–30 min. The casein and some of the whey proteins coagulate, entrapping air, and float to the surface from which they are scooped off into perforated containers to drain for 4–6 h in a cold room. Typical compositions of some of the products, which are used in lasagna, ravioli, whipped desserts and pancake fillings, are shown in Table V.

Manufacture of good quality Ricotta from milk concentrated by ultrafiltration appears to be possible.[81]

TABLE V
Composition of Ricotta and Ricottone cheeses[a]

Type of cheese	Fat (%)	Protein (%)	Lactose (%)	Moisture (%)
Whole milk Ricotta (3·0–3·5% fat milk)	12·7	11·2	3·0	72·2
Part skim Ricotta (2% fat milk)	8·4	13·2	3·6	76·4
Part skim Ricotta (1% fat milk)	5·2	12·1	3·4	77·6
Ricottone (whey + skim milk)	0·5	11·3	1·5	82·5

[a] From Kosikowski.[19]

6.6 Mysost and Gjetost [82]

The method of manufacture of these Norwegian cheeses is unique and merits mention. They are produced by thermally concentrating whey (cheese or casein) to which milk or cream has been added; after concentration, controlled crystallization of lactose occurs. When made from cows' milk whey, the product is called Mysost, and Gjetost if made from goats' milk whey. The most common brand of Mysost, Gudbrandsdalsost (8000 tonnes p.a.), is made from a mixture of cow's whey and goats' whey (minimum of 1 litre/kg cheese) with added fat. Mysost made exclusively from goats' whey, Ekte Geitost, is produced in relatively small amounts (~ 2000 tonnes p.a.) while ~ 6500 tonnes of Mysost (Flotemysost) is made from cows' milk whey only.

Traditionally, the whey, with added cream, was concentrated in open iron kettles to the desired solids content, poured into troughs to cool with stirring to induce uniform lactose crystallization and then poured into moulds; considerable Maillard browning occurred. Modern production methods use vacuum pans for initial concentration followed by concentration to $\sim 80\%$ solids in special open kettles during which the characteristic brown colour develops. Cooling has to be carefully controlled to ensure the formation of small lactose crystals and avoid a sandy texture. The traditional product was rich in iron from the cooking kettles and it is now standard practice to add 10 mg iron per 100 g cheese, which makes Mysost an important source of iron in the Norwegian diet.

Mysost, which has a sweetish, caramelized taste, accounts for $\sim 25\%$ ($\sim 17\,000$ tonnes p.a.) of total cheese production in Norway. It is eaten, sliced, on bread at breakfast or lunch or as a snack. The cheese is not ripened and if properly packaged has a very long shelf-life. The typical composition of Gudbrandsdalsost is: fat $\sim 30\%$; lactose $\sim 37\%$; protein $\sim 11\%$; moisture $\sim 14\%$; and ash $\sim 9\%$.

7. CLASSIFICATION OF CHEESE

A considerable international trade exists in cheese, the principal varieties are produced in several countries but may not be identical. Principally to assist international trade but also for other reasons, e.g. research, a number of attempts have been made to develop a classification system for cheese varieties. Davis[7] discussed the problems encountered in attempting to classify cheese and suggested a number of possible schemes. One

TABLE VI
Suggested rheological classification of cheese[a]

Type	Moisture, %[b]	pV	pM	pS
Very hard	<25	>9	>6·3	>2·3
Hard	25–36	8–9	5·8–6·3	2–2·3
Semi-hard	36–40	7·4–8	<5·8	1·8–2
Soft	>40	<7·4	<5·8	>1·8

[a] From Ref. 7.
[b] Suggested moisture levels appear very low.
pV = viscosity factor, logarithmic scale.
pM = elasticity factor, logarithmic scale.
pS = springiness factor, logarithmic scale.

scheme was based on rheological properties (Table VI); the suggested moisture ranges appear rather low.

In a second scheme,[7] based on a complex matrix of manufacturing parameters, cheese was classified into 8 types: hard, semi-hard, soft, surface slime, surface mould, interior mould, acid coagulated, cream. A simplified version of this scheme is shown in Fig. 1; Davis[7] gave examples for most groups.

Davis[7] also considered the possibility of classifying cheese according to the extent of chemical breakdown during ripening or according to flavour and expressed the view that it might be possible within a few years (from

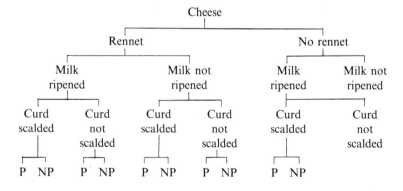

P = pressed
NP = not pressed

Fig. 1. Classification of cheese according to salient manufacturing features (modified from Ref. 7).

1965) to classify cheese on the basis of chemical fingerprints; 20 years later it is still not possible to do so.

Burkhalter[3] classified 510 varieties by the criteria summarized in Table VII.

Scott[4] classified cheeses primarily on the basis of moisture content, hard, semi-hard and soft, and sub-divided these groups on the basis of cooking (scalding) temperature and/or secondary microflora (Table VIII).

Walter and Hargrove[2] suggest that there are probably only about 18 distinct types or kinds of natural cheese, no two of which are made by the same method, i.e. they differ with respect to: setting the milk, cutting, stirring, heating, draining, pressing and salting of the curd and curing of the cheese. He lists the following varieties as typical examples of the 18 types: Brick, Camembert, Cheddar, Cottage, Cream, Edam, Gouda, Hand, Limburger, Neufchatel, Parmesan, Provolone, Romano, Roquefort, Sapsago, Swiss, Trappist and whey cheeses. The authors acknowledge the imperfection and incompleteness of such a classification and indeed a cursory glance at the list of examples highlights this, e.g. listing Edam and Gouda and Parmesan and Romano as clearly distinct families appears highly questionable; exclusion of Feta and Domiati appear to be major omissions.

Walter and Hargrove[2] suggest an alternative classification into 8 families, generally similar to those of Burkhalter:[3]

1. Very hard (grating):
    1.1 Ripened by bacteria: Asiago (old), Parmesan, Romano, Sapsago, Spalen.
2. Hard:
    2.1. Ripened by bacteria, without eyes: Cheddar, Granular, Caciocavallo.
    2.2 Ripened by bacteria, with eyes: Emmental, Gruyère.
3. Semi-soft:
    3.1. Ripened principally by bacteria: Brick, Munster.
    3.2 Ripened by bacteria and surface micro-organisms: Limburger, Port du Salut, Trappist.
    3.3 Ripened principally by blue mould in the interior: Roquefort, Gorgonzola, Danablu, Stilton, Blue Wensleydale.
4. Soft:
    4.1. Ripened: Bel Paese, Brie, Camembert, Hand, Neufchatel.
    4.2 Unripened: Cottage, Pot, Baker's, Cream, Ricotta, Mysost, Primost.

TABLE VII

Classification of cheese according to source of milk, moisture content, texture and ripening agent[a]

1. Cow's milk

1.1 Hard (<42% H_2O)	1.2 Semi-hard/semi-soft (43–55% H_2O)	1.3 Soft (>55% H_2O)	1.4 Fresh, rennet	1.5 Fresh, acid	1.6 Fresh
1.1.1 Grating cheese (extra hard)	1.2.1 Small round openings	1.3.1 Blue veined			
1.1.2 Large round openings	1.2.2 Irregular openings	1.3.2 White surface mould			
1.1.3 Medium round openings	1.2.3 No openings	1.3.3 Bacterial surface smear			
1.1.4 Small round openings	1.2.4 Blue veined	1.3.4 No rind			
1.1.5 Irregular openings					
1.1.6 No openings					

2. Sheep's milk
Hard; semi-hard; soft, blue-veined: fresh

3. Goat's milk

4. Buffalo's milk

[a] Modified from Ref. 3; unless otherwise stated, the cheeses are internally bacterially ripened.

TABLE VIII

Classification of cheese according to moisture content, cook temperature and secondary microflora[a]

Hard cheese (moisture content 20–42%)

Low scald Ns	Medium scald Ns	High scald Ns or Pr	Plastic curds Ns or Pr
Edam (N)	Cheddar (UK)	Grana	Scamorza (I)
Gouda (N)	Gloucester (UK)	(Parmesan) (I)	Provolone (I)
Cantal (F)	Derby (UK)	Emmental (Sw)	Caciocavallo (I)
Fontina (I)	Leicester (UK)	Gruyère (Sw)	Mozzarella (I)
Cheshire (UK)	Svecia (S)	Beaufort (F)	Cecil (USSR)
	Dunlop (UK)	Herregaardsost (S)	Kasseri (Gr)
	Turunmaa (Fin)	Asiago (I)	Kashkaval (B)
		Sbrinz (Sw)	Perenica (C)

Semi-hard cheese (moisture content 44–55%)

Ns	Sm	Bv
St. Paulin (F)	Herve (Bel)	Stilton (UK)
Caerphilly (UK)	Limburger (Bel)	Roquefort (F)
Lancashire (UK)	Romadur (G)	Gorgonzola (I)
Trappist (H)	Munster (F)	Danablu (D)
Providence (F)	Tilsit (G)	Mycella (D)
	Vacherin-Mont	Wensleydale (UK)
	d'Or (Sw)	Blue Vinny (UK)
	Remoudou (Bel)	Gammelost (Nor)
	Steinbuscher Käse (G)	Adelost (S)
	Brick (USA)	Tiroler-Graukäse (G)
		Edelpilzkäse (A)
		Aura (Ice)
		Cabrales (E)

Soft cheese (moisture content > 55%)

Sm or Hm	Hm	Ns	Un, Ac
Brie (F)	Camembert (F)	Colwich (UK)	Coulommier (F)
Bel Paese (I)	Carré d'est (F)	Lactic (UK)	York (UK)
Maroilles (F)	Neufchatel (F)	Bondon (F)	Cambridge (UK)
	Chaource (F)		Cottage (UK)
			Quarg
			Petit Suisse (F)
			Cream (UK)

Key letters on column heads:
Pr = secondary ripening (propionic eyeholes).
Ns = normal lactic starter or milk flora.
Sm = smear coat (*Brevibacterium linens*).
Hm = surface mould (*Penicillium candidum* or *P. camemberti*).
Bv = blue-veined internal mould (*P. glaucum* or *P. roqueforti*).
Ac = acid coagulated.
Un = normally unripened, fresh cheese.
[a] Modified from Scott.[4]

While the published classification schemes appear to be inadequate, this author is unable to offer a significantly improved classification scheme. However, I would like to suggest a classification scheme into super-families based on the coagulation agent:

1. Rennet cheeses: most of the major international varieties.
2. Acid cheeses: e.g. Cottage, Quarg, Queso Blanco, Cream.
3. Heat/acid: e.g. Ricotta, some forms of Queso Blanco, Sapsago, Ziger, Schottenziger.
4. Concentration/crystallization: e.g. Mysost.

Obviously, the classification schemes of Davies,[7] Walter and Hargrove[2] and Burkhalter[3] can be applied to the Rennet cheeses but are not really applicable to the other three super-families since most are high-moisture, soft cheeses and most are not normally ripened. However, it would appear reasonable that the very heavily salted varieties (which are normally stored in brine or brined whey) including Domiati, Feta, Brinza, Lightvan, Bulgarian pickled white cheese, should be classified as a separate family within any of these classification schemes.

Standards for 30 major varieties are described in various editions of Code of Quality Standards for Cheese as part of its Code of Principles covering milk and milk products by the Joint FAO/WHO Codex Alimentarius.

A further set of standards arises from the Stresa Convention of 1951 on the use of 'applications d'origine' and cheese designations. Under this convention 'Roquefort' may be produced only in France, Stilton only in England and Gorgonzola, Pecorino Romano and Parmigiano Reggiano only in Italy. Several varieties may be imitated in countries other than that of its origin, provided the name of the producing country is included, e.g. Emmental, Gruyère, Gouda, Edam, Provolone, Camembert, Brie, St. Paulin, Fontina, Svecia, Danablu, Samsoe, Danbo, Fynbo.

REFERENCES

1. Sandine, W. E. and Elliker, P. R., *J. Agr. Food Chem.*, 1981, **18**, 557.
2. Walter, H. E. and Hargrove, R. C., *Cheeses of the World*, 1972, Dover, New York.
3. Burkhalter, G., *Catalogue of Cheeses*, International Dairy Federation, Document 141, 1981.
4. Scott, R., *Cheesemaking Practice*, 2nd edn, 1986, Elsevier Applied Science Publishers, London.

30   P. F. Fox

5. Cheke, V., *The Story of Cheesemaking in Britain*, 1959, Routledge & Kegan Paul, London.
6. Squire, E. H. (ed.), *Cheddar Gorge: A Book of English Cheeses*, 1937, Collins, London.
7. Davis, J. G., *Cheese, Vol. 1, Basic Technology; Vol. 2, Bibliography*, 1965, Churchill Livingstone, London.
8. Food & Agricultural Organization, *Production Yearbook*, 1982, Vol. 36, p. 247.
9. International Dairy Federation, *The World Market for Cheese*, International Dairy Federation, Document 146, 1982.
10. International Dairy Federation, *Consumption Statistics for Milk and Milk Products*, International Dairy Federation, Document 160, 1983.
11. Sammis, J. L., *Cheesemaking*, 1948, Cheesemaker Book Co., Madison, Wisconsin, USA.
12. Van Slyke, L. L. and Price, W. V., *Cheese*, 1949, Orange Judd, New York.
13. Kosikowski, F. V. and Mocquot, G., *Advances in Cheese Technology*, 1958, FAO Studies 38, FAO, Rome.
14. Simon, A. L., *Cheeses of the World*, 1956, Faber & Faber, London.
15. Layton, J. A., *The Cheese Handbook*, 1973, Dover, New York.
16. Mair-Waldburg, H., *Handbook of Cheese; Cheeses of the World A to Z*, 1974, Volkwertschaftlecher Verlag GmbH, Kempten Allgan, Germany.
17. Davis, J. G., *Cheese, Vol. III, Manufacturing Methods; Vol. IV, Bibliography*, 1967, Churchill Livingstone, London.
18. Eekhof-Stork, N., *World Atlas of Cheese*, 1976, Paddington Press Ltd, London.
19. Kosikowski, F. V., *Cheese and Fermented Milk Foods*, 1977, Edwards Bros. Inc., Ann Arbor, Michigan.
20. Cantin, C., *Guide Pratique des Fromages*, 1976, Solar Editeur, Paris.
21. Eck, A. (ed.), *Le Fromage*, 1984, Lavoisier, Paris.
22. Lloyd, G. T., *Dairy Sci. Abstr.*, 1971, **33**, 411.
23. Reiter, B., *J. Soc. Dairy Technol.*, 1972, **26**, 3.
24. Stadhouders, J., *Milchwissenschaft*, 1974, **29**, 329.
25. Lawrence, R. C., Thomas, T. D. and Tarzaghi, B. E., *J. Dairy Res.*, 1976, **43**, 141.
26. Sandine, W. E., *J. Dairy Sci.*, 1977, **60**, 322.
27. Daly, C., *Ir. J. Fd Sci. Technol.*, 1983, **7**, 39.
28. Daly, C., *Antonie van Leeuwenhoek*, 1983, **49**, 297.
29. Accolas, J. P. and Auclair, J., *Ir. J. Fd Sci. Technol.*, 1983, **7**, 27.
30. Auclair, J. and Accolas, J. P., *Antonie van Leeuwenhoek*, 1983, **49**, 313.
31. Accolas, J. P., Veaux, M., Vassal, L. and Mocquot, G., *Le Lait*, 1978, **58**, 118.
32. Sardinas, J. L., *Adv. appl. Microbiol.*, 1972, **15**, 39.
33. Ernstrom, C. A. In: *Fundamentals of Dairy Chemistry*, 2nd edn, B. H. Webb, A. H. Johnson and J. A. Alford (eds), 1974, Avi Publishing Co. Inc., Westport, CT, p. 662.
34. Nelson, J. H., *J. Dairy Sci.*, 1975, **58**, 1739.
35. Sternberg, M., *Adv. appl. Microbiol.*, 1976, **20**, 135.
36. Green, M. L., *J. Dairy Res.*, 1977, **44**, 159.
37. Martens, R. and Naudts, M., *International Dairy Federation Annual Bulletin*, Document 180, 1978, p. 51.

38. De Koning, P. J., International Dairy Federation, Document 126, 1979, p. 11.
39. Phelan, J. A., Ph.D. thesis, National University of Ireland, 1985.
40. Berridge, N. J., *Nature, Lond.*, 1942, **149**, 194.
41. Fox, P. F. In: *Developments in Food Proteins—3—Proteins*, B. J. F. Hudson (ed.), 1984, Applied Science Publishers, London, p. 69.
42. Waugh, D. F. and von Hippel, P. H., *J. Am. Chem. Soc.*, 1956, **78**, 4576.
43. Wake, R. G., *Aust. J. Biol. Sci.*, 1959, **12**, 479.
44. Delfour, A., Jolles, J., Alais, C. and Jolles, P., *Biochim. Biophys. Res. Commun.*, 1965, **19**, 452.
45. Humme, H. E., *Neth. Milk Dairy J.*, 1972, **26**, 180.
46. Schmidt, D. F. In: *Developments in Dairy Chemistry—1—Proteins*, P. F. Fox. (ed.), 1982, Applied Science Publishers, London, p. 61.
47. McMahon, D. J. and Brown, R. J., *J. Dairy Sci.*, 1984, **67**, 499.
48. Pyne, G. T. and McGann, T. C. A., *Proc. 16th Int. Dairy Congr. (Copenhagen)*, 1962, **A**, p. 611.
49. Emmons, D. B., *Dairy Sci. Abstr.*, 1963, **25**, 129 and 175.
50. Emmons, D. B. and Tuckey, S. L., *Cottage Cheese and Other Fermented Milk Products*, Chas. Pfizer Inc., New York.
51. Dean, D. D. and Hammond, E. G., *J. Dairy Sci.*, 1960, **43**, 1421.
52. Ernstrom, C. A. and Kale, C. G., *J. Dairy Sci.*, 1975, **58**, 1008.
53. Fox, P. F., *Dairy Sci. Abstr.*, 1978, **40**, 727.
54. White, C. H. and Ray, B. W., *J. Dairy Sci.*, 1977, **60**, 1236.
55. Demott, B. J., Hitchcock, J. P. and Sanders, O. G., *J. Dairy Sci.*, 1984, **67**, 1539.
56. Cross, S. D., Henderson, J. M. and Dunkley, W. L., *J. Dairy Sci.*, 1977, **60**, 1820.
57. Dunkley, W. L. and Patterson, D. R., *J. Dairy Sci.*, 1977, **60**, 1824.
58. Chua, T. E. H. and Dunkley, W. L., *J. Dairy Sci.*, 1979, **62**, 1216.
59. Emmons, D. B. and Beckett, D. C., *J. Dairy Sci.*, 1984, **67**, 2192.
60. Emmons, D. B. and Beckett, D. C., *J. Dairy Sci.*, 1984, **67**, 2200.
61. Covacevich, H. R. and Kosikowski, F. V., *J. Dairy Sci.*, 1978, **61**, 529.
62. Kosikowski, F. V., *J. Dairy Sci.*, 1982, **65**, 1705.
63. Dybing, S. T., Parson, J. G., Martin, J. H. and Spurgeon, K. R., *J. Dairy Sci.*, 1982, **65**, 544.
64. Mohamed, F. O. and Bassette, R., *J. Dairy Sci.*, 1979, **62**, 222.
65. Aylward, E. B., O'Leary, J. and Langlois, B. E., *J. Dairy Res.*, 1980, **63**, 1819.
66. Glasser, J., Carroad, P. A. and Dunkley, W. L., *J. Dairy Sci.*, 1979, **62**, 1058.
67. Korolczuk, J., Crzelak, D., Zmarkicki, S. and Yanicki, Q., *N.Z. J. Dairy Sci. Technol.*, 1983, **18**, 101.
68. Lang, F., *Milk Industry*, 1980, **82**(11), 21.
69. Kroger, M., *Cult. Dairy Prod. J.*, 1980, **15**(3), 11.
70. Mann, E. J., *Dairy Ind. Internat.*, 1982, **47**(3), 33.
71. Winwood, J., *J. Soc. Dairy Technol.*, 1983, **36**, 107.
72. Siggelkow, M. A., *Dairy Ind. Internat.*, 1984, **49**(6), 17.
73. Mann, E. J., *Dairy Ind. Internat.*, 1984, **49**(12), 13.
74. Siapantas, L. G. and Kosikowski, F. V., *J. Dairy Sci.*, 1965, **48**, 764.
75. Siapantas, L. G. and Kosikowski, F. V., *J. Dairy Sci.*, 1967, **50**, 1589.
76. Siapantas, L. G. and Kosikowski, F. V., *J. Dairy Sci.*, 1973, **56**, 631.
77. Chandan, R. C., Marin, H., Nakrani, K. R. and Zehner, M. D., *J. Dairy Sci.*, 1979, **62**, 691.

78. Torres, N. and Chandan, R. C., *J. Dairy Sci.*, 1981, **64**, 552.
79. Torres, N. and Chandan, R. C., *J. Dairy Sci.*, 1981, **64**, 2161.
80. Parnell-Clunies, E. M., Irvine, D. M. and Bullock, D. H., *J. Dairy Sci.*, 1985, **68**, 789.
81. Maubois, J.-L. and Kosikowski, F. V., *J. Dairy Sci.*, 1978, **61**, 881.
82. Oterholm, A., *Nordish Mejeriinustri*, 1983, **10**(6), 287.

Chapter 2

General and Molecular Aspects of Rennets

Bent Foltmann

Institute of Biochemical Genetics,
University of Copenhagen, Denmark

1. INTRODUCTION

Cheesemaking and fermentation represent the first examples of applied biochemistry and biology. Whereas living micro-organisms are used in fermentation processes, the clotting of milk for cheesemaking has always required soluble enzymes. The milk-clotting enzyme from the fourth stomach of the calf was one of the first enzymes of which purification was attempted, and Deschamps[1] suggested the name chymosin derived from the Greek word for gastric liquid 'chyme'. This designation was later used in continental European languages, whereas in English, the name rennin, derived from rennet, was used.[2] Misunderstandings often occurred between rennin and renin from the kidneys, and therefore the designation chymosin was recently adopted in English[3] and it is now used in the recommended international enzyme nomenclature.[4]

Calf chymosin is still the prevailing milk coagulant used in cheesemaking but due to the shortage of calf stomachs, animal rennets are sometimes fortified by addition of pepsins. Furthermore, proteases of microbial origin are now widely used for cheesemaking.

In some countries, vegetable rennets are traditionally used and bacterial proteases may also have milk-clotting properties (reviews, Refs 5–8), but compared to animal and fungal rennets, little is known about vegetable and bacterial rennets and hence they will not be considered further in this review.

The proteases in animal and fungal rennets all belong to the group of aspartic proteases (previously called acid proteases). In the international

TABLE I
Nomenclature and sources of major proteases in rennets

	IUB-name	*Other names*	*Sources*
Pepsin	Pepsin A (EC 3.4.23.1)	Pepsin II[9]	Ruminants Pigs Chicken
Gastricsin	Pepsin C (EC 3.4.23.3)	Pepsin I[9] Parapepsin II[10] Pepsin B[11]	Ruminants Pigs
Chymosin	Chymosin (EC 3.4.23.4)	Rennin[12]	Ruminants
M. miehei protease (MMP)	(EC 3.4.23.6)	*Trade names* Rennilase (Novo) Hanilase (Chr. Hansen) Fromase (Wallerstein) Marzyme (Miles)	*Mucor miehei*
M. pusillus protease (MPP)	(EC 3.4.23.6)	Emporase (Dairyland) Meito (Meito Sangyo) Noury (Vitex)	*Mucor pusillus* var. Lindt
E. parasitica protease (EPP)	(EC 3.4.23.6)	Sure curd Suparen (Pfizer)	*Endothia parasitica*

Notes:
Pepsin: Chicken pepsin is tentatively classified together with the mammalian pepsins though the evolutionary and physiological relationships are not yet firmly established. Suffixes of Roman numerals have been used to characterize the individual gastric proteases in their order of elution by ion-exchange chromatography on DEAE-cellulose.

Gastricsin: The mammalian gastricsins form a separate group of gastric proteases that are different from both the predominant pepsin and chymosin. In order to emphasize this, the present trends among biochemists are to use the term gastricsin instead of pepsin C.

Chymosin: The mammalian chymosins are neonatal proteases, see also Section 6.

Fungal proteases: Though these proteases show great differences in structures and specificities, all microbial aspartic proteases have the same EC number.

enzyme classification,[4] this group carries the number EC 3.4.23. Table I presents a list of proteases of major importance for rennets. The aim of this review is to give a survey with representative references, mainly from 1970 to 1984. Further references and references to the older literature may be found in reviews on the following topics: microbial rennets,[7,8] aspartic proteases,[13] gastric proteases,[14] chymosin,[3,12] pepsin,[10,14-17] rennets and cheese.[18-21]

2. PREPARATION, PURIFICATION AND CHARACTERIZATION

2.1 Preparation

Animal rennets

Frozen calf stomachs are now sold in bulk, but large-scale extraction procedures based on frozen starting material have not been published. The traditional method of preparation from dried or salted vells is described by Placek *et al.*[22] The stomachs are cut into small pieces and mixed with Excelsior. Counter-current extraction is carried out with a 10% NaCl solution. The crude extracts consist of a mixture of zymogens and active enzymes. After activation by addition of acid to a pH between 2 and 4·6, the pH is adjusted to 5·5–5·7 (see also Sections 4 and 5); the salt concentration is increased to about 20% NaCl and preservatives, e.g. sodium benzoate or sodium propionate, are added. Finally, the rennet is filtered and the activity is adjusted ready for use.

For research purposes, several small-scale extraction procedures have been published. If fresh or frozen material is available, it is convenient to dissect the mucosa from the muscular sheet before extraction. Extraction may take place after passage through a meat grinder or directly in a blender. For preparation of zymogens, it may be an advantage to carry out the extraction under neutral or weakly alkaline conditions (bicarbonate[12] or phosphate buffers of pH 7·3–7·5[23]). Under such conditions, active enzymes are denatured, whereas the zymogens are stable (Section 4). If no buffers are added, the buffering capacity of a fresh mucosal extract will generally result in a pH about 6. For small-scale extraction, salt solutions containing up to 0·5 M NaCl have been used[24] but in other preparations of gastric zymogens, salt has not been added during the extraction and for purification, the zymogens and enzymes have been adsorbed on DEAE-cellulose directly from the extraction liquid,[25] or after activation and dialysis.[26]

Microbial rennets

Best yields of the milk-clotting protease from *M. pusillus* are obtained from semi-solid cultures containing 50% of wheatbran, whereas *M. miehei* and *E. parasitica* are well suited for submerged cultivation. From the former, good yields of milk-clotting protease may be obtained in a medium containing 4% potato starch, 3% soybean meal and 10% barley. During growth, lipase is secreted together with the protease; the lipase activity is destroyed by treatment at low pH values before the preparation can be used as cheese rennet.[8,27]

2.2 Purification

Calf chymosin may be crystallized after repeated precipitations from solutions saturated with NaCl (review, Ref. 12). The crystals are rectangular plates but unless the solutions are seeded with crystals from a previous preparation, it is often difficult to obtain crystallization. Today, crystallization of a protein is not regarded as a criterion of homogeneity, and chromatographic or electrophoretic analyses,[12,28,29] have shown that crystalline chymosin may contain at least 3 different components. However, it should be noted that crystalline chymosin is by far the most stable form of the enzyme. At this Institute, we have a batch of crystalline chymosin suspended in 4 M NaCl, and stored at $-10°$ to $-20°C$; when samples of these crystals are dissolved, we have for 24 years observed no significant decrease in the ratio of the milk-clotting activity relative to absorbancy at 278 nm.

Ion-exchange chromatography on columns of DEAE–cellulose or DEAE–Sephadex has been used successfully for both preparative purification and analytical characterization of extracts of gastric mucosa, of solutions of fungal proteases and of commercial rennets. The milk-clotting proteases are stable at pH 5–6 and buffers within this pH range are used in most of the chromatographic fractionations. Typical examples of conditions used for ion-exchange chromatography are summarized in Table II.

Afinity chromatography using inhibitors like pepstatin,[34] ε-amino capronyl-D-phenylalanine methyl ester, gramicidin or bacitracin[35,36] has been used successfully for the preparation of chymosin and other aspartic proteases. Affinity chromatography with inhibitors is especially suitable for the isolation of enzymes from crude extracts. Though different binding constants occur, these methods will generally not specify the individual proteases.

TABLE II
Examples of chromatographic systems used for purification and characterization
of rennets on columns of DEAE-ion exchangers

Equilibration buffer	*Elution*	*Comments*	*Ref.*
0·1 M sodium phosphate, pH 5·8	Linear gradient of the equilibration buffer and 0·4 M sodium phosphate, pH 5·5	Optimum conditions for separation of prochymosin and the individual components of chymosin	12
0·05 M sodium phosphate, pH 5·8	Linear gradient of the equilibration buffer and 0·5 M NaCl in the same buffer	Fractionation of chymosin and pepsin in bovine rennet	11
0·02 M piperazine, pH 5·3	Linear gradient of 0·15 M NaCl and 0·6 M NaCl in the equilibration buffer	Fractionation of chymosin and pepsin in bovine rennets; also used for analytical separation of fungal proteases and pepsin	30 31
0·05 M citrate buffer, pH 4·0	Isocratic	Initial purification of *M. miehei* protease	32
0·05 M sodium acetate, pH 5·0	Linear gradient of the equilibration buffer and 0·5 M KCl in the same buffer	Final purification of *M. pusillus* protease	33

2.3 Quantitation and Identification

The essential property of a rennet is its milk-clotting activity. The milk-clotting process is described in detail in Chapter 3 of this volume. At this Institute, we use radial diffusion in agarose–skim milk gels[37] for a semiquantitative and rapid screening of the milk-clotting activity in preparations or chromatographic fractionations; clotting tests with 10 ml of reconstituted skim milk in bifurcated glass tubes are used for accurate determinations.[3] Our coagulation or chymosin unit (CU) is defined from chromatographically purified chymosin B: a solution of freshly prepared chymosin B with an absorbancy at 278 nm of 1·00 contains 100 CU/ml; this corresponds to 1·43 CU/mg of chymosin B.[3] As the chromatographic fractionation of chymosin is very reproducible, this unit could be used by others also.

The milk-clotting activity of a solution is a measure of the total amount of milk-clotting proteases. Whether the question concerns a sample of rennet or an evaluation of a purification procedure, the activity test must be followed up by analyses that characterize the enzymic composition of the samples.

Indirect information about the contents of the individual enzymes may be obtained by utilizing the differences in milk-clotting activities at different pH values,[11] or by selective denaturation of the individual components,[38] preferably combined with chromatographic fraction-ation.[31] In an IDF report, de Koning[39] has suggested a systematic procedure for identification of milk-clotting enzymes. This scheme involves tests for enzymic activity and inactivation as well as several types of electrophoresis. Separations by ion-exchange chromatography or electrophoresis provide direct information about the enzyme profile of rennets. Ion-exchange chromatography is rather time consuming and a single experiment gives only a limited separation of the individual components. Thus, under the conditions of Garnot *et al.*[30] chymosin and gastricsin co-elute. Electrophoretic separations are rapid and several samples may be tested simultaneously. Samples of rennets have been evaluated by polyacrylamide gel electrophoresis or isoelectric focusing[39] followed by staining of the proteins. Such methods give a detailed picture of the protein content, but with crude samples they do not discriminate between enzymic components and inert proteins; however, if the gels are developed as zymograms, the enzymically active components, only, show up. Detection of proteases after incubation with haemoglobin followed by precipitation and staining of undigested proteins[40] has been widely used in clinical investigations on pepsins and pepsinogens (review, Ref. 41). The method is also suitable for detection of pepsins in rennets, but due to its weak general proteolytic activity it is difficult to observe chymosin in haemoglobin zymograms. The milk-clotting proteases may be detected by pouring skim-milk on top of the electrophoresis gel;[42] a more accurate method that allows permanent documentation has recently been described.[43] As the precipitates consist mainly of casein, this method is designated a caseogram. Figure 1 illustrates caseograms of different milk-clotting enzymes after electrophoresis on agar gel; it should be pointed out that the caseogram detection works well after all kinds of non-denaturating gel electrophoresis, including immunoelectrophoresis.

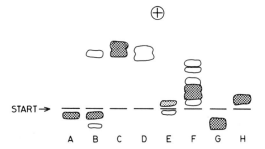

Fig. 1. Tracings of caseograms of different rennets. Electrophoresis was performed in a 1% agar gel, 0·05 M sodium acetate pH 5·0 at 15 V/cm for 1·5 h. All samples were diluted to a milk-clotting activity of approx. 0·1 CU/ml; 5 μl was used in each slot. A: calf chymosin (the apparent cathionic mobility is due to electro-osmotic flow in the system); B: calf rennet (a faint zone is observed below the chymosin band, which may correspond to degradation products, probably the chromatographic fraction designated chymosin C cfr.,[12] a small amount of pepsin is also observed). C: bovine rennet (pepsin only); D: porcine pepsin; E: lamb rennet; F: chicken pepsin; G: *M. miehei* rennet; H: *M. pusillus* rennet.[43,44]

Immunochemical methods represent efficient tools for characterization and identification of proteins (review, Ref. 45). Early applications on rennets are reviewed by de Koning.[46] Using monospecific antisera, quantitative determinations may be obtained by radial diffusion or by rocket immunoelectrophoresis; good agreement between immunochemical determinations and other analytical methods have been reported.[11,47] There are, however, certain reservations which must be considered in an evaluation of the immunochemical determinations. As pointed out in the following section, the gastric proteases are highly homologous proteins and pepsins from different species may have common antigenic determinants. Such common antigenicity may not be expressed in all antisera but partial immunochemical identity has been observed among pepsins from different species.[48] Hence, if one wants to determine bovine pepsin in the presence of porcine pepsin, the common antigen binding sites in anti-(bovine pepsin) should be removed by adsorption with porcine pepsin prior to use. Conversely, anti-(porcine pepsin) may be purified by adsorption with bovine pepsin before determination of porcine pepsin by immunochemical methods. No cross-reactivity has been observed among bovine chymosin, pepsin or gastricsin by gel immunoelectrophoresis. In this connection, it may be noted that most analyses of rennets disregard gastricsin though the content in bovine rennets may be about 10% of the content of pepsin.[11] Furthermore, it should be observed that the milk-clotting enzymes may undergo denaturation in such a way that activity is lost but at least some of the antigenic determinants are retained. Thus, some types of rennet do not show proportionality between milk-clotting activity and immunological tests.[49]

As regards the microbial rennets, partial immunochemical identity has also been observed between *M. miehei* and *M. pusillus* proteases.[50]

3. STRUCTURE

3.1 Amino Acid Compositions and Molecular Weights

The amino acid compositions of aspartic proteases are generally characterized by a high content of dicarboxylic and hydroxy amino acids and a low content of basic amino acids.[12–17,50–54]

Molecular weights from 30 400 to 40 000 have been reported for chymosin and pepsin.[3,10] After determination of the primary structures, the molecular weights of calf chymosin and pig pepsin turned out to be 35 600 and 34 600, respectively.[51,52]

Among the fungal proteases, a molecular weight of about 38 000 has been reported for the protein moiety of the glycosylated *M. miehei* protease,[53] and 30 000 was found for the *M. pusillus* protease.[33] For *E. parasitica* protease,[54] a molecular weight of 37 500 was reported, whereas 33 800 has been calculated from the amino acid sequence (Fig. 2). If one considers the structural homology among these enzymes, the general feature appears that all the proteases in question consist of about 325–360 amino acid residues, and, depending on their amino acid compositions, the molecular weights add up to between 33 000 and 38 000.

3.2 Primary Structure

The gastric proteases are synthesized and secreted as zymogens which are converted into active enzymes by a limited proteolysis that removes about 45 amino acid residues from the N-terminal end of the peptide chain (see also Section 5). Figure 2 presents an alignment of known primary structures of proteases from rennets, together with examples of related proteases. Proparts of the zymogens are shown where such sequences are known. In order to facilitate discussion about the structures of these homologous proteins, the residues in N-terminal sequences of the zymogens are numbered from the longest of the peptide chains (prochymosin), introducing gaps and insertions in order to obtain the largest number of identities. Further it is common practice to number the residues of the active enzymes as in pig pepsin. The numbering therefore starts again from the N-terminus of pig pepsin. However, it should be observed that relative to pig pepsin the other proteases have their N-terminal sequences extended by 1–5 amino acid residues. In the tertiary structure (see next section) the N-termini are located at the back of the molecule relative to the active site cleft. Of bovine pepsinogen and progastricsin only partial amino acid sequences are known. In order to illustrate the structural relationships among these groups of proteases, the primary structures of porcine, human and monkey pepsinogens are shown in Fig. 2 together with the primary structures of human and monkey progastricsins. The two primate pepsinogens show about 95% identity, whereas the primate pepsinogens show about 80% identity with porcine pepsinogen; the known sections of bovine pepsinogen have 78% identity with the corresponding parts of porcine pepsinogen. These results are consistent with the observed partial immunochemical identity among the pepsins.

The primate gastricsins likewise have 95% identity whereas the N-terminal sequences of their zymogens have about 80% identity with the N-terminal sequence of bovine progastricsin.

Chymosins from different species show pronounced immunochemical cross-reactions.[48] The N-terminal amino acid sequences of chymosins from cat and pig indicate 75–80% identity with calf chymosin, whereas the identities with the pepsins amount to only about 45%.

From these observations it appears that the mammalian pepsins, gastricsins and chymosins form 3 groups of proteases in which one enzyme is structurally more closely related to an enzyme of the same group in another species than to an enzyme from another group from the same species. The primary structure of chicken pepsin[58] is apparently more closely related to that of pig pepsin than to that of the primate gastricsins or calf chymosin. In Table I chicken pepsin is tentatively placed together with the mammalian pepsin A. But more knowledge about the structures of other avian gastric proteases is required before a final classification of the avian gastric proteases is established.

As one might expect, the vertebrate gastric proteases are more closely related to each other than to the proteases of fungal origin. Though the alignment of distantly related proteins implies a choice, the amino acid sequences of the fungal proteases clearly demonstrate homology with the gastric proteases. A tentative amino acid sequence of *M. miehei* protease has been published.[63] Minor corrections have been introduced after nucleotide sequencing of c-DNA.[63a,b] The latter investigations also show

```
             N-term.                                              N-term.
             proparts                                             enzymes
             pl    *      ^              ^            ^    p38^          1
P  PgA       LVKVPLVRKKSLRQNLIKDGKLKDFLKTHKHNPASKYFPE--AAAL----IG
B  PgA       SVVKIPLVKKKSLRQNLIENGKLKEFMRTHKYNLGSKYIRE--AATL----V̄S
H  PgA       IMYKVPLIRKKSLRRTLSERGLLKDFLKKHNLNPARKYFPQWEAPTL----V̄D
M  PgA       IIYKVPLVRKKSLRRNLSEHGLLKDFLKKHNLNPASKYFPQAEAPTL----ĪD

B  PgC       LVKIPLKKFKSIREIMKEKGLLZBFLRTYKHNPAEKYRFGDF-------IVA
H  PgC       AVVKVPLKKFKSIRETMKEKGLLGEFLRTHKYDPAWKYRFGDL-------S̄VT
M  PgC       AVVKVPLKKFKSIRETMKEKGLLGEFLRTHKYDPAWKYHFGDL-------S̄VS

P  Pch                                                            GEVA
B  Pch       AEITRIPLYKGKSLRKALKEHGLLEDFLQKQQYGISSKYSGF--------GĒVA
F  Pch       SEITRVPLHKGKSLRKALKEHGLLEBF/                       D̄KVS
G  Pg        SIHRVPLKKGKSLRKQLKDHGLLEDFLKKHPYNPASKYHPVL------ĪĀTES

PJP                                                              AASGV
EPP                                                              S̄TGSA
MMP          RPVSKQSESKDKLLALPLTSVSRKFSQTKFGQQQLAEKLAGLKFPSEAAĀDGSV

Com Gas      PL    KS R      G L   F          KY
Com all             K                         K

             ^*a        ^         ^ 32     ^       a     *  53
P  PnA       DEPLENYLD-TEYFGTIGIGTPAQDFTVIFDTGSSNLWVPSVYC-SSLACSDH
B  PnA       EQPLQNYLD-TEYFGTIGIGTPAQDFTVIFDTGSSNLWVPSIYC-SSEACTNH
H  PnA       EQPLENYLD-MEYFGTIGIGTPAQDFTVVFDTGSSNLWVPSVYC-SSNACTNH
M  PnA       EQPLENYLD-VEYFGTIGIGTPAQDFTVIFDTGSSNLWVPSVYC-SSLACTNH

B  PnC       TEPM-DY/    /FGZISIGTPPZBF/
H  PnC       YEPM-AYMD-AAYFGEISIGTPPQNFLVLFDTGSSNLWVPSVYC-QSQACTSH
M  PnC       YEPM-AYMD-AAYFGEISIGTPPQNFLVLFDTGSSNLWVPSVYC-QSQACTSH

P  Ch        SZPLTNYLD-TZYF/
B  Ch        SVPLTNYLD-SQYFGKIYLGTPPQEFTVLFDTGSSDFWVPSIYC-KSNACKNH
F  Ch        NZPLADFLD-SEYFGKIYIGTPPZ/
G  Pn        YEPMTNYMD-ASYYGTISIGTPQQDFSVIFDTGSSNLWVPSIYC-KSSACSNH

PJP          ATNTPTAND-EEYITPVTIGGTT--NLLNFDTGSADLWVFSTEL-PASQQSGH
EPP          TTTPIDSLD-DAYITPVQIGTPAQTLNLDFDTGSSDLWVFSSET-TASEVDGQ
MMP          DTDTYYDFDLEEYAIPVSIGTPGQDFLLLFDTGSSDTWVPHKGCTKSEGCVGS

Com Gas   P      D    Y G I   GTP    F V FDTGSS   WVPS YC   S AC   H
Com all          D    Y       G          FDTGS    WV
```

Fig. 2.

```
                   ^     a    ^         a^      *abcd        100
P PnA    NQFNPDDSSTFEA-TSQELSITYGTGS-MTGILGYDTVQ----VGGISDTNQI
B PnA    NRFNPQDSSTYE/               /MTG/
H PnA    NRFNPEDSSTYQS-TSETVSITYGTGS-MTGILGYDTVQ----VGGISDTNQI
M PnA    NLFNPQDSSTYQS-TSGTLSITYGTGS-MTGILGYDTVQ----VGGISDTNQI

H PnC    SRFNPSESSTYST-NGQTFSLQYGSGS-LTGFFGYDTLT----VQSIQVPNQE
M PnC    SRFNPSESSTYST-NGQTFSLQYGSGS-LTGFFGYDTLT----VQSIQVPNQE

B Ch     QRFDPRKSSTFQN-LGKPLSIHYGTGS-MQGILGYDTVT----VSNIVDIQQT
G Pn     KRFDPSKSSTYVS-TNETVYIAYGTGS-MSGILGYDTVA----VSSIDVQNQI

P JP     SVYNPSATGKE-L-SGYTWSISYGDGSSASGNVFTDSVT----VGGVTAHGQA
E PP     TIYTPSKSTTAKLLSGATWSISYGDGSSSSGDVYTDTVS----VGGLTVTGQA
M MP     RFFDPSASSTFKA-TNYNLNITYGTGGANGLYFEDSIAIGDITVTKQILAYVD

Com Gas  F P    SST           YG G    G GYDT     V   I    Q
Com all         P             YG G            V
```

```
                    ^      ^122     ^       abc   ^  abc    147
P PnA    FGLSETEPGSFLYYAPFDGILGLAYPSISASGATPV---FDNLWD---QGLVS
B PnA    /LSETEPGSF/                            /IWD---QGLVS
H PnA    FGLSETEPGSFLYYAPFDGILGLAYPSISSSGATPV---FDNIWN---QGLVS
M PnA    FGLSETEPGSFLYYAPFDGILGLAYPSISSSGATPV---FDNIWD---QGLVS

H PnC    FGLSENEPGTNFVYAQFDGIMGLAYPALSVDEATIA---MQGMVQ---EGALT
M PnC    FGLSENEPGTNFVYAQFDGIMGLAYPTLSVDGATTA---MQGMVQ---EGALT

B Ch     VGLSTQEPGDVFTYAEFDGILGMAYPSLASEYSIPV---FDNMMN---RHLVA
G Pn     FGLSETEPGSFFYYCNFDGILGLAFPSISSSGATPV---FDNMMS---QHLVA

P JP     VQAAQQISAQFQQDTNNDGLLGLAFSSINTVQPQSQTTFFDTVKSS-------
E PP     VESAKKVSSSFTEDSTIDGLLGLAFSTLNTVSPTQQKTFFDNAKAS-----LD
M MP     NVRGPTAEQSPNADIFLDGLFGAAYPDNTAMEAEYGSTYNTVHVNLYKQGLIS

Com Gas  GLS    EPG    Y   FDGI  G A P
Com all                     DG    G A
```

```
                    ^    *ab   ^            ^          ^   a   ^   195
P PnA    QDLFSVYLSS--NDDSGSVVLLGGIDSSYYTGSLNWVPV-SVEGYWQITLD
B PnA    ZBL/   /LSS--NEESGXVVIFGDIBSSYYXGSLNWVPV-XV//YWQI/
H PnA    QDLFSVYLSA--DDQSGSVVIFGGIDSSYYTGSLNWVPV-TVEGYWQITVD
M PnA    QDLFSVYLSA--DDQSGSVVIFGGIDSSYYTGSLNWVPV-SVEGYWQISVD

H PnC    SPVFSVYLSN-QQGSSGGAVVFGGVDSSLYTGQIYWAPV-TQELYWQIGIE
M PnC    SPIFSVYLSD-QQGSSGGAVVFGGVDSSLYTGQIYWAPV-TQELYWQIGIE

B Ch     QDLFSVYMDR---DGQESMLTLGAIDPSYYTGSLHWVPV-TVQQYWQFTVD
G Pn     QDLFSVYLSK---GETGSFVLFGGIDPNYYTKGIYWVPL-SAETYWQITMD

P JP     LAQPLFAVAL--KHQQPGVYDFGFIDSSKYTGSLTYTGVDNSQGFWSFNVD
E PP     SPVFTADLGY----HAPGTYNFGFIDTTAYTGSITYTAVSTKQGFWEWTST
M MP     SPLFSVYMNTNSGTGEVVFGGVNNTLLSGDIAYTDVMSRYGGYYFWDAPVT

Com Gas  FSVY               G  D         W P      YWQ
Com all                     W
```

Fig. 2—*contd*.

(continued)

```
        *     ^      a      ^ 215   ^              ^        ^a 244
P PnA   SITMDGETI-ACSGGCQAIVDTGTSLLTGPTSAIAINIQSDIGASE-NSDG
B PnA   /ITMDGESI-ACSNGCEAIVDTGTSL/
H PnA   SITMNGEAI-ACAEGCQAIVDTGTSLLTGPTSPIA-NIQSDIGASE-NSDG
M PnA   SITMDGEAI-ACAEGCQAIVDTGTSLLTGPTSPIA-NIQSDIGASE-NSDG

H PnC   EFLIGGQASGWCSEGCQAIVDTGTSLLTVPQQYMS-ALLQATGAQE-DEYG
M PnC   EFLIGGQASGWCSEGCQAIVDTGTSLLTVPQQYMS-ALLQATGAQE-DEYG

B Ch    SVTISGVVV-ACEGGCQAILDTGTSKLVGPSSDIL-NIQQAIGATQ-NQYG
G Pn    RVTVGNKYV-ACFFTCQAIVDTGTSLLVMPQGAYN-RIIKDLGVS---SDG

PJP     SYTA-GS---QSGDGFSGIADTGTTLLLLBDSVVSQYYSQVSGAQQDSNAG
EPP     GYAV-GSGT-FKSTSIDGIADTGTTLLYLPATVVSAYWAQVSGAKSSSSVG
MMP     GITVDGSAAVRFSRPQAFTIDTGTNFFIMPSSAASKIVKAALPDATETQQG

Com Gas          C    C AI DTGTS L  P              G        G
Com all                    DTGT                             G


        *     ^         ^            ^       *abcdefghij ^   285
P PnA   EMVISCSSIDSLPDIVFTIDGVQYPLSPSAYILQ----------DDDSCTS
B PnA   /INSLPD/
H PnA   DMVVSCSAISSLPDIVFTINGVQYPVPPSAYILQ----------SEGSCIS
M PnA   EMVVSCSAISSLPDIVFTINGIQYPVPPSAYILQ----------SQGSCTS

H PnC   QFLVNCNSIQNLPSLTFIINGVEFPLPPSSYILS----------NNGYCTV
M PnC   QFLVNCNSIQNLPTLTFIINGVEFPLPPSSYILN----------NNGVCTV

B Ch    EFDIDCDNLSYMPTVVFEINGKMYPLTPSAYTSQ----------DQGFCTS
G Pn    E--ISCDDISKLPDVTFHINGHAFTLPASAYVLN----------EDGSCML

PJP     GYVFDCST--NLPDFSVSISGYTATVPGSLINYG-------PSGDGSTCLG
EPP     GYVFPCSA--TLPSFTFGVGSARIVIPGDYIDFG------PISTGSSSCFG
MMP     -WVVPCASYQNSKSTISIVMQKSGSSSDTIEISVPVSKMLPVDQSNETCMF

Com Gas          C     P   F I G      S Y                 C
Com all          C                                        C


               ^           a ab^ 303    ^        a ^      327
P PnA   GFEGMDVPTSSGE-L--WILGDVFIRQYYTVFDRAN-NKVGLAPVA
B PnA                /L--WILGDVFIRQYFTVFDRGN-NQIGLAPVA
H PnA   GFQGMNLPTESGE-L--WILGDVFIRQYFTVFDRAN-NQVGLAPVA
M PnA   GFQGMDVPTESGE-L--WILGDVFIRQYFTVFDRAN-NQVGLAPVA

H PnC   GVEPTYLSSQNGQPL--WILGDVFLRSYYSVYDLGN-NRVGFATAA
M PnC   GVEPTYLSAQNSQPLVYWILGDVFLRSYYSVYDLSN-NRVGFATAA

B Ch    GFQS----ENHSQ-K--WILGDVFIREYYSVFDRAN-NLVGLAKAI
G Pn    GFENMGTPTELGE-Q--WILGDVFIREYYVIFDRAN-NKVGLSPLS

PJP     GIQSN----SGIG-F--LIFGDIFLKSQYVVFDSD-GPQLGFAPQA
EPP     GIQSS----AGIG-I--NIFGDVALKAAFVVFNGATTPTLGFASK
MMP     IILP-----NGGN-Q--YIVGNLFLRFFVNVYDFGN-NRIGFAPLASAYENE

Com Gas G                   WILGDVF R Y     D  N N  G
Com all                     I G                      G
```

Fig. 2—*contd.*

that though zymogens for the fungal aspartic proteases never have been observed, the *M. miehei* protease is synthesized with a propart that is homologous to the proparts of the gastric proteases. The functional significance of this is discussed below. Among the other aspartic proteases from fungi those from *E. parasitica* and *P. janthinellum* are the only ones that have been fully sequenced. The latter has only a very weak milk-clotting activity, but its structure is included for comparison, and because this enzyme has been of great importance for elucidation of the tertiary structure of the aspartic proteases. The *E. parasitica*, *P. janthinellum* and *M. miehei* proteases show no immunochemical cross-reactions. The partial immunochemical identity between *M. pusillus* and *M. miehei* protease is consistent with preliminary information about their primary structures. Shoun and Beppu (University of Tokyo, personal communication) have identified 186 amino acid residues in the *M. pusillus* protease, and these

---

Fig. 2. Alignment of amino acid sequences of proteases from rennets and some related proteases. P PgA, P PnA: porcine pepsinogen and pepsin.[52,55-57] B PgA, B PnA: bovine pepsinogen and pepsin.[59,60] H PgA, H PnA: human pepsinogen and pepsin.[61] M PgA, M PnA: monkey pepsinogen and pepsin.[61a] B PgC: bovine progastricsin (Ref. 60a, Harboe and Foltmann, this Institute). H PgC, H PnC: human progastricsin and gastricsin.[25,61b] M PgC, M PnC: monkey progastricsin and gastricsin.[61c] P Ch: pig chymosin (Lønblad and Foltmann, this Institute). B Pch, B Ch: calf prochymosin and chymosin.[51] F Pch, F Ch: cat prochymosin and chymosin.[62] G Pg, G Pn: chicken pepsinogen and pepsin.[58] PJP: *Penicillium janthinellum* protease.[66] EPP: *Endothia parasitica* protease (V. Barkholt, this Institute. MMP: *Mucor miehei* protease.[63,63a,b] Com Gas: residues that are identical in gastric zymogens and proteases. Com all: residues that are identical in all the structures. 'This Institute' indicates work in progress for which documentation has not been published.

The results are expressed in the single letter code A:Ala; B:Asx; C:Cys; D:Asp; E:Glu; F:Phe; G:Gly; H:His; I:Ile; K:Lys; L:Leu; M:Met; N:Asn; P:Pro; Q:Gln; R:Arg; S:Ser; T:Thr; V:Val; W:Trp; X:Unknown; Y:Tyr; Z:Glx; '-': gap; '/': end of fragment. Prefix 'p' indicates propart numbering, starting from the longest peptide chain (prochymosin). Numbering starts again from the N-terminus of pig pepsin, insertions relative to pig pepsin are marked by lower case letters. In addition to numbers mentioned in the text and to numbers ending a line, every number of 10 is marked by '^'. The vertebrate proteases have S-S bridges from C(45) to C(50), C(206) to C(210), and C(250) to C(283), MMP has bridges from C(45) to C(50) and C(250) to C(283), EPP and PJP have an S-S bridge from C(250) to C(283) only. Underlined residues are N-termini in active enzymes. '*' marks location of introns (see Section 7). For further comments see the text.

show about 85% identity with the corresponding residues in the *M. miehei* protease.

3.3 Tertiary Structure

Several aspartic proteases have now been analysed by X-ray crystallography[64–69] and the results show that the homology of the folding of their peptide chains is even more pronounced than the homology that is observed by comparison of their primary structures. A schematic, generalized model is shown in Fig. 3. The molecule is bilobal, consisting of an N-terminal and a C-terminal domain separated by a cleft that runs perpendicular to the largest dimension of the molecule. It is noteworthy that the cleft and its immediate surroundings comprise most of the amino acid residues which are non-conditionally conserved in the primary structures. This applies especially to two aspartic acid residues (numbers 32 and 215) and their neighbouring residues. These are located

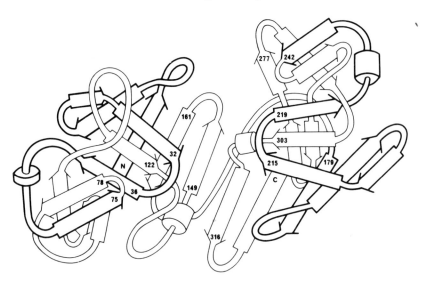

Fig. 3. Schematic and expanded drawing of the folding of the peptide chain of an aspartic protease molecule. The model is opened along the cleft, in order to illustrate the two-domain structure. The arrows indicate β structures and the cylinders short stretches of α-helices. N-terminus and C-terminus are marked by N and C, respectively; relative to the active site cleft, these are located at the 'back' of the molecule. The numbering of residues corresponds to that of Fig. 2. The figure is drawn on basis of data from Refs 64–69.

in the so-called psi-shaped structures, i.e. two bends from the N-terminal and the C-terminal domains with side chains of Asp-32 and Asp-215 pointing out toward the cleft. Behind each bend run the peptide chains with the conservative residues around Gly-122 and Gly-303. All evidence indicates that the cleft constitutes the active site with Asp-32 and Asp-215 participating in the catalytic mechanism, whereas the rest of the cleft serves as an extended binding site that may accommodate up to 7 or 8 amino acid residues of the substrate peptide chain.

3.4 Post-translational Modifications

Several mammalian pepsins occur in both unphosphorylated and phosphorylated forms. In porcine and bovine pepsins the phosphorylated forms are predominant. After determination of the amino acid sequence of porcine pepsin, Ser-68 was identified as the site of phosphorylation.[52] Bovine pepsin may contain up to 3 phosphate groups[70,71] but their locations in the structure have not been determined. The presence of phosphate and sialic acid has been reported in bovine gastricsin[72] but structural analyses were not made. Chicken pepsin is glycosylated at Asn-68 and the carbohydrate moiety may be sulphated.[58] As regards calf chymosin, no post-translational modifications have been observed. Glycosylation of the fungal rennet enzymes apparently depends on the culture conditions. The commercial enzymes from *M. pusillus* and *E. parasitica* are not glycosylated, whereas the enzyme from *M. miehei* is glycosylated at Asn-72 and Asn-167 (Ref. 63).

4. PROPERTIES

4.1 General Proteolytic Activity and Stability

All the milk-clotting enzymes have pH optima for general proteolysis at acidic conditions, but it must be recalled that for these proteases the pH optimum is not an absolute value. The observed values for the pH of optimum activity depend on experimental conditions such as denaturation of substrates, ionic strength of the solutions, duration and temperature of the experiments, and the methods used to follow the progress of the proteolysis like, for instance, the conditions for precipitation of undigested substrate. Hence, though the general trends are the same in different experiments, a detailed comparison among these proteases is only possible with one common set of conditions. With these reservations in mind, the following values for pH optima for general proteolytic activities may be stated: pepsin, pH 2 (Refs 9, 10, 15–17); gastricsin, broad optimum about pH 3 (Refs 9, 17); chymosin, pH 3–4 (Refs 9, 12); fungal proteases, pH 3–4 (Refs 33, 54, 73). When tested with haemoglobin as substrate and at the pH of optimum activity, solutions of equal milk-clotting activities against bovine milk show the following approximate ratios of general proteolytic activities: calf chymosin/bovine pepsin/porcine pepsin; 1/3/6 (Refs 9, 12).

As regards stability, the observed limits for pH stability may also depend on the experimental conditions like ionic strength of solutions, temperature, duration of the experiment and concentration of enzymes. Pepsin and chymosin undergo autolysis at the pH of optimum proteolytic activity[12] whereas the fungal proteases are stable down to pH 2·5 (Refs 32, 33, 54). In the neutral or alkaline ranges, pig pepsin and calf chymosin lose activity at pH values above 6·5, but the rate of inactivation is different for the two enzymes and pig pepsin has a sharp drop in stability at pH 7 (Refs 9, 12). Bovine and chicken pepsins are stable at pH 7 but are inactivated at pH 8 (Refs 9, 74). Inactivation of bovine gastricsin occurs at pH values about 7·5 (Ref. 9). For the *M. miehei* protease a considerable loss of activity was observed at pH 9 after 1 h at 38°C,[32] but at 20°C both the *M. miehei* and the *M. pusillus* proteases withstood pH 9 for 1 h without observable loss of activity.[31] The mammalian gastric proteases show different susceptibilities to inactivation by urea, the pepsins being rather stable. This has been used for differentiation among the bovine enzymes.[38]

4.2 Catalytic Mechanism and Specificity

During investigations on the enzymic properties of porcine pepsin, Knowles and collaborators found that two groups with pK_a values about 1·5 and 4·5 participated in the catalytic mechanism.[75] It has also been observed that pepsin and related proteases are inhibited after reaction with diazoacetyl-DL-norleucine methyl ester (abbreviated DAN)[76] or 1,2-epoxy-3-(p-nitrophenoxy) propane (abbreviated EPNP).[77] Determinations of the primary structure showed that the inhibition with DAN is due to esterification of Asp-215 whereas the inhibition with EPNP preferentially occurs by esterification of Asp-32. The importance of these two residues is consistent with their locations in the molecule. In the primary structure, both are surrounded by highly conservative residues. In the tertiary structure, they are located in the middle of the cleft, close to each other and are highly hydrogen bonded. Furthermore, the peptide inhibitor, pepstatin, is bound in the cleft.[64-68]

Thus, all experiments indicate that the cleft is an extended substrate binding site and that the two aspartic acid residues constitute the active centre as such; however, the catalytic mechanism itself is not well elucidated. Asp-32 is buried in the cleft in such a way that its side-chain can not come in direct contact with the substrate, and in spite of many attempts, it has not been possible to observe any covalent intermediate during the enzymic catalysis. Hence, it has been suggested that a nucleophilic attack of a negative charge from the two aspartic acid residues on the carbonyl group of the scissile peptide bond is mediated via a water molecule that is hydrogen bonded to the two aspartic acid residues.[14,78-80] From the latest X-ray crystallographic refinements, on the other hand, James and Sielecki[81] have concluded that the peptide substrate will displace the water molecule between the two aspartates, and that the electron transfer occurs via another water molecule. The question of a mechanistic model is not finally settled, but a covalent intermediate appears unlikely.

Calf chymosin may be inhibited by reaction with dansyl chloride. It was first suggested that the inhibition was due to modification of a lysine residue[82] but reactivation experiments[83] made modification of a histidine residue more probable. Unpublished results from our Institute (Agerlin Olsen, M.Sc. thesis) have shown that His-74 is modified by dansylation. Although His-74 does not belong to the non-conditionally conserved residues, it is located in very conservative surroundings from Ile-73 to Gly-78. These residues form a flap that is essential for substrate binding; thus, modification of a group in this flap may prevent catalysis.

Calf chymosin and *M. pusillus* protease may also be inactivated by photo-oxidation of a histidine residue,[84,85] and NMR spectroscopy of *M. pusillus* protease has shown that a histidine residue is located close to one of the two essential aspartic acid residues. It was therefore suggested that a histidine group interacts directly with one of the aspartic acid residues in the active centre.[86]

But the amino acid sequence of *M. pusillus* protease (Beppu and collaborators, personal communication) shows that the only two histidine residues are located at positions which correspond to the histidines in the *M. miehei* protease (His-42 and His-140). At these positions no histidines are found in calf chymosin. Thus, the significance of the histidine residues in these enzymes can not be compared directly.

In a long series of experiments, Fruton and coworkers showed that the length of the substrate peptide chain was of great importance for the catalytic efficiency of pig pepsin[16] and subsequent investigations have shown that the same holds true for chymosin[21] (and for other aspartic proteases also). In order to explain the enhancement of the catalytic efficiency by increased substrate peptide length, Pearl[80] recently suggested that the binding energy of the substrate is transferred to the scissile peptide bond and thereby facilitates cleavage.

Kinetic as well as X-ray crystallographic studies show that the binding cleft may accommodate a substrate peptide chain with 4 residues before and 3 residues after the scissile peptide bond. The extended binding site, with possible cooperative interaction of the individual sub-sites, opens the possibility of a high degree of specificity, but the molecular details of the substrate binding are not yet worked out for any of the milk-clotting proteases.

Digestion of the B-chain of oxidized insulin has been used in several investigations on the specificities of these enzymes; although minor differences are observed, the overall pattern of degradation is quite similar for all.[12,73,87–89] The influence of ionic strength and composition of buffers has been investigated by degradation of ribonuclease with bovine and porcine pepsins.[89] In this case, the activity of bovine pepsin is lower and more dependent on ionic strength than that of porcine pepsin. Calf chymosin does not cleave ribonuclease.[12] Cleavage of α and β-caseins by chymosin and pepsin has also been investigated.[90–92b] The experiments show that the milk-clotting proteases preferentially cleave between amino acid residues with apolar side-chains. Cleavages after Asp or Glu have also been observed, but under acidic conditions the carboxylic acids in the side chains become protonated and thus are able to fit into an apolar binding site.

The clotting of bovine milk depends primarily on a limited proteolysis involving cleavage of the bond Phe-105–Met-106 in κ-casein. Several studies have been carried out with synthetic peptides that mimic this peptide bond and its neighbouring amino acid sequence in κ-casein. These will be dealt with in Chapter 3 of this book. Here it should be mentioned that the tryptic fragment of κ-casein His-98–Lys-111 is cleaved with a K_{cat}/K_m value which is about 75 times larger than the value for the peptide His-102–Ile-108 (Refs 21, 93). This means that interactions of residues outside the cleft also influence the catalytic efficiency.

Calf chymosin occurs as at least two isoenzymes. Chymosin A has an aspartic acid residue at position 244, while chymosin B has glycine at this position. In the tertiary structure depicted in Fig. 3, this residue is located in the upper, right part of the cleft. Interaction between Asp-244 in chymosin A and His-102 of κ-casein may explain why the milk-clotting activity of chymosin A is about 20% higher than that of chymosin B.[12] A third chymosin fraction from chromatography on DEAE–cellulose is designated chymosin C. This is a mixture of several components, and has not been analysed in detail. Among other components, chymosin C includes a degradation product of chymosin A. The general proteolytic activity of this degradation product is 50% of that of chymosin A but its milk-clotting activity is only 25%.[12]

5. ACTIVATION OF ZYMOGENS

The vertebrate gastric proteases are all secreted as inactive precursors. The fungal aspartic proteases are apparently secreted as active forms, but nothing is known about their pathways of activation.

Manufacturers of cheese rennets ensure that the maximum milk-clotting activity is developed in the rennet before it is sold. Hence, the activation process is not of importance in cheesemaking, but from a biochemical point of view, the activation of the gastric zymogens has interesting aspects.

The zymogens for the vertebrate extracellular proteases are activated by limited proteolysis which, generally, is brought about by other proteases, but the activation of zymogens of the gastric proteases may be initiated by the action of hydrogen ions only. This may be explained by the following mechanism, first suggested for the activation of prochymosin.[12]

From the primary structure of the zymogens (Fig. 2) it is seen, (1) that the majority of the basic amino acid residues are located in the N-terminal regions of the peptide chains, and (2) that the distribution of these amino acids is homologous. Lys or Arg may substitute each other at the positions p5 and p10, but the positive charge of a basic amino acid is retained. Arg-p15 is common in all vertebrate zymogens, whereas Lys-p12 and Lys-p38 are found in the propart for *M. miehei* protease as well. Determination of the tertiary structure of porcine pepsinogen[93a] has confirmed that at neutral pH the zymogen molecules are held in a stable and inactive conformation through apolar interactions as well as electrostatic interactions between positive charges of the basic amino acid residues in propart, and negative dicarboxylic amino acid residues in the enzyme. In porcine pepsinogen the side chain of Lys-p38 points towards the active site

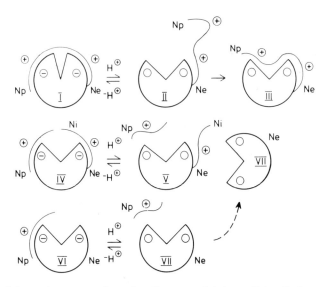

Fig. 4. Schematic presentation of pathways and intermediates that may occur during the activation of gastric zymogens. Np, Ni and Ne indicate N-termini of proenzyme, intermediate and active enzyme, respectively. I: Zymogen at neutral pH, stabilized in an inactive conformation (symbolized by a narrow cleft). II: Zymogen under acidic conditions (active conformation is symbolized by open cleft). III: Zymogen in active conformation with the propart folded back in the cleft, ready for intra-molecular cleavage. IV and V: Equilibrium between intermediate in complex with the N-terminal fragment of the propart and free intermediate. VI and VII: Equilibrium between active enzyme in complex with the N-terminal fragment of the propart and free enzyme. All active forms may give rise to proteolytic cleavage at any stage of the activation process (symbolized by VII right to V). In the final stages, the propart is hydrolysed to small peptides that do not form a complex with the enzymes.

During the activation of pepsinogen and progastricsin, I, IV, VI and VII have been observed as discrete zones after gel electrophoreses at pH 5·5–6·0 (Ref. 25, Foltmann, unpublished). V may be trapped if the activation takes place in the presence of pepstatin.[95,97] Non-complexed intermediates have been observed by gel electrophoresis in presence of SDS.[97] The milk-clotting activity of the complexes are partly suppressed. It is not known how the propart peptides are bound in a non-covalent complex. (Reproduced, with permission, from Ref. 97a.)

cleft and its ε-amino group is located between Asp-32 and Asp-215. Lys-p38 is common in all the structures shown in Fig. 2, and it appears most probable that the positive charge of its ε-amino group is important for bringing the negative charges of Asp-32 and Asp-215 together during the initial folding of the peptide chain. Under acidic conditions, the carboxylic acids become protonated, the salt bridges are weakened and the zymogen molecules undergo conformational changes leading to the formation of the active centre without cleavages of peptide bonds. The activation will then proceed by a limited proteolysis that finally removes about 45 amino acid residues from the N-terminal part of the peptide chain, which is designated the propart or the activation segment. The liberated propart peptides may still inhibit the milk-clotting activity of some of the gastric proteases (see Ref. 93b for further references).

The main features of the activation process are the same for all the gastric zymogens, but depending on pH, ionic strength, concentration of the zymogen, the amino acid sequence of the propart and the specificity of the active enzyme, the activation process may follow different pathways, and the individual pathways may be partly overlapping. Furthermore, under physiological conditions and during the production of cheese rennet different zymogens and active enzymes are present. These will probably also interact with each other. Thus, the system is very complex and all details have not been elucidated.

Figure 4 illustrates in a schematic way some pathways and intermediates that have been observed during activation of purified zymogens. When calf prochymosin is activated at pH 2 the first cleavage occurs between Phe-p27 and Leu-p28; the process is predominantly intermolecular but may also occur as an intramolecular reaction.[12,94] The resulting intermediate (corresponding to Fig. 4V) has been designated pseudochymosin. Nothing is known about the folding of the remaining fragment of the propart in pseudochymosin, but for 20 h at pH 2 and 0°C no further proteolysis was observed.[94] However, at pH 4–5·5, the limited proteolysis proceeds. When a solution of pseudochymosin was transferred to pH 5·5 only chymosin was found after 20 h at 25°C.[94] Pseudochymosin and chymosin are not inhibited by the propart peptides. In solutions of 0·1 mg/ml at pH 2, porcine or bovine pepsinogens are first cleaved between Leu-p18 and Ile-p19; under these conditions the reaction is predominantly monomolecular (Fig. 4 III).[96] In contrast to the activation of prochymosin, the degradation of pseudopepsin to pepsin proceeds at pH 2. At higher initial concentrations of porcine pepsinogen, activation may also occur in a single step that removes the entire propart.[97] The propart peptides from the pepsinogens have pronounced inhibitory effects and complexes between the peptides and intermediates or active enzyme behave as single components on ion exchange chromatography.[97] At pH 2, chicken pepsinogen is cleaved at the same site as prochymosin, the propart peptide has inhibitory properties, but the stability of any non-covalent complex has not been investigated.[95]

During the production of cheese rennet activation may take place at about pH 4·6 (Ref. 22). At this pH only a minor part of the zymogen molecules are in an active conformation, but still sufficient to start the activation process. Thereafter, the activation is mainly autocatalytic in the sense that the rate is determined by molecules which have undergone the limited proteolysis. On activation at pH between 2 and 4·7, a combination of the different pathways may occur simultaneously; the resulting mixtures have not been analysed.

6. PHYSIOLOGY OF MAMMALIAN GASTRIC PROTEASES

Pepsinogen, progastricsin and prochymosin are secreted by the chief cells in the fundic part of the gastric mucosa.[14,41,98] These are located mainly in the lower half of the oxyntic glands which are tubular structures with a narrow lumen oriented almost perpendicular to the muscular sheet surrounding the stomach. The acid-producing parietal cells are located mainly above the chief cells. This means that the zymogens of the gastric proteases are secreted directly into a highly acidic liquid, and under physiological conditions, the initial limited proteolysis of the activation process presumably occurs already in lumen of the glands. This is important for the clotting of milk in the stomachs of young mammals: milk has a rather high buffering capacity, so after suckling the contents of the lumen may have a pH up to 5 or 6 (Refs 99, 100) and at such pH, it would take hours to activate the zymogens.

Until a few years ago it was often assumed that the production of chymosins was characteristic for young ruminants (e.g. Ref. 12) but electrophoretic and immunochemical investigations have shown that the production of gastric proteases changes from young to adult mammals, and that several species have gastric proteases which show partial immunochemical identity with calf chymosin.[48]

Quantitative analyses of the ontogeny of gastric proteases was carried out with pigs.[101] The results show that chymosin is produced in large amounts from birth with a rapid decrease after the first week of life. Pepsin is virtually absent during this period but a rapid increase in the production of pepsin starts after about two weeks. A less detailed analysis of the production of chymosin and pepsin in calves showed, in principle, the same pattern of secretion, though with the difference that in cattle the production of chymosin never comes to a complete stop.[102]

To illustrate the physiological significance of chymosin it should be recalled, firstly, that piglets and calves, as well as other mammals in which chymosin-like enzymes have been observed, also have a postnatal uptake of immunoglobulins from colostrum;[48,103] secondly that pepsin may cleave the immunoglobulins in the hinge region between the Fab and the Fc fragments. The degradation of immunoglobulins by pepsin or chymosin has not been investigated under physiological conditions but it appears likely that secretion of pepsin would damage the uptake of immunoglobulins in newborn mammals whereas the weaker general proteolytic activity of chymosin will cause less damage.

The physiological significance of clot formation has not · been investigated. The significance may be that the newborn, toothless mammal has the advantage of taking liquid food that solidifies as a rubberlike clot in the stomach. The clot may then act as a mechanical stimulus for the subsequent reactions in the digestive tract. In this context, it is interesting that the clotting activity of pig chymosin against porcine milk is about 6 times that against bovine milk and, conversely, the clotting activity of calf chymosin against porcine milk is about half of the activity against bovine milk.[101] This means that in spite of a close structural relationship between the two chymosins, an adaptation between the specificity of the chymosins and the structures of the caseins has taken place.

7. CLONING OF CHYMOSIN AND STRUCTURE OF ITS GENE

Due to the shortage of calf stomachs and the economic value of cheese rennet, calf chymosin was one of the first mammalian enzymes of which cloning in micro-organisms was carried out.[104–110] After cloning of the gene for prochymosin and expression in *E. coli*, about 99·8% of the synthesized proenzyme may be bound in an insoluble form.[105] After disintegration of the cells, the zymogen can be recovered by dissolving the washed cell debris in 9 M urea/0·05 M Tris-HCl pH 8/0·5 M NaCl, the solution is dialysed, a precipitate is removed by centrifugation, and the supernatant is purified by chromatography on DEAE-cellulose.[108] The resulting prochymosin behaves like that isolated from calf stomachs and can be activated in a similar manner. The gene for prochymosin has also been cloned in yeast (Saccharomyces cerevisiae) and the amounts of expression correspond to 0·5–2% of total yeast protein.[109,110] In yeast, about 20% of the prochymosin can be released in a soluble form which can be activated directly, the remaining 80% is still associated with cell debris. The experiments of Mellor et al.[109] also comprised cloning of chymosin without the propart. Though the level of chymosin m-RNA was similar to that of prochymosin m-RNA, no milk-clotting activity was observed in clones containing the chymosin gene. The results suggest that the propart is essential for correct folding of the peptide chain.

Up to July 1986, rennets produced from cloned chymosin have not been marketed but the experiments have provided interesting results about the structure of the prochymosin gene. The code for the prochymosin gene is preceded by a series of nucleotides coding for a signal peptide consisting of 16 amino acid residues. The structure of this is typical for a signal peptide that facilitates the transport of a secreted protein through the membrane of the endoplasmic reticulum. After the initiating methionine residue follows an arginine and then a long stretch of apolar amino acid residues.[106,107]

With minor exceptions, the observed nucleotide sequence of c-DNA for prochymosin corresponds to the primary structure as determined by amino acid sequencing. At position 244, either Asp[105,107] or Gly[106] have been found which is consistent with the two isoenzymes observed previously. At position 171, Asp was found by amino acid sequencing and in two of the nucleic acid sequences,[104,107] but Asn was reported by Harris et al.[106] Asp was found at position 158 by amino acid sequencing but all the nucleotide sequences indicate Asn at this position. It is possible that deamidation occurred during amino acid sequencing, although the possibility of isoenzymes can not be ruled out.

Moir et al.[107] reported that the genes for the individual prochymosins represent different alleles at a single locus. At least two alleles are predominant, but other forms may occur in minor amounts. As regards introns, it is most interesting that the genes for calf prochymosin,[111] human pepsinogen[61] and mouse prorenin, EC 3.4.23.15[112] have a total of 8 introns located at identical positions in their nucleotide sequences. This means that the location of introns appears more conservative than the homology observed in the primary structures of the genes. The significance of this has not yet been elucidated, but it is interesting that several of the suggested insertions in the alignment of the amino acid sequences (Fig. 2) are located in the immediate vicinities of the observed introns.

REFERENCES

1. Deschamps, J. B., *J. Pharm.*, 1840, **26**, 412.
2. Lea, A. S. and Dickinson, W. L., *J. Physiol. Lond.*, 1890, **11**, 307.
3. Foltmann, B., *Methods in Enzymology*, Vol. 19, G. E. Perlmann and L. Lorand (eds), 1970, Academic Press, New York—London, p. 421.
4. IUB-IUPAC, *Enzyme Nomenclature*, 1978.
5. Veringa, H. A., *Dairy Sci. Abstr.*, 1961, **23**, 197.
6. Sardinas, J. L., *Adv. appl. Microbiol.*, 1972, **15**, 39.
7. Sardinas, J. L., *Process Biochem.*, 1976, **11**(4), 10.
8. Sternberg, M., *Adv. appl. Microbiol.*, 1976, **20**, 135.
9. Antonini, J. and Ribadeau Dumas, B., *Biochemie*, 1971, **53**, 321.
10. Ryle, A. P., *Methods in Enzymology*, Vol. 19, G. E. Perlmann and L. Lorand (eds), 1970, Academic Press, New York—London, p. 316.
11. Rothe, G. A. L., Axelsen, N. H. Jøhnk, P. and Foltmann, B., *J. Dairy Res.*, 1976, **43**, 85.
12. Foltmann, B., *C. R. Trav. Lab. Carlsberg*, 1966, **35**, 143.
13. Hofmann, T., *Adv. Chem. Ser.*, 1974, **136**, 146.
14. Foltmann, B., *Essays in Biochemistry*, Vol. 17, P. N. Campbell and R. D. Marshall (eds), 1981, Academic Press, New York—London, p. 52.
15. Fruton, J. S., In: *The Enzymes*, 2nd edn, P. D. Boyer (ed.), Vol. 3, 1971, Academic Press, New York—London, p. 119.
16. Fruton, J. S., *Adv. Enzymol.*, 1976, **44**, 1.
17. Tang, J., *Methods in Enzymology*, G. E. Perlmann and L. Lorand (eds), Vol. 19, 1970, Academic Press, New York—London, p. 406.
18. Scott, R. In: *Topics in Enzyme and Fermentation Biotechnology*, Vol. 3, A. Wiseman (ed.), 1979, John Wiley, New York, p. 103.
19. Ernstrom, C. A. In: *Fundamentals of Dairy Chemistry*, 2nd edn, B. H. Webb, A. H. Johnson and J. A. Alford (eds), 1974, AVI Publ. Co., Westport, Conn., p. 662.
20. Green, M. L., *J. Dairy Res.*, 1977, **44**, 159.
21. Visser, S., *Neth. Milk Dairy J.*, 1981, **35**, 65.
22. Placek, C., Bavisotto, V. S. and Jadd, E. C., *Ind. Engng Chem.*, 1960, **52**(1), 2.
23. Meitner, P. A. and Kassell, B., *Biochem. J.*, 1971, **121**, 249.
24. Harboe, M., Andersen, P. M., Foltmann, B., Kay, J. and Kassell, B., *J. Biol. Chem.*, 1974, **249**, 4487.
25. Foltmann, B. and Jensen, A. L., *Eur. J. Biochem.*, 1982, **128**, 63.
26. O'Leary, P. A. and Fox, P. F., *J. Dairy Res.*, 1975, **42**, 445.
27. Aunstrup, K. In: *Microbial Enzymes and Bioconversions*, A. H. Rose (ed.), 1980, Academic Press, London—New York, p. 50.

58   *Bent Foltmann*

28. De Koning, P. J. and Draaisma, J. Th. M., *Neth. Milk Dairy J.*, 1973, **27**, 368.
29. Ernstrom, C. A., *J. Dairy Sci.*, 1958, **41**, 1663.
30. Garnot, P., Thapon, J. L., Mathieu, C. M., Maubois, J. L. and Ribadeau Dumas, B., *J. Dairy Sci.*, 1972, **55**, 1641.
31. O'Leary, P. A. and Fox, P. F., *J. Dairy Res.*, 1974, **41**, 381.
32. Ottesen, M. and Rickert, W., *C. R. Trav. Lab. Carlsberg*, 1970, **37**, 301.
33. Arima, K., Yu, J. and Iwasaki, S., *Methods in Enzymology*, Vol. 19, G. E. Perlmann and L. Lorand (eds) 1970, Academic Press, New York—London, p. 446.
34. Kobayashi, H. and Murakami, K., *Agric. Biol. Chem.*, 1978, **42**, 2227.
35. Stepanov, V. M., Lavrenova, G. I., Adly, K., Gonchar, M. V., Balandina, G. M., Slavinskaya, M. M. and Strongin, A. Ya., *Biochemia*, 1976, **41**, 294.
36. Stepanov, V. M., Rudenskaya, G. N., Gaida, A. V. and Osterman, A. L., *J. Biochem. Biophys. Meth.*, 1981, **5**, 177.
37. Lawrence, R. C. and Sanderson, W. B., *J. Dairy Res.*, 1969, **36**, 21.
38. Douillard, R., *Biochemie*, 1971, **53**, 447.
39. De Koning, P. J., *Int. Dairy Fed. Ann. Bull.*, 1974, Document 80.
40. Uriel, J., *Nature, Lond.*, 1960, **188**, 853.
41. Kreuning, J., Samloff, I. M., Rotter, J. I. and Eriksson, A. W. (eds), *Pepsinogens in Man*, 1985, Alan R. Liss, Inc., New York.
42. Shovers, J., Fossum, G. and Neal, A., *J. Dairy Sci.*, 1972, **35**, 1532.
43. Foltmann, B., Szecsi, P. B. and Tarasova, N. I., *Anal. Biochem.*, 1985, **146**, 353.
44. Foltmann, B., Tarasova, N. I. and Szecsi, P. B. In: *Aspartic Proteinases and their Inhibitors*, V. Kostka (ed.), 1985, W. de Gruyter, Berlin—New York, p. 491.
45. Axelsen, N. H. (ed.), Handbook of immunoprecipitation in gel techniques, *Scand. J. Immunol.*, 1983, **17**, suppl. 10.
46. De Koning, P. J., *Int. Dairy Fed. Ann. Bull.*, 1972, part IV, 1.
47. Rothe, G. A. L., Harboe, M. K. and Martiny, S. C., *J. Dairy Res.*, 1977, **44**, 73.
48. Foltmann, B. and Axelsen, N. H. In: *Trends in Enzymology, FEBS Proceedings*, Vol. 60, 1980, p. 271.
49. Harboe, M. K. In: *Aspartic Proteinases and their Inhibitors*, V. Kostka (ed.), W. de Gruyter, Berlin—New York, 1985, p. 537.
50. Etoh, Y., Shoun, H., Beppu, T. and Arima, K., *Agric. Biol. Chem.*, 1979, **43**, 209.
51. Foltmann, B., Pedersen, V. B., Jacobsen, H., Kauffman, D. and Wybrandt, G., *Proc. Nat. Acad. Sci. USA*, 1977, **74**, 2321.
52. Tang, J., Sepulveda, P., Marciniszyn, J., Chen, K. C. S., Huang, W. Y., Tao, N., Liu, D. and Lanier, J. P., *Proc. Nat. Acad. Sci. USA*, 1973, **70**, 3437.
53. Rickert, W. S. and Elliott, J. R., *Can. J. Biochem.*, 1973, **51**, 1638.
54. Whitaker, J. R., *Methods in Enzymology*, Vol. 19, G. E. Perlmann and L. Lorand (eds), 1970, Academic Press, New York—London, p. 436.
55. Ong, E. B. and Perlmann, G. E., *J. Biol. Chem.*, 1968, **243**, 6104.
56. Pedersen, V. B. and Foltmann, B., *FEBS Lett.*, 1973, **35**, 255.
57. Moravek, L. and Kostka, V., *FEBS Lett.*, 1974, **43**, 207.
58. Baudys, M. and Kostka, V., *Eur. J. Biochem.*, 1983, **136**, 89.

59. Harboe, M. K. and Foltmann, B., *FEBS Lett.*, 1975, **60**, 133.
60. Rasmussen, K. T. and Foltmann, B., *Acta Chem. Scand.*, 1971, **25**, 3873.
60a. Klemm, P., Poulsen, F., Harboe, M. K. and Foltmann, B., *Acta Chem. Scand.*, 1976, **B30**, 979.
61. Sogawa, K., Yoshiaki, F. K., Mizukami, Y., Ichihara, Y. and Takahashi, K., *J. Biol. Chem.*, 1983, **258**, 5306.
61a. Kageyama, T. and Takahashi, K., *J. Biol. Chem.*, 1986, **261**, 4395.
61b. Wong, R. N. S. and Tang, J., *J. Biol. Chem.*, submitted for publication.
61c. Kageyama, T. and Takahashi, K., *J. Biol. Chem.*, 1986, **261**, 4406.
62. Jensen, T., Axelsen, N. H. and Foltmann, B., *Biochim. Biophys. Acta*, 1982, **705**, 249.
63. Bech, A.-M. and Foltmann, B., *Neth. Milk Dairy J.*, 1981, **35**, 275.
63a. Boel, E., Bech, A.-M., Randrup, K., Dræger, B., Fiil, N. P. and Foltmann, B., *Proteins*, 1987 (in press).
63b. Gray, G., *et al.*, *Gene*, 1987 (in press).
64. Tang, J., James, M. N. G., Hsu, I. N., Jenkins, J. A. and Blundell, T. L., *Nature, Lond.*, 1978, **271**, 618.
65. Blundell, T. L., Jones, H. B., Khan, G., Taylor, G., Sewell, B. T., Pearl, L. H. and Wood, S. P. In: *Trends in Enzymology, FEBS Proceedings*, Vol. 60, 1980, p. 281.
66. James, M. N. G. and Sielecki, A., *J. Molec. Biol.*, 1983, **163**, 299.
67. Andreeva, N. S., Zdanov, A. S., Gustchina, A. E. and Fedorov, A. A., *J. Biol. Chem.*, 1984, **259**, 11 353.
68. Blundell, T. L., Jenkins, J., Pearl, L., Sewell, T. and Pedersen, V. In: *Aspartic Proteinases and their Inhibitors*, V. Kostka (ed.), 1985, W. de Gruyter, Berlin—New York, p. 151.
69. Safro, M. G., Andreeva, N. S. and Zhdanov, A. S. In: *Aspartic Proteinases and their Inhibitors*, V. Kostka (ed.), 1985, W. de Gruyter, Berlin—New York, p. 183.
70. Martin, P., *Biochemie*, 1984, **66**, 371.
71. Martin, P. and Corre, C., *Anal. Biochem.*, 1984, **143**, 256.
72. Martin, P., Tricu-Cuot, P., Collin, J. C. and Ribadeau Dumas, B., *Eur. J. Biochem.*, 1982, **122**, 31.
73. Rickert, W., *C. R. Trav. Lab. Carlsberg*, 1970, **38**, 1.
74. Bohak, Z., *Meth. Enzymology*, 1970, **19**, 347.
75. Knowles, J. R., *Phil. Trans. Roy. Soc. Lond. B*, 1970, **257**, 135.
76. Rajagopalan, T. G., Stein, W. H. and Moore, S., *J. Biol. Chem.*, 1966, **241**, 4295.
77. Tang, J., *J. Biol. Chem.*, 1971, **246**, 4510.
78. Antonov, V. K., Ginodman, L. M., Kapitannikov, Yu. V., Barshevskaya, T. N., Gurova, A. G. and Rumsh, L. D., *FEBS Lett.*, 1978, **88**, 87.
79. Pearl, L. and Blundell, T., *FEBS Lett.*, 1984, **174**, 96.
80. Pearl, L. In: *Aspartic Proteinases and their Inhibitors*, V. Kostka (ed.), 1985, W. de Gruyter, Berlin—New York, p. 189.
81. James, M. N. G. and Sielecki, A. R., *Biochemistry*, 1985, **24**, 3701.
82. Hill, R. D. and Laing, R. R., *Biochim. Biophys. Acta*, 1967, **132**, 188.
83. Rickert, W., *Biochim. Biophys. Acta*, 1970, **220**, 628.

84. Hill, R. D. and Laing, R. R., *Biochim. Biophys. Acta*, 1965, **99**, 352.
85. Etoh, Y., Shoun, H., Arima, K. and Beppu, T., *J. Biochem. (Tokyo)*, 1982, **91**, 747.
86. Etoh, Y., Shoun, H., Ogino, T., Fujiwara, S., Arima, K. and Beppu, T., *J. Biochem. (Tokyo)*, 1982, **91**, 2039.
87. Oka, T., Ishino, K., Tsuzuki, H., Morihara, K. and Arima, K. *Arg. Biol. Chem.*, 1973, **37**, 1177.
88. Sternberg, M., *Biochim. Biophys. Acta*, 1972, **285**, 383.
89. Pedersen, U. D., *Acta Chem. Scand. B*, 1977, **31**, 149.
90. Pelissier, J. P., Mercier, J. C. and Ribadeau Dumas, B., *Ann. Biol. Anim. Biochim. Biophys.*, 1974, **14**, 343.
91. Visser, S. and Slangen, K. J., *Neth. Milk Dairy J.*, 1977, **31**, 16.
92. Carles, C. and Ribadeau Dumas, B., *Biochemistry*, 1984, **23**, 6839.
92a. Mulvihill, D. M. and Fox, P. F., *Milchwissenschaft*, 1979, **34**, 680.
92b. Mulvihill, D. M., Collier, T. M. and Fox, P. F., *J. Dairy Sci.*, 1979, **62**, 1567.
93. Visser, S., van Rooijen, P. J. and Slangen, Ch. J., *Eur. J. Biochem.*, 1980, **108**, 415.
93a. James, M. N. G. and Sielecki, A. R., *Nature, Lond.*, 1986, **319**, 33.
93b. Kay, J. In: *The Enzymology of Post-translational Modification of Proteins*, Vol. 1, R. B. Freedman and H. C. Hawkins (eds), 1980, Academic Press, New York, p. 423.
94. Pedersen, V. B., Christensen, K. A. and Foltmann, B., *Eur. J. Biochem.*, 1979, **94**, 573.
95. Keilova, H., Kostka, V. and Kay, J., *Biochem. J.*, 1977, **167**, 855.
96. Christensen, K. A., Pedersen, V. B. and Foltmann, B., *FEBS Lett.*, 1977, **76**, 214.
97. Kageyama, T. and Takahashi, K., *J. Biochem. (Tokyo)*, 1983, **93**, 743.
97a. Foltmann, B. In: *Molecular and Cellular Basis of Digestion*, P. Desnuelle, H. Sjöström and O. Norén (eds), 1986, Elsevier, Biomedical Press, Amsterdam, p. 491.
98. Andrén, A., Björck, L. and Claesson, O., *J. Physiol.*, 1982, **327**, 247.
99. Decuypere, J. A., Bossuyt, R. and Henderickx, H. K., *Br. J. Nutr.*, 1978, **40**, 91.
100. Cranwell, P. D., Noakes, D. E. and Hill, K. J., *Br. J. Nutr.*, 1976, **36**, 71.
101. Foltmann, B., Jensen, A. L., Lønblad, P., Smidt, E. and Axelsen, N. H., *Comp. Biochem. Physiol.*, 1981, **68B**, 9.
102. Andrén, A., Björck, L. and Claesson, O., *Swedish J. Agric. Res.*, 1980, **10**, 123.
103. Brambell, F. W. R. *The Transmission of Passive Immunity from Mother to Young*, 1970, North-Holland, Amsterdam—London.
104. Nishimori, K., Kawaguchi, Y., Hidaka, M., Uozumi, T. and Beppu, T., *J. Biochem. (Tokyo)*, 1982, **91**, 1085.
105. Nishimori, K., Kawaguchi, Y., Hidaka, M., Uozumi, T. and Beppu, T., *Gene*, 1982, **19**, 337.
106. Harris, T. J. R., Lowe, P. A., Lyons, A., Thomas, P. G., Eaton, M. A. W., Millican, T. A., Patel, T. P., Bose, C. C., Carey, N. H. and Doel, M. T., *Nucleic Acid Res.*, 1982, **10**, 2177.
107. Moir, D., Mao, J., Schumm, J. W., Vovis, G. F., Alford, B. L. and Taunton-Rigby, A., *Gene*, 1982, **19**, 127.

108. Emtage, J. S., Angal, S., Doel, M. T., Harris, T. J. R., Jenkins, B., Lilley, C. and Lowe, P. A., *Proc. Nat. Acad. Sci. USA*, 1983, **80**, 3671.
109. Mellor, J., Dobson, M. J., Roberts, N. A., Tuite, M. F., Emtage, J. S., White, S., Lowe, P. A., Patel, T., Kingsman, A. J. and Kingsman, S. M., *Gene*, 1983, **24**, 1.
110. Goff, C. G., Moir, D. T., Kohno, T., Gravius, T. C., Smith, R. A., Yamasaki, E. and Taunton-Rigby, A., *Gene*, 1984, **27**, 35.
111. Hidaka, M., Sasaki, K., Uozumi, T. and Beppu, T., *Gene*, 1986, **43**, 197.
112. Holm, J., Ollo, R., Panthier, J. J. and Rougeon, F., *EMBO J.*, 1980, **3**, 557.

Chapter 3

The Enzymatic Coagulation of Milk

D. G. Dalgleish

Hannah Research Institute, Ayr, Scotland, UK

1. INTRODUCTION

It is well established that the formation of curd in the first step of cheesemaking is the result of two processes: the first of these is the attack on the κ-casein of the casein micelles by the proteolytic enzymes contained in rennet, and the second is the clotting of the micelles which have been destabilized by this enzymic attack. The two processes are defined as the primary and secondary stages of renneting, respectively. This treatment of the reaction is perhaps over-simplified, since it is known that the secondary stage may be well advanced before the enzymic reaction is complete. Indeed, the milk may be clotted before the κ-casein has been more than 85% destroyed.[1,2]

Since the two processes of enzymic reaction and the subsequent aggregation can occur simultaneously during the later stages of the enzyme reaction, this chapter will deal with both. Without the primary enzyme action, no clotting can occur, so that the greater part of the chapter will indeed by concerned with the enzymes responsible for the splitting of κ-casein and their behaviour. However, the description of the enzymic reaction will not be considered in isolation from the effects which it has on the casein micelles, not merely in chemical but in physical and mechanistic terms. The properties of curd formed by the coagulation will not be described, but the approach to clotting will be considered in some detail. To understand this, a suitable model for the casein micelle must be defined.

For most of our purposes, the casein micelle may be considered as being a particle, approximately spherical in shape, composed of several thousand individual molecules of all four types of caseins and containing, as part of its structure, calcium phosphate in one of its insoluble states.[3] The different caseins, however, are not evenly distributed throughout the particle: in particular, the κ-casein appears to be located mainly at the surface of the micelle,[4,5] so that it can exercise a stabilizing effect upon the native micelles and prevent them from coagulating. The stabilizing effect arises from the fact that κ-casein, according to its primary sequence,[6] is divided into two distinct regions, namely the hydrophobic para-κ-casein and the hydrophilic macropeptide or glycomacropeptide (CMP or GMP): in its natural position on the surface of the micelle, the κ-casein binds to the remainder of the micelle via the para-κ-casein, with the macropeptide protruding into the surrounding solution. This hydrophilic moiety interacts with the solvent to stabilize the micelle.[7,8] Successful milk clotting agents split the κ-casein at the junction between the para-κ-casein and macropeptide moieties, that is, in bovine κ-casein, at the bond between the phenylalanine residue 105 and the methionine residue 106.[9] When this occurs, the macropeptide diffuses off into the serum, its stabilizing influence is lost, and the micelles can begin to coagulate once sufficient of their κ-casein has been split.

The enzymes which are successful in bringing about the specific splitting of the Phe–Met bond of bovine κ-casein belong to the group of acid proteases. The enzymes of this class traditionally used in the manufacture of cheese are chymosin and pepsin, the former extracted from calf stomach and the latter from adult cows. However, in recent years, the use of enzymes of the same class from micro-organisms or from other higher animals has been developed, for economic, religious or cultural reasons. In the main, this chapter will deal with the bovine enzymes, since they are the best studied and may be considered fairly typical of the class, but some discussion of the non-bovine proteases will also be given.

The activity of the proteases should not be defined in terms of the rate at which they clot milk under different conditions, because the clotting is a two-stage process, and any variation in conditions can affect the two stages differently. An example of this is the fact that milk does not clot at temperatures below 15°C.[10] This must not be interpreted as being caused by a loss of activity of the enzyme, but is the result of the inability of renneted micelles to clot at or below this temperature. Therefore, when considering the enzymic reaction itself, I have chosen not to use measurements of clotting time as indicators of the progress of the reaction, nor to consider the effects of additives or processing on the clotting time as definite evidence that the enzymic reaction is being altered.

2. ANALYSIS OF THE PROTEASE ACTION

A number of methods are available for the quantitative estimation of the attack of the acid proteases on κ-casein, for studying the protein either in an isolated state or as a component of casein micelles as it is found in milk. None of the methods presently available is simple and rapid enough to be used as a 'real-time' analysis which can be performed during the course of the reaction. The most obvious method of following the reaction, namely by measuring the disappearance of κ-casein, is complicated by the fact that κ-casein contains a number of components. Not only does the protein occur as genetic variants[11] (a problem which can be avoided in the laboratory by using the milk of individual animals), but each of these genetic variants contains fractions which are glycosylated to different extents.[12,13] Thus, on column chromatography by ion exchange[14] or on electrophoresis on starch or polyacrylamide gels the κ-casein appears as a number of fractions, which complicates its estimation. Therefore it has generally been found more convenient to isolate the products of the reaction, namely the macropeptide or the para-κ-casein fractions.

Para-κ-casein is not readily soluble, but may be solubilized using urea, and subsequent quantitation is possible using electrophoresis on polyacrylamide gels[15] or cellulose acetate strips,[2] staining the bands and using photometric scanning of the para-κ-casein band. The advantage of this method is that the glycosylated residues of κ-casein are all found in the macropeptide moiety (see Fig. 1), so that para-κ-casein generally appears as a single band in the electrophoretogram. Moreover, para-κ-casein is positively charged at pH values around neutrality, whereas all the other caseins have a net negative charge: the para-κ-casein migrates in the opposite direction to the other caseins, making its identification and quantitative estimation relatively simple. Alternative analyses of para-κ-casein have depended upon the fact that, in the absence of calcium ions, para-κ-casein is insoluble and precipitates whereas the other caseins do not. Proteolysis of milk followed by the chelation of the Ca^{2+} present can then be used to assess the formation of para-κ-casein.[16] It is also possible to exploit the higher isoelectric point of renneted κ-casein ($>$pH 5·0) compared with native κ-casein (pH 4·5) to precipitate the para-κ-casein specifically.[17]

1
PyroGlu–Glu–Gln–Asn–Gln–Glu–Gln–Pro–Ile–Arg–Cys–Glu–Lys–Asp–Glu–

16
Arg–Phe–Phe–Ser–Asp–Lys–Ile–Ala–Lys–Tyr–Ile–Pro–Ile–Gln–Tyr–

31
Val–Leu–Ser–Arg–Tyr–Pro–Ser–Tyr–Gly–Leu–Asn–Tyr–Tyr–Gln–Gln–

46
Lys–Pro–Val–Ala–Leu–Ile–Asn–Asn–Gln–Phe–Leu–Pro–Tyr–Pro–Tyr–

61
Tyr–Ala–Lys–Pro–Ala–Ala–Val–Arg–Ser–Pro–Ala–Gln–Ile–Leu–Gln–

76
Trp–Gln–Val–Leu–Ser–Asp–Thr–Val–Pro–Ala–Lys–Ser–Cys–Gln–Ala–

91
Gln–Pro–Thr–Thr–Met–Ala–Arg–His–Pro–His–Pro–His–Leu–Ser–Phe–*

106
Met–Ala–Ile–Pro–Pro–Lys–Lys–Asn–Gln–Asp–Lys–Thr–Glu–Ile–Pro–

121
Thr–Ile–Asn–Thr–Ile–Ala–Ser–Gly–Glu–Pro–Thr–Ser–Thr–Pro–Thr–Thr–

137
Glu–Ala–Val–Glu–Ser–Thr–Val–Ala–Thr–Leu–Glu–Asp–SerP–Pro–Glu–

152
Val–Ile–Glu–Ser–Pro–Pro–Glu–Ile–Asn–Thr–Val–Gln–Val–Thr–Ser–

167
Thr–Ala–Val–OH

Fig. 1. Primary structure of bovine κ-casein-A. The B genetic variant has Ile for Thr in position 136 and Ala for Asp at position 148. Sites of glycosylation are at positions 131, 133, 135 and 136 (variant A only). The site of cleavage by rennet is marked by *.

The quantitative estimation of the macropeptides liberated during the reaction is somewhat more complex. Use is generally made of the fact that all the proteins in milk, with the exception of the macropeptides, are precipitated by 2% trichloroacetic acid (TCA).[18] Therefore, all of the material remaining in the supernatant of renneting milk after treatment with TCA is macropeptide. However, the differently glycosylated forms of the macropeptide have different solubilities in TCA: if the concentration of TCA is increased to >2%, the less glycosylated peptides are precipitated while the more highly glycosylated forms remain soluble.[19]

The estimation of macropeptide is therefore subject to variation, depending upon the exact concentration of TCA used to precipitate the caseins, and also on the relative amounts of the differently glycosylated fractions present in the macropeptide, and in the original κ-casein. This variation may be exploited to differentiate between the non-glycosylated and the glycosylated fractions, by measuring the different amounts of peptides soluble in 2% and 12% TCA.[20] A further complication is that the estimation of the macropeptide is hindered by its lack of aromatic amino acids: estimation by the absorbance of the peptide at 220 nm or by the determination of the nitrogen content of the TCA filtrate must be used, which may necessitate lengthy dialysis to remove traces of other interfering materials. A recent development, however, allows much more rapid estimation of the macropeptide using high-performance liquid chromatography (HPLC),[21] obviating the need for extensive dialysis. An alternative rapid method is to use fluorescence techniques. Fluorescamine (4-phenylspiro[furan-2(3H),1-phthalan]-3,3'-dione) binds to amino groups in proteins,[22] especially to the N-termini, and in the process becomes fluorescent. During the renneting reaction new N-termini are produced by the formation of macropeptide, and therefore the fluorescence of samples taken during the course of the reaction will increase.[23] Treatment of the milk with TCA is still necessary to separate the peptides of interest, since the background fluorescence arising from all of the other proteins present in milk is too high.

HPLC can be used to study κ-casein and possibly the formation of para-κ-casein;[24] another rapid method, which requires no extensive prior treatment of the samples, is fast protein liquid chromatography (FPLC). Using this method, it is possible to estimate the amounts of the different forms of κ-casein in renneting samples relatively rapidly.[25] This method and the HPLC method have the advantage that they measure the loss of the protein itself, rather than analysing the products of the reaction. There is no method of quantifying the formation of products of the renneting reaction as it happens, since all analyses depend on the subsequent study of samples taken during the reaction and treated with TCA or dissociating solutions.

It is of course simple to make approximate estimates of enzyme activity by observing the time that a particular enzyme preparation takes to clot a standardized sample of reconstituted skim milk powder under defined conditions.[26] An approximately linear relationship exists between the enzyme activity and the time required for the sample to clot.[27,28] Such methods cannot, however, allow a detailed analysis of the kinetics or mechanism of the enzymic reaction, since the clotting time is compounded of the time required for a considerable extent of enzymic reaction and the time taken by the renneted micelles to form visible clots. The clotting time depends on the structure of the casein micelles as well as on the enzymic reaction. However, under strictly defined conditions, the activities of different enzyme preparations can be compared using such measurements of clotting time.

To study the potential activity of the acid proteases, rather than their reaction with κ-casein, it is possible to use synthetic peptides, especially those which possess a light-absorbing group whose absorbance changes when the peptide is cleaved by the enzymes. The peptide Leu–Ser–Phe(NO$_2$)–Nle–Ala–Leu–OMe is a suitable peptide whose breakdown can be followed photometrically,[29] and other similar peptides have been proposed.[30] Alternatively, peptides containing phenylalanine rather than nitrophenylalanine may be used with the reaction being followed by estimation of the products using ninhydrin.[31] These peptide substrates can be used to measure general proteolytic activity which can then be compared with milk-clotting activity to define the usefulness of the enzyme as a milk-clotting agent, where high clotting activity must be linked to generally low proteolytic activity.

Since commercial rennets contain varying proportions of chymosin and pepsin, it is often desirable to estimate the amounts of the two enzymes separately, since they have different proteolytic properties. This has been attempted in several ways and can be achieved by a combination of chromatographic separation of the enzymes and the subsequent analysis of the enzymic activity using the synthetic peptide described above.[32,33] Such measurements can be related, if care is taken, to a standard milk-clotting assay, so that the assay using the reference peptide need not always be used.[33] Attempts have also been made to determine the amounts of active enzymes in rennets by using immuno-electrophoresis or immunodiffusion techniques.[34-36] While qualitative identification of the enzymes is possible using the appropriate antisera,[35] the presence of an immunological reaction does not guarantee that the enzyme is active.[34,36] The techniques must therefore be used with care.

3. OVERALL KINETICS OF THE PROTEASE REACTION

Since the acid proteases are enzymes and the breakdown of the κ-casein substrate is essentially a single-step reaction, it seems reasonable that the kinetics of the proteolysis should obey the standard Michaelis–Menten formulation. In this, the instantaneous rate of the reaction (i.e. the rate at which substrate is converted into product), v, is given by the relation:

$$v = - d[S]/dt = V_{max}[S]/(K_m + [S])$$ (1)

In this equation, V_{max} is the maximum rate at infinite concentration of the substrate (i.e. it depends on the concentration of the enzyme) and K_m is the dissociation constant for the enzyme–substrate complex. The renneting reaction has been analysed in this way in a number of studies,[2,15,37–40] and the reaction of synthetic peptides with chymosin has also been shown to obey the Michaelis–Menten behaviour.[41] However, it should be noted that overt behaviour of this type is not always observed, because of the relation between the concentration of substrate and the constant, K_m. It can be seen from Eqn. (1) that if [S] is much larger than K_m, effectively a reaction which is zero-order with respect to the concentration of substrate will be observed, at least in the early part of the reaction. Conversely, if $K_m \gg [S]$ the reaction becomes apparently first order, i.e.

$$- d[S]/dt = V_{max}[S]/K_m$$ (2)

Various analyses of the time-course of the reaction have been made using both isolated and micellar κ-casein as substrates, with rather different results. Determinations of the value of K_m range from 7×10^{-6} mole litre^{-1} to about 5×10^{-4} mole litre^{-1}. In milk, the course of the reaction appears to be approximately first order,[39] and attempts to fit the time-course of the reaction gave values of K_m which were greater, although values were not quoted, than the substrate concentration which is of the order of $1–1.5 \times 10^{-4}$ M in unconcentrated milk. This appears to rule out the lower values for K_m which would by no means fulfil this condition, and would tend to predict a zero-order reaction. Thus, to describe the reaction which occurs in milk, it seems to be possible to use either a first-order formulation or a Michaelis mechanism with a relatively high K_m. The decision as to whether or not the reaction is truly a Michaelis reaction must depend on the method by which the results are analysed. If the enzyme kinetics are to be considered thoroughly, the reaction must be analysed only during its early stages, and with a variety of enzyme and substrate concentrations. This avoids criticism that the Michaelis approximation is valid only at the point in the reaction at which there is no possibility that the products may inhibit the reaction. There is another method of using the Michaelis kinetics which can be used over the whole course of the reaction, and this is to use the integrated form of Eqn (1):

$$K_m \ln([S]_0/[S]) + ([S]_0 - [S]) = V_{max}t \qquad (3)$$

This has been used in some studies,[2,15] and it is these, in general, which give the highest values of K_m. However, it is possible that the inaccuracy of experimental results may make the distinction between Michaelis and first-order behaviour difficult to judge, since the difference between the time-courses of the two reactions may be small.

There remains the question as to whether the Michaelis–Menten mechanism is the correct formulation to use in any case. By using the formulation, an implicit assumption is made that enzyme and substrate are able to equilibrate at all times, and this ideally carries the implication that both enzyme and substrate are mobile throughout the solution. This is a problem which requires some attention, since it may have implications for the mechanism of clotting after proteolysis. The proteases, being relatively small in comparison with the casein micelles, are free to move through the solution, but this cannot be true of the κ-casein which is bound to the micelles and which must be constrained to move through the solution as the micelles move, that is, slowly in comparison to the enzyme. It is in principle possible that the enzyme molecules, once they have bound to the micelles, could create patches of para-κ-casein by attacking adjacent κ-casein molecules one after the other rather than producing randomly distributed individual molecules of para-κ-casein, as would be the case if both enzyme and substrate were mobile. Thus, it might be expected that the modes of proteolysis of micellar and soluble κ-casein could be different, although studies of the aggregation behaviour appear to preclude this.[2] It is not certain that these differences would be reflected in the kinetics of the enzyme attack, but it is perhaps significant that the lower values of K_m which have been measured have mainly derived from studies on isolated κ-casein or on peptides,[37,40,41] and the higher values have been mainly measured using micellar material.[2,15,39] The possibility of non-random proteolysis must however be borne in mind when the clotting reaction is to be studied.

In Eqn (1), the value of V_{max} can be replaced by the expression $k_{cat}[E]$, where [E] is the concentration of the enzyme; k_{cat} is then the catalytic constant. Values for this vary, as do the values for K_m. The highest value, $216 \, s^{-1}$, was found for the reaction of chymosin with skim milk powder,[39] and lower values of about $60 \, s^{-1}$ were found for peptides,[41] and $30 \, s^{-1}$ for isolated κ-casein.[37] The highest value was obtained from the same experiments as those which gave high values of K_m. Since this result was obtained using milk and the others used isolated κ-casein or peptides, it appears that there may be significant differences between the behaviour of chymosin or rennet in milk and in model systems.

The dependence of the clotting time of milk on the concentration of rennet is well known, and this variation can be related in part to the concentration of the enzyme, as it affects the rate of proteolysis. The rate of the enzymic reaction has been shown to increase linearly with the concentration of the enzyme, which accords with either a Michaelis–Menten or a first-order mechanism.[39] Temperature also affects the clotting time, and although much of this variation can be attributed to the change in the rate of aggregation of renneted micelles, at least some can be attributed to the enzymic reaction. For isolated κ-casein, there appears to be little change in K_m with temperature, and k_{cat} approximately doubles between 25° and 40°C.[37] In milk, the same appears to be true for the value of k_{cat}, at least.[39] Certainly, the κ-casein of milk can be hydrolysed by rennet even at 0°C, at which temperature the clotting reaction does not occur.[10]

4. SENSITIVITY OF THE PHE–MET BOND IN PEPTIDES AND IN κ-CASEIN AND FACTORS WHICH AFFECT THE RATE OF HYDROLYSIS

To clot bovine casein micelles effectively, the κ-casein component must be split in the region of the Phe_{105}–Met_{106} bond.[9] Cleavage at other points may, and in fact does, occur subsequently, but any general proteolysis of the caseins during the clotting reaction is a disadvantage, leading to losses of soluble peptides. The acid proteases are all remarkably specific for the requisite bond, attacking it many times faster than other peptide bonds in the caseins. This specificity may be defined by two factors; the sequence of the substrate about the sensitive bond (i.e. the primary structure of the substrate) and the overall conformation of the substrate (i.e. its secondary and tertiary structure). The first of these will define the specific interactions between individual amino acids in the substrate and in the enzyme, and certain residues in the region of the sensitive bond can be shown to be important in this respect. The second factor is of more general importance in that the conformation of the κ-casein must be such that the sensitive bond is located in a region of the protein readily accessible to the enzymes.

The important part of the sequence of bovine κ-casein (Fig. 1) appears to be the residues between 97 and 129 of the protein and changes in this region can cause changes in the reactivity of the sensitive bond.[42,43] There appears to be no especial quality of a Phe–Met bond which renders it susceptible, insofar as the dipeptide itself is not split by chymosin,[44] nor is the bond hydrolysed when it is in tri- or tetrapeptides.[45,46] However, incorporation of the bond into a pentapeptide, viz. Ser–Leu–Phe–Met–Ala–OMethyl, renders it active with respect to hydrolysis, and when the serine and leucine are interchanged to give the correct sequence appearing in κ-casein, the rate of hydrolysis is enhanced.[45,47] Presumably in this peptide the residues in the immediate vicinity of the sensitive bond begin to serve a role of holding the substrate in its correct orientation in the active site of the enzyme. Extension of this pentapeptide in either direction shows that amino acids towards the N- and C-terminals of the protein exercise influence on the reactivity of the sensitive bond.[46,48,49] The effect of elongating the chain towards the C-terminal by three amino acids to give the peptide Ser_{104}–Lys_{111} increases the catalytic ratio, k_{cat}/K_m. Greater effects are produced by incorporating the N-terminal Leu_{103}, giving an increase of about 600-fold in the catalytic ratio, and extension to incorporate His_{102} and Pro_{101} leads to further increases in the activity of chymosin towards the substrates.[49]

In these studies, the sequences of the model peptides followed exactly that of the original κ-casein. Other substrates have been used to define the importance of either the phenylalanine or the methionine on the efficiency of the peptides as substrates. Norleucine is isosteric with methionine and can be used as a replacement; its incorporation increases the ratio k_{cat}/K_m by a factor of about 3.[50] Conversely, the replacement of phenylalanine by p-nitrophenylalanine reduces the catalytic efficiency of the enzyme on the peptide substrate by about 3.[48] From the results on the synthetic peptides, it appears that a good substrate must possess hydrophobic residues at positions 103 and 108 (occupied by Leu and Ile in the natural protein). The hydroxyl group of Ser_{104} is also strongly involved in the binding and in the catalytic reaction, and the two proline residues at positions 109 and 110 have similar importance.[51] The shorter synthetic substrates do not show the same values for k_{cat} and K_m as are found for κ-casein, but a peptide derived from tryptic hydrolysis and containing residues 98–112 of κ-casein gives a rate of hydrolysis similar to intact κ-casein,[41] so that the addition of the residues in positions 98–102 (His–Pro–His–Pro–His) is of great importance in defining the binding of the substrate to the enzyme. As evidence of this, the value of K_m for the longer peptide is considerably smaller than that of the peptide 103–112.

The sequence 98–102 contains the only histidine residues in bovine κ-casein, and it has already been shown that these residues are important to the reaction. Confirmation of the results on the peptides comes from studies of the photo-oxidation of histidyl and other residues of κ-casein, which results in a much reduced sensitivity of the protein to renneting.[52,53] It may be that only one of the histidyl residues performs an essential function[52] and the others may play a role in the aggregation of para-κ-casein. Surprisingly, iodomethylation of the methionine in intact κ-casein did not apparently reduce the sensitivity of the Phe–Met bond,[53] so that, as found for the synthetic substrates, it is not necessary for the residue in position 106 to be methionine, so long as the sequence around it is correct. This is also confirmed by the rennetability of both human and porcine κ-caseins, neither of which possess a Phe–Met bond.[54,55] Porcine κ-casein has a Phe–Ile bond in the sensitive position and is attacked by calf chymosin, although somewhat less rapidly than bovine κ-casein.

Thus far, we have considered the binding of the various substrates to the enzymes as being governed by the interaction of specific residues with particular sites on the enzyme. However, increases in the efficiency of the binding may be achieved if the three-dimensional structure of κ-casein is such as to present the relevant peptide segment to the enzyme in an 'optimum' conformation. Many of the small peptide substrates are structureless because they are too short to fold significantly: this is not the case in the intact protein. It is possible to speculate (since no definite structural information is available for κ-casein) as to what the conformation of the sensitive area is. By using calculations for predicting the conformations of proteins, it has been suggested that the Phe–Met bond is situated in a region of the protein which can form a β-structure,[56] and which can interact with the enzyme by participating in β-sheet formation.[57] An alternative prediction of the secondary structure suggests that the Phe–Met bond is situated between two β-turns, which would render it accessible to enzymic attack.[167]

There are of course naturally-occurring variations in the structure of κ-casein which may be used to gauge the effect of modification of sites more distant from the Phe–Met bond on its susceptibility towards hydrolysis. The effect of glycosylation has been considered in a number of studies, and it has been suggested that glycosylated forms of κ-casein are hydrolysed somewhat more slowly than the non-glycosylated form.[39,58] This is not universally agreed, however, and other evidence suggests that glycosylation has no effect.[15,25] A second natural modification is the difference between the A and B genetic variants of κ-casein, where again the modification is some distance from the site of enzymic attack (Fig. 1).

Again, there seems to be little effect of this modification on the rate of hydrolysis.[25] A further possible source of variation in the rate of hydrolysis of the sensitive bond appears to be the size of the micelles in which the κ-casein is to be found. From experiments where micelles of different sizes were separated and renneted, it appeared that the clotting times of the largest and smallest micelles were longer than those of medium size.[59,60] Since it is also known that the rate of aggregation of fully-renneted micelles does not depend on the micellar size,[61] it appears therefore that the different micelles must rennet at different rates. The evidence for this is based on measurements of the clotting time only and probably reflects factors such as the concentrations of the micelles and the extent of aggregation required to give visible clotting as well as the possibly different mode of attack of the enzyme on the κ-casein.

The activities of the acid proteases are dependent on both pH and ionic strength, which makes comparisons of rate constants difficult since in many cases measurements have been made under different conditions. Measurement of the maximal activity of the proteases is hampered by the precipitation of the substrate caseins at pH values below 5. It appears that the pH optimum for the attack of chymosin on κ-casein is in the range 5·0–5·5,[62] with the activity decreasing as the pH is increased. Sufficient activity of chymosin remains at the natural pH of milk (about 6·7) to allow clotting of the milk, but some other acid proteases lose their activity about this pH value. The ionic strength of the renneting medium is also important in defining the activity of the protease. This may be because the enzyme and substrate are both negatively charged and tend to repel each other: this can be overcome by increasing the ionic strength. If the ionic strength is increased too far, however, it will interfere with specific charge interactions which are essential for enzyme activity, and consequently the activity will fall. The activity therefore goes through a maximum as the ionic strength is increased.[63]

The concentration of specific ions, notably Ca^{2+}, has an effect on the rate of the enzymic reaction. It is an established fact that the addition of Ca^{2+} to milk accelerates the clotting process, principally because of the effect on the aggregation stage of the reaction. It has also been demonstrated that these ions increase the rate of the enzymic reaction.[64,65]

As described in an earlier section, the values for K_m and k_{cat} for the attack of chymosin on the rennet-sensitive bond are subject to some uncertainty, although this may be partly because of different experimental conditions. Garnier[37] quotes 33 μM for K_m, which is in good agreement with the 27 μM suggested by Visser *et al.*,[41] but is higher than some of the values given by Castle and Wheelock[38] which were in some cases as low as 6 μM. All of these values are considerably lower than the values of 500 μM given by Dalgleish[2] and 283 μM given by Chaplin and Green.[15] A value of 66 μM has been reported by Azuma et al.[40] According to Garnier,[37] the K_m was not dependent on temperature between 25 and 40°C, otherwise some of the discrepancies might have been reconciled by postulating that K_m increases with decreasing temperature. All of the values, except those of Visser et al.,[41] were obtained at pH values between 6·6 and 7·0, so that the differences cannot all be explained by variations in pH. The values obtained by Garnier[37] and Visser et al.,[41] for k_{cat} are in surprisingly good agreement, being 36 s^{-1} at 35°C and pH 6·9 and approximately 65 s^{-1} at 30°C and pH 4·7, respectively. This is of interest, insofar as they do not show the expected variation with pH which is shown by the overall enzyme activity.[62]

5. ATTACK OF ACID PROTEASES ON OTHER CASEINS

The acid proteases are generally highly specific in their action on the bond 105–106 of the κ-caseins. During clotting, any other proteolytic reaction will render the process less efficient because small soluble peptides will be released into solution and lost from the coagulum. Thus, it is important that the enzymes used for coagulation be as specific as possible, at least in the short term, i.e. possessing the maximum clotting activity and the minimum general proteolytic activity. Although the acid proteases in general fulfil this function well, even these enzymes attack caseins other than κ-casein, albeit considerably more slowly than the primary attack. During clotting, such proteolysis is unimportant because of the short period of time involved, but during the ripening of cheese the residual clotting agents which are retained in the curd play an essential part in breaking down the caseins. They may also, if the proteolysis is too severe, produce undesirable bitter peptides in the cheese.[66]

Chymosin attacks both α_s- and β-caseins in solution. The attack occurs at a number of specific sites in both proteins, although of course neither of the proteins possesses a Phe–Met bond as part of their structures. The primary site for the cleavage of β-casein is in the region of peptide 189–193, being variously identified as the bond 189–190[67,68] or 192–193;[69] in fact both these bonds are hydrolysed.[70] The larger resultant peptide residues 1–189 are defined as β-I casein. This peptide can be further degraded to β-II casein by breaking the bond 166–167 or 164–165, and the β-II can then be attacked at bond 139–140 to give β-III casein.[67,69] Splitting of the bond 127–128 is also possible on prolonged hydrolysis at low pH.[69] These different reactions may be sequential rather than competitive, and it may be impossible to form β-III casein directly from β-casein without the intermediate formation of β-I and β-II peptides.[67] This may arise because the conformation of the β-casein makes the relevant bonds unavailable as primary sites of attack. Alternatively, the apparently sequential nature of the formation of the peptides may arise simply because of the different rates of attack on the different bonds.[69] The effect of the primary attack is to render the β-I casein incapable of self-association[71] and this may also explain the differences in the rates of attack on the three susceptible bonds, at least in solution. In contrast to the behaviour in solution, chymosin and pepsin do not appear to attack β-casein in ripening cheese,[71,72] perhaps because of low water activity,[73] or perhaps because of the immobilized state of the β-casein.

The proteolysis of β-casein in this way is dependent on the pH and the ionic strength of the solution, and upon the temperature. Decreasing the pH increases the rate of proteolysis, in accordance with the pH-dependence of the primary reaction with κ-casein.[67] The rates of production of β-II and β-III peptides are slowed even more than the rate of formation of β-I by increasing pH, but at low temperature the dependence on pH is less than at 37°C. Ionic strength has the effect of slowing the reaction on β-casein, although the rates of reaction to form β-II and β-III are less affected. As with the dependence on pH, the effects of ionic strength are greater at higher temperatures. These results are consistent with the suggestion that polymeric β-casein is relatively resistant to attack by the enzyme, as do results showing that addition of Ca^{2+} (which increases the aggregation of the protein) slows down the rate of cleavage of the first bond.[74,75]

It has been pointed out by Visser[51] that the sites of attack by chymosin on α_s- and β-caseins appear to occur at bonds involving either phenylalanine or leucine. The primary site of attack by chymosin on α_{s1}-casein is Phe_{23}–Phe_{24} or Phe_{24}–Val_{25}, to give the peptide α_{s1}-I casein.[68,76] Further proteolysis is possible and occurs in cheese[76] as well as in solution. The products have been identified as α_{s1}-II (residues 24/25–199 of α_{s1}-casein), α_{s1}-III and α_{s1}-IV (residues 24/25–149/150), α_{s1}-V (residues 29/33–199) and α_{s1}-VII (residues 56–179),[77] but alternative positions for the hydrolysis (as many as 20) have been suggested.[68] The formation of each of these peptides depends upon the particular conditions of pH used:

for example at pH values above 5·8 the hydrolysis follows the sequence α_{s1}-I → α_{s1}-II → α_{s1}-III/IV, while at lower pH α_{s1}-I is hydrolysed directly to α_{s1}-V.[78] Hydrolysis of the first peptide bond is, in contrast to the hydrolysis of β-casein, only slightly dependent on the ionic strength of the medium,[79] whereas the subsequent degradation of the α_{s1}-I casein is dependent on the salt concentration. As with β-casein, the state of aggregation of the casein appears to affect the proteolysis and in particular micellar α_{s1}-casein is degraded much more slowly than when it is in solution.[80] During cheese maturation, α_{s1}-casein is completely degraded, possibly because the proteolytic reactions involved are less dependent upon the concentration of salt present than is the hydrolysis of β-casein.

In all cases, these secondary reactions of chymosin on the α_{s1}- and β-caseins are slower than the attack on κ-casein by a considerable amount. Data available for the attack of chymosin on α_{s1}-casein in solution[81] give a value of K_m of $4·5 \times 10^{-4}$ M and k_{cat} of $3·8 \, s^{-1}$. Thus, the binding appears to be weaker than the binding of κ-casein and the catalytic constant is less. An alternative measurement[70] gives values for the ratio k_{cat}/K_m for α_{s1}-, β- and κ-caseins of 1·8, 20·6 and 1405, respectively. Thus, proteolysis of α_{s1}- and β-caseins is unimportant during the formation of the curd during cheesemaking, but significant as far as α_{s1}-casein is concerned during cheese ripening.

Bovine chymosin is of course specific for the clotting of bovine milk: other acid proteases are less specific in their action on this material. Porcine pepsin is more proteolytic than chymosin, but bovine pepsin is more similar to chymosin in its attack on κ-casein.[82] Microbial enzymes cause degradation patterns different from those produced by chymosin and pepsin.[83-85] Comparisons are often difficult since even within the enzyme group, the reactivities of the individual members depend differently on pH and ionic strength, as well as being affected by the aggregation state of the caseins. In general terms, it appears that the non-bovine proteases are more proteolytic than chymosin but that for all the acid proteases the primary site of attack is the Phe–Met bond in κ-casein.

6. ACID PROTEASES OTHER THAN CHYMOSIN

The world supply of calf rennet is inadequate to supply the needs of the cheese industry and other acid proteases have been developed for use as rennet substitutes. These can conveniently be divided into two classes: the pepsins (obtained from the stomachs of ruminants and other species) and acid proteases of microbial or fungal origin. Among the first group are pepsins from sheep, goat, pig and chicken and the most important members of the second group are the acid proteases of *Mucor miehei, M. pusillus* and *Endothia parasitica*. The most important criterion to be applied to these enzymes in relation to cheesemaking is their general proteolytic activity compared with their activity towards the rennet-sensitive bond of κ-casein. Only acid proteases appear to be suitable, since proteases such as trypsin have the wrong specificity and degrade the milk clot almost as soon as it has formed. In addition to individual proteases, mixtures of different proteases can be used as rennet substitutes. The distribution of use of rennet substitutes appears to be variable worldwide, since it has been estimated that in 1974 about 60% of the cheese manufactured in the United States was produced using microbial enzymes,[86] whereas in Europe, microbial rennets are less widely used. A number of reviews are available on the different rennets and rennet substitutes.[86-91]

All the acid proteases used have the ability to split κ-casein at the required position, but they are not identical in their properties. For example, they have different pH optima and indeed different stabilities and pH-dependence of activity.[92] Pig pepsin is unstable above pH 6·0,[93] compared with chymosin (pH 6·5[94]), *Mucor miehei* protease (pH 6·7[95]) and chicken pepsin (pH 8·0[96]). Since the effects of pH are different, it may be necessary to modify the cheesemaking process to account for this, especially if mixtures of proteases are used.[97] A second difference between the coagulants is their stability towards heat, which is important if the cheese whey is to be processed. Chymosin shows maximum activity at about 40°C, as does pepsin, and both enzymes are largely inactivated > 50°C whereas for *M. miehei* protease the temperature required to initiate inactivation is about 65°C.[88] A series of experiments shows that the order of inactivation of various acid proteases is pig pepsin, bovine pepsin, chymosin, *M. pusillus* protease and *M. miehei* protease, and that the heat stability of all is increased by decreasing pH.[98-100] The enzymes can all be inactivated by prolonged heating but care must be taken that the whey proteins are not also denatured by too high a temperature during this process. Two protease preparations from *M. miehei* are available, one of which is heat-labile,[101] and to which the above remarks do not apply.

The proteolytic and clotting activities of the enzymes have been compared and show that almost all the rennet substitutes compare unfavourably with chymosin. A clear comparison is given by the clotting to proteolytic ratios of chymosin (40·9) and bovine pepsin (4·3), showing the markedly greater general proteolysis caused by pepsin.[102] Another study using synthetic substrates showed that pepsin is considerably more proteolytic than chymosin and that *Mucor* proteases are somewhat less proteolytic than pepsin but considerably more active than chymosin.[103] The heat-labile *Mucor* protease, however, compares very favourably with chymosin in respect to its proteolytic activity.[104] *M. pusillus* protease powder, rather than enzyme extract, is reported to be less proteolytic than chymosin,[105] while all other preparations tested were more proteolytic, both on κ-casein and on α_s- and β-caseins.

The products of the attack of non-chymosin proteases on the caseins have not been analysed in great detail. The enzymes have been shown to attack the B-chain of insulin with different specificities,[86] so they may be expected to have different specificities on the caseins also. This is true for the *Mucor* enzymes: electrophoretic patterns of the breakdown products of β-casein are different from those obtained with calf rennet,[84,106] although one product from α_{s1}-casein was common to all enzymes. The peptides produced by chymosin and by *Mucor* protease are, however, relatively similar, whereas proteolysis by the protease of *E. parasitica* gives a very different pattern.[107] The different proteolytic patterns are evident during cheese ripening and may give rise to undesirable bitter peptides. A good example of this is evident from a number of studies on the suitability of chicken pepsin for the manufacture of Cheddar cheese: off flavours and bitterness developed much faster than when calf rennet was used.[108,109]

Therefore, given that the proteolytic activities of non-chymosin acid proteases are almost invariably greater than that of chymosin, there may be problems associated with long-maturing cheeses. The ideal solution is to use as coagulants mixtures of proteases which contain enzymes less proteolytic and more proteolytic than chymosin. Of the available enzymes, pig pepsin is the only one which is potentially less proteolytic than chymosin, since it is readily denatured during the cheesemaking process.[110] Such approaches have been made,[111,112] and were used as the so-called Fifty-Fifty coagulants which found commercial use.[97] In general, however, the enzymes used as coagulants are chosen so as to minimise their proteolytic activities.

7. IMMOBILIZED PROTEASES FOR THE CLOTTING OF MILK

In economic terms, it would be valuable to possess a clotting agent which was reusable, and therefore there has been research to investigate the possibilities of immobilizing chymosin or pepsin on solid supports for use in column reactors to perform the proteolysis of the κ-casein. In principle, the concept is simple: that milk would be cooled to prevent aggregation, passed through a column of the immobilized protease and emerge from the column with all of its κ-casein converted to para-κ-casein. Warming the milk would then allow the curd to form. Such types of reactors are already used for other enzyme processes.

There are, as will be discussed below, a number of claims that such reactors are practicable. However, there are reasons why the use of immobilized proteases is impracticable for a process such as milk clotting. Experiments have shown that the efficiency of the hydrolysis of κ-casein by pepsin which had been bound to dextrans of different sizes, decreased with the size of the dextran–pepsin conjugate. If these results are extrapolated to the limit where the pepsin is completely immobilized, the activity of the protease is expected to be very low.[113] Successful processes using immobilized enzymes usually involve small, mobile substrates, which can diffuse rapidly around the immobilized enzyme; in milk, the casein micelles are large particles and their diffusion is slow. In the normal renneting of milk, the enzyme is small in relation to the casein micelles and can thus diffuse rapidly to cause rapid reaction. But, if the enzyme is immobilized and the substrate can diffuse to it only slowly, the reaction is likely to be very slow. This has been demonstrated in some studies: Beeby[114] found only limited hydrolysis of micellar κ-casein, even when the protease was linked to the immobile support via a flexible link, and suggested that it was possible to hydrolyse only the soluble fraction of κ-casein by such a system. Somewhat similarly, Dalgleish[2] found that only very prolonged treatment of milk with immobilized chymosin led to sufficient κ-casein being split to allow aggregation of the casein micelles. It must be borne in mind that the reactors must be run at low temperature to prevent coagulation of the milk[10] in the reactor itself and this tends to cause loss of β- and κ-caseins from the micelles into the soluble phase and thereby to render them more susceptible to the protease.

Since there are a number of reports of apparently successful coagulation of milk by immobilized proteases, it is necessary to explain why, if the arguments given above are true, coagulation of milk can occur after it has been passed through an immobilized rennet reactor. The simplest explanation which can be given is that, in addition to the proteolysis of solubilized κ-casein, enzyme is released from the column and remains active in the milk.[115] The quantities of protease liberated in this way need only be small to give eventual clotting when the milk is warmed. Desorption of the proteases from hydrophobic carriers has been demonstrated,[115] and the desorption of the enzymes has been estimated to be the cause of most of the apparently successful results.[116] It is a not uncommon occurrence that loss of enzyme activity occurs as the reactors are used extensively and that some or indeed most of this loss of activity cannot be recovered; desorption of the proteases readily explains this phenomenon. The loss of enzyme activity in this way will depend on the method by which the enzyme is coupled to its support and also on the materials present in the solutions being used. For example, Ca^{2+} can be very effective in removing enzyme coupled using $TiCl_2$.[117]

Desorption of the proteases may be regarded as being the main reason for clotting in many studies where sufficient information is given on the experimental method. Since it is known[2,15] that extensive proteolysis of the κ-casein is required before the micelles will aggregate, it is probable that any experiments which demonstrate that coagulation can take place at small extents of proteolysis must be doubted.[118,119] This is confirmed by the study where truly immobilized chymosin split only the soluble κ-casein and where no clotting was observed.[114] Likewise, the clotting of milk when it had been mixed with ultracentrifugate which had been passed through a column of immobilized pepsin[118] can only be explained by assuming that a quantity of the enzyme had been released into the solution.

A number of supports and methods of linking the enzymes to them have been tried, and a review of some of the techniques has been published.[120] Hydrophobic adsorption on hexyl-substituted Sepharose 6B, on phenoxyacetyl cellulose or on activated carbon gave active preparations but activity decreased rapidly with use due to desorption of the enzymes. Covalent binding to Sepharose 4B likewise gave very rapid loss of activity.[121] Controlled-pore glass beads were used in several studies[2,114,117,119,122,123] and appeared to give the most satisfactory results within the constraints given above of slight leakage of enzyme. Other supports used include titania, stainless steel, iron oxide, teflon,[124] alumina[124,125] and polystyrene.[126] None of these were found to be particularly successful. The attachment of the enzymes to glass supports can be achieved by coupling the enzymes via glutaraldehyde to the glass after treatment with 3-aminopropyltriethoxysilane and sodium borohydride.[120] Glutaraldehyde treatments have, however, also been found to decrease the activity of the bound enzymes.[127] The use of esters of triethoxysilylbutyric acid has been claimed to give a preparation which remained active during 21 successive milk treatments but subsequently showed a decrease in activity.[127] This appears to be the best performance of a column of immobilized enzyme, although the enzyme itself was not defined and the possibility of enzyme leakage was not studied. A series of supports has also been studied for applicability,[128,129] and paraffin wax was eventually selected for cheesemaking.[130] The preparation was stable for 15 assays with skim milk and showed no leakage of enzyme during a 2-h period; in addition, enzymic activity could be restored by washing the column with HCl.

If such preparations as the last two described above are sufficiently viable to produce the results claimed, then the theoretical reasons for the lack of success of immobilized enzyme preparations appear to be invalid. It remains to be seen whether such preparations are indeed industrially practicable.

8. EFFECT OF PRETREATMENT OF MILK ON THE ENZYMIC REACTION

Heating milk prior to renneting renders it difficult to clot by normal renneting procedures.[131] The effects are not significant until the milk has been heated to temperatures which cause the denaturation of β-lacto-globulin.[132] There are a number of possible reasons for this loss of clottability: the denaturation of β-lactoglobulin and its interaction with κ-casein may cause the κ-casein to be less accessible and/or susceptible to rennet action; conversely, the enzyme may split the κ-casein but the renneted micelles may be unable to clot because of the denatured β-lactoglobulin bound to their surfaces. Alternatively, the heating may cause more far-reaching changes in the micellar structure itself such that neither of these can be considered as primary causes of the loss of clottability of the milk: it is possible that the heating causes changes in the distribution of calcium phosphate in the micelles and the serum which render even renneted micelles unaggregable. That some such structural factor may be involved is evidenced by the fact that the effect of the heating can be almost totally reversed by dropping the pH of the milk to 5·8 and then readjusting it to pH 6·3 before adding rennet.[133] The effect of changing the pH in this way is to dissociate the calcium phosphate of the micelles as the pH is lowered,[134] followed by its reformation (and possible reconstitution of the micelles) as the pH is raised again. Caseins are probably lost from the micelles at the same time,[135] principally β-casein, but presumably reassociate as the pH is raised. The effect of heating can also be reversed, at least partially, by the addition of Ca^{2+}, again suggesting that heating interferes, at least, with the coagulation mechanism of the renneted micelles, as well as with the enzymic reaction.

The enzymic reaction appears to be inhibited in heated milk,[136] but inhibition does not appear to be complete, as gauged by the release of peptides by the enzyme.[132,137] The inhibition appears to prevent a portion (between one-third and one-half) of the κ-casein from being hydrolysed after skim milk has been heated for 1 h at 90°C,[132] or by heating casein/β-lactoglobulin mixtures for short times at 85°C.[136] The conclusion to be drawn may be that inhibition of the enzyme prevents it from hydrolysing sufficient κ-casein on the surfaces of the micelles to make them aggregable, since it is known[2,15] that rennet must hydrolyse a considerable proportion of the κ-casein before aggregation at a measurable rate can occur. The adjustment of pH described above may, by altering the structure of the micelles, render them more susceptible to aggregation at limited extents of splitting of the κ-casein, or may, by reforming the micelles, render all of the κ-casein susceptible to rennet. Although the cause of the inhibition is expected to be the reaction of β-lactoglobulin with κ-casein, the effect of adding reducing agents is small and the enzyme cannot hydrolyse all of the κ-casein.[138] α-Lactalbumin also may play a part in the effect of heat, since it also inhibits the release of peptides by rennet.[139]

Cooling of the milk before renneting tends to increase the clotting time,[140,141] and this has been demonstrated to arise in part from the decrease in the rate of the renneting reaction.[39] This decrease can be partly reversed by pasteurization,[39] or by holding at temperatures up to 60°C[141] but recovery is not complete.

A further factor which might influence the renneting of milk is homogenization. After the homogenization process, casein micelles are attached to the surface of the fat globules and some of the micelles may be partly dissociated before binding.[142] The change in the surroundings of the κ-casein might therefore induce changes in its behaviour during renneting. This does not seem to be the case: a study in which the kinetics of rennet-induced aggregation of skim and homogenized milks were compared[143] showed that maximal rates of aggregation were attained at the same time, suggesting that rennet acted similarly on both systems. This presumably reflects the fact that the micelles are relatively intact when bound to the surfaces of the fat globules in homogenized milk.[144] A different situation has been found to obtain if κ-casein is bound directly to the fat globule surfaces: in this case, the action of the rennet was considerably altered,[145] presumably because the κ-casein binds to the surface in such a conformation that the susceptible bond is not available to the enzyme.

9. RENNETING AND THE MECHANISM OF AGGREGATION

Before they are renneted, the casein micelles in milk show no tendency to aggregate. Two mechanisms have been invoked to explain this. First, the micelles carry negative charges on their surfaces, partly, but not completely, derived from the macropeptide regions of κ-casein. Since the like charges repel one another, DLVO theory can be used to account for the stability of the micelles.[146-148] This principle cannot, however, account for all aspects of the micellar stability,[149] especially since the densities of surface charge may be rather too low to prevent aggregation. An alternative mechanism by which stability may be conferred on the micelles is that of steric stabilization,[150] where the macropeptide segments of the κ-casein project into the solution from the surfaces of the micelles. The macropeptides are flexible and hydrophilic, and aggregation of the micelles is prevented, in effect, because the 'hairy' outer layers of the micelles cannot interpenetrate. This latter cause of stabilization has been favoured by a number of authors.[7,8,151,152]

During renneting, the charges on the surfaces of the casein micelles are reduced. Measurements of the electrophoretic mobility of the particles[146,153-155] show that approximately half of the charge is lost, so that it is possible that this is at least a contributor to the loss of stability. Moreover, the charge decreases approximately proportionately with the extent of proteolysis of the κ-casein;[156] the relationship is not linear, since the rate of change of the surface charge with the extent of renneting is faster towards the end of the reaction.[156] The radii of the micelles also decrease by approximately 5 nm during renneting[8] and the decrease appears to be linear with the change in surface charge;[156] the viscosity of the milk also decreases during this period,[157] as does its turbidity.[158] The decrease in radius, which seems to have the same value irrespective of the initial radii of the micelles, is consistent with the loss of the 'hairy' macropeptide surface of the particles.[159] Therefore, the changes which occur in the micelles involve possible losses of both charge stabilization and steric stabilization. The experimental measurements, especially the change in radius caused by renneting, strongly suggest that the κ-casein must be largely on the surface of the micelles, a theory supported by other evidence.[4,5]

Para-κ-casein is insoluble and so renneting of isolated κ-casein causes precipitation almost immediately. The kinetics of the aggregation have been described by Payens[158,160] and have been shown to describe the reaction in detail.[161] However, the aggregation behaviour of isolated κ-casein during renneting may not serve as an adequate model for the clotting of casein micelles. As soon as an individual molecule of κ-casein has been hydrolysed by chymosin, it is free to aggregate; the effect of chymosin is therefore to provide a steady stream of monomeric material for a subsequent aggregation reaction.[160] This can indeed be seen when κ-casein is hydrolysed by pepsin.[161] However, in casein micelles the proteolysis of a small number of κ-casein molecules does not affect the aggregation properties of the micelles, since they contain many hundreds or even thousands of such molecules. The para-κ-casein produced in the micelles by renneting can only aggregate when the whole micelle is capable of aggregating, and it is this which causes the lag stage before aggregation is observed.[152,162] A short lag phase is seen when isolated κ-casein is renneted but the origin of this is different: the concentration of particles capable of aggregation is low at the start of the reaction and then increases rather rapidly.[160] Renneted micelles appear to be incapable of aggregating until about 80% of their κ-casein has been destroyed, after which the concentration of micelles capable of aggregating increases rapidly.[2] This behaviour can be explained either by the loss of surface charge during renneting or by loss of steric stabilization; both of the predicted curves have much the same overall shape and it is not easy to definitively conclude that only one mechanism is operative, although the model based on steric stabilization appears to be favoured.[152,159]

During the last 20% of the proteolytic reaction both the concentration of micelles which are capable of aggregation and the rate at which they can aggregate increase rapidly as the last of the stabilizing surface is removed.[2] Finally, when the micelles have been completely denuded of their κ-casein macropeptide a limiting rate for the aggregation is reached and the micelles aggregate by a Smoluchowski[163] mechanism, i.e. the growth of molecular weight with time is linear.[160] This certainly applies in dilute solutions, in which most of the measurements have been made; it is possible that in the more concentrated dispersion represented by milk, the aggregation mechanism may be rather different because the micelles are fairly close to each other (within one or two diameters). In such cases, Smoluchowski theory is not strictly applicable, although it may be so in practice. Most theoretical treatments of the renneting reaction[152,160,162] have assumed that Smoluchowski kinetics apply. In milk during normal cheesemaking, the aggregation is very rapid and it is demonstrable that not all of the κ-casein has been hydrolysed before clotting occurs at 30°C,[164] so that the micelles are not aggregating at their maximum rate during clotting at the temperatures normally used for cheesemaking, nor is it necessarily true that all of the casein micelles in the milk actually participate in the formation of the curd initially.

The aggregation rate of renneted micelles is unaffected by the concentration of rennet[165] or by the size of the micelles.[61] It is however very sensitive both to the concentration of calcium ions present in the solution and to temperature.[166] Milk itself will not clot at less than about 15°C,[10] and this can be shown to be a direct consequence of the slowness of the aggregation reaction at low temperatures. It is not possible to draw a linear Arrhenius plot for the reaction, such a plot being curved very sharply at the low-temperature end. However, at temperatures of above 45°C the aggregation is very efficient indeed and approaches the theoretical maximum rate at which particles can collide. To some extent, the effect of temperature below 45°C can be overcome by increasing the concentration of Ca^{2+} present in the solution but above 45°C the concentration of Ca^{2+} has little effect upon the reaction because it is already near its maximum rate.[166] These results on temperature apply equally to measurements made when micelles are suspended in synthetic buffers[166] or in ultrafiltrate from the same milk.[165]

The reasons for the aggregation of renneted micelles are not fully understood. It is probable that there is more than one cause since a number of factors are known to affect the rate of aggregation. In the absence of repulsive forces, van der Waals attraction may be sufficient to hold the micelles together, but a number of other forces may act as well. From the temperature-dependence of the rate of aggregation or coagulation,[165,166,168] it is plausible to assume that hydrophobic interactions may be important. However, the known change in the rate of aggregation with the concentration of Ca^{2+} suggests that these ions play a role in the aggregation,[65] which is incompatible with the aggregates being held together only by hydrophobic interactions.[166] Furthermore, the rate of aggregation is decreased when the ionic strength is increased,[166] suggesting that specific ion-pair formation may be important. Such specific interactions have been proposed.[65,158,169,170] An additional factor appears to be the state of the micellar calcium phosphate. It is well established that a decrease in pH leads to a decrease of the rennet coagulation time[171] but the bulk of this is probably caused by the increase in enzyme activity as the pH is lowered.[62] However, it has also been shown that pH does exert a small effect on the rate of coagulation of the renneted micelles.[168] It has been suggested[154] that this type of effect arises from the increase in the activity of Ca^{2+} as the pH is lowered but an alternative explanation may be found by considering the effect of pH on the micellar (or colloidal) calcium phosphate;[172] Pyne and McGann[173] proposed this some 25 years ago and recent work[174] has shown that dissolution of micellar calcium phosphate leads to a decrease in the efficiency with which the micelles coagulate. As the pH is lowered, more calcium phosphate is dissolved, but in milk this only serves to increase the concentration of Ca^{2+}. The effects may therefore tend to cancel out to give only a small pH-dependence of the aggregation.

However, the dissolution of micellar calcium phosphate may not in itself be important in determining how the micelles aggregate. Since calcium phosphate is an integral component of the casein micelles,[3] its breakdown also liberates caseins from the micelles, the effect being apparent at pH values as high as 6·3.[174] The micellar structure at pH 6·3 is therefore not the same as that at pH 6·7 and the pH-dependence of aggregation may reflect this rather than the calcium phosphate content per se.

The fact that micellar charge is important in the clotting of the renneted micelles is further evidenced by the effect of cations such as Ca^{2+} on the clotting time[65] and the effect of polyions. Lysozyme appears to bind to casein micelles and to catalyse clotting,[175] probably by acting as a polycation.[147] Other polycations which have been used are cetyltrimethylammonium bromide[154] and salmine.[147] Polycations can cause milk to clot in the absence of rennet[176] and so it is not surprising that subcritical amounts can enhance the rate of coagulation.[177] The effect is produced by materials which bind to the casein micelles[164] and the important factor appears to be the relative charge concentration of polycations.[178] Since the mean sizes and the surface potentials of the casein micelles appear to be largely unaltered by the binding of the ionic materials, it is possible that they bind in the interiors of the micelles. Binding may also occur via hydrophobic interactions and it appears that the casein, rather than the calcium phosphate, is the primary binding site.[179] The effect of additives such as proline show the importance of hydrophobic interactions,[164] although they may also disrupt the micelles, and additives which decrease the clotting time tend to be of this type or positively charged and strongly bound to the micelles.[164] Additives which decrease the clotting time tend to remain bound to the micelles after coagulation and most (with the notable exception of sodium dodecyl sulphate) do not affect the rate of proteolysis by rennet.[164]

All of these results tend towards a view that the enhancement of the rate of coagulation arises from the neutralization of negative charge within the micelles, diminishing the charge repulsions and allowing hydrophobic interactions to occur.

10. OVERALL KINETICS OF THE CLOTTING PROCESS

The earliest attempt to describe the kinetics of the clotting process was that of Storch and Segelcke.[180] This simply stated that the clotting time was inversely related to the concentration of rennet used to clot the milk, i.e. that

$$CT = k/[E] \qquad (4)$$

To a first approximation, this is true, but a further refinement was postulated by Holter[181] and rearranged by Foltmann[27] to give the familiar equation:

$$CT = (k/[E]) + A \qquad (5)$$

where A is a constant. This preserves the linearity of the relation between clotting time and the inverse of the enzyme concentration. In this form, it is acceptable for use with a wide range of enzyme concentration.[28] It may be taken of a test of any theoretical model that it reduces to the Holter formulation, which is amply supported by experimental evidence. However, the relationships given in Eqns (4) and (5) are empirical in nature and recent studies have sought to describe the reaction in a more mechanistic manner. There have been three main approaches to the problem, which have come to somewhat different conclusions, although they have certain assumptions in common.

The first of these mechanisms was proposed by Payens and co-workers in a series of papers.[158,160,165,182–184] To explain the lag time before clotting is seen, it was suggested that the micelles only became aggregable at a slow rate. Thus, in the early stages of the reaction, proteolysis only creates small concentrations of micelles which can aggregate. Since the growth of the particles is a bimolecular process, this can only occur slowly in the early stages of the reaction. Thus, if the only criterion of the coagulation is the clotting time, there will be a period during which no effect of the enzyme will be apparent. On more sensitive criteria of particle size, the size (or, more precisely, the molecular weight) will decrease by a small amount because of the loss of the macropeptides from the micelles. According to this theory, the micelles can aggregate, albeit slowly, from the earliest stages of the reaction. As the reaction proceeds, the micelles will become more aggregable because of the increased proteolysis of

κ-casein. This model has been found to describe well the kinetics of coagulation of renneted κ-casein[161] and predicts that for milk a characteristic time (which may be identified as the clotting time) may be defined by the simple relation:

$$t_c = \sqrt{2/k_s V} \tag{6}$$

where k_s is the rate constant for flocculation and V is the enzymic velocity. This equation predicts that the clotting time will be inversely proportional to the square root of the enzyme concentration, rather than to the enzyme concentration itself. The major problem with the treatment is that, to describe the coagulation of milk, the rate constant for the flocculation of renneted micelles is very low compared with that which is measured directly.[61,165,166] This is essentially because the value of k_s which must be used in the calculations represents an average over all values, from the low value at the start of the reaction to the high value at the end.

The manner in which the value of k_s can vary during the proteolytic reaction was addressed by Darling and van Hooydonk.[152] They sought to model the reaction by considering the micelles as being originally sterically stabilized, this stabilization being lost as the renneting proceeded. At the start of the reaction, rennet has a negligible effect upon the aggregation and effectively no aggregation can take place until about 70% of the κ-casein has been hydrolysed. At this point, the aggregability of the micelles increases fairly rapidly with the extent of proteolysis and Smoluchowski aggregation can take place, at an increasing rate. The description of the reaction in this way is important, since it provides a reason for the micelles to change their aggregation rate with the degree of proteolysis and is also in accord with experimental observations that the micelles cannot aggregate until a very large fraction of their κ-casein has been hydrolysed.[2,162]

Using these observations, Dalgleish[2,162] used a model which simplified the description of the dependence of micelle aggregation upon the extent of the proteolytic reaction by defining k_s as being zero until a defined critical extent of proteolysis had occurred on any particular micelle. After this, the value of k_s was taken to be maximal. The numbers of micelles which had achieved the critical state at any degree of proteolysis could be computed by probability theory if the overall extent of the reaction was known. The complete mathematical description of the system is relatively complex but it could be shown to simplify in many cases to the Holter approximation of Eqn (5).[185]

Thus, all of the models in their various ways describe the overall reaction as consisting of a lag stage followed by rapid aggregation. In two of the models, the lag time is explained as arising from the time required for aggregable micelles to be formed, giving the impression of a primary (enzymatic) stage followed by a secondary (coagulation or flocculation) stage. However, all of the models show that the onset of coagulation will occur before the exhaustion of the κ-casein substrate by the enzyme. None of the models is complete, inasmuch as they cannot explain all of the changes which can be caused in the coagulation process by such factors as temperature, pH, ionic strength and concentrations of different ions such as Ca^{2+}. What they have achieved is a rationale for the reaction in fairly general terms, within which framework more detailed investigations of the behaviour of the casein micelles and the enzyme–substrate reactions can be made.

A particular aspect of the kinetics of real rennet coagulation of milk which has received no attention is the use of starter cultures to lower the pH during the renneting reaction. In such a case, there is, in addition to the factors described above, the added dimension of how the structures of the casein micelles change as the pH is lowered. Since the kinetics of the pH-induced changes in the casein micelles are almost unknown, as are their consequences in terms of rennetability and aggregation, it will obviously be some time before mechanisms such as those described above can be refined sufficiently to give a full description of curd formation during the cheesemaking process.

11. CONCLUSION

We have considered in this chapter the factors which influence rennet clotting and the reactions which are believed to occur during the process. Clotting times can be measured in a variety of ways, ranging from simple observation of the formation of visible particles to more sophisticated methods. The discussion of the behaviour of the system during clotting is more complex than the description which has been given here, which related only to the events giving rise to clotting. Once the aggregation of the renneted micelles is well advanced, it is almost certain that the description of the system in terms of Smoluchowski kinetics cannot be accurate and more complex theories of gel formation and properties must be used. Therefore, we cannot, from the theories described above, develop models to describe such factors as gel strength and syneresis. An attempt has been made to describe the coagulation of milk using theories developed for the vulcanization of rubber[186] and, although the theory can be criticized in terms of whether it is applicable to the milk system,[187] it appears to be able to explain some of the changes which occur in the gel. Electron microscopy has shown that the coagulating micelles form a network of strands,[1,188] with gaps between them of considerable size, a process which has been described by computer modelling.[189] Whether or not all of the casein micelles are involved at the time of gel formation is not certain, although extrapolation of the models discussed in the previous section would suggest that, at the gel point, a quantity of the casein is likely not to be incorporated in the framework.[190] It is the properties of this framework which determine the properties of the gel.

To travel from the properties of renneting milk as a suspension to those of renneting milk as a gel requires changes in the types of experiments which can be done and also the development of different theoretical backgrounds within which to discuss the results. The point of division between the two regimes is one which requires further study since there are as yet no certain theoretical developments, nor indeed experimental techniques, which will allow the details of the suspension–gel transition to be investigated successfully.

REFERENCES

1. Green, M. L., Hobbs, D. G., Morant, S. V. and Hill, V. A., *J. Dairy Res.*, 1978, **45**, 413.
2. Dalgleish, D. G., *J. Dairy Res.*, 1979, **46**, 653.
3. Schmidt, D. G. In: *Developments in Dairy Chemistry—1*, P. F. Fox (ed.), 1982, Applied Science Publishers, London, p. 60.
4. McGann, T. C. A., Donnelly, W. J., Kearney, R. D. and Buchheim, W., *Biochim. Biophys. Acta*, 1980, **630**, 261.
5. Donnelly, W. J., McNeill, G. P., Buchheim, W. and McGann, T. C. A., *Biochim. Biophys. Acta*, 1984, **789**, 136.
6. Mercier, J.-C., Brignon, G. and Ribadeau Dumas, B., *Eur. J. Biochem.*, 1973, **35**, 222.
7. Holt, C., *Proc. Int. Conf. Surf. Sci.*, E. Wolfram (ed.), 1975, Akademiai Kiado, Budapest, p. 641.
8. Walstra, P., Bloomfield, V., Wei, J. G. and Jenness, R., *Biochim. Biophys. Acta*, 1981, **669**, 258.
9. Jollès, J., Alais, C. and Jollès, P., *Biochim. Biophys. Acta*, 1968, **168**, 591.
10. Berridge, N. J., *Nature, Lond.*, 1942, **149**, 194.
11. Mackinlay, A. G. and Wake, R. G. In: *Milk Proteins: Chemistry and Molecular Biology: Vol. II*, H. A. McKenzie (ed.), 1971, Academic Press, New York, p. 175.
12. Pujolle, J., Ribadeau Dumas, B., Garnier, J. and Pion, R., *Biochim. Biophys. Acta*, 1966, **25**, 285.

13. Schmidt, D. G., Both, P. and De Koning, P. J., *J. Dairy Sci.*, 1966, **49**, 776.
14. Vreeman, H. J., Both, P., Brinkhuis, J. A. and van der Spek, C., *Biochim. Biophys. Acta*, 1977, **491**, 93.
15. Chaplin, B. and Green, M. L., *J. Dairy Res.*, 1980, **47**, 351.
16. Lawrence, R. C. and Creamer, L. K., *J. Dairy. Res.*, 1969, **36**, 11.
17. Bingham, E. W., *J. Dairy Sci.*, 1975, **58**, 13.
18. Wake, R. G., *Aust. J. Sci.*, 1957, **20**, 147.
19. Armstrong, C. E., Mackinlay, A. G., Hill, R. J. and Wake, R. G., *Biochim. Biophys. Acta*, 1967, **140**, 123.
20. Hindle, E. J. and Wheelock, J. V., *J. Dairy Res.*, 1970, **37**, 389.
21. Van Hooydonk, A. C. M. and Olieman, C., *Neth. Milk Dairy J.*, 1982, **36**, 153.
22. Udenfriend, S., Stein, S., Bohlen, P., Dairman, W., Leimgruber, W. and Weigele, M., *Science*, 1972, **178**, 891.
23. Beeby, R., *N.Z. J. Dairy Sci. Technol.*, 1980, **15**, 99.
24. Humphrey, R. S. and Newsholme, L. J., *N.Z. J. Dairy Sci. Technol.*, 1984, **19**, 197.
25. Dalgleish, D. G., *J. Dairy Res.*, 1986, **53**, 43.
26. Berridge, N. J., *Analyst*, 1952, **77**, 57.
27. Foltmann, B., *Proc. XV Intern. Dairy Congr.*, 1958, Vol. II, p. 655.
28. McMahon, D. J. and Brown, R. J., *J. Dairy Sci.*, 1983, **66**, 341.
29. Raymond, M. N., Bricas, E., Salesse, R., Garnier, J., Garnot, P. and Ribadeau Dumas, B., *J. Dairy Sci.*, 1973, **56**, 419.
30. Raymond, M. N. and Bricas, E., *J. Dairy Sci.*, 1979, **62**, 1719.
31. De Koning, P. J., Van Rooijen, P. J. and Visser, S., *Neth. Milk Dairy J.*, 1978, **32**, 232.
32. Martin, P., Collin, J.-C., Garnot, P., Ribadeau Dumas, B. and Mocquot, G., *J. Dairy Res.*, 1981, **48**, 447.
33. Collin, J.-C., Martin, P., Garnot, P., Ribadeau Dumas, B. and Mocquot, G., *Milchwissenschaft*, 1981, **36**, 32.
34. Andren, A. and De Koning, P. J. In: *Use of Enzymes in Food Technology*, P. Dupuy (ed.), 1982, Technique et Documentation Lavoisier, Paris, p. 275.
35. Collin, J.-C., Muset de Retta, G. and Martin, P. In: *Use of Enzymes in Food Technology*, P. Dupuy (ed.), 1982, Technique et Documentation Lavoisier, Paris, p. 159.
36. Garnot, P. and Molle, D., *Lait*, 1982, **62**, 671.
37. Garnier, J., *Biochim. Biophys. Acta*, 1963, **66**, 366.
38. Castle, A. V. and Wheelock, J. V., *J. Dairy Res.*, 1972, **39**, 15.
39. Van Hooydonk, A. C. M., Olieman, C. and Hagedoorn, H. G., *Neth. Milk Dairy J.*, 1984, **37**, 207.
40. Azuma, N., Kaminogawa, S. and Yamauchi, K., *Agric. Biol. Chem.*, 1984, **48**, 2025.
41. Visser, S., Van Rooijen, P. J. and Slangen, C. J., *Eur. J. Biochem.*, 1980, **108**, 415.
42. Hill, R. D. and Hocking, V. M., *N.Z. J. Dairy Sci. Technol.*, 1978, **13**, 195.
43. Beeby, R., *J. Dairy Res.*, 1976, **43**, 37.
44. Voynick, I. M. and Fruton, J. S., *Proc. Nat. Acad. Sci. USA*, 1971, **68**, 257.
45. Hill, R. D., *Biochem. Biophys. Res. Comm.*, 1968, **33**, 659.
46. Schattenkerk, C. and Kerling, K. E. T., *Neth. Milk Dairy J.*, 1973, **27**, 286.

47. Hill, R. D., *J. Dairy Res.*, 1969, **36**, 409.
48. Raymond, M. N., Bricas, E. and Mercier, J.-C., *Neth. Milk Dairy J.*, 1973, **27**, 286.
49. Visser, S., Van Rooijen, P. J., Schattenkerk, C. and Kerling, K. E. T., *Biochim. Biophys. Acta*, 1976, **438**, 265.
50. Visser, S., Van Rooijen, P. J., Schattenkerk, C. and Kerling, K. E. T., *Biochim. Biophys. Acta*, 1977, **481**, 171.
51. Visser, S., *Neth. Milk Dairy J.*, 1981, **35**, 65.
52. Kaye, N. M. C. and Jolles, P., *Biochim. Biophys. Acta*, 1978, **536**, 329.
53. Hill, R. D. and Laing, R. R., *J. Dairy Res.*, 1965, **32**, 193.
54. Chobert, J.-M., Mercier, J.-C., Bahy, C. and Hazé, G., *FEBS Lett.*, 1976, **72**, 155.
55. Fiat, A.-M. and Jolles, P., *C.R. Acad. Sci. Paris*, 1977, **284D**, 393.
56. Raap, J., Kerling, K. E. T., Vreeman, H. J. and Visser, S., *Arch. Biochem. Biophys.*, 1983, **221**, 117.
57. Jenkins, J. A., Tickle, I., Sewell, T., Ungaretti, L., Wollmer, A. and Blundell, T. L., *Adv. Exp. Med. Biol.*, 1977, **95**, 43.
58. Sinkinson, G. and Wheelock, J. V., *Biochim. Biophys. Acta*, 1970, **215**, 517.
59. Ekstrand, B., Larsson-Raznikiewicz, M. and Perlmann, C., *Biochim. Biophys. Acta*, 1980, **630**, 361.
60. Ekstrand, B. and Larsson-Raznikiewicz, M., *Milchwissenschaft*, 1984, **39**, 591.
61. Dalgleish, D. G., Brinkhuis, J. and Payens, T. A. J., *Eur. J. Biochem.*, 1981, **119**, 257.
62. Humme, H. E., *Neth. Milk Dairy J.*, 1972, **26**, 180.
63. Payens, T. A. J. and Both, P. In: *Biochemistry: Ions, Surfaces, Membranes*, M. Blank (ed.), 1980, American Chemical Society, Advances in Chemistry Series No. 188, p. 129.
64. Kato, I., Mikawa, K., Kim, Y. M. and Yasui, T., *Mem. Fac. Agr. Hokkaido Univ.*, 1970, **7**, 477.
65. Green, M. L. and Marshall, R. J., *J. Dairy Res.*, 1977, **44**, 521.
66. Visser, S., Slangen, K. J. and Hup, G., *Neth. Milk Dairy J.*, 1975, **29**, 319.
67. Creamer, L. K., *N.Z. J. Dairy Sci. Technol.*, 1976, **11**, 30.
68. Pélissier, J. P., Mercier, J. C. and Ribadeau Dumas, B., *Ann. Biol. Anim. Biochim. Biophys.*, 1974, **14**, 343.
69. Visser, S. and Slangen, K. J., *Neth. Milk Dairy J.*, 1977, **31**, 16.
70. Carles, C. and Ribadeau Dumas, B., *FEBS Lett.*, 1985, **185**, 282.
71. Berry, G. P. and Creamer, L. K., *Biochemistry*, 1975, **14**, 3542.
72. Foster, P. M. D. and Green, M. L., *J. Dairy Res.*, 1974, **41**, 259.
73. Phelan, J. A., Guiney, J. and Fox, P. F., *J. Dairy Res.*, 1973, **40**, 105.
74. Creamer, L. K. and Mills, O. E., *J. Dairy Res.*, 1971, **38**, 269.
75. De Jong, L. and De Groot-Mostert, A. E. A., *Neth. Milk Dairy J.*, 1977, **31**, 296.
76. Creamer, L. K. and Richardson, B. C., *N.Z. J. Dairy Sci. Technol.*, 1974, **9**, 9.
77. Mulvihill, D. M. and Fox, P. F., *J. Dairy Res.*, 1979, **46**, 641.
78. Mulvihill, D. M. and Fox, P. F., *J. Dairy Res.*, 1977, **44**, 533.
79. Mulvihill, D. M. and Fox, P. F., *Ir. J. Food Sci. Technol.*, 1980, **4**, 13.
80. Fox, P. F. and Guiney, J., *J. Dairy Res.*, 1973, **40**, 229.
81. Hill, R. D., Lahav, E. and Givol, D., *J. Dairy Res.*, 1974, **41**, 147.

82. Mulvihill, D. M. and Fox, P. F., *Milchwissenschaft*, 1979, **34**, 11.
83. Vamos-Vigyazo, L., El-Hawary, M. and Kiss, E., *Acta Alimentaria*, 1981, **10**, 278.
84. El-Shibiny, S. and Abd-El-Salam, M. H., *J. Dairy Res.*, 1976, **43**, 443.
85. El-Shibiny, S. and Abd-El-Salam, M. H., *J. Dairy Sci.*, 1977, **60**, 1519.
86. Sternberg, M., *Adv. appl. Microbiol.*, 1976, **20**, 135.
87. Green, M. L., *J. Dairy Res.*, 1977, **44**, 159.
88. Scott, R., *Topics in Enzyme and Fermentation Biotechnology*, 1979, **3**, 103.
89. Martens, R. and Naudts, M., *Bulletin, International Dairy Federation*, 1978, No. 108, 51.
90. De Koning, P. J., *Bulletin, International Dairy Federation*, 1980, No. 126, 11.
91. Kay, J. and Valler, M. J., *Neth. Milk Dairy J.*, 1981, **35**, 281.
92. Hofmann, T. In: *Food Related Enzymes*, J. R. Whitaker (ed.), 1974, American Chemical Society Advances in Chemistry Series No. 136, p. 146.
93. Fruton, J. S. In: *The Enzymes*, P. Boyer (ed.), Vol. 3, 1971, Academic Press, New York, p. 119.
94. Foltmann, B., *C.R. Trav. Lab. Carlsberg*, 1966, **35**, 143.
95. Alais, C. and Lagrange, A., *Lait*, 1972, **52**, 407.
96. Bohak, Z., *J. Biol. Chem.*, 1969, **244**, 4638.
97. Jesperson, N. J. T. and Dinesen, V., *J. Soc. Dairy Technol.*, 1979, **32**, 194.
98. Duersch, J. W. and Ernstrom, C. A., *J. Dairy Sci.*, 1974, **57**, 590.
99. Thunell, R. K., Duersch, J. W. and Ernstrom, C. A., *J. Dairy Sci.*, 1979, **62**, 373.
100. Hyslop, D. B., Swanson, A. M. and Lund, D. B., *J. Dairy Sci.*, 1975, **58**, 795.
101. Wallace, D. L., *Proceedings of the Second Biennial Marschall International Cheese Conference*, 1981, p. 289.
102. De Koning, P. J., *Dairy Industries International*, 1978, **43**(7), 7.
103. Martin, P., Raymond, M.-N., Bricas, E. and Ribadeau Dumas, B., *Biochim. Biophys. Acta*, 1980, **612**, 410.
104. Ramet, J. P. and Weber, F., *Lait*, 1981, **61**, 381.
105. Philippos, S. G. and Christ, W., *Milchwissenschaft*, 1976, **31**, 349.
106. Vanderpoorten, R. and Weckx, M., *Neth. Milk Dairy J.*, 1972, **26**, 47.
107. Kovacs-Prost, G. and Sanner, T., *J. Dairy Res.*, 1973, **40**, 263.
108. Green, M. L., Valler, M. J. and Kay, J., *J. Dairy Res.*, 1984, **51**, 331.
109. Stanley, D. W., Emmons, D. B., Modler, H. W. and Irvine, D. M., *Can. Inst. Food Sci. Tech.*, 1980, **13**, 97.
110. Green, M. L. and Foster, P. M. D., *J. Dairy Res.*, 1974, **41**, 269.
111. Phelan, J. A., *Dairy Industries*, 1973, **38**, 418.
112. Green, M. L. and Stackpoole, A., *J. Dairy Res.*, 1975, **42**, 297.
113. Chaplin, B. and Green, M. L., *J. Dairy Res.*, 1982, **49**, 631.
114. Beeby, R., *N.Z. J. Dairy Sci. Technol.*, 1979, **14**, 1.
115. Voutsinas, L. P. and Nakai, S., *J. Dairy Sci.*, 1983, **66**, 694.
116. Carlson, A., *Diss. Abstr. Int. B*, 1983, **43**, 3671.
117. Baijot, B., Oliart, M., Paquot, M. and Thonart, P. In: *Use of Enzymes in Food Technology*, P. Dupuy (ed.), 1982, Technique et Documentation Lavoisier, Paris, p. 321.
118. Hicks, C. L., Ferrier, L. K., Olson, N. F. and Richardson, T., *J. Dairy Sci.*, 1975, **58**, 19.

119. Lee, H. J., Olson, N. F. and Richardson, T., *J. Dairy Sci.*, 1977, **60**, 1683.
120. Taylor, M. J., Olson, N. F. and Richardson, T., *Process Biochem.*, 1979, **14**(2), 10.
121. Angelo, I. A. and Shahani, K. M., *J. Dairy Sci.*, 1979, **62**, 64.
122. Cheryan, M., Van Wyk, P. J., Olson, N. F. and Richardson, T., *Biotech. Bioeng.*, 1975, **17**, 585.
123. Paquot, M., Thonart, P. and Deroanne, C., *Lait*, 1976, **56**, 154.
124. Taylor, M. J., Cheryan, M., Richardson, T. and Olson, N. F., *Biotech. Bioeng.*, 1977, **19**, 683.
125. Skogberg, D., Richardson, T. and Olson, N. F., *Abstracts of Papers, Am. Chem. Soc.*, 1977, **173**, AGFD67.
126. Wejwoda, S., Fischer, J., Behnke, U. and Schellenberger, A., *Nahrung*, 1980, **24**, 309.
127. Borisova, V. N., Stal'naya, I. D., Menyailova, I., Motina, L. I., Nakhapetyan, L. A., Fedotov, N. S. and Rybalka, I. G., *Appl. Biochem. Microbiol.*, 1978, **14**, 548.
128. Shindo, K. and Arima, S., *J. Fac. Agr. Hokkaido Univ.*, 1979, **59**, 284.
129. Shindo, K. and Arima, S., *J. Fac. Agr. Hokkaido Univ.*, 1979, **59**, 294.
130. Shindo, K., Sakurada, K., Niki, R. and Arima, S., *Milchwissenschaft*, 1980, **35**, 527.
131. Morrissey, P. A., *J. Dairy Res.*, 1969, **36**, 333.
132. Wheelock, J. V. and Kirk, A., *J. Dairy Res.*, 1974, **41**, 367.
133. Banks, J. M., personal communication to author.
134. Davies, D. T. and White, J. C. D., *J. Dairy Res.*, 1960, **27**, 171.
135. Snoeren, T. H. M., Klok, H. J., Van Hooydonk, A. C. M. and Damman, A. J., *Milchwissenschaft*, 1984, **39**, 461.
136. Damicz, W. and Dziuba, J., *Milchwissenschaft*, 1975, **30**, 399.
137. Wilson, G. A. and Wheelock, J. V., *J. Dairy Res.*, 1972, **39**, 413.
138. Shalabi, S. I. and Wheelock, J. V., *J. Dairy Res.*, 1977, **44**, 351.
139. Shalabi, S. I. and Wheelock, J. V., *J. Dairy Res.*, 1976, **43**, 331.
140. Quist, K. B., *Milchwissenschaft*, 1979, **34**, 467.
141. Ali, A. E., Andrews, A. T. and Cheeseman, G. C., *J. Dairy Res.*, 1980, **47**, 371.
142. Oortwijn, H., Walstra, P. and Mulder, H., *Neth. Milk Dairy J.*, 1977, **31**, 134.
143. Robson, E. W. and Dalgleish, D. G., *J. Dairy Res.*, 1984, **51**, 417.
144. Green, M. L., Marshall, R. J. and Glover, F. A., *J. Dairy Res.*, 1983, **50**, 341.
145. Dickinson, E., Whyman, R. and Dalgleish, D. G., *Chem. Soc. Special Publications*, 1986, in press.
146. Green, M. L. and Crutchfield, G., *J. Dairy Res.*, 1971, **38**, 151.
147. Green, M. L., *Neth. Milk Dairy J.*, 1973, **27**, 278.
148. Kirchmeier, O., *Neth. Milk Dairy J.*, 1973, **27**, 191.
149. Payens, T. A. J., *J. Dairy Res.*, 1979, **46**, 291.
150. Napper, D. H., *J. Coll. Int. Sci.*, 1977, **58**, 390.
151. Walstra, P., *J. Dairy Res.*, 1979, **46**, 317.
152. Darling, D. F. and Van Hooydonk, A. C. M., *J. Dairy Res.*, 1981, **48**, 189.
153. Darling, D. F. and Dickson, J., *J. Dairy Res.*, 1979, **46**, 441.
154. Pearce, K. N., *J. Dairy Res.*, 1976, **43**, 27.
155. Dalgleish, D. G., *J. Dairy Res.*, 1984, **51**, 425.
156. Holt, C. and Dalgleish, D. G., *J. Coll. Int. Sci.*, 1986, 513.

157. Scott-Blair, G. W. and Oosthuizen, J. C., *J. Dairy Res.*, 1961, **28**, 165.
158. Payens, T. A. J., *Biophys. Chem.*, 1977, **6**, 263.
159. Horne, D. S., *Biopolymers*, 1984, **23**, 989.
160. Payens, T. A. J., Wiersma, A. K. and Brinkhuis, J., *Biophys. Chem.*, 1977, **6**, 253.
161. Hyslop, D. B., Richardson, T. and Ryan, D. S., *Biochim. Biophys. Acta*, 1979, **566**, 390.
162. Dalgleish, D. G., *Biophys. Chem.*, 1980, **11**, 147.
163. Von Smoluchowski, M., *Z. Physik. Chem.*, 1917, **92**, 129.
164. Marshall, R. G. and Green, M. L., *J. Dairy Res.*, 1980, **47**, 359.
165. Brinkhuis, J. and Payens, T. A. J., *Biophys. Chem.*, 1984, **19**, 75.
166. Dalgleish, D. G., *J. Dairy Res.*, 1983, **50**, 331.
167. Loucheux-Lefebvre, M.-H., Aubert, J.-P. and Jollès, P., *Biophys. J.*, 1978, **32**, 323.
168. Kowalchyk, A. W. and Olson, N. F., *J. Dairy Sci.*, 1977, **60**, 1256.
169. Slattery, C. W., *J. Dairy Sci.*, 1976, **59**, 1547.
170. Knoop, A. M. and Peters, K. H., *Milchwissenschaft*, 1976, **31**, 338.
171. Cheryan, M., Van Wyk, P. J., Olson, N. F. and Richardson, T., *J. Dairy Sci.*, 1975, **58**, 477.
172. Shalabi, S. I. and Fox, P. F., *J. Dairy Res.*, 1982, **49**, 153.
173. Pyne, G. T. and McGann, T. C. A., *Proc. 16th Intern. Dairy Congr.*, 1962, Vol. B611.
174. Roefs, S. P. F. M., Walstra, P., Dalgleish, D. G. and Horne, D. S., *Neth. Milk Dairy J.*, 1985, **39**, 119.
175. Bakri, M. and Wolfe, F. H., *Can. J. Biochem.*, 1971, **49**, 882.
176. Di Gregorio, F. and Sisto, R., *J. Dairy Res.*, 1981, **48**, 267.
177. Green, M. L. and Marshall, R. J., *J. Dairy Res.*, 1979, **46**, 365.
178. Green, M. L., *J. Dairy Res.*, 1982, **49**, 87.
179. Green, M. L., *J. Dairy Res.*, 1982, **49**, 99.
180. Storch, V. and Segelcke, T., *Milchzeitung*, 1874, **3**, 997.
181. Holter, H., *Biochem. Z.*, 1932, **255**, 160.
182. Payens, T. A. J., *Farad. Disc. Chem. Soc.*, 1978, **65**, 164.
183. Payens, T. A. J. and Wiersma, A. K., *Biophys. Chem.*, 1980, **11**, 137.
184. Payens, T. A., *J. appl. Biochem.*, 1984, **6**, 232.
185. Dalgleish, D. G., *J. Dairy Res.*, 1980, **47**, 231.
186. Johnston, D. E., *J. Dairy Res.*, 1984, **51**, 91.
187. Payens, T. A. J., *Neth. Milk Dairy J.*, 1984, **38**, 195.
188. Kalab, M. and Harwalker, V. R., *J. Dairy Sci.*, 1973, **56**, 835.
189. Sutherland, J., *J. Colloid Sci.*, 1967, **22**, 373.
190. Dalgleish, D. G., *J. Dairy Res.*, 1981, **48**, 65.

Chapter 4

Secondary (Non-enzymatic) Phase of Rennet Coagulation and Post-coagulation Phenomena

Margaret L. Green and Alistair S. Grandison

AFRC Institute of Food Research (University of Reading), Shinfield, Reading, UK

1. INTRODUCTION

Cheesemakers often state that a good curd is required to make a quality cheese, one which is highly acceptable in both flavour and texture. This implies that the initial stages of casein aggregation to form a network influence the characteristics of the cheese. The mechanisms involved in network formation have been probed over the last 10 years, microscopic methods and, more recently, rheological techniques being especially useful. It has been shown that the structure of the curd determines its properties and, thus, the retention of fat and moisture on which depend cheese yield and composition. The curd structure is also a direct precursor of the cheese structure, which must be the basis of its texture.

The formation of the curd is itself influenced by the composition and treatment of the milk. Ideally, the milk should coagulate quickly after addition of rennet to produce a firm curd which drains well and retains a high proportion of the fat. Much progress has been made during the last few years in elucidating the factors which influence this process, mainly because of improvements in methods for measuring the different stages of cheesemaking in isolation.

In this chapter, the formation of curd and its conversion to cheese and the effects of compositional and processing factors will be reviewed. This will involve discussion of the methods now available for studying the formation, properties and structure of curd and cheese and the way in which their application has led to some understanding of the mechanisms involved. From this basis, explanation of the diverse influences of factors

97

in the milk and the manufacturing process will be attempted. Emphasis will be given to work published during the last 5 years and the review will extend and update an earlier one by Green.[1]

2. EXPERIMENTAL METHODS

2.1 Curd Formation

Gels formed by the action of rennet in milk are viscoelastic materials constantly changing with time. To obtain information on their structure and to allow comparison with gels of other materials, absolute rheological measurements are required. These are now beginning to be made. For a time-dependent gel system, Bohlin *et al.*[2] argue that a dynamic test is most suitable. They describe an oscillating coaxial-cylinder rheometer which permits continuous measurement of the loss and storage moduli, G' and G'', and the phase shift at constant shear strain amplitude. Tokita *et al.*[3] used a rather simpler torsion pendulum apparatus to measure G' and G'' continuously at a fixed frequency. A variable frequency rheometer was used for acid milk gels.[4] G' can also be determined from the displacement of a column of curd in a U-tube by an applied pressure.[5] A stress relaxation modulus has been determined with an Instron Food Tester (Instron Corp., Canton, Mass., USA) from the relaxation of a gel with time after a small displacement.[6]

However, most measurements of curd firmness are empirical. This is satisfactory only if the instrumental output can be related to some useful property of the milk gel, or for strictly comparative measurements. If any alteration is made in the conditions, such as varying the casein concentration or using homogenized milk, the output may not necessarily relate to the extent of micellar aggregation.[7] Further, different instruments do not usually give comparable outputs (Fig. 1), because they measure different aspects of the gel's properties. In fact, the outputs of different instruments may move in opposite directions when the conditions are changed. For instance, the curd firming rate increased with temperature when measured with a vibrating reed viscometer or an oscillating diaphragm apparatus[8] but was either unaffected or declined with temperature when measured as yield force with an Instron.[9] This makes it difficult to compare the effect of using different milks if curd firmness measurements were made with different instruments. Thus, it would seem

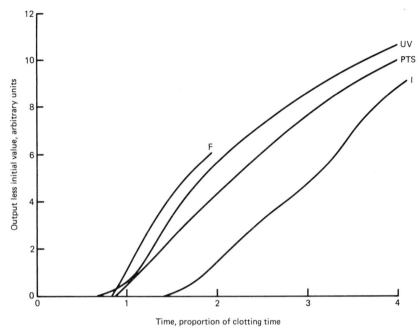

Fig. 1. Typical curves of increase in curd firmness with time. The Ultra Viscoson (UV) and pressure transmission system (PTS) were used on pasteurized whole and skim milk, respectively, as described by Marshall *et al.*[8] The Formograph (F) was used as recommended by the manufacturers and the Instron (I), as described by Storry and Ford,[18] on pasteurized whole milk.

hazardous to attempt to use such measurements to derive fundamental information.

The empirical measurement of curd formation has become much easier in recent years with the development of a number of instruments enabling reproducible measurements and giving continuous outputs. Most of those which have become available since Prokopek's[10] review of the subject and which seem to be generally useful are described below. Of the instruments incorporating a slow oscillating cylinder or probe, an upgraded version of the Plint torsiometer, incorporating transducers to measure the angle and the movement, has been described.[11] However, the Formograph (Foss & Co., Hellerup, Denmark) is based on the same principle as the torsiometer and lactodynamograph but is a simpler and cheaper instrument. It involves the oscillation of stainless steel pendula and measures 10 samples simultaneously. The manufacturers claim that it parallels curd formation in the vat. Although preliminary trials have been reported,[12] the authors have not yet seen a full independent assessment of the instrument. Variations of this apparatus are a slowly oscillating sphere attached to an Instron probe and suspended in a sample of milk[13] and an oscillating vertical steel disc.[14] The latter instrument can be used in a cheese vat.

The hydraulically-operated oscillating diaphragm apparatus, developed by Vanderheiden,[15] measures the rigidity of the curd by its ability to transmit a pressure wave. It can be used directly in the vat and preliminary trials suggest that it would be useful in indicating the optimum cutting time for Cheddar curd.[16] An electronically-operated version has been developed.[17] It was used successfully in preliminary trials in the vat, and also compared with a vibrating-reed viscometer (Ultra Viscoson 1800, Bendix Corp. Inc., Lewisburg, W. Virginia, USA).[8] This and another instrument of the same type (Unipan 505, Unipan Scientific Instruments, Warsaw, Poland) vibrates much more rapidly than those described previously. They are particularly useful for detecting the early stages of aggregation, before visible coagulation (Fig. 1). A more recent instrument, the Gelograph R (Gel Instrumenti AG Rüschlikon, FDR), involving damping the vibrations of a needle by the curd, appears to be available, but the authors have not seen the instrument or an independent assessment of its effectiveness.

Most other methods for the continuous assessment of gel firmness in current use involve measuring the force required to break the curd. Storry and Ford[18] used the traverse of a wire probe through undisturbed curd by means of an Instron. Matěj[19] used a spherical sensor, electrically polarized to avoid coagulum adhesion, to travel spirally through the curd and Kulkarni and Vishweshwariah[20] derived curd strength from the force and time required to move a knife through curd.

2.2 Syneresis of Curd

Syneresis, which is curd shrinkage and loss of whey, occurs very readily[21] and so is extremely sensitive to the experimental conditions. The purpose of its measurement in model experiments is usually to indicate the probable effect of a variable on whey loss during cheesemaking, so it is desirable to try to simulate the conditions pertaining in a cheese vat as closely as possible. This is perhaps most readily achieved by forming and cutting identical curds in a number of vessels, the contents of which are separated by a sieve at intervals.[22] However, the necessity to conserve time and materials often demands that all points on a syneresis–time curve are derived from a single sample of curd and whey. One method[23] involves pouring off the whey from the curd at intervals. This is simple and reproducible, and the effects of variables are at least qualitatively as expected, but the method suffers in that the curd does not remain suspended in the whey and cannot easily be stirred. Tracer dilution methods overcome these disadvantages, but the problem is to select a tracer which does not interfere with the process nor adsorb to the curd. Zviedrans and Graham[24] report that blue dextran is suitable. Pearse *et al.*[25] used clarified whey as the tracer; this became more turbid as syneresis proceeded because of the presence of fat globules not retained by the curd. These workers describe a suitable apparatus for stirring the curd and whey, consisting of 6 vials held on a wheel which is rotated at 20 rpm in a water bath.

2.3 Moisture Content of Curd and Cheese

Modern, semi-continuous methods of cheese production require a rapid method for determining the moisture content of curd. A method for various cheeses using a specific microwave oven was reported to be very reproducible.[26] However, a more thorough collaborative study indicated that drying of samples in microwave ovens can be beset by a number of problems,[27] the most serious of which are the influence of the salt content of the sample and the variability between ovens, even of the same model, with respect to optimal power setting and sample positioning. Extensive calibration against the British Standards Institution standard method of drying in an electrically-heated oven is recommended.

2.4 Curd Fusion

A direct method for determining the stickiness of cheese grains has been described.[28] It involves pressing two cups containing cheese curd together and measuring the force required to separate them. In a more involved method, the frequency of holes, originally containing whey, in electron micrographs of curd at the required stage has been measured (R. J. Marshall, personal communication). A photographic method for detecting curd granule junctions in cheese has been described.[29] It should be adaptable for use with cheddared curd.

No method has been described for measuring salt uptake by curd, and it is not known whether curd samples differ in this respect. However, there has been speculation that differences may exist and the view has been expressed that such measurements are desirable.

2.5 Curd and Cheese Structure

During the last few years, a number of experimental and theoretical advances have been made which appear to be useful in studying curd and cheese structure. It is too early yet to assess the value of some of them, because they have not yet been applied extensively enough. In fact, some have only been used with other protein gel systems, although all appear to the authors to hold promise for use with curd or cheese. Different methods can often be used to give complementary information on a system.

Now that methods are beginning to be available for determining the rheological properties of curd (Section 2.1) and cheese (Chapter 8) in absolute terms, it is timely that theoretical advances are being made to enable the results to be interpreted in structural terms. Bohlin et al.[2] suggest that the complex modulus of rigidity of curd is a measure of the network density and that the phase shift between the applied deformation and resultant force reflects the elastic and viscous contributions to the linkage. Johnston[30] has applied polymer cross-linking theory to rheological measurements of renneted curd. This also suggests that the shear modulus is a measure of the number of cross-links in the gel. Haddad[31] has developed a theoretical analysis for the steady-state deformation of fibrous systems, which takes the microstructure into account and gives information on the distribution of internal stresses.

The main information on curd and cheese structure to date has been derived from microscopic methods. Kimber et al.[32] used transmission microscopy (TEM) to follow the transition of curd to cheese and Green et al.[33] applied scanning electron microscopy (SEM) and light microscopy (LM) after staining of the fat or protein, to the same process. It was shown that the distribution of fat in the protein matrix of cheese was similar when measured by LM and SEM. However, it seems probable that the freezing process applied to fixing the curd for LM distorted the true structure,[34] although the results obtained with different curds suggested that valid comparisons could be made. Shimmin[35] described the application of water-soluble fluorochromes to the staining of cheese for examination of the samples by light fluorescence microscopy.

Means for quantitation of some of the structures observed by microscopy have been described. Tombs[36] deduced the mean pore size and strand thickness in protein gels from measurements on transmission electron micrographs. Green *et al.*[33] described methods for assessing the fat/protein interfacial area from transmission electron micrographs and the coarseness of the protein matrix from light micrographs, both applicable to curd and cheese. It is not known whether these methods give valid absolute data, so they are probably best confined to comparative studies.

Ultrasonics, which should give information on the size and distribution of the fat particles, is beginning to be applied to the study of cheese structure.[37] Small angle X-ray scattering combined with computer modelling has been used on globular protein gels.[38] It has shed light on the assembly of the gel, and the strand thickness and degree of uniformity of the network. In principle, such methods should be applicable to cheese curds.

Proton nuclear magnetic resonance (NMR) can be used to give information on the extent and strength of water-binding in materials, and has been applied to both curd[39] and cheese.[40] An NMR method has also been described for determining the mean size and variance of distribution of liquid droplets in a solid phase, and has been applied to the fat in cheese.[40]

3. MECHANISMS INVOLVED IN FORMATION OF CURD AND ITS CONVERSION TO CHEESE

3.1 Curd Assembly

The curd starts to form at about the visually-observed clotting time (RCT) (Fig. 1) and the process can be followed quantitatively thereafter by measuring the increase in firmness. It is rather slow, so can also be followed by electron microscopy of samples taken at intervals. It is characterized by a steady aggregation of the rennet-treated casein micelles. Chains of micelles are formed at first.[41] By the RCT, these have begun to link into a loose network (Fig. 2a). The network then extends and becomes more differentiated, with the chains of micelles aligning together (Fig. 2b). During this time, the linkages between the micelles also appear to strengthen. Initially, many micelles are joined by bridges (Fig. 2a), but later these appear to contract, bringing the micelles into contact and eventually causing partial fusion. These observations suggest that the increase in curd

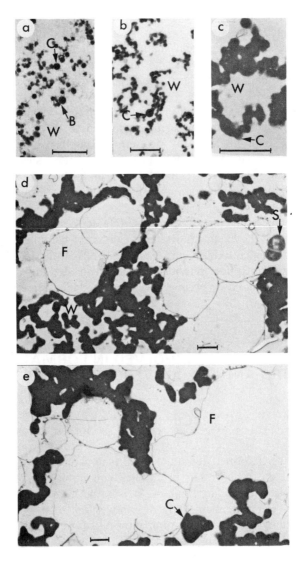

Fig. 2. Thin section electron micrographs of curd during the early stages of normal Cheddar cheesemaking. (a) At about 1·3 × clotting time, 15 min after renneting; (b) just before cutting, 40 min after renneting; (c) at maximum scald, 1·7 h after renneting; (d) 2·7 h after renneting; (e) at pitching, 3·5 h after renneting. C, casein; F, fat; W, whey; S, starter bacteria; B, bridge between micelles. Scale bar = 1 μm. (Modified from Kimber *et al.*[32])

firmness is due to increases in both the number and strength of linkages between micelles. Further light has been shed on the process by means of rheological measurements. Curd formation can be described by a single first-order reaction,[3] as expected if it is a continuation of the initial aggregation of the casein micelles (Chapter 3). It can be explained by application of a general cross-linking theory of gel formation.[30] According to this, curd formation starts when the number of cross-links reaches a critical value, then material is incorporated into the curd at a rate depending on the number of links eventually formed, and finally curd strength increases due to internal cross-linking. The time-course of shear modulus development or the incorporation of material into the curd would be predictable from the initial number of reacting units and the final number and rate of formation of cross-links. It is suggested that several cross-links may eventually be present between 2 micelles in contact, providing a means for increasing the strength of such contacts. It has been noted that the firming rate of curd formed from small micelles is faster than that formed from large ones at the same casein concentration.[42] This may indicate, as expected intuitively, that the same number of cross-links would be formed more readily by a large number of small particles than by fewer large ones.

The presence of fat in the milk decreases the initial shear modulus and exerts a plasticizing action enabling greater deformation of the gel,[43] as expected if fat limits, but also directs and supports, the casein strands without inhibiting their movement in relation to one another.

The chemical nature of the cross-links is not yet entirely clear, but the phosphoryl side chains of casein, especially β-casein, are probably involved.[44] These may be linked by Ca^{2+} bridges. In cheese, α_{S1}-casein appears to play the major structural role,[123,196] but this is much affected by the early stages of hydrolysis to α_{S1}-I-casein. Thus, it seems likely that groups near the N-terminal end, probably in the region of residues 14–24[123] may be involved in linking α_{S1}-casein into the network.

Other mathematical models for explaining curd formation have been suggested, notably by Scott Blair and Burnett[45] and Douillard,[46] but have not been of much use in illuminating the mechanisms involved. Both models fit the output of various curd measuring instruments.[47,48] However, it is important to remember that instrumental outputs are often empirical (Section 2.1) and that attempts to fit them to mathematical equations can lead to improbable predictions.[49]

If a rennet gel is left undisturbed, the shear modulus continues to increase for a period of hours.[30] This must reflect a continuing increase in the number and/or strength of the links between casein micelles. This has been observed directly by microscopy over a 24-h period as an increase in the amount of contact between micelles.[50] The casein strands became shorter and thicker and eventually fused into large masses. Similar changes in the casein were observed in Cheddar cheesemaking (Fig. 2); the casein micelles lost their individuality and steadily fused into masses of increasing size.[32] There is also a steady increase in the size of the casein particles during Cottage cheesemaking.[51] Thus, casein aggregation is not terminated by cutting, but continues throughout cheesemaking. It is now clear that this process is fundamental to the conversion of milk to cheese and that its manipulation is essential for the control of cheese manufacture.

3.2 Syneresis

Calorimetric, sorption[52] and NMR measurements[39] have shown that whey loss is not accompanied by a change in the hydration of the casein. Thus, the whey must be actively expelled, presumably because the continuing aggregation of the casein causes curd shrinkage. This mechanism can easily be envisaged by examination of Figs. 2d,e, which indicate that the pressure exerted by the shrinking curd is sufficient to cause deformation and rupture of the fat globules.

If curd formation and syneresis are two aspects of the same basic process of casein aggregation, they should respond similarly to changes in conditions. A number of variables do indeed change the two parameters in the same direction (Table I), and they are also affected to a similar extent. Increased acidity, temperature and pasteurization temperature and modification of casein amino groups tend to have a large effect on both curd formation and syneresis, while fat content, added $CaCl_2$, cold storage, psychrotroph growth and homogenization tend to have less effect on both parameters.

Increasing the fat content of the milk probably also decreases the rate of whey loss by physical means. As well as limiting casein aggregation, fat globules may act as 'plugs', blocking the flow of whey through channels in the curd.

If it is driven by casein aggregation, whey expulsion from the curd should show a positive pressure. This has been verified, but the pressure is very low, only about 1 Pa or 0·1 mm of water.[21] If whey expulsion is prevented by blocking shrinkage, the permeability of the curd increases with time,[58] as expected from continuing casein aggregation. The time course of syneresis can be explained by a theoretical model including a low

TABLE I
Factors influencing formation, syneresis and fusion of curd

Factors	Curd formation	Syneresis	Curd fusion
Curd treatment			
Lower pH	I[8]	I[23]	
Increase temperature	I[8]	I[23]	
Milk treatment			
Store cold	D[53]	D[53]	
Grow psychrotrophs	D[54]	D[54]	
Homogenize	D[7]	D[7]	D[7]
Increase pasteurization temperature	D[55]	D[55]	D*
Increase fat content	D[43]	D[23]	
Add CaCl$_2$	I[8]	I[23]	I[56]
Chemical modification of casein			
Block—NH$_2$	D[56]	D[57]	

I = increase; D = decrease.
* R. Marshall (personal communication).

endogenous pressure combined with gradually increasing external pressure and permeability.[58]

3.3 Subsequent Cheesemaking Stages

Present indications are that the fusion of the curd particles after whey removal also occurs by casein aggregation. Variations in the cheesemaking procedure appear to have similar influences on curd fusion to those they have on curd formation and syneresis (Table I). Further, the junctions between curd granules are more deficient in fat globules than the bulk of the granule,[59] as expected if fusion is dependent on protein interactions.

Casein continues to aggregate during cheese ripening. For instance in Ras cheese, a Kashkaval-type of hard cheese, casein aggregation and whey exudation occur over at least the first 2 months of ripening.[60]

The manufacture of most types of cheese involves, as a last step, salt flux through the curd. This appears to occur by diffusion, in that it accords with Fick's law, but the diffusion coefficient is about 0·2 cm^2/day, 20% of the value in pure water.[61,62] This discrepancy has been explained by the observation that salt uptake is accompanied by water loss, and the supposition that the salt and water flux would occur through tortuous pores in the cheese.[61] The pulsed field NMR measurement of the diffusion coefficient of water in cheese, $0.35\,\text{cm}^2/\text{day}$,[40] is consistent with these observations. In accord with the proposed mechanism, the rate of salt flux was increased when the moisture content of the cheese was raised.[61] Further, when the fat content of the cheese was increased, the fluxes of both salt and water were decreased and the difference between them was reduced. This could be explained if the role of the fat is to block some of the pores through which the fluxes occur and to prevent shrinkage of the cheese matrix, analogous to the proposed mechanism for the effect of fat on syneresis. Aspects of salt diffusion in cheese are considered in Chapter 7.

3.4 Influence of Curd Structure and Composition on Curd Properties and Cheese Structure

As expected from the inhibiting effect of fat on syneresis, higher fat concentrations in milk result in higher moisture in non-fat solids (MNFS) in cheese.[63] Lower casein levels also give higher MNFS in the cheese, suggesting that casein aggregation probably occurs more slowly in low-casein milks.

There appears to be a direct influence of curd structure on the structure and texture of the derived cheese. Both the curd and Cheddar cheese formed with bovine pepsin have more open, looser structures than those formed with rennet.[64,65] Fat losses during cheesemaking were higher with pepsin, indicating that the curd with the more open structure retained less fat. When Cheddar cheese was made from milk concentrated by ultrafiltration (UF), both the curd and the cheese had an abnormally coarse protein network.[33] The network became coarser as the concentration factor (CF) of the milk was increased, the relative differences being the same throughout cheesemaking into the mature cheese. Less fat was recovered and the MNFS was lower in the cheeses from the more concentrated milks,[66] presumably because the curds with the coarser protein network were less effective in retaining fat and moisture. This accords with the observations of Sone et al.[67] on whey protein gels. Stronger protein interactions in forming the network were associated with a coarser structure and reduced water holding capacity.

The question arises as to why curds vary in the coarseness of the protein network. Knoop and Peters[68] suggested that casein micelles would tend to link together to form chains rather than clumps under ideal conditions. This is because, for negatively-charged renneted micelles, the electrostatic repulsive forces against lateral interaction between a single particle and a chain or between 2 chains are greater than against end-to-end addition.[69]

However, the mean free path of micelles decreases in concentrated milk in proportion to the CF, from about one micelle diameter in native milk. Thus, as the concentration of casein micelles in the milk increases, it may be that the conditions for aggregation become progressively less ideal with a greater tendency to lateral aggregation and, consequently, a coarser protein network is formed.

Lawrence *et al.*[70] have drawn attention to the importance of curd composition in determining cheese structure and texture. They point out

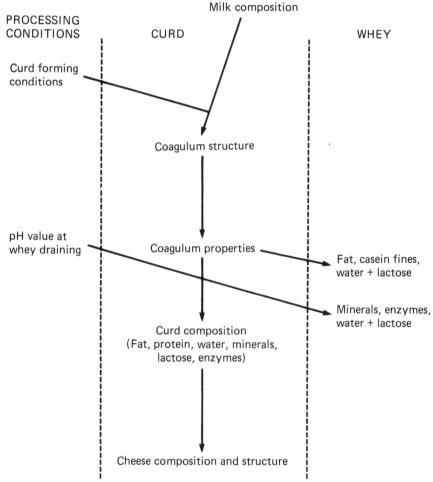

Fig. 3.   Factors influencing the composition and structure of curd and cheese.

that cheese types can be broadly distinguished by their pH values and concentrations of minerals. Both these factors are largely controlled by the acidity at whey draining which determines the extent of removal of Ca, inorganic phosphate (P_i) and water, with dissolved components such as lactose, from the casein. Cheeses which are highly acid and have a low mineral content, such as Cheshire, tend to have a structure consisting of smaller protein aggregates, which may affect the perceived texture. Further, the acidities at both coagulation and whey draining influence the extent to which the enzymes of the coagulant and the milk are retained in the cheese and, thus, participate in ripening. A possible synthesis of the known manufacturing influences on the composition and structure of cheese is summarized in Fig. 3.

In Cottage cheesemaking, a period of hours is generally allowed before cutting, so that coagulation occurs under more acid conditions than in the manufacture of most other types of cheese. Acid coagulation of milk results in less aggregation of the casein than is obtained with rennet.[71] Probably, the acid coagulation which occurs in Cottage cheesemaking also results in slower and less complete aggregation of casein than is obtained in the manufacture of other cheese types. If so, this would account for the high stability of the curd particles against fusion and loss of moisture.

4. FACTORS AFFECTING MILK COMPOSITION OR DISTRIBUTION OF COMPONENTS

4.1 Composition

The suitability of milk for cheesemaking is affected by its composition. This, in turn, depends on a number of factors including the husbandry of the animals and technological treatments of the milk prior to cheese manufacture.

Different breeds of cow produce milks of widely differing composition. The concentrations of fat and protein decrease in the order: Jersey, Guernsey, Ayrshire, British Friesian, British Holstein.[72] Further marked changes in gross composition can arise from selective breeding within a specific breed.[73]

The contents of fat, protein and lactose in milk fall slightly as the age of the cow increases,[74] but this is not relevant to a bulk milk supply where the age ranges of herds cannot be manipulated readily. Stage of lactation can exert a large effect on milk composition and is especially important for a milk supply where the contributing herds are predominantly synchronized to either spring or autumn calving. The most dramatic changes occur in early lactation when levels of fat, casein, Ca and P fall markedly.[75] However, in late lactation the concentrations of casein[76] and fat[77] tend to rise and to be accompanied by considerable changes in the mineral composition.[78] In late lactation, the amount of plasmin-like proteinase secreted into the milk also tends to rise[79] and this causes degradation of part of the β-casein to γ-caseins and proteose peptones.

Seasonal changes in bulk milk composition arise from a combination of lactational and dietary effects. In the UK, the most dramatic variations result from sudden dietary changes, especially during the spring when the cows are put out to pasture and to a lesser extent when they are brought inside for the winter.[72,80] The composition of the diet is a major determinant of milk composition and is the subject of much literature. The effects of nutrition on milk protein were reviewed by Rogers and Stewart[74] and Thomas[81] and the dietary effects on milk fat by Storry[82] and Sutton.[83]

Milking interval or frequency may affect the composition at a single milking, but is unlikely to affect a bulk supply.[84] Milk composition is also affected by climate[85] and excitement or stress.[74]

The presence of diseased animals in a herd can result in compositional changes in the milk which are detrimental to its use for cheesemaking. Although other diseases, such as ketosis, may affect the milk, mastitis is by far the most important disease to the dairy industry. Changes in milk composition due to mastitis result from both changes in the composition of the secreted milk and through the post-secretory action of enzymes derived from somatic cells, blood plasma and the mammary gland epithelium. These changes have been extensively reviewed by Kitchen[86] and Munro *et al.*[87] Increased somatic cell counts are associated with losses in milk total solids content[88] and depressed concentrations of lactose.[89] Total milk fat is not greatly altered,[90] but changes have been reported in the composition of the fat fraction, for example increased free fatty acid levels,[91] during mastitis. While total protein levels remain constant during mastitic infections, the proportions of proteins which are synthesized in the mammary gland (α_{s1}-, α_{s2}-, β- and κ-caseins, β-lactoglobulin, α-lactalbumin) are reduced, while the increased permeability of the mammary gland results in increased levels of immunoglobulins and serum albumin. Mastitis also causes an increase in the ratio, soluble/micellar casein,[92,93] which may result in increased casein proteolysis. The changes in the permeability of the udder also affect the mineral composition of the milk. Most significantly for cheesemaking, the total [94] and micellar[95] concentrations of Ca and P are considerably reduced during mastitis.

Milk composition may also be altered deliberately by ultrafiltration (UF) of the milk. Fat and protein are completely retained in the retentate by the membrane, but vitamins and salts are only partly retained, the extent depending on the proportion bound to the protein.[96] Thus, concentration by UF leads to changes in the relative amounts of the various components in the milk and in the bound/free ratio for macromolecule-bound materials. Further, at high total solids levels, there is a perceptible change in the ratio of the aqueous and particulate phases, so that the concentration of lactose is reduced in the whole milk though unaltered in the milk serum. Treatment of milk in a UF-plant may also cause some disruption of the fat globules, rendering the fat susceptible to lipase action unless this enzyme is destroyed by heating. This problem can be worse during reverse osmosis (RO), when higher pressures are required as the membranes are permeable only to water.

The final concentration of water-soluble components in a UF-retentate can be influenced by additional treatments. Acidification of the initial milk, which causes dissociation of both salts[97] and vitamins,[98] can be used to reduce the concentrations of these components in the retentate. Diafiltration, i.e. the addition and removal of extra water during the UF process, can be used to decrease the final concentration of any or all of the water-soluble components in the retentate.[99]

4.2 Distribution of Components

Storage of milk at refrigeration temperatures allows proteolysis and lipolysis to occur by the action of psychrotrophic bacteria and indigenous milk enzymes, as well as by somatic cells. Law[100] has reviewed the action of psychrotrophic enzymes in milk. Cold storage, at 4 or 7°C for up to 48 h, also causes the caseins, particularly β-casein, Ca and P_i to dissociate from the micelles.[101] Solubilization increases the susceptibility of the casein to proteolysis in the milk. The process is partially reversed by prolonged storage, and completely reversed by heat treatment, 60°C/30 min or 72°C/1 min.[101] There is also a change in the micelle size distribution after holding milk at 4°C for 48 h, with a decrease in the proportion of small micelles.[102]

Heat treatments in excess of pasteurization, in the range 90°C/15 s to

140°C/4 s, can be used as preludes to cheesemaking. These conditions cause partial denaturation of most of the whey proteins,[103] which then participate in SS/SH interchange reactions to precipitate as aggregates or bind to the κ-casein on the outside of the casein micelles.[104] Such heating also reduces the concentrations of soluble Ca and P_i, although these recover, at least partially, on subsequent storage in the cold.

Milk may also be homogenized prior to cheesemaking. The fat globules become smaller and the total surface area larger, to an extent depending on the pressure.[105] The new fat surface becomes covered with milk proteins, mostly casein micelles and submicelles.

5. MILK COMPOSITIONAL AND TREATMENT FACTORS AFFECTING CHEESEMAKING PROPERTIES

The structure and characteristics of a particular cheese are determined by the composition and treatment of the milk and the variables during cheese manufacture. It is by the deliberate control and manipulation of these factors that different cheese varieties are made. There may be influences on the structure of the curd, which then determines the cheese structure. The properties of the curd may be affected, thus influencing the retention of fat or water in the finished product and hence its composition. Alternatively, the retention of minor components such as rennet, minerals or starter in the curd can have large influences on the rate and type of proteolysis during ripening. In this section and the next, we shall attempt to explain the mechanisms underlying the influence of most of the variables normally encountered on the cheesemaking process and the structure of the product.

5.1 Breed and Genetics

Different species of ruminant produce milks of widely differing renneting properties,[108,133] reflecting their different compositions. While particular properties of milks from non-bovine species may be exploited in the manufacture of specific cheeses, this discussion will concentrate on cows' milk.

The major effect of breed on the cheesemaking properties of milk probably results from variations in casein content.[106–108] Curd firmness and structure are directly affected by the casein concentration.[108] The casein and fat in the milk, being the major solid components, also largely determine the cheese yield.[55,109,110] In fact, various equations have been published for predicting cheese yield from the fat and casein (or protein) levels in the milk.[55,110,111] As expected from the casein and fat contents, the yields of Cheddar cheese decrease in the order: Jersey, Guernsey, Ayrshire, Holstein.[112] Genetic improvement in cows in the UK has tended to be concerned with increasing milk yield by replacing traditional English breeds by the Friesian and, more recently, by the North American Holstein.[113] With the recent increases in the proportion of milk being used for processing, where the composition is important, questions must be raised as to whether the higher yielding Holstein–Friesian is the optimal breed or whether reintroduction of more Channel Island characteristics may be economically beneficial to the dairy industry.[114]

One possibility for improving the properties of milk with respect to cheesemaking lies in the fact that individuals secrete genetically determined variants of the caseins and β-lactoglobulin. Even though the variants differ by only a few amino acid substitutions, these differences cause significant changes in renneting and cheesemaking properties. Some of these changes may result directly from physical changes in the milk caused by differences in the physical properties of the protein molecules, but in most cases the variant seems to be genetically linked to some other compositional factor and therefore just acting as a marker trait.

Several authors have noted the effects of the different κ-casein variants in milks during cheesemaking. The B and AB variants are associated with shorter clotting times and higher curd firmness than the A variants.[115–117] Schaar[118] found that the rennet-to-cut time was reduced by more than 30% and fat recovery from the milk was slightly greater when cheese was made from milk containing κ-casein B rather than the A variant, but there was little difference in the yield or composition of the finished cheeses. However, Mariani et al.[119] reported that the B variant resulted in improved texture of Parmesan cheese. The B variant of κ-casein is therefore desirable, at least for the renneting stage of cheesemaking. This is probably not a direct effect but due to associated compositional factors. In particular, milk containing κ-casein B has higher contents of casein, Ca and P and lower contents of citrate than milk containing κ-casein A.[119] Each of these characteristics will tend to favour the association of casein into the micellar form and promote micelle stability. In agreement with this, El-Negoumy[120] observed that casein micelles were more stable in milks containing the B variant rather than the A variant of κ-casein. The B variant of β-casein has also been reported to be associated with higher curd firmness than the A variant.[115] This may be due to differences in the distribution between serum and micelles or to linkage between the genes for the B variants of β- and κ-casein.

Milk containing α_{s1}-casein A gave slower acid development than that containing the B or BC variants, while curd firmness decreased in the order of variants, BC, B, AB, AA.[121] Grandison *et al.*[122] found that curd firmness is closely related to the content of α_{s1}-casein in milk and Creamer *et al.*[123] showed that the hydrolysis of α_{s1}-casein correlated with changes in the rheological properties of young cheeses. Therefore, it seems likely that α_{s1}-casein is basic to the formation of the network in the curd, analogous to its known structural role in the micelle, and that variants of differing physical properties may cause direct changes in curd rheology.

Different genotypes of β-lactoglobulin also seem to be important in cheesemaking although this whey protein has no direct role in curd formation. Milk containing the B variant produced firmer curds than that containing the AA or AB variants[124] and greater cheese yield and dry matter content were obtained with β-lactoglobulin B milk compared with that containing the A variant, with the protein loss in the whey decreasing in the order: AA, AB, BB.[118] These results can be explained by the observation that the proportion of casein in the protein fraction of milks decreases in the order: β-lactoglobulin BB, AB, AA.[118,125]

Thus, there seems to be potential to the cheese industry in including considerations of milk protein genotypes in future breeding programmes. Further research is needed, however, to check that the improvements in cheesemaking associated with the different variants are not linked with undesirable traits.

5.2 Mastitis

Inclusion of high levels of mastitic milk in the milk supply is clearly detrimental to renneting properties and cheese yield and quality.[55] Very severe mastitis results in doubling of the clotting time and halving of the curd firmness of the milk[87] but as little as 10% mastitic milk in the milk supply has been shown to prolong curd formation and give unsatisfactory curd.[126] Curd properties appear to deteriorate in direct proportion to the severity of mastitis, in the range of somatic cell counts $0 \cdot 3$–$7 \cdot 3 \times 10^6$/ml,[127] and therefore to the compositional defects in the milk. Probably, the decreased casein content of the milk and alterations in the mineral balance leading to higher than normal casein solubility are both influential, since curd formation from mastitic milk could be improved, while still remaining sub-normal, by dialysis against normal milk.[128]

As expected, the formation of weak curds from mastitic milk is associated with high moisture retention and excessive fat losses in the whey.[55] These high fat losses and the low casein concentration in the milk were also found to reduce cheese yields by about 5%.[129,130] With treatment of the mastitis, the cheese yield returned to normal levels. There may also be some potential for increasing cheese yields by improving cow health further, since milks of very low cell counts (5×10^4/ml) gave better yields of curd than milks with counts typical of bulk milk supplies (5×10^5/ml).[93]

5.3 Environmental, Seasonal, Lactational and Dietary Effects

Most cheesemakers are aware of seasonal variations in the cheesemaking properties of milk. These result from variations in milk composition, which in turn result mainly from lactation and dietary effects.

Variations in the clotting times of milks during lactation appear to result mainly from variations in the pH value, with the more acid milk clotting more rapidly.[131,132] Curd firmness tends to be highest very early in lactation and declines to a fairly constant level within a few weeks, in parallel with the fall in casein concentration in the milk.[75,133] However, the rate of syneresis increases during this period, perhaps related to the fall in fat concentration in the milk.[75] Syneresis tends to be slow in late lactation milks[134] and to be accompanied by high moisture levels in the derived cheeses.[135] This has been traced to proteolysis in the milk.[136]

Dietary factors can have a marked effect on the renneting behaviour of milk. Several authors[80,137,138] have noted that curd firmness is greater during pasture feeding than when animals are kept indoors. Curd firmness also increases with the proportion of concentrate in the diet.[139] These changes resulted from variations in the casein concentrations in the milks. The effects of diet on clotting times and syneresis were less well defined. It has also been suggested that climatic changes affect renneting properties[140] and cheese quality,[85] but it seems probable that these effects are mediated through dietary changes, particularly resulting from compositional changes in the pasture.

The resultant effect of these variables on seasonal changes in a bulk milk supply is difficult to assess. It is dependent on the proportion of the contributing herds which are autumn or spring calving combined with the timing of putting the animals out to pasture and returning them indoors as well as the basic composition of pasture and winter rations on the individual farms. Generally, the effect of bulking the milk from a number of herds is to smooth out the extremes of composition and properties so that problems such as slow-renneting milks may be removed by bulking. However, seasonal variation in cheesemaking properties does still exist in bulked supplies. Olson[141] reported that cheese yield varied with seasonal changes in (fat + protein) concentration and that slight deviations from this were due to changes in the proportions of milk proteins. Milks that produce good curds give better cheese yields and quality[55,142] whereas weak coagula result in cheese of lower quality and increased moisture.[135,143] Probably, maintenance of a high casein concentration throughout the year is the most important consideration for good yield and quality of cheese.

The composition of the fat fraction of the diet probably only influences cheesemaking in extreme cases. Cheese made from milk containing 19% linoleic acid in the milk fat, resulting from feeding protected sunflower seed oil, had poor texture and flavour.[144] Churning of fat during milk handling can also cause reduced yields.[141]

It is still not clear exactly how changes in composition affect the cheesemaking potential of milk, because much of the data is conflicting. However, the main positive factors appear to be high casein concentration, low pH and high micellar calcium phosphate.[145,146] Of these, the last is the most complex and difficult to determine. There is now reasonable agreement on its composition[147,148] but, as there appear to be direct links between the Ca of the calcium phosphate and casein phosphate groups,[149] there is no clear distinction from casein-bound Ca. Further, as the same factors appear to favour association of Ca with P_i to form micellar calcium phosphate and with casein phosphate groups, these two effects cannot be separated at present.

A clear understanding of the relation between milk composition and cheesemaking potential really depends on precise knowledge of the components present. A start has been made in this direction by the development of computer models describing the distribution of minerals in a milk ultrafiltrate among the various possible complexes and the influence thereon of pH and temperature.[150,151] Now that the micellar calcium phosphate composition is established,[147,148] extension of this to the casein micelle requires information on the various ionic binding sites in casein complexes.

However, in qualitative terms, it is clear that compositional factors favourable for cheesemaking are also those that promote both association of casein into micelles and coagulum formation. Both reactions are also facilitated by the binding of a number of polycations to casein.[152] Thus, the association of caseins to micelles and of para-casein to a coagulum may operate by similar mechanisms.

5.4 Cold Storage

Storage of the milk may affect cheesemaking by both the physical effect of casein solubilization from the micelles and proteolysis of casein by enzymes in the milk, mainly from psychrotrophic bacteria but also from somatic cells or blood. In some cases it is difficult to distinguish the two effects.

Milk stored at 4° or 7°C, having increased soluble casein, shows slower clotting, higher losses of fat and curd fines into the whey, weaker curds and lower curd yield than that stored at 10–20°C.[101] This suggests that soluble casein may not be incorporated into the curd matrix, but the results are confounded by bacterial growth and proteolysis in the milks stored at the higher temperatures. The effects of cold storage are at least partially reversed by holding the milk at 60–65°C, which reduces the clotting time and improves curd properties.[153]

5.5 Psychrotroph Action

The action of enzymes from psychrotrophic bacteria during cold storage can cause lipolysis and proteolysis in the milk. The main effects noted on the cheesemaking properties are rancid off-flavours due to lipolysis and reduced yields resulting from proteolysis. In Cottage cheesemaking, yield losses only become significant after the total bacterial count has reached 10^6/ml and are related to increased non-casein N formed by proteolysis.[154] When the bacterial count had reached 10^8/ml, clotting occurred more slowly and Cottage cheese curds were softer.[155] This level of bacterial growth also caused serious losses in yield. Psychrotroph growth in milk also causes significant losses in Cheddar cheese yield.[156] However, the numbers of psychrotrophic bacteria occurring in stored raw milks under commercial conditions are unlikely to cause significant losses in yield.[100,118] High psychrotrophic counts also cause the micelle size distribution to change[157] which may influence the coagulating properties of the milk.

Reduced cheese yields due to extended cold storage may be avoided by on-farm heat treatment of milk prior to cooling and storage. Heating to 74°C for 10 s was reported to result in 5% more Cottage cheese after storage of the milk for 7 days at 3°C.[158] However, yields of Cheddar cheese from thermized milks stored cold for 8 days were only 1·5% higher than from unheated control milks, which was not statistically significant.[159] Yields of Edam and Limburg cheeses were increased 1·5–2% by heating to 73°C for 30 s, cooling to 8–10°C and reheating to 67°C for 30 s before cooling overnight and pasteurization.[160] Thus, it seems that thermization of milk before cold storage is only really beneficial if the milk is to be stored for a long period. Probably, the heat treatments used result in improved microbiological quality rather than cause whey protein–casein interactions, as suggested by Dzurec and Zall.[158]

5.6 Carbon Dioxide Addition

Another possible means of improving the keeping quality of raw milk by reducing the growth of psychrotrophs is to add about 30 mM CO_2 to milk, decreasing the pH value to about 6·0.[161] The CO_2 can be removed by sparging with nitrogen, but this would seem to be unnecessary where the milk is to be converted to cheese as acid production is required and all the CO_2 is driven off by the time of pitching, so as to have no effect on the later stages of cheesemaking (J. S. King, personal communication).

In model experiments with milk containing CO_2 but without starter, using rennet levels to give the same RCT, both curd formation and whey loss were faster than with the controls, but the differences were entirely accounted for by the difference in pH value (M. L. Green, unpublished work). Reducing the pH value from 6·6 to 6·0 by either CO_2 or lactic acid had no perceptible effect on curd structure. As expected from these findings, milk preserved with CO_2 created no problems in pilot-scale Cheddar cheesemaking trials, provided allowance was made for the faster curd formation by cutting the curd at the optimal point (L. A. Mabbitt and J. S. King, personal communication). This might cause difficulties in factory-scale cheesemaking, because the concentration of CO_2 in the milk in the vat at renneting is likely to be variable, so that the optimal time for cutting the curd may vary between vats. Cutting too early or too late may cause fat losses or excessive moisture retention, respectively.[162] However, one advantage would be that the amount of rennet required could be reduced.

5.7 High Heat Treatment

Heating milk above pasteurization temperatures causes loss of coagulability without necessarily affecting the enzymic action of rennet (R. J. Marshall, personal communication), presumably due to steric hindrance by the β-lactoglobulin bound to the surface of the casein micelles. The curd from such milk also shows reduced syneresis, which has been shown to be due to β-lactoglobulin binding.[163] These processes are not a simple function of (time × temperature), since whey proteins undergo other interactions in the milk at high temperatures. The cheesemaking parameters appear to be affected more at higher heating temperatures,[164] even if the level of whey protein denaturation is kept constant (R. J. Marshall, personal communication).

Acidification and Ca^{2+} addition can be used to facilitate the formation of curd from high-heat-treated milks.[165] This suggests that the best types of cheese to make from such milks may be those in which the curd is formed under acid conditions. In agreement with this, satisfactory Mozzarella cheese was made from milk heated for 2 s at up to 130°C by allowing coagulation to occur at pH 5·6;[166] there was a 3–4% increase in cheese yield. Cheshire cheese, which is a crumbly, semi-hard variety, was also made satisfactorily from high-heat-treated milk (R. J. Marshall, personal communication). In this instance, heat treatment was at 97°C for 15 s and coagulation occurred at pH 6·4. The curd tended to retain moisture and fuse poorly, which correlated with slower aggregation of the casein masses observed by electron microscopy. To overcome this, it was scalded at a higher temperature than normal and the manufacturing time extended to encourage curd fusion. By this means, a product of normal composition and properties could be prepared but with an increase in yield in terms of dry matter of 4–5%.

In contrast, most attempts to prepare satisfactory Cheddar cheese, a variety containing lower moisture and requiring coagulation at a higher pH value, from high-heat-treated milk have not been successful[167] (R. J. Marshall, personal communication). However, Poznanski *et al.*[168] patented a method for making several varieties of cheese in increased yield from milk heated at 92°C for 15 s.

An alternative to heating the milk to be used for cheesemaking is to recover the proteins from whey for addition to the next batch of cheesemilk. A number of methods have been tried, including recovery of the proteins by heat treatment,[169] by heating after concentration[170] or as a complex with carboxymethyl cellulose.[171] However, although yields were higher in all instances, the moisture content of the cheeses containing the extra whey proteins was significantly above normal, often causing flavour and texture defects.

5.8 Homogenization

When milk is homogenized, the rate of aggregation of the casein particles is reduced, the biomolecular rate constant (k) being about 10^{-2} of that for skim milk.[172] This is unlikely to be due to the change in size of the casein particles, since k is little affected by this factor. Curd is also formed more slowly from homogenized milk and the curd also synereses more slowly,[173] so that the final cheese retains more moisture than normal. In curds formed from concentrated milk, homogenization also reduces the ability of the curd particles to fuse.[7]

Homogenization of the milk also influences the structure of the curd[7] and young cheese[174] formed from it. Both have a less coarse protein network than normal; this may contribute to the improvement in soft cheese texture observed with homogenized milk.[175]

It seems likely that the effects of homogenization of the milk on curd formation, structure and properties all stem from the same basic mechanism. There is no evidence for a change in the surface of the casein particles, since the electrophoretic mobility is unaffected by homogenization.[176] However, many micelles are linked to fat particles in homogenized milk[105] without altering the micelle size distribution. This may reduce the total surface area of the casein, decreasing the amount available for interaction and so slowing it.

5.9 Membrane Concentration

The concentration of milk by UF has little effect on the clotting time[177] and the aggregation rate of micelles does not appear to be much affected by concentration.[7] However, the curd firmness, measured by empirical methods, increases markedly with concentration. This apparent discrepancy probably results from the higher total solids content of the curds from concentrated milks compared with unconcentrated ones, reducing the relative ease of movement of the strands in the protein network and thus increasing the viscosity and rigidity.

As the concentration of fat and protein in the milk increases, the structure of the curd changes, the protein network becoming more coarse.[33] This appears to be accompanied by an alteration in the rheological properties, the viscosity increasing faster than the elastic modulus as the milk becomes more concentrated.[178] The structural change is probably the basis of poor retention of fat and moisture by curds from concentrated milks.[66] Further, the structure of the curd leads directly to that of the cheese, so that cheeses from more concentrated milks have coarser protein networks.[33] The atypical structures are perceived as textural defects, cheeses from more concentrated milks tending to be more crumbly, grainy and dry.[179]

The structure of curd from concentrated milks can be improved to some extent by reducing the temperature and, thus, the aggregation rate.[179] However, the mechanisms by which the curd structure is determined are still unclear. Aggregation of the casein micelles in concentrated milks starts when a smaller proportion of κ-casein has been hydrolysed than for normal milk[180] and can occur at lower temperatures[181] which may lead to a change in the balance of small and large aggregates.[182] Alternatively, the decreased mean free path of casein micelles as the milk becomes more concentrated may reduce the proportion of the energetically-favoured end-to-end linking of chains of micelles and increase lateral interactions, thus creating coarser protein strands.[1]

UF-concentration and high heat treatment (Section 5.7) tend to have opposite effects on cheesemaking parameters. This suggests that combining the two processes may be desirable. Certainly, the yields of cheese should be greater than from either process alone, as denaturation of the whey proteins should increase the proportion retained in the curd from UF-concentrated milk. Maubois and Mocquot[183] stated that UF-concentration of UHT-milk either before or after heating allows the retention of curd-forming ability. A more detailed study of the effect of UF-concentration before heating milk at 90–97°C for 15 s (M. L. Green, unpublished work) has shown that the proportion of whey protein denatured increased and the coagulability and curd formation were less affected by heat as the milk concentration increased. However, the rate of syneresis was slowed to an increasing extent as the milk became more concentrated. Prokopek *et al.*[184] found that the texture of Camembert cheese made from UF-concentrated milk could be improved by heat treating the concentrate above pasteurization temperatures.

A study has been made of the use for Cheddar cheesemaking of milk in which all the solids have been concentrated by reverse osmosis (RO).[185,186] It was found that a 15% reduction in milk volume gave satisfactory results provided a few changes were made in the cheesemaking technology and the RO plant did not damage the fat. Increased retention of fat, casein and whey solids was achieved.

5.10 Reconstitution and Recombination

Whole milk powder or skim milk powder and cream or anhydrous milk fat reconstituted in clean water to the same TS and fat/casein ratio as whole milk with added $CaCl_2$ can be used reasonably successfully for cheesemaking provided the powders are prepared under low heat conditions so that interaction of whey proteins with the casein is minimized. Both Camembert[187] and soft brine cheeses[188] tended to have a more open structure than normal, with the casein less evenly distributed, giving more rapid loss of whey and penetration of brine. This was probably due to relatively poor aggregation of the casein resulting from heat damage during the drying process, since the problem was accentuated with milks dried under high heat conditions.[187]

In a thorough study of cheesemaking from recombined milk prepared by homogenizing anhydrous milk fat into reconstituted skim milk powder with $CaCl_2$ addition, Gilles and Lawrence[189] found that coagulation, firming and syneresis were all slower than normal and the curds tended to retain moisture, probably due to the effects of both heat treatment and homogenization. The typical fibrous structures of Cheddar and Mozzarella cheeses were not developed, perhaps because the reduced aggregation potential of the casein decreased the tendency of the curd to flow during the texturization steps. However, Dutch cheeses, made by a process not involving texturization, could be produced satisfactorily from recombined milks.

One possible way to simplify cheesemaking from reconstituted milk would be to carry out some of the normal cheesemaking processes before the milk is dried. In a study of the effects of acidification and renneting of the milk prior to drying on its subsequent cheesemaking properties, Ehsani *et al.*[190] found that curd giving satisfactory rates of firming and whey loss could be prepared.

A quite different approach to the use of dried milk fractions is to combine them to form a mix of the same composition as required in the final cheese, similar to the rationale used by Maubois and Mocquot[183] for making soft cheeses from milk concentrated by ultrafiltration. Davis[191] first tried this approach, mixing skim milk powder, sodium caseinate and ripened cream to the composition of hard, semi-hard and soft cheeses, though no really satisfactory product was prepared. It was developed further by Ali[192] who prepared a soft cheese of the Domiati type which developed acceptable flavour and a typical conchoidal texture on maturation in brine. The changes in structure throughout cheesemaking and ripening were followed by electron and light microscopy. In the first stage, combination of skim milk powder with anhydrous milk fat, casein micelles were adsorbed onto the globule surface as in homogenized milk. This cream was ripened and sodium caseinate was added to give a mixture having a denser matrix, with a fuzzy background of caseinate. When rennet was added to this, aggregation occurred at only about 10% of the expected rate. After 1 h, the caseinate was less evenly dispersed in the matrix, appearing to have moved towards the micelles, and a firm curd was formed in about 6 h. Some whey expulsion started after 15–20 h and this was increased by the addition of NaCl. In the 1-day old cheese, the caseinate and casein micelles were coalesced into aggregates containing entrapped fat, with whey-filled spaces between them. During ripening, the protein masses broke down into smaller units still separated by whey-filled areas. The structure of the ripened cheese prepared by the new method was comparable with that of the authentic product.

5.11 Alteration of Fat Levels

When milk for Cheddar cheesemaking is standardized to within a narrow range of casein/fat ratios, which tends to involve a reduction in the proportion of fat, a slightly higher proportion of the fat tends to be retained in the cheese.[110] Thus, a smaller proportion of the fat escapes from the curd into the whey, perhaps because it is more effectively entrapped. Johnston and Murphy[43] have shown that the fat present in curd acts as a plasticizer and inhibits the formation of cross-links between the casein chains. The weaker and more porous protein network would tend to lose fat more readily.[162]

When the fat in the milk is markedly reduced, so as to produce a low-fat cheese containing about half the normal proportion of fat, the cheese tends to be harder, more crumbly[193] and less smooth.[194] Presumably these characteristics are derived from increased cross-linking within the curd, which is carried into the cheese, together with loss of the plasticizing action of the fat. However, an increase in the softening of cheese has been noted when the fat is reduced.[195] This is to be expected since the cheese contains a higher proportion of protein, the hydrolysis of which is probably responsible for softening.[196]

5.12 Addition of Positively-charged Materials

$CaCl_2$ is frequently used as an additive in cheesemaking because it stimulates coagulation, curd firming and whey loss (Table I). This is probably because it binds to the casein micelles[197] in such a way as to reduce the repulsive forces between them, perhaps by promoting hydrophobic interactions.[152] In this circumstance, all the stages of cheesemaking depending on casein aggregation would probably be stimulated.

Many other positively-charged materials have similar effects to Ca^{2+}, their efficacy being dependent on the extent of binding and on the charge.[198] It appears that their actions also mimic that of Ca^{2+}.[152] In fact, some cationic polyelectrolytes can almost completely coagulate native casein,[199] probably because of the extent of their binding and charge neutralizing abilities.

6. INFLUENCE OF VARIABLES DURING CHEESEMAKING ON CURD AND CHEESE STRUCTURE

6.1 Curd Formation

As indicated in Section 3.4, the nature of the coagulant may affect the structure and properties of the curd and the cheese. The main action is probably on the extent of proteolysis during manufacture and ripening. The more proteolytic enzymes appear to cause the curd to be formed more slowly.[200] There is also decreased fat retention and cheese yield, presumably due to hydrolysis of the curd matrix. Cheeses made with chicken pepsin did not differ in structure from the controls initially, but differences were evident after 9 months.[201]

As the temperature at which the curd is formed is raised, the casein micelles aggregate more readily and extensively.[202] As expected, the protein network became coarser as the temperature of curd formation was raised for both normal and UF-concentrated milks (Fig. 4) (M. L. Green, unpublished observations). More fat tended to be lost in the whey from the coarser curds (Table II).

When the milk was pre-renneted at 5°C, so as to effect the enzymic reaction without coagulation, and then warmed by plunging into a bath at the required temperature, the curd formed more rapidly than normal

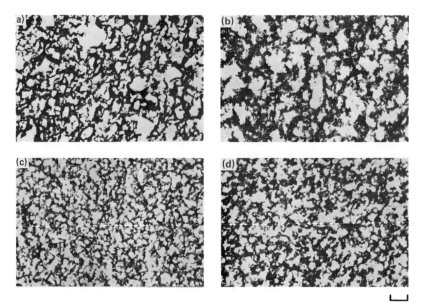

Fig. 4. Light micrographs of curds from milk concentrated 3·25-fold by UF. Conditions of formation: (a) Renneted at 30°C; (b) renneted at 38°C; (c) pre-renneted at 5°C then raised to 30°C; (d) pre-renneted at 5°C then raised to 38°C. Scale bar = 20 μm.

(Table II). However, with milk concentrated 3·25-fold by UF, the protein network was less coarse than when formed by normal renneting at the same temperature (Fig. 4) and the fat losses in the whey were reduced (Table II). This unexpected result can probably be explained by the slowness of the heating process. Curd formation actually started well before the final temperature was reached, probably under the minimum conditions required for aggregation. Thus, the views that the initial stages of formation strongly influence the curd structure, and that curds formed under less favourable conditions have a less coarse protein network are consistent with these observations.

6.2 Curd Handling

A number of recent studies have been made on the effect of firmness at cutting on curd properties and cheese yields.[142,143,162,203] It was generally concluded that the cutting time has little influence unless it falls outside the range of about 85–200% of normal. The amount of fat in the whey

TABLE II

Effect of temperature and pre-renneting at 5°C on the rate of formation, structure and properties of curd from milk concentrated 3·25-fold by ultrafiltration

	Renneted at curd forming temperature		Pre-renneted at 5°C, then warmed	
Temperature, °C	30	38	30	38
Temperature at which viscosity started to rise, °C			14	14
Maximum curd firming rate, arbitrary units	55	86	62	123
Coarseness of protein network, arbitrary units	3·8	6·0	3·2	3·4
Fat loss in whey, % of milk fat	2·9	7·1	2·6	4·9

decreased and the moisture content of the cheese increased linearly with increase in the cutting time.[162] The loss of fat from soft curd was explained by the inability of a poorly-developed network to retain it, and the retention of moisture by the difficulty of a very rigid highly cross-linked curd subsequently forming sufficient cross-links to expel the required amount of whey.

In Cheddar cheesemaking, the high cooking temperature liquefies the fat, so that it can flow in the curd.[204] During cheddaring, the protein chains become oriented, causing the fat globules, still containing liquid fat, to elongate in the same direction and aggregate.[59] The protein and fat are also oriented in Mozzarella and Provolone cheeses, which are stretched at temperatures above the melting point of the fat, but not in Edam and Gouda cheeses, where flow during manufacture is not induced.

Openness in Cheddar cheese can be minimized by the use of vacuum pressing.[205] This process also helps to obscure the curd junctions at which openness tends to occur.[206]

6.3 Cheese Ripening

Ripening of both soft and hard cheeses is accompanied by disintegration of the casein network to form a smoother, more homogeneous structure.[207,208] This occurs more readily if little Ca is present,[71] presumably because Ca helps to cross-link the protein. The extent of proteolysis is also an important factor. In one soft cheese, the softening has been correlated with α_{s1}-casein hydrolysis by residual rennet.[196] This results in reduced hydrophobic interactions between molecules, which could cause the protein network to weaken.[123] Mould development may be more important in the ripening of Camembert cheese, since proteolysis occurs most rapidly near to the fungal hyphae.[209]

6.4 Cheese Processing

In processed cheesemaking, the cheese is heated with salts which complex Ca and thus remove it from the protein matrix, causing this to disintegrate.[210] The salts also emulsify the fat, so that a uniform gel-like structure is formed.[211]

7. CONCLUSION

Although it is now possible to describe the conversion of milk to cheese at the microscopic level in some detail, the forces involved still remain to be understood sufficiently to enable full control of the process. Much data has been collected on the effect of composition on the cheesemaking properties of milk, but the complex interaction of multiple components has sometimes been difficult to disentangle. A coherent theory linking the composition and cheesemaking potential of a milk would be of great benefit. We need to be able to specify the factors in a milk which determine the efficiency of its conversion to cheese so as to be able to select for them. This would enable either the use of milk of the optimal composition or processing before cheesemaking to give the required composition and properties. By these means it should be possible to optimize the recovery of solids, the utilization of equipment and the quality of the product.

REFERENCES

1. Green, M. L. In: *Advances in the Microbiology and Biochemistry of Cheese and Fermented Milk*, F. L. Davies and B. A. Law (eds), 1984, Elsevier Applied Science Publishers, London and New York, p. 1.
2. Bohlin, L., Hegg, P. O. and Ljusberg-Wahren, H., *J. Dairy Sci.*, 1984, **67**, 729.
3. Tokita, M., Hikichi, K., Niki, R. and Arima, S., *Biorheology*, 1982, **19**, 209.
4. Van Vliet, T. and Dentener-Kikkert, A., *Neth. Milk Dairy J.*, 1982, **36**, 261.
5. Scott Blair, G. W. and Burnett, J., *J. Dairy Res.*, 1958, **25**, 297.
6. Johnston, D. E., *Milchwissenschaft*, 1984, **39**, 405.
7. Green, M. L., Marshall, R. J. and Glover, F. A., *J. Dairy Res.*, 1983, **50**, 341.
8. Marshall, R. J., Hatfield, D. S. and Green, M. L., *J. Dairy Res.*, 1982, **49**, 127.
9. Storry, J. E. and Ford, G. D., *J. Dairy Res.*, 1982, **49**, 469.
10. Prokopek, D., *Deutsche Milchwirtschaft*, 1978, **29**, 534.

11. Gervais, A. and Vermeire, D., *J. Texture Studies*, 1983, **14**, 31.
12. Zannoni, M., Mongardi, M. and Annibaldi, S., *Scienza e Tecnica Lattiero-Casearia*, 1981, **32**, 153.
13. Ramet, J. P., El Mayda, E. and Weber, F., *Lait*, 1982, **62**, 511.
14. Richardson, G. H., Okigbo, L. M. and Thorpe, J. D., *J. Dairy Sci.*, 1985, **68**, 32.
15. Vanderheiden, G., *CSIRO Fd. Res. Q.*, 1976, **36**, 45.
16. Kowalchyk, A. W. and Olson, N. F., *J. Dairy Sci.*, 1978, **61**, 1375.
17. Hatfield, D. S., *J. Soc. Dairy Technol.*, 1981, **34**, 139.
18. Storry, J. E. and Ford, G. D., *J. Dairy Res.*, 1982, **49**, 343.
19. Matěj, V., cited from: *Dairy Sci. Abstr.*, 1984, **46**, 200.
20. Kulkarni, S. and Vishweshwariah, L., *J. Food Sci. Technol. (Mysore)*, 1983, **20**, 214.
21. Van Dijk, H. J. M., Walstra, P. and Geurts, T. J., *Neth. Milk Dairy J.*, 1979, **33**, 60.
22. Lawrence, A. J., *Aust. J. Dairy Technol.*, 1959, **14**, 166.
23. Marshall, R. J., *J. Dairy Res.*, 1982, **49**, 329.
24. Zviedrans, P. and Graham, E. R. B., *Aust. J. Dairy Technol.*, 1981, **36**, 117.
25. Pearse, M. J., Mackinlay, A. G., Hall, R. J. and Linklater, P. M., *J. Dairy Res.*, 1984, **51**, 131.
26. Pieper, H., Stuart, J. A. and Renwick, W. R., *J. A.O.A.C.*, 1977, **60**, 1392.
27. Barbano, D. M. and Della Valle, M. E., *J. Food Protect.*, 1984, **47**, 272.
28. Ilyushkin, V. S., Lepilkina, O. V. and Tabachnikov, V. P., cited from: *Food Sci. Technol. Abstr.*, 1983, **15**, P1887.
29. Kalab, M., Lowrie, R. J. and Nichols, D., *J. Dairy Sci.*, 1982, **65**, 1117.
30. Johnston, D. E., *J. Dairy Res.*, 1984, **51**, 91.
31. Haddad, Y. M., *J. Colloid Interface Sci.*, 1984, **100**, 143.
32. Kimber, A. M., Brooker, B. E., Hobbs, D. G. and Prentice, J. H., *J. Dairy Res.*, 1974, **41**, 389.
33. Green, M. L., Turvey, A. and Hobbs, D. G., *J. Dairy Res.*, 1981, **48**, 343.
34. Hermansson, A.-M. and Buchheim, W., *J. Colloid Interface Sci.*, 1981, **81**, 519.
35. Shimmin, P. D., *Aust. J. Dairy Technol.*, 1982, **37**, 33.
36. Tombs, M. P., *Faraday Disc.*, 1974, **57**, 158.
37. Orlandini, I. and Annibaldi, S., *Scienza e Tecnica Lattiero-Casearia*, 1983, **34**, 20.
38. Clark, A. H. and Tuffnell, C. D., *Int. J. Peptide Protein Res.*, 1980, **16**, 339.
39. Lelievre, J. and Creamer, L. K., *Milchwissenschaft*, 1978, **33**, 73.
40. Callaghan, P. T., Jolley, K. W. and Humphrey, R. S., *J. Colloid Interface Sci.*, 1983, **93**, 521.
41. Green, M. L., Hobbs, D. G., Morant, S. V. and Hill, V. A., *J. Dairy Res.*, 1978, **45**, 413.
42. Niki, R. and Arima, S., *Jpn J. Zootech. Sci.*, 1984, **55**, 409.
43. Johnston, D. E. and Murphy, R. J., *Milchwissencahft*, 1984, **39**, 585.
44. Yun, S. E., Ohmiya, K. and Shimizu, S., *Agric. Biol. Chem.*, 1982, **46**, 443.
45. Scott Blair, G. W. and Burnett, J., *Biorheology*, 1963, **1**, 183.
46. Douillard, R., *J. Texture Studies*, 1973, **4**, 158.
47. Qvist, K. B., *Proc. 21st Intern. Dairy Congr., Moscow*, 1982, Vol. 1(2), p. 238.

48. Gervais, A. and Cerf, O., *J. Texture Studies*, 1983, **14**, 47.
49. McMahon, D. J., Richardson, G. H. and Brown, R. J., *J. Dairy Sci.*, 1984, **67**, 1185.
50. Knoop, A. M., *Deutsche Milchwirtschaft*, 1977, **28**, 1154.
51. Glaser, J., Carroad, P. A. and Dunkley, W. L., *J. Dairy Sci.*, 1980, **63**, 37.
52. Ruegg, M., Luscher, M. and Blanc, B., *J. Dairy Sci.*, 1974, **57**, 387.
53. Knoop, A. M. and Peters, K. H., *Proc. 20th Intern. Dairy Congr.*, *Paris*, 1978, p. 808.
54. Lelievre, J., Kelso, E. A. and Stewart, D. B., *Proc. 20th Intern. Dairy Congr.*, *Paris*, 1978, p. 760.
55. Davis, J. G., *Cheese*, Vol. 1, 1965, J. &. A. Churchill Ltd, London.
56. Beeby, R., Hill, R. D. and Snow, N. J. In: *Milk Proteins*, H. A. McKenzie (ed.), Vol. 2, 1971, Academic Press, New York and London, p. 421.
57. Wallace, G. M. and Aiyar, K. R., *Proc. 18th Intern. Dairy Congr.*, *Sydney*, 1970, Vol. 1E, p. 48.
58. Van Dijk, H. J. M. and Walstra, P., *Chem. Eng. J.*, 1984, **28**, B43.
59. Kalab, M., *Milchwissenschaft*, 1977, **32**, 449.
60. Omar, M. M., *Food Chem.*, 1984, **15**, 19.
61. Geurts, T. J., Walstra, P. and Mulder, H., *Neth. Milk Dairy J.*, 1974, **28**, 102.
62. Guinee, T. P. and Fox, P. F., *J. Dairy Res.*, 1983, **50**, 511.
63. Whitehead, H. R., *J. Dairy Res.*, 1948, **15**, 387.
64. Eino, M. F., Biggs, D. A., Irvine, D. M. and Stanley, D. W., *J. Dairy Res.*, 1976, **43**, 113.
65. Eino, M. F., Biggs, D. A., Irvine, D. M. and Stanley, D. W., *Canad. Inst. Food Sci. Technol. J.*, 1979, **12**, 149.
66. Green, M. L., Glover, F. A., Scurlock, E. M. W., Marshall, R. J. and Hatfield, D. S., *J. Dairy Res.*, 1981, **48**, 333.
67. Sone, T., Dosako, S. and Kimura, T., *Snow Brand Milk Prod. Co. Rep. Res. Lab.*, 1984, **79**, 371.
68. Knoop, A. M. and Peters, K. H., *Kiel. Milch. Forsch.*, 1975, **27**, 227.
69. Thomas, I. L. and McCorkle, K. H., *J. Colloid Interface Sci.*, 1971, **36**, 110.
70. Lawrence, R. C., Gilles, J. and Creamer, L. K., *N.Z.J. Dairy Sci. Technol.*, 1983, **18**, 175.
71. Knoop, A. M. and Buchheim, W., *Milchwissenschaft*, 1980, **35**, 482.
72. Crabtree, R. M., British Society of Animal Production, Occasional Publication No. 9, 1984, p. 35.
73. Mulholland, J. R., British Society of Animal Production, Occasional Publication No. 9, 1984, p. 27.
74. Rogers, G. L. and Stewart, J. A., *Aust. J. Dairy Technol.*, 1982, **37**, 26.
75. Grandison, A. S., Ford, G. D., Millard, D. and Owen, A. J., *J. Dairy Res.*, 1984, **51**, 407.
76. Ng-Kwai-Hang, K. F., Hayes, J. F., Moxley, J. E. and Monardes, H. G., *J. Dairy Sci.*, 1982, **65**, 1993.
77. Phelan, J. A., O'Keeffe, A. M., Keogh, M. K. and Kelly, P. M., *Irish J. Food Sci. Technol.*, 1982, **6**, 1.
78. Keogh, M. K., Kelly, P. M., O'Keeffe, A. M. and Phelan, J. A., *Irish J. Food Sci. Technol.*, 1982, **6**, 13.

79. Donnelly, W. J. and Barry, J. G., *J. Dairy Res.*, 1983, **50**, 433.
80. Grandison, A. S., Ford, G. D., Owen, A. J. and Millard, D., *J. Dairy Res.*, 1984, **51**, 69.
81. Thomas, P. C., British Society of Animal Production, Occasional Publication No. 9, 1984, p. 53.
82. Storry, J. E. In: *Recent Advances in Animal Nutrition*, W. Haresign (ed.), 1981, Butterworth, London, p. 3.
83. Sutton, J. D., British Society of Animal Production, Occasional Publication No. 9, 1984, p. 43.
84. Dodd, F. H., British Society of Animal Production, Occasional Publication No. 9, 1984, p. 77.
85. Zannoni, M., *Industria del Latte*, 1984, **20**, 99.
86. Kitchen, B. J., *J. Dairy Res.*, 1981, **48**, 167.
87. Munro, G. L., Grieve, P. A. and Kitchen, B. J., *Aust. J. Dairy Technol.*, 1984, **39**, 7.
88. Ashworth, U. S., Forster, T. L. and Luedecke, L. O., *J. Dairy Sci.*, 1967, **50**, 1078.
89. Renner, E., *IDF Bull.*, 1975, **85**, 53.
90. Needs, E. C. and Anderson, M., *J. Dairy Res.*, 1984, **51**, 239.
91. Randolph, H. E. and Erwin, R. E., *J. Dairy Sci.*, 1974, **57**, 865.
92. Sharma, K. K. and Randolph, H. E., *J. Dairy Sci.*, 1974, **57**, 19.
93. Ali, A. E., Andrews, A. T. and Cheeseman, G. C., *J. Dairy Res.*, 1980, **47**, 393.
94. Bogin, E. and Ziv, G., *Cornell Veterinarian*, 1973, **63**, 666.
95. Singh, L. N. and Ganguli, N. C., *Milchwissenschaft*, 1975, **30**, 17.
96. Green, M. L., Scott, K. J., Anderson, M., Griffin, M. C. A. and Glover, F. A., *J. Dairy Res.*, 1984, **51**, 267.
97. Brule, G., Maubois, J. L. and Fauquant, J., *Lait*, 1974, **54**, 600.
98. Salter, D. N., Scott, K. J., Slade, H. and Andrews, P., *Biochem. J.*, 1981, **193**, 469.
99. Sutherland, B. J. and Jameson, G. W., *Aust. J. Dairy Technol.*, 1981, **36**, 136.
100. Law, B. A., *J. Dairy Res.*, 1979, **46**, 573.
101. Ali, A. E., Andrews, A. T. and Cheeseman, G. C., *J. Dairy Res.*, 1980, **47**, 371.
102. Ali, A. E., Ph.D. thesis. University of Reading, England, 1979.
103. Farah, Z., *Milchwissenschaft*, 1979, **34**, 484.
104. Parry, R. M. In: *Fundamentals of Dairy Chemistry*, B. H. Webb, A. H. Johnson and J. A. Alford (eds), 1974, Avi Publishing Co. Inc., Westport, p. 603.
105. Walstra, P. and Jenness, R., *Dairy Chemistry and Physics*, 1984, John Wiley, New York, p. 266.
106. Jairam, B. T., Vijayalakshmi, B. T. and Nair, P. G., *Indian J. Dairy Sci.*, 1980, **33**, 17.
107. Tervala, H. L., Antila, V., Syväjärvi, J. and Lindström, U. B., *Meijeritieteellinen Aikakauskirja*, 1983, **41**, 24.
108. Storry, J. E., Grandison, A. S., Millard, D., Owen, A. J. and Ford, G. D., *J. Dairy Res.*, 1983, **50**, 215.
109. Howells, J. C., *Dairy Ind. Int.*, 1982, **47**(3), 13, 15, 17, 19, 22.
110. Banks, J. M., Muir, D. D. and Tamime, A. Y., *Dairy Ind. Int.*, 1984, **49**(4), 14.

111. Callanan, T. and Lewis, K. In: *Proceedings of IDF Symposium: Physico-Chemical aspects of dehydrated protein-rich milk products,* Helsingør, Denmark, p. 160.
112. Custer, E. W., *J. Dairy Sci.,* 1979, **62** (Suppl. 1), 48.
113. Wilson, P. N. and Lawrence, A. B., British Society of Animal Production, Occasional Publication No. 9, 1984, p. 95.
114. Kindstedt, P. S., Duthie, A. H. and Nilson, K. M., *Cultured Dairy Prod. J.,* 1984, **19**(1), 20, 23.
115. Feagan, J. T., Bailey, L. F., Hehir, A. F., McLean, D. M. and Ellis, N. J. S., *Aust. J. Dairy Tech.,* 1972, **27**, 129.
116. Morini, D., Losi, G., Castagnetti, G. B. and Mariani, P., *Scienza e Tecnica Lattiero-Casearia,* 1979, **30**, 243.
117. Schaar, J., *J. Dairy Res.,* 1984, **51**, 397.
118. Schaar, J., *J. Dairy Res.,* 1985, **52**, 429.
119. Mariani, P., Losi, G., Russo, V., Castagnetti, G. B., Grazia, L., Morini, D. and Fossa, E., *Scienza e Tecnica Lattiero-Casearia,* 1976, **28**, 208.
120. El-Negoumy, A. M., *J. Dairy Res.,* 1972, **39**, 373.
121. Sadler, A. M., Kiddy, C. A., McGann, E. and Mattingly, W. A., *J. Dairy Sci.,* 1968, **51**, 28.
122. Grandison, A. S., Ford, G. D., Millard, D. and Anderson, M., *J. Dairy Res.,* 1985, **52**, 41.
123. Creamer, L. K., Zoerb, H. F., Olson, N. F. and Richardson, T., *J. Dairy Sci.,* 1982, **65**, 902.
124. Sherbon, J. W., Ledford, R. A. and Regenstein, J., *J. Dairy Sci.,* 1967, **50**, 951.
125. McLean, D. M., Graham, E. R. B. and Ponzoni, R. W., *J. Dairy Res.,* 1984, **51**, 531.
126. Abdel-Galil, H. and Nassib, T. A., *Assiut Vet. Med. J.,* 1980, **7**, 149.
127. Butkus, K. D., Butkene, V. P. and Potsyute, R. Y., *Prikladnaya Biokhimiya i Mikrobiologiya,* 1973, **9**, 473.
128. Erwin, R. E., Hampton, O. and Randolph, H. E., *J. Dairy Sci.,* 1972, **55**, 298.
129. Dean, M. E., *Dairy and Ice Cream Field,* 1974, **157**, 81.
130. O'Leary, J. and Leavitt, B., *Kentucky Agric. Exp. Stn Prog. Rep.,* No. 264, 1982, p. 25.
131. White, J. C. D. and Davies, D. T., *J. Dairy Res.,* 1958, **25**, 267.
132. McDowell, A. K. R., Pearce, K. N. and Creamer, L. K., *N.Z.J. Dairy Sci. Technol.,* 1969, **4**, 166.
133. Rao, R. V., Chopra, V. C., Stephen, J. and Bhalerao, V. R., *J. Food Sci. Technol. (Mysore),* 1964, **1**, 19.
134. O'Keeffe, A. M., Phelan, J. A., Keogh, K. and Kelly, P., *Irish J. Food Sci. Technol.,* 1982, **6**, 39.
135. O'Keeffe, A. M., *Irish J. Food Sci. Technol.,* 1984, **8**, 27.
136. Donnelly, W. J., Barry, J. G. and Buchheim, W., *Irish J. Food Sci. Technol.,* 1984, **8**, 121.
137. Zienkiewicz-Skulmowska, T., Michalakowa, W., Michalak, W., Sinda, H., Jasinska, L. and Goszczynski, J., *Prace i Materialy Zootechniczne,* 1978, **16**, 85.
138. Chapman, H. R. and Burnett, J., *Dairy Ind.,* 1972, **37**, 207.

139. Bartsch, B. D., Graham, E. R. B. and McLean, D. M., *Aust. J. Agric. Res.*, 1979, **30**, 191.
140. Fossa, E., Pecorari, M. and Mariani, P., *Industria del Latte*, 1984, **20**, 87.
141. Olson, N. F., *Dairy Ind. Int.*, 1977, **42**(4), 14.
142. Bynum, D. G. and Olson, N. F., *J. Dairy Sci.*, 1982, **65**, 2281.
143. Banks, J. M. and Muir, D. D., *Dairy Ind. Int.*, 1984, **49**(9), 17.
144. Ahmad, N., *Aust. J. Dairy Technol.*, 1978, **33**, 50.
145. El-Shibiny, S. and Abd-El-Salam, M. H., *Egyptian J. Dairy Sci.*, 1980, **8**, 35.
146. Shalabi, S. I. and Fox, P. F., *J. Dairy Res.*, 1982, **49**, 153.
147. Holt, C., *J. Dairy Res.*, 1982, **49**, 29.
148. Chaplin, L. C., *J. Dairy Res.*, 1984, **51**, 251.
149. Holt, C., Hasnain, S. S. and Hukins, D. W. L., *Biochim. Biophys. Acta*, 1982, **719**, 299.
150. Lyster, R. L. J., *J. Dairy Res.*, 1981, **48**, 85.
151. Holt, C., Dalgleish, D. G. and Jenness, R., *Anal. Biochem.*, 1981, **113**, 154.
152. Green, M. L., *J. Dairy Res.*, 1982, **49**, 87.
153. Reimerdes, E. H., Pérez, S. J. and Ringqvist, B. M., *Milchwissenschaft*, 1977, **32**, 154.
154. Aylward, E. B., O'Leary, J. and Langlois, B. E., *J. Dairy Sci.*, 1980, **63**, 1819.
155. Yan, L., Langlois, B. E., O'Leary, J. and Hicks, C., *Milchwissenschaft*, 1983, **38**, 715.
156. O'Leary, J., Hicks, C. L., Aylward, E. B. and Langlois, B. E., *Proc. 6th Int. Congr. of Food Sci. and Technol.*, J. V. McLoughlin and B. M. McKenna (eds), 1983, Boole Press Ltd, Dublin, Vol. 1, p. 150.
157. Burlingame-Frey, J. P. and Marth, E. H., *J. Food Protect.*, 1984, **47**, 16.
158. Dzurec, D. J. and Zall, R. R., *J. Dairy Sci.*, 1982, **65**, 2296.
159. Zall, R. R., Chen, J. H. and Dzurec, D. J., *Milchwissenschaft*, 1983, **38**, 203.
160. Bochtler, K., *North European Dairy J.*, 1982, **48**, 127.
161. King, J. S. and Mabbitt, L. A., *J. Dairy Res.*, 1982, **49**, 439.
162. Mayes, J. J. and Sutherland, B. J., *Aust. J. Dairy Technol.*, 1984, **39**, 69.
163. Pearse, M. J., Linklater, P. M., Hall, R. J. and Mackinlay, A. G., *J. Dairy Res.*, 1985, **52**, 159.
164. Humbert, G. and Alais, C., *Rev. Lait Fr.*, 1975, **337**, 793.
165. Humbert, G. and Alais, C., *Rev. Lait Fr.*, 1976, **344**, 407.
166. Schafer, H. W. and Olson, N. F., *J. Dairy Sci.*, 1975, **58**, 494.
167. Melachouris, N. P. and Tuckey, S. L., *J. Dairy Sci.*, 1966, **49**, 800.
168. Poznanski, S., Smietana, Z., Jakubowski, J. and Rymaszewski, J., *Acta Alimentaria Polonica*, 1979, **5**, 125.
169. Banks, J. M. and Muir, D. D., *J. Soc. Dairy Technol.*, 1985, **38**, 27.
170. Brown, R. J. and Ernstrom, C. A., *J. Dairy Sci.*, 1982, **65**, 2391.
171. Baky, A. A. A., Elfak, A. M., El-Ela, W. M. A. and Farag, A. A., *Dairy Ind. Int.*, 1981, **46**(9), 29.
172. Robson, E. W. and Dalgleish, D. G., *J. Dairy Res.*, 1984, **51**, 417.
173. Emmons, D. B., Lister, E. E., Beckett, D. C. and Jenkins, K. J., *J. Dairy Sci.*, 1980, **63**, 417.
174. Knoop, A. M. and Peters, K. H., *Milchwissenschaft*, 1972, **27**, 153.
175. Jameson, G. W., *CSIRO Fd. Res. Q.*, 1983, **43**, 57.

176. Dalgleish, D. G., *J. Dairy Res.*, 1984, **51**, 425.
177. Dalgleish, D. G., *J. Dairy Res.*, 1980, **47**, 231.
178. Culioli, J. and Sherman, P., *J. Texture Studies*, 1978, **9**, 257.
179. Green, M. L., *J. Dairy Res.*, 1985, **52**, in press.
180. Garnot, P. and Corre, C., *J. Dairy Res.*, 1980, **47**, 103.
181. Van Leeuwen, H. J., *Proc. 21st Intern. Dairy Congr., Moscow*, 1982, Vol. 1(1) p. 457.
182. Dalgleish, D. G., *J. Dairy Res.*, 1981, **48**, 65.
183. Maubois, J. L. and Macquot, G., *J. Dairy Sci.*, 1975, **58**, 1001.
184. Prokopek, D., Knoop, A. M. and Buchheim, W., *Kiel. Milch. Forsch.*, 1976, **28**, 245.
185. Barbano, D. M. and Bynum, D. G., *J. Dairy Sci.*, 1984, **67**, 2839.
186. Bynum, D. G. and Barbano, D. M., *J. Dairy Sci.*, 1985, **68**, 1.
187. Peters, K.-H. and Knoop, A. M., *Milchwissenschaft*, 1975, **30**, 205.
188. Omar, M. M. and Buchheim, W., *Food Microstructure*, 1983, **2**, 43.
189. Gilles, J. and Lawrence, R. C., *N.Z.J. Dairy Sci. Technol.*, 1981, **16**, 1.
190. Ehsani, R., Bennasar, M. and Tarodo de la Fuente, B., *Lait*, 1982, **62**, 276.
191. Davis, J. G., *Dairy Ind. Int.*, 1980, **45**(10), 7.
192. Ali, M., Ph.D. thesis, University of Reading, UK, 1984.
193. Emmons, D. B., Kalab, M., Larmond, E. and Lowrie, R. J., *J. Texture Studies*, 1980, **11**, 15.
194. Kerr, T. J., Washam, C. J., Evans, A. L. and Todd, R. L., *J. Food Protect.*, 1981, **44**, 496.
195. Grappin, R., Rank, T. C., Johnson, M. E. and Olson, N. F., *J. Dairy Sci.*, 1983, **66** (Suppl. 1), 76.
196. De Jong, L., *Neth. Milk Dairy J.*, 1977, **31**, 314.
197. Green, M. L. and Marshall, R. J., *J. Dairy Res.*, 1977, **44**, 521.
198. Marshall, R. J. and Green, M. L., *J. Dairy Res.*, 1980, **47**, 359.
199. Di Gregorio, F. and Sisto, R., *J. Dairy Res.*, 1981, **48**, 267.
200. McMahon, D. J. and Brown, R. J., *J. Dairy Sci.*, 1985, **68**, 628.
201. Findlay, C. J., Stanley, D. W. and Emmons, D. B., *Canad. Inst. Food Sci. Technol. J.*, 1984, **17**, 97.
202. Knoop, A. M., *Deutsche Molkerei-Z.*, 1976, **97**, 1092, 1167.
203. Tabachnikov, V. P. and Dudnik, P. N., cited from: *Dairy Sci. Abstr.*, 1980, **42**, 56.
204. Hall, D. M. and Creamer, L. K., *N.Z.J. Dairy Sci. Technol.*, 1972, **7**, 95.
205. Hoglund, G. F., Fryer, T. F. and Gilles, J., *N.Z.J. Dairy Sci. Technol.*, 1972, **7**, 150.
206. Lowrie, R. J., Kalab, M. and Nichols, D., *J. Dairy Sci.*, 1982, **65**, 1122.
207. Stanley, D. W. and Emmons, D. B., *Canad. Inst. Food Sci. Technol. J.*, 1977, **10**, 78.
208. De Jong, L., *Neth. Milk Dairy J.*, 1978, **32**, 1, 15.
209. Knoop, A. M. and Peters, K.-H., *Milchwissenschaft*, 1971, **26**, 193.
210. Heertje, I., Boskamp, M. J., Van Kleef, F. and Gortemaker, F. H., *Neth. Milk Dairy J.*, 1981, **35**, 177.
211. Rayan, A. A., Kalab, M. and Ernstrom, C. A., cited from: *Dairy Sci. Abstr.*, 1981, **43**, 931.

Chapter 5

The Syneresis of Curd*

P. Walstra, H. J. M. van Dijk† and T. J. Geurts

*Department of Food Science, Agricultural University,
Wageningen, The Netherlands*

1. INTRODUCTION

Gels formed from milk by renneting or acidification under quiescent conditions may subsequently show syneresis, i.e. expel liquid (whey) because the gel (curd) contracts. Under quiescent conditions, the gel may lose two thirds of its volume, and up to nine tenths or even more if external pressure is applied. Often syneresis is undesired, e.g. during storage of products like yoghurt, sour cream, cream cheese or quarg; hence, it is useful to know under what conditions syneresis can be (largely) prevented. In making cheese from renneted or acidified milk, syneresis is an essential step. Consequently, it is useful to understand and quantitatively describe syneresis as a function of milk properties and process conditions, particularly when new methods or process steps are introduced in cheesemaking. This concerns several aspects:

—regulation of water content of the cheese implies controlling syneresis;
—the rate of syneresis affects the method of processing, and thereby the

* At the request of the editor, and by kind permission of the editors of *The Netherlands Milk and Dairy Journal*, the article: P. Walstra, H. J. M. van Dijk and T. J. Geurts, 'The syneresis of curd. 1. General considerations and literature review', *Neth. Milk Dairy J.*, 1985, **39**, 209, has been reprinted here almost unaltered. Since that article did not contain the authors' more recent results, Section 9 has been added, which is a summary of: H. J. M. van Dijk and P. Walstra, The syneresis of curd. 2. One-dimensional syneresis of rennet curd in constant conditions, *Neth. Milk Dairy J.*, 1986, **40**, 3–30.
† Present address: Central Laboratory, Melkunie-Holland, Woerden, The Netherlands.

equipment and time needed, and the losses of fat and protein in the whey;

— the rate of syneresis in relation to other changes (e.g. acidification, proteolysis, inactivation of rennet enzymes) affects cheese composition and properties;

— the way in which syneresis of curd grains proceeds may affect the propensity of the grains to fuse into a continuous mass during shaping and/or pressing;

— differences in syneresis throughout a mass of curd cause differences in composition of the cheese between loaves of one batch and between sites in one loaf;

— after a cheese loaf has been formed, it may still show syneresis and hence moisture loss.

(Note: throughout this chapter we will use the word 'moisture' for any liquid that may move through curd or cheese; it is thus generally an aqueous solution and not just water.)

Thus, the importance of syneresis is obvious. Accordingly, numerous research reports have been published, providing many important data on the influence of various factors on the rate, and sometimes on the endpoint, of syneresis. However, there are considerable quantitative discrepancies between the results of various authors, and sometimes even trends differ. Moreover, the results provide little understanding of the underlying mechanisms and of the causes of the differences observed. Some of our experimental results and considerations have already been published, partly in a preliminary form.[1-4]

2. GEL FORMATION AND PROPERTIES

The casein micelles in milk, consist mainly of protein (α_{s1}-, α_{s2}-, β- and κ-caseins), calcium phosphate and water.[3,5] The casein molecules are probably present in small aggregates (submicelles, 15–20 nm in diameter), each containing different casein species and having a predominantly hydrophobic core and a predominantly hydrophilic outer layer. The submicelles are clustered into approximately spherical aggregates (micelles), for the most part 50–300 nm in diameter, and with interstitial moisture; they are most probably kept together by the undissolved or colloidal calcium phosphate. There is, however, a dynamic equilibrium between casein and particularly calcium phosphate in the micelles and in solution. If milk is brought below physiological temperature, some casein (predominantly β) and some calcium phosphate go into solution. If the casein micelles are ruptured, the fragments reassociate into particles like the original micelles.

Van der Waals attraction would cause the casein micelles to flocculate if there were no repulsive interaction energy between them.[5,6] These interactions are electrostatic and steric in nature. Most of the κ-casein of the micelles is at the outside[5] and the strongly hydrophilic C-terminal part of these molecules apparently sticks out from the micelle surface as a flexible chain that perpetually changes its conformation by Brownian motion,[7] thereby causing steric repulsion. During the renneting of milk, the proteolytic enzymes in the rennet (mainly chymosin) split the κ-casein molecules into para-κ-casein and soluble caseinomacropeptides (the C-terminal region), thereby largely removing the protruding chains and greatly diminishing steric and electrostatic repulsions. The micelles can now approach one another closely and it is observed that they flocculate, i.e. remain close together. It is not yet clear what forces keep the paracasein micelles together since van der Waals attraction most probably is insufficient to achieve this, at least for the smaller micelles. (Assuming the Hamaker constant to be little over 10^{-21} J and the interparticle distance caused by the presence of 'bound' solvent molecules, etc., to be a few times 0·1 nm, the attraction energy would be only a few times kT for micelles of 50 nm diameter.) Both electrostatic interaction (salt bridges) and the hydrophobic effect have been held responsible.[6] It may be argued that the outside of the paracasein micelles (predominantly) consists of para-κ-casein and that this protein is insoluble under conditions as in milk (e.g. Ref. 8). The latter statement, however, appears to be questionable: para-κ-casein in the presence of other caseins is insoluble at a free Ca^{2+} ion activity over ~ 7 mM[126] and the combined free ion activity of Ca^{2+} and Mg^{2+} in milk is generally less than 2 mM.[3] Consequently, it is unlikely that the flocculation can be explained by milk serum being a poor solvent for para-κ-casein.

The kinetics of renneting are difficult to interpret since two reactions are involved. The enzymic reaction is essentially first order[9] and the flocculation can be described by Smoluchowski kinetics.[6,10] The caseinomacropeptide segments are one by one removed from the micelles (since each micelle contains in the order of 10^3 κ-casein molecules and since the number of micelles is roughly 10^2 times the number of chymosin molecules). Consequently, the reactivity of the micelles, i.e. the probability that micelles that meet each other become flocculated, at first remains low,

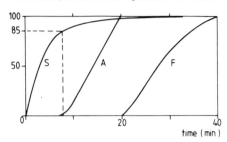

Fig. 1. Changes occurring in milk after adding rennet. Degree of splitting of κ-casein (S), aggregation of paracasein micelles as measured by turbidity (A) and firmness (approximately a yield stress) of the gel formed (F) as a percentage of their value after 40 min, as a function of time (from Ref. 3).

strongly increasing when a greater proportion of the κ-casein has been split, becoming noticeable when this proportion is on average about 0·85, but still increasing markedly after that[10,128] (see also Fig. 1). The reactivity of fully renneted micelles, i.e. those that are fully converted into paracasein micelles, depends little on pH, increases with Ca^{2+} concentration, decreases with increasing ionic strength (NaCl), and increases markedly with temperature, especially from e.g. 15 to 30°C.[11] Above 50°C, the flocculation rate becomes independent of temperature, being roughly equal to that predicted by Smoluchowski's equation for diffusion-controlled coagulation.[11] The temperature dependence is often taken as indicative of hydrophobic bonds being responsible for the reaction between the paracasein micelles,[6,11] but this is difficult to reconcile with the observation that the shear modulus of a rennet-induced skim-milk gel increases markedly with decreasing temperature.[12] Consequently, it is more likely that with decreasing temperature only the activation free energy for flocculation increases, possibly because of protrusion of β-casein chains.

After a while, the flocculation leads to the formation of a gel (see Fig. 1). Microscopically, one can observe that at first irregular, but mostly somewhat threadlike aggregates are formed; these grow in size until they start to touch and form a continuous network.[13,14] Electron microscopy reveals (e.g. Refs. 15, 16, 17) that the network can be described as consisting of strands of micelles, 1–4 micelles in thickness and some 10 micelles long, alternated by thicker nodes of micelles and leaving openings up to 10 μm in diameter. It is sometimes assumed (e.g. Ref. 6) that a gel, rather than a precipitate is formed, because the flocculating particles temporarily have a limited number of reactive sites on their surface.

However, if the casein is fully converted into paracasein at low temperature, and the temperature is subsequently raised so that the paracasein micelles can flocculate, a normal gel (which exhibits normal syneresis) is formed.[41] Sutherland[18] and Meakin[127] have shown by computer simulation that even if homodisperse, smooth spheres meet by Brownian motion and flocculate, flocs of an irregular, often partly threadlike shape are formed, much as observed with renneted micelles; the flocs become less dense (more porous) as they grow. If flocculation proceeds unhindered, i.e. in the absence of liquid flow and with negligible sedimentation of the particles, it must therefore lead, in our opinion, to the formation of a continuous network, hence a gel. It is well known that stirring milk during renneting leads to a precipitate, not a gel. We have observed that a precipitate (or at least not a gel throughout the whole liquid) is obtained if so little rennet is added that the coagulation time is as long as 3 days; apparently, the slowly growing aggregates now had sufficient time to sediment somewhat before they could form a continuous network.

The gel induced by renneting alters considerably with time. Electron microscopy shows (e.g. Ref. 19) that the micelles, which can, initially, still be distinguished clearly lose their identity in the course of several hours, as they seem to fuse into uneven strands of paracaseinate. In other words, the contact area between two micelles in the network is small at first, but gradually increases. It is tempting to explain this by a rearrangement of calcium phosphate and submicelles. The shear modulus of the gel increases rapidly at first (Fig. 1), but continues to increase for about 6 h at $30°C^2$ and for longer times at lower temperatures;[12] eventually it decreases somewhat.

If the gel is formed undisturbed and if it completely sticks to the wall of the vessel in which it is formed (e.g. clean glass), it usually shows no syneresis, at least if the vessel is not too large and has vertical walls, and if the temperature is not too high (e.g. 30°C). Apparently, the gel is now constrained and cannot shrink. We have observed spontaneous syneresis if the milk was renneted in a conical flask: presumably, the gel tears loose from the glass wall by gravity before it is fully set. Similarly, spontaneous syneresis may occur in a cylindrical glass if it is tilted slightly for a moment during setting. After the gel has become firmer, it can withstand a heavier disturbance without exhibiting spontaneous syneresis. Usually it does not show syneresis at the milk surface, either; presumably, the surface is covered by a thin lipid-rich layer which causes the contact angle between milk serum, air and the paracaseinate matrix (as measured in the serum) to be obtuse so that capillary forces prevent the serum from leaving the matrix. As soon as the gel is cut or the surface (locally) is wetted, syneresis occurs. This effect permits experimentally starting syneresis at any desired moment after a gel is formed.

So far we have considered only rennet-induced gels. Quiescent acidification to pH ~4·6 of (skim) milk leads to a gel that looks microscopically rather similar to an aged rennet gel,[15,16] despite the fact that the building blocks must be different,[104] as virtually all colloidal calcium phosphate has dissolved.[3] An acid milk gel, formed by cold acidification and subsequent quiescent heating, has a higher shear modulus than a rennet gel, and the modulus keeps increasing with time (for at least a week), albeit at an ever decreasing rate.[20] Such an acid gel shows little or no syneresis when it is kept undisturbed for some hours at 30°C, even if it is then cut or wetted. Acid gels formed by permitting lactic acid bacteria to grow in skim-milk may, however, exhibit syneresis after cutting or when put under external pressure.[93,107,108]

3. POSSIBLE CAUSES OF SYNERESIS

3.1 Change in Solubility

Syneresis of cross-linked polymer gels can often be described in terms of a change in solubility of the polymer,[21,22] but, as discussed above and elsewhere,[129] we must consider curd to be a particle gel. One may argue that a small region around the contact area between flocculated paracasein micelles can be considered as a kind of polymer gel, to which a modified theory of polymer gel syneresis can be applied. Nothing is known about the properties (e.g. an effective chi parameter) of the hypothetical mini-gel, but even if this were different, we expect such an approach to be ineffectual since it would relate to at most a minor part of the mechanisms of syneresis (see below). Some authors (e.g. Cheeseman[23] and Dimov and Mineva[24]) have considered syneresis of rennet curd to be caused by a dehydration of the casein when transformed into paracasein. Even if dehydration is ill-defined in this context, the notion is in fact equivalent to the mentioned solubility change. The difference in water 'binding' between caseinate and paracaseinate, as determined by different methods[25,26] is, however, marginal. Considering, for instance, sorption isotherms, the change in equilibrium water content caused by renneting is only about 3%

at high water activities.[26] Neither did pulsed wide-line proton-NMR studies show a significant change in the mobility of the water protons in skim milk owing to renneting.[27] Moreover, the composition of the whey does not change in the course of syneresis and, as was observed by Stoll,[28] this also points to an insignificant change in 'bound' water.

In acid milk gels, particularly those produced by the action of lactic acid bacteria, a change in solubility cannot be ruled out. Conceivably, slow proteolysis may alter the casein particles in such a way that they become more reactive, the casein becoming more like paracasein. This may well be the cause for the widely different practical experience with syneresis in sour milk products, since such proteolysis would depend on several conditions.

3.2 Rearrangement

Syneresis can be due to rearrangement of the network of (para)casein particles. These particles form only a limited number (mostly 2–5) of bonds with others. However, they are expected to be reactive over their entire surface (or to contain numerous reactive sites smeared out over their surface) and in the network as described in Section 2, by far the greater part of the surface of each particle does not touch (form a bond with) another one. Rearrangement of the particles into a more compact network would thus increase the number of bonds and hence decrease the total free energy (the counteracting loss in conformational entropy is very small). But the particles cannot easily attain a more compact configuration because they are almost immobilized in the network. In other words, the network has to be deformed locally to form new bonds, which implies an activation free energy for rearrangement. We can think of the following mechanisms that may cause the number of bonds to increase:

1. Long-range attractive forces between the particles. However, van der Waals attraction and electrostatic forces can effectively act over at most a few nm[3,6] and it is very unlikely that any interactions caused by protruding molecular chains can act over much longer distances. Since the interparticle distances are in the order of a few μm, long-range forces can be ruled out.

2. Micelle flow. The same forces as mentioned above may, however, cause attraction between the parts of two flocculated micelles that are near the area of contact between them, since there the mutual distance is small. If the particles are rigid, this will have no further consequences. But if the particles can show lasting deformation (viscous flow), this may lead to a gradually increasing area of contact between them, hence to a more compact network. Virtually nothing is known about the rheological properties of casein micelles. It has been estimated that the stress needed to disrupt them, which may be related to a yield stress, is roughly 2×10^4 Pa.[29] This appears a rather high stress, but it concerns a very short deformation time (about 10^{-7} s), and at longer time scales the yield stress probably is much smaller. Consequently, a mechanism whereby shrinkage of the network occurs because the constituting particles increase their area of contact owing to attractive forces cannot be ruled out.

3. Thermal motion of strands. In a gel consisting of long cross-linked macromolecules, thermal motion of the strands between cross-links can lead to mutual contact and hence possibly to an increase in the number of cross-links.[21] As will be clear from the discussion on gel structure in Section 2, this is an unlikely mechanism for milk gels because of the thickness and shortness of the strands. Rheological measurements on rennet[2,12] and acid[20] milk gels show that the shear modulus is linear with deformation for a relative deformation of about 0·03; if the theory of entropic (rubber) gels[30] would hold, it would imply only about one statistical chain element between cross-links; in other words, the strands are fairly rigid. Nonetheless, a limited additional cross-linking due to thermal motion of the strands cannot be ruled out. It will certainly occur during the early stages after a gel has formed, as is borne out by the very large increase in dynamic shear modulus with time,[2] which must primarily be caused by an increase in the number of bonds.

4. Spontaneous breaking of strands. If the mechanisms described under items 2 and 3 above are active, this must lead to a tensile stress in at least part of the strands. Consequently, strands may break; there must be several weak spots in the rather irregular network. The breaking of a strand creates the opportunity for forming more new bonds, thereby causing a denser network to develop (and possibly leading to a tensile stress in other strands). This is illustrated in Fig. 2. Breaking of bonds between caseinate particles, and thereby of strands, conceivably can also occur by Brownian motion. The breaking stress of a rennet gel at slow deformation is of the order of 10 Pa.[2] From the number and size distribution of casein micelles,[31] a regular network consisting of strands of

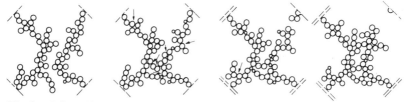

Fig. 2. Schematic representation of strands of paracasein micelles forming new cross links, leading to breaking of one of the strands (from Ref. 2).

one micelle thickness is calculated to have 2×10^{13} strands/m^2 cross section. Taking into account the irregularity of the network, 10^{12} strands/m^2 may be a reasonable estimate. This would yield a breaking force of a strand of the order of 10^{-11} N. Assuming that breakage of a bond between paracasein micelles involves their moving apart over 4 nm, the breaking energy would amount to 4×10^{-20} J $= 10kT$, which, in turn, gives a probability of breaking of $e^{-10} = 5 \times 10^{-5}$. Although this calculation is a very rough one and involves several uncertainties, it shows that spontaneous breaking of strands due to Brownian motion cannot be ruled out. In all probability, breaking will usually be due to a combination of a local stress and thermal energy. Fluctuations in thermal energy add to the probability of breaking a strand under some stress, and the existence of a tensile stress before breaking diminishes the probability of reformation of the same bond after breaking, as the loose ends tend to contract somewhat. That breaking of strands indeed occurs, follows from our results on the change in permeability with time.[2,4]

5. Breaking of strands due to external forces. An external pressure applied to a network, be it caused by gravity, centrifugation or mechanical means, causes the liquid held in the network to flow out, as is experienced when squeezing a wet sponge. This may also happen with a network of casein particles. But the sponge swells again after releasing the pressure, and we are unaware of a similar observation on a milk gel. Stressing a milk gel easily leads to flow,[2] which implies that bonds are ruptured and others formed. Consequently, the stress will cause a rearrangement of the network, leading to a more compact configuration, hence syneresis. This apparently accounts for the well-known strong effect of external pressure on (rate of) syneresis.[1] As the gel shrinks further because of syneresis, geometrical constraints make it more and more unlikely that spontaneous rearrangement of the network can occur; consequently, as syneresis proceeds, external pressure may become relatively more important.

3.3 Shrinkage of Casein Particles

If the building blocks of a network shrink, the whole network will shrink proportionally. As long as conditions remain unaltered, it is unlikely that (para)casein micelles will shrink after flocculation. The change in the micelles that causes flocculation (acidification, renneting) may well cause them to shrink, but because of their small size, shrinkage will be so rapid as to be virtually complete before the network is formed. During renneting, a little shrinkage of the micelles caused by splitting of κ-casein in the micelle interior, may conceivably occur after flocculation (see also Fig. 1), and this may perhaps induce an (additional) small stress in the network.

Changing conditions after a gel is formed may cause shrinkage of the casein particles, hence of the gel. For instance, a drop in pH and a rise in temperature both considerably enhance syneresis, and this may be due partly to shrinkage of the particles. The effects of some variables on the equilibrium swelling state of (para)casein micelles are further discussed in Section 7.

4. SYNERESIS AS A RATE PROCESS

The tendency of a gel network to shrink can be expressed as the pressure exerted by the network on the entrapped moisture. The moisture, therefore, tends to flow out but the flow is hindered by the viscous resistance exerted by the gel network on the liquid streaming through its pores. The classical treatment for flow through a porous medium due to a pressure gradient is by Darcy (e.g. Scheidegger[32]), who's law states:

$$v = \frac{B \Delta p}{\eta l} \qquad (1)$$

The various quantities are discussed below.

v is the linear flow rate (m/s) of the liquid, defined as the volume flow rate in the direction of l, divided by the cross sectional area perpendicular to l through which the liquid flows. If the effective volume fraction of the material forming the network is φ (porosity = $1 - \varphi$), and if the network is isotropic (has the same properties in all directions), the actual average liquid velocity equals $v/(1 - \varphi)$.

B is the permeability (coefficient) of the network (m^2) and can be envisaged as a kind of average cross section of the pores. Its value depends on the geometry of the network and numerous equations have been derived for various models of porous structures;[32,33] in all of these, B decreases sharply with increasing φ, hence with syneresis. B may depend on the flow rate: flow irregularities affect the viscous drag, and the flow itself may alter the network if the latter is not rigid. But for gentle flow (Re $\ll 1$ and shearing stress < 0.1 Pa) we can hardly expect much effect. However, deformation of the curd may well alter B.

η is the viscosity (Pa s) of the moisture flowing through the network; we can safely take this as the viscosity of the whey, which depends somewhat on temperature and acidification.

Δp is the pressure (Pa) exerted by the network on the moisture. The pressure may be due to an endogenous tendency to syneresis or to external causes, either gravity or mechanical pressure. At any point in the gel, the pressure on the moisture is isotropic, but it may vary with location. Δp is a net pressure: deformation of the network because of endogenous or external forces will be counteracted to some extent by elastic reaction forces building up in the network. In the early stages of syneresis, these reaction forces may be slight (unless the whole gel is geometrically constrained or if it is made from concentrated milk), but they must become stronger as syneresis proceeds and increases; eventually, the net pressure becomes zero, when the gel cannot shrink any further. However, this all depends on the external forces applied, on the rheological properties of the network (elastic modulus, stress relaxation spectrum) and on the time-scale considered.

l is the distance (m) over which the moisture must flow. Cutting of the curd greatly enhances syneresis because the smaller l causes a higher v, according to Eqn (1), and because v acts over a larger surface area, thus increasing the volume flow.

B, Δp and l all may vary with φ (hence syneresis), with location and with time. Consequently, Eqn (1) has to be applied to small volume elements in the gel; combination with the equation of continuity then gives an expression for syneresis rate. The resulting equation has been numerically solved (finite difference method for space and time) for one-dimensional syneresis, i.e. flow in one direction.[4] For three-dimensional syneresis (i.e. the normal situation), solution is much more difficult, since liquid flow and shrinkage are not always in the same direction and B and l may vary according to direction; moreover, the counteracting stress in the network tends to depend on direction, since local increases in density (increasing φ) cause the rheological properties to depend on direction. In practical terms, a shrinking piece of curd forms a kind of rind that is more rigid than the

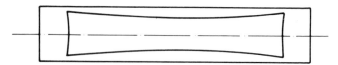

Fig. 3. Cross section through a cylindrical piece of curd before and after syneresis under quiescent conditions and in the absence of external pressure (author's observation).

inside of the piece. The result on syneresis is clearly reflected in the shape that a piece of curd attains after quiescent syneresis, since shrinkage in directions parallel to the skin is hindered; an example is shown in Fig. 3.

Equation (1) is, to a considerable extent, model-independent, but it implicitly assumes that conditions are constant in a volume element that thus must be much larger than the largest pores (say $10\,\mu$m). This condition will usually be met, except for rapid syneresis (e.g. due to a high external pressure) in small pieces of curd.

The considerations given above lead to the conclusion that the rate of syneresis is unlikely to follow a simple relationship. Kirchmeier[34] reported that the change in the volume, V, of a piece of curd is, under 'constant' conditions, given by:

$$V = V_0 \exp(-Kt) \qquad (2)$$

where V_0 = original volume, t = time after the start of syneresis and K is a rate constant linearly dependent on temperature. A similar relation, albeit with some 'extra' syneresis immediately after cutting, was observed by Marshall.[53] Apart from the lack of theoretical justification for Eqn (2), it predicts that V approaches zero for very high t, which is clearly impossible. Weber[35] therefore modified Eqn (2) to:

$$V = V_0(0.15 + 0.85 \exp(-Kt)) \qquad (3)$$

where it was assumed that the curd eventually shrinks to 0·15 times its original volume (actually, Weber used mass rather than volume). Lawrence and Hill[36] found that the amount of whey expelled ($V_0 - V$) from pieces of curd was proportional to $t^{1/2}$, and concluded that 'rate of syneresis is substantially diffusion-controlled'. Such a conclusion had also been reached for syneresis in cross-linked polymer gels.[37] We can, however, not conceive any mechanism of diffusion-controlled syneresis in curd.

The results of other workers (e.g. Refs. 68, 28) also roughly fit a proportionality with $t^{1/2}$ for rennet curd. It can be shown[4] that solution of

Eqn (1) for constant B and Δp gives results analogous to those for solution of the diffusion equation, hence an initial proportionality of syneresis to $t^{1/2}$. But for longer times and for changing conditions, more complicated relations result.

The results quoted above are incompatible: for $Kt \ll 1$, Eqns (2) and (3) predict that $(V_0 - V)$ is proportional to t, not $t^{1/2}$. Results for the rate of syneresis strongly depend on conditions (see Section 6) and even on the experimental method employed (Section 5). The only conclusion can be that, under constant external conditions, the rate of syneresis $(-\mathrm{d}V/\mathrm{d}t)$ mostly decreases as syneresis proceeds. This need not always be true for the relative rate of syneresis $(-\mathrm{d}\ln V/\mathrm{d}t)$, although this quantity ultimately becomes zero also.

5. ESTIMATING SYNERESIS

The ultimate result of syneresis can easily be determined from the water content of the cheese made or from the quantity of whey separated from a cup containing a sour milk gel. To study the syneresis process, other ways have to be found and numerous techniques have been applied. It concerns predominantly syneresis of renneted milk or skim milk, to which we will confine ourselves in Sections 5.1 and 5.2; acid curd is considered in Section 5.3.

5.1 Methods

Table I gives a summary of methods employed to determine syneresis, mostly as a function of time. Some authors are not fully clear about experimental conditions.

Relatively few workers have directly measured shrinkage of the curd (Method 1), for instance the height of a slab, the size of a cube or the mass of a piece of shrinking curd. It is not easy to measure shrinkage accurately; the method can be used for fundamental studies of the early stages of undisturbed syneresis. Evaluation of Thromboelastograph traces[38] only gives a qualitative indication of syneresis. Repeatedly determining the mass of curd once shaped into a loaf, combined with determining water content at the end, gives a possibility to estimate syneresis accurately during the final stages of cheesemaking.[43]

The amount of whey expelled (Method 2) can be measured easily, especially during the early and middle stages. Usually, the volume of whey

TABLE I

Methods used to determine syneresis (the numbers given are references)

Method	Conditions				
	Uncut, in whey	Uncut, in air	Pieces, in whey, at rest	Pieces, in whey, stirring	Drained curd
1. Shrinkage of curd					
(a) Height or volume	38[e], 2		39, (28), 24	n	n
(b) Mass	40[d]	41	42[d], 49	i	43
2. Amount of whey					
(a) Volume drained	44, 68, 45, 28, 46[r]	47, 48, 38	44[r], 68, 42, 45, 50, 81, 51[t], 52[t], 125, 53[r], 54[r], 55[t], 109[r], 90[t], 87[r]	56, 24?, 28, 66[t], 71	57, 84
(b) Tracer dilution	n	n	i	(40), 58, 36, 59, (28), 60, 61, 62, 63, 35, 64, 71	n
3. Dry matter of curd	i	i	65, 52[t]	66, 67, 69, 40, 70, 65[s], 1, 61	66, 52, 70, 43, 63
4. Density of curd	n	n	i	67, 28	i

Notes: (): tried but discarded. d: disturbed (e.g. lifting of curd). e: in Thromboelastograph. i: inconvenient. n: not possible. r: repeated drainage. s: stir while setting. t: temperature increase.

is estimated. A problem is that the whey never drains off completely, which implies that syneresis is underestimated. Another way is to add a tracer to the whey once a certain amount has separated and to determine tracer concentration in the whey as a function of time, and thereby the volume of whey expelled. The tracer may consist of formaldehyde-treated casein micelles,[58,36,59] or some suitable polymer.[61,62] A problem is that a certain quantity of tracer usually appears to become associated with the curd, particularly after some time,[36,61,62] thereby causing the extent of syneresis to be overestimated. The method of Pearse *et al.*,[64] in which a quantity of clarified whey is added and the subsequent increase in turbidity—owing to the expulsion of normal, turbid whey—is measured, is claimed to be free from this problem and may give accurate results; however, it cannot be ruled out that the first whey contains more fat globules, and is thus more turbid, than that expelled later.

Estimating the water (or dry matter) content of the curd (Method 3) is particularly useful in the middle and later stages of syneresis; the volume of whey expelled can be calculated from water loss from the curd and the water content of the whey. A problem is, again, that a certain quantity of whey inevitably adheres to the curd grains. For instance, a 0·1 mm layer of whey covering a 5 mm diameter curd grain tends to increase its apparent water content by about 15% of the actual value. Drying the curd grains with blotting paper or by suction on a Buchner filter introduces the uncertainty of pressing or sucking out whey.[69]

During syneresis of a piece of curd, its density increases (Method 4) and this can be used to calculate the loss of whey, although it is difficult to do so with great accuracy. Stoll[28] used density measurements extensively, but did not calculate the extent of syneresis from the results. An apparatus devised to determine the 'pitching point' during curd treatment in the vat[73] employs a kind of density measurement of a mass of drained curd grains.

Few authors have actually compared the results of different methods on the same curd, although some have observed that different methods at least give the same trend.[28,38] Figure 4 gives some results from our department[61,63] and it is seen that using tracer dilution (Method 2b) a lower water content of the curd is calculated than is found by actual determination (Method 3); the difference could be due to an assumed layer of whey, about 80 μm thick, adhering to the curd grains. Nilsen and Abrahamsen[71] compared tracer dilution with volume drained off (Method 2a) on a number of samples of goat milk and found the ratio (whey volumes) to vary from 0·94 to 1·26; they sometimes found by tracer

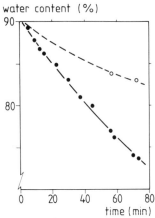

Fig. 4. Water content of curd from skim milk renneted and kept at 31°C as a function of time after cutting, determined from the concentration in the whey of added polyvinyl alcohol (●) and by oven drying of pieces of curd strained off (○) (after Ref. 61).

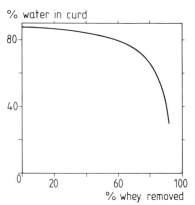

Fig. 5. Calculated relation between the water content of curd (from whole milk of 12·3% dry matter) and the quantity of whey (6·8% dry matter) expelled as % (w/w) of the original milk.

dilution a greater apparent volume of whey expelled than was present in the curd.

The calculated example given in Fig. 5 shows that at the beginning of syneresis large quantities of whey are expelled, while the water content of the curd decreases only slightly; at the end, a small loss of whey corresponds to a considerable decrease in the water content of the curd. This observation has some relevance for the accuracy of the various methods at various stages of syneresis (for instance, measuring only the amount of whey expelled may lead to the erroneous conclusion that syneresis is virtually complete after, say, half an hour). It also poses the problem of how to express syneresis; this becomes particularly important when the effects of variation in milk composition (e.g. fat content or preconcentration of milk) are studied.

5.2 Conditions

The conditions under which the syneresis experiments are performed may strongly affect the results (see Section 6) and may vary widely, as seen in

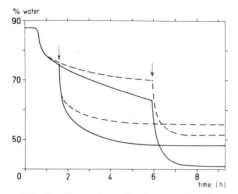

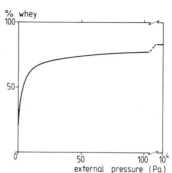

Fig. 6. Examples of changes in the water content of curd (determined by oven drying) as a function of time after renneting. The gel was cut after 0·5 h. At two moments (indicated by arrows), curd was taken out of the whey and put into a cheese mould. Experiments with (——) and without (– – –) added starter. The curd and whey mixture was continually stirred. Temperature of the whey was 32°C throughout, temperature in the mould gradually fell to 20°C. (recalculated after Refs 74 and 61).

Fig. 7. The amount of whey expelled from curd (as % of the original milk volume) after 2 h at 30°C as a function of the external pressure applied to the curd. Approximate results, recalculated from Ref. 1 $(100\,Pa = 10^{-3}\,bar)$.

Table I. Important variables are: size of the piece(s) of curd; whether curd is kept under the whey or not; stirring of the whey–curd mixture or not; and application of external pressure, including pressue due to gravity. Taking curd out of the whey induces considerable differences (Fig. 6); taking it out for even a short period affects the results: Thomé *et al.*[40] found, for instance, that removing a slice of curd 4 times from the whey, for 30 s on each occasion, resulted in a 13% lower weight of curd than removing it only once. Repeated drainage (for 30 s) of whey from a curd–whey mixture resulted in a few per cent more syneresis than draining once.[53] Temperature and acidification during syneresis may strongly affect its extent (Fig. 6). In some studies, conditions were kept as constant as possible, in order to study the effect of certain variables, while in others, the cheesemaking practice was more or less mimicked, which implies changing conditions. In still other cases, a condition (generally temperature) was deliberately changed to speed up syneresis (see Table I).

If experiments are done under such conditions that syneresis is slow, they may take several (up to 24) hours. This poses the problem of changing conditions, such as acidification or proteolysis caused by bacterial growth. Addition of preservatives may lead to a change in the casein, and hence to unreliable results.

It may be concluded that several combinations of measuring methods and conditions can be applied, although not all combinations are easy to perform or are even feasible. The results found will depend on the technique applied, which implies that results from different authors cannot be compared directly; considerable inaccuracy may be encountered. Nevertheless, there is a fair agreement among different studies as to trends, as can be seen in Section 6. Regretfully, none of the methods as such gives much understanding of the cause of the effects observed.

5.3 Acid Gels

For gels formed by acidification of skim-milk, syneresis has been measured by method 1a of Table I, i.e. following the height of a thin slab of curd under its own whey.[2] Method 2a has also been applied, either by measuring drainage from a quantity of cut curd under its own weight[107,108] or by centrifuging the whole (uncut) gel.[93,107] The latter method may be more like an estimation of the end point of syneresis (Section 7.1).

6. FACTORS AFFECTING SYNERESIS RATE

Numerous authors have studied the effects of product and process variables on syneresis rate, beginning with Sammis *et al.*[66] in 1910. Other extensive studies were by, successively, Wurster,[44] Koestler and Petermann,[68] Van der Waarden,[45] Thomé *et al.*[40] and Stoll.[28] Several others have studied one or a few variables. Harwalkar and Kalab[93,107] studied syneresis of set yoghurt.

As will be seen below, the results often vary somewhat. Results that are obviously in error in view of our present understanding have generally been left out. But even then, differences in the individual milk samples, in the methods used and in the conditions employed, cause variation. Particularly, the stage at which syneresis is measured affects the results. Moreover, the effect of one variable may be influenced greatly by the level of another one, and altering one factor often causes other conditions to change also.

6.1 Geometrical factors

If the gel sticks to the surface of the vessel in which it has been made, it expels no whey at that surface[44,68,40] and it has to be cut loose to achieve syneresis. It depends on the nature and the cleanliness of the surface whether the gel sticks to it (see e.g. Ref. 75), but in a vessel with sloping walls or due to some slight shaking of the vessel during renneting, the gel may come off the surface and syneresis occurs.[44,68] For quiescent conditions, a temperature $\leq 30°C$ and a not too large air–milk surface, neither rennet[85,2] nor acid[2,107] milk gels showed spontaneous syneresis at that surface; putting a tiny drop of whey or water on the gel usually induces syneresis, although in the case of a well-set acid gel this may not be so. If milk containing rennet was put on top of a rennet-induced gel, the newly forming gel did not stick to the old one, and syneresis of the latter was rapid.[44]

Initially, syneresis (volume flow rate) is proportional to the area of the surface exhibiting syneresis[44,68,45] and also during practical cheese-making, cutting the curd into smaller pieces gives faster (initial) syneresis.[66,44,40,84] The same holds true for set yoghurt.[107] In a thin layer of rennet curd, syneresis soon slows down because of 'exhaustion' of moisture;[45] in an experiment with thin layers, the amount of whey expelled after 2 h at 35°C was proportional to the layer thickness up to 15 mm, while thicker layers did not expel more whey within that time.[45]

6.2 Clotting

Most authors agree that rennet concentration has no effect on syneresis.[66,44,28,52] Others found that more rennet gave a slight increase[42,84,27] or a decrease[82] in syneresis, or observed an optimum concentration.[35] These effects should be considered in relation to the time of cutting;[28,35,52] as made clear by, for instance, Weber,[35] it is the stage of the coagulation process or the firmness of the curd at the moment of cutting that is the variable: if cutting is very late, syneresis may be somewhat less.

Disturbance of the gel during setting may considerably enhance syneresis rate because it causes enlargement of the free surface[44] (see Section 6.1). But also when the free surface was kept constant, such disturbance caused syneresis rate to increase by 20–30% in some experiments.[51,41]

Curd formed solely by acidification shows very little syneresis, if left undisturbed (e.g. Refs 46, 2). Syneresis became progressively slower if the gel was left for a longer time after setting before it was cut or wetted.[2] In skim milk gelled by growth of yoghurt bacteria to a pH in the range of 3·8–4·5, however, cutting of the gel led to considerable syneresis, up to ~40% of the original volume being expelled as whey.[107,108] In milk clotted below about pH = 5, the presence of rennet was found to considerably enhance syneresis, the more so when the amount of added rennet was increased.[81] Presumably, this signifies a gradual change from an acid to a rennet-induced gel and is of importance in the production of fresh cheese types[35] and for the understanding of syneresis in acid milk products.

6.3 Pressure

If the curd is kept in the whey, any external pressure applied greatly enhances syneresis.[66,1] This is illustrated in Fig. 7; here the lowest pressures are due to velocity differences during stirring and to the weight of the curd itself, while for the higher pressures, perforated plates were put on the layer of curd grains in the whey. Although the pressures as given in Fig. 7 are somewhat uncertain (say by a factor of two), it is clear that particularly the first increase in external pressure (compare the endogenous syneresis pressure of about 1 Pa) has a very large effect. In gels of soured skim milk, applying pressure by means of centrifugation considerably enhanced syneresis,[93,107] but a quantitative interpretation of the results obtained is difficult.

Taking the curd out of the whey often has a rapid and strong enhancing effect on syneresis;[66,42,40,41,50,74,27] an example is shown in Fig. 6. It must be assumed that the far greater pressures exerted on the curd when it is taken out of the whey are primarily responsible. If the curd directly after formation is removed from the whey, for instance in a continuous curd making process, initial syneresis is very rapid (for instance 3 times faster than in the whey while stirring) and applying further pressure even enhanced the rate.[41]

Stirring curd grains in whey considerably enhances syneresis[40,56,28,84] (e.g. Fig. 8). The effect of stirring is probably two-fold. First, it prevents the curd grains from sedimenting and in a sedimented curd layer, particularly during the early stages of syneresis, curd grains deform each other, leaving only narrow channels between them that hinder whey drainage and hence syneresis. Second, some pressure is applied to the curd grains, because of velocity gradients in the liquid (which cause pressure differences in the order of 10 Pa) and because curd grains collide with one another. Above a

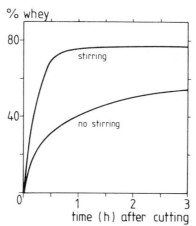

Fig. 8. The volume of whey expelled (as % of the original milk volume) from curd kept in the whey at 38°C as a function of time after cutting, with or without stirring (after Lawrence [56]).

stirring rate sufficient to prevent sedimentation, increasing the rate may cause a small but significant increase in syneresis.[65] Diluting the curd–whey mixture by adding water or whey, slows down syneresis,[56,70] presumably because the pressure gradients caused by collision of curd grains are smaller or occur less frequently. Removing much of the whey enhances the effect of stirring. Incidentally, vigorous stirring may also cause rupture of curd grains (particularly if they still contain much moisture), thus enlarging their surface area and enhancing syneresis (and the losses of 'fines' and fat in the whey).

Some authors have studied possible relations between rheological properties of the curd and its tendency to synerese (e.g. Refs 66, 78, 52, 27, 2, 109, 110) and found somewhat different results. Here we need to mention only two points. Under conditions where deformation (flow) of the curd particles tends to promote their fusion or very close packing, and hence hinder syneresis, a lower apparent viscosity of the curd tends to correspond to less syneresis. Under conditions where individual curd particles can be deformed under stress, a lower modulus leads to more deformation and this tends to promote syneresis.[52]

6.4 Temperature

Temperature greatly affects syneresis rate of rennet curd; some results are summarized in Fig. 9. All authors agree as to the trend and all results show that the rate of change of syneresis with temperature (Q_{10} or $-d \ln V/dT$) decreases with increasing temperature, but otherwise the results are fairly different. At 25°C reported values of Q_{10} vary from about 2·5 to 15, at 45°C from about 1·1 to 1·5.

It appears that the rate at which temperature is changed (dT/dt) does not, as such, affect syneresis.[44,65] Keeping the milk for some time at low temperature before renneting has been reported to have no effect,[55] a small detrimental effect on syneresis[80] or a considerable effect: holding for 20 h at 5°C reduced syneresis by about 30%.[84] Probably, any detrimental effect of precooling is reversed by prewarming the milk to a fairly high temperature before renneting, as is commonly done in cheesemaking to ensure normal setting.

For acid gels, the effect of temperature on syneresis appears not to have been determined, but it has been observed that in gels of skim milk soured

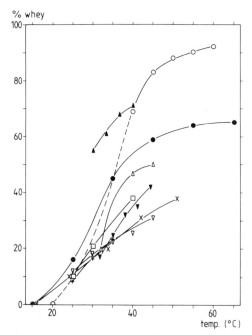

Fig. 9. The volume of whey expelled (as % of the original milk volume) from curd set, kept and treated at different (constant) temperatures. Most results were obtained 1 h after cutting. Recalculated after Sammis et al.[66] ▲; Wurster[44] ▽; Koestler and Petermann[68] ●; Gyr[42] ○; Lawrence[56] ▼; Stoll[28] △; Kirchmeier[34] ×; Kammerlehner[84] □; Marshall[53] +.

by bacteria, considerable syneresis occurred after cutting the gel at $6°C^{107}$ or $3°C.^{108}$

6.5 Acidity

If milk has been acidified to a lower pH before renneting, syneresis rate is faster. Some observations are summarized in Fig. 10; other authors have reported similar results.[66,68,45,40,78,27] Although the observed trends were mostly the same, there were, again, considerable quantitative differences. The deviating relation found by Berridge and Scurlock[41] is not due to inaccuracy but may be related to the different experimental set up (syneresis of a cylinder of curd attached to a grid, in air). The inflection points in the curves near pH 6 are also realistic. Stoll[28] observed that the

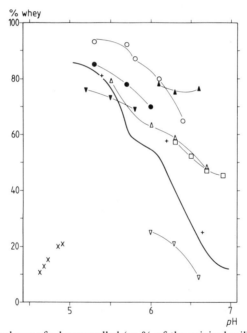

Fig. 10. The volume of whey expelled (as % of the original milk volume) from curd set, kept and treated at different pH; in some cases, pH decreased slightly during the experiment. Most results were obtained 1 h after cutting. Recalculated after Wurster,[44] heavy line = average of several experiments; Gyr[42] ○; Cheeseman[23] ●; Stoll[28] △; Berridge and Scurlock[41] ▲; Patel *et al.*[65] ▼; Marshall[53] ▽; Pearse *et al.*[64] □; Weber[35] +. See text for the results of Emmons *et al.*[81] ×.

effect of pH was relatively greater at lower temperature and in the absence of stirring, i.e. if syneresis was slower. There were no appreciable differences according to the acid used.[45]

If the pH falls during syneresis this may enhance syneresis rate to a greater extent than is found when the pH is previously brought to the same value,[28,74] because the building blocks of the protein network tend to shrink due to the change in pH. This is also exemplified in some results by Emmons *et al.*,[18] shown in Fig. 10. Here the milk contained variable numbers of starter bacteria and the pH values indicated in the figure are those at the moment of cutting. A higher pH at that stage implies a greater drop in pH after cutting, hence more syneresis. Milk that has already been soured to a very low pH (e.g. 4·5) exhibits only weak syneresis, even after renneting.[66,81] However, as mentioned before, set yoghurt did exhibit syneresis after cutting and the amount of whey expelled did not vary significantly in the pH range of 3·8–4·5.

6.6 Principal Constituents of Milk

This concerns either addition or subtraction of fat, protein, water, etc., or natural variations. The general trend for milk clotted by rennet is that a higher water content gives a higher syneresis rate (expressed as proportion of whey expelled per unit time), but has little effect on the water content of the fat-free curd after syneresis is virtually complete. Also, for set yoghurt, syneresis rate was much reduced if total solids content[107] or protein content[108] was increased.

A higher fat content in the milk coincides with slower syneresis (Refs 40, 58, 24, 28, 84, 125, 54, 35, 109, 90). For instance, if fat percentage was increased from 2 to 6, syneresis rate was reduced by about 15%.[24,28,90] In samples from individual cows, either no[66,68] or a slight negative correlation[24,110] was found between fat content and syneresis rate.

A higher casein content was found to have a negative[66,35] or a negligible effect[68] on syneresis. Diluting milk somewhat (e.g. 20%) with water increased syneresis rate.[66]

6.7 Various Additions

We will not consider additions meant to modify specific residues of the milk proteins, in order to study the clotting reaction. Adding sugars, that are fairly unreactive, has been reported to cause no effect,[28,109] a slight decrease[45] or a slight increase[23] in syneresis rate. About the same holds for addition of up to 10% urea.[45,23,28]

In cheesemaking, some (~ 1 mM) $CaCl_2$ is frequently added to enhance clotting. Most authors report that small additions (e.g. up to 10 mM) of $CaCl_2$ somewhat enhanced syneresis,[44,45,28,84,27] while others found little or no effect;[23,65,125] larger additions were generally found to reduce syneresis.[44,42,23,78] Van der Waarden[45] clearly showed that the main enhancing effect of $CaCl_2$ is due to its lowering the pH; when the pH was kept constant, addition of $CaCl_2$ caused syneresis to decrease, while $MgCl_2$ gave a marked increase.[45,28] Presumably, one has to consider two points (besides pH): the calcium ion activity (or rather the activity of divalent cations) which should be at a certain level to achieve syneresis; and the colloidal calcium phosphate, a high amount of which (as caused, for example, by addition of $CaCl_2$) may tend to reduce syneresis. Lowering the pH causes, of course, a dissolution of colloidal phosphate and an increase in Ca^{2+} activity. Addition of phosphate,[45,28] citrate,[45,28] oxalate[45] or EDTA[28] at constant pH, all caused decreased syneresis; these additions considerably reduce Ca^{2+} activity. The salt equilibria in milk are intricate, depend on several conditions and often exhibit slow changes, as discussed by, for instance, Walstra and Jenness.[3]

Increasing the ionic strength of milk with univalent ions (e.g. NaCl) has been reported to give at first no change[23] or a slight increase in syneresis;[28] it tends to reduce the amount of colloidal phosphate and possibly the Ca^{2+} activity. Large increases in ionic strength caused a decrease in syneresis,[45,23,28] but then, milk with added salt clots very poorly on renneting. Addition of $AlCl_3$ caused syneresis to decrease.[28]

In the production of set yoghurt, some gelatin is often added to enhance firmness and to reduce syneresis. Adding 0·5% gelatin to skim milk before acidification by yoghurt bacteria was found to be very effective in reducing syneresis after cutting the gel.[108] Presumably, the gelatin gel formed on cooling immobilizes the network of casein particles, thereby preventing their rearrangement and thus syneresis (see Section 3.2).

6.8 Different Milk Samples

Considering the effects of milk composition on syneresis, it is not surprising that different milk samples show differences in syneresis after renneting. Moreover, stirring, foaming or prolonged storage of the milk may cause changes. For instance, considerable growth of *Pseudomonas* species in milk was shown to markedly diminish syneresis.[83] Some variables studied are:

Species. Other conditions being equal, renneted goats' milk showed greater syneresis than cows' milk, and ewes' milk syneresed less.[54] The effect of several variables on syneresis of renneted cows' milk, as discussed above, was often different for either ewes' or buffaloes' milk.[24]

Breed. Little influence has been observed,[76] except that Jersey milk appears to exhibit faster syneresis than that of other breeds, despite its high fat and protein contents.[86]

Individual cow. Differences are often considerable,[68,40,84,110] with initial syneresis rate varying by a factor of 3. Addition of $CaCl_2$ diminishes variability.

Stage of lactation. Minor differences have been observed.[84] Particularly during the first two months of lactation, syneresis rate has been found to increase, although rennet clotting time did not change significantly.[110] In Ireland, syneresis was found to be reduced in November–December[124] and this was attributed to cows being in late lactation.

Feed. Minor[76] or no differences[87] have been found.

Mastitis. Milk from cows suffering from severe mastitis exhibits poor clotting by rennet and somewhat diminished syneresis.[76,122,123]

6.9 Treatment of Milk

Heat treatment of milk to such an extent that serum proteins are denatured, increasingly diminishes syneresis rate of renneted milk, according to many authors (Refs 44, 45, 24, 28, 84, 80, 79). Some found even a slight decrease caused by milder heat treatments,[48,28,80] but the others did not. Pearse *et al.*[79] found the decrease in syneresis to be almost linearly correlated with denaturation of β-lactoglobulin. Heat treatment of synthetic milk free of serum proteins hardly affected syneresis. Addition of κ-casein to milk diminished the detrimental effect of heating, presumably because β-lactoglobulin now reacted primarily with κ-casein in the serum during heating, thus affecting the casein micelles less.[79]

Syneresis of set yoghurt is reduced but not prevented by intense heat treatment.[107] Presumably, the increased voluminosity of the whey proteins in combination with their association with casein, causes a higher effective volume fraction of the protein network, thus diminishing the possibility for syneresis.

Homogenization or recombination of milk significantly decreases syneresis rate (Refs 77, 84, 125, 91, 92, 54). This is related to the incorporation of micellar casein in the surface coat of the fat globules, which causes the fat globules to become part of the paracasein network, which, in turn, may hinder shrinking of the network. A comparable effect on syneresis was observed if milk was concentrated by evaporation and diluted again before clotting,[88] which has a similar consequence for the fat globules.[89] If fat is homogenized into whey, so that the fat globules do not contain much casein in their surface layers, the detrimental effect of homogenization on syneresis is clearly less.[125]

Concentration of milk (either by evaporation, by reverse osmosis, or by adding dried milk) decreased syneresis rate,[66,84,78,125] as discussed above. Concentration by ultrafiltration also gave less whey,[54,92] but a similar final moisture content.[54]

6.10 Concluding Remarks

It may be concluded that the main variables affecting syneresis rate are:

— the geometrical constraints (surface area of curd, distance over which the whey has to flow);
— pressure applied to the curd (grains), where the relative effect is greatest in the low pressure range;
— pH in the case of rennet-induced curd;
— temperature for rennet-induced gels, where the relative effect is greatest in the low temperature range.

The effect of the other variables is generally small (with the exception of intense heat treatment) and tends to be relatively smaller as overall syneresis rate is higher. Stoll[28] observed, for instance, that stirring the curd–whey mixture almost eliminated differences caused by some variables observed when studying syneresis under quiescent conditions.

7. END POINT OF SYNERESIS

After some time syneresis stops because the curd cannot shrink any further and it may be said that there is an equilibrium moisture content for given conditions of temperature and composition. It is, however, questionable whether such an equilibrium state of swelling can be determined, since syneresis will proceed slower and slower, possibly never coming to an end. More important may be the objection that syneresis rate, also in its final stage, greatly increases with external pressure (see Section 6.3). After the external pressure is removed, the curd may not swell again to attain a hypothetical equilibrium volume, for instance, because the swelling is far too slow or because the curd has been taken out of the whey.

One may try to derive equilibrium swelling from the water content of the cheese obtained under various conditions, but this is mostly not reliable, as may become clear from Section 8. We roughly estimate that for whole-milk rennet curd, at a temperature of 35°C and a pH of 5·2 during pressing, the lowest moisture content that can be obtained corresponds to 1·2 g water/g paracasein.

7.1 Methods

Estimation of an equilibrium state of swelling is beset with difficulties. To begin with, common terminology is confusing. Several authors speak of bound water in a milk gel or of its solvation or hydration, where clearly a state of swelling is meant. True solvation, i.e. water bound to specific groups on the protein molecules, concerns only small quantities. We showed earlier[94,25] that the greater part of the so-called non-solvent water is in fact not bound, but results from negative adsorption of solute onto the protein. More recently it has become clear (see, for example, Franks[95]) that the greater part of non-freezing water is not bound either, but is merely prevented from freezing because the solution has passed the glass transition point, which implies that the freezing rate has become infinitely slow. Consequently, we now interpret our earlier results[25] even more strictly and conclude that paracasein binds perhaps something like 0·1 g water/g, and certainly less than 0·2 g under all relevant conditions. The water we are considering here is thus primarily imbibed in the curd, and its quantity follows from the spatial arrangement of the protein molecules or particles. The latter will, in turn, depend on such conditions as ionic environment and temperature.

The determination of the sorption of moisture on or in (para)caseinate at a high water activity (e.g. 0·99), has been assumed to be representative for equilibrium swelling as in curd. However, the amount of water 'sorbed' primarily depends on the osmotic effect of the counterions and low-molecular weight impurities, and the quantities of these may vary greatly with conditions such as pH, particularly for micellar caseinate. For pure Na-caseinate, where the disturbing factors perhaps are smallest, it was observed, for instance, that the quantity of sorbed water markedly decreased (at 25°C) if the pH was lowered from 6·1 to 5·6 and was at a minimum near the isoelectric pH.[96] The relevance of this for conditions as in a milk gel is questionable, in our opinion.

The voluminosity of casein micelles, defined as their volume per unit mass of (para)casein, can be estimated from hydrodynamic measurements, by electron microscopy or from the sediment after high-speed centrifugation; these methods give different results, as was discussed and to some extent explained by one of us.[97] Interpretation of the results may cause problems. First, if part of the casein dissociates from the micelles while leaving the volume of the micelle intact, this is recorded as an increase in voluminosity. Second, variables affecting the voluminosity of casein micelles may well have a different effect on paracasein micelles, of which the voluminosity is not easily determined. Hydrodynamic voluminosity of the micelles is reduced to about 2/3 of its original value by renneting, mainly because of the splitting off of the protruding parts ('hairs') of the κ-casein molecules.[7,97] Darling[102] also found a small reduction in voluminosity due to renneting, as determined by sedimentation; here one would expect the 'hairs' to largely collapse. From the results reviewed[97] it may be concluded that paracasein micelles would contain at room temperature and physiological pH about 1·4 g water/g protein; to this, some interstitial moisture for a gel of closely packed micelles may have to be added.

Wurster[98] renneted milk with various additions in centrifuge tubes and sedimented the curd at approximately $2000 \times g$ for 15 min; he measured the volume of curd obtained. The problem here is that syneresis is not complete: at the bottom of the tube, the centrifugal pressure acting on the gel was about 10^4 Pa but it is zero at the top of the curd layer. Consequently, the results will at least partly reflect syneresis rate. A similar method was applied to set yoghurt by Harwalkar and Kalab,[93,107] who centrifuged at various accelerations (up to $2000\,g$) and times (up to 1 h). Here, the maximum pressure was at most 5 kPa.

Stoll[28] freeze-dried pieces of curd obtained after 2 h of syneresis and afterwards put them in whey or some other liquid and let them take up moisture. He recorded the weight as a percentage of the original (before drying); the results were poorly reproducible. In our laboratory, pieces of freshly made (unsalted) cheese were put in various liquids and the length and/or mass of the pieces after some time were recorded.[99,100] The problem with these studies is that components of the curd or cheese dissolve in the excess of liquid present, and a true equilibrium is never attained; under some conditions the whole curd tends to dissolve.

One may try to let syneresis proceed until it stops. One of us[2] did some experiments with renneted skim milk at 30°C, pH 6·7, and no external pressure (except that caused by gravity) and found that the curd had shrunk to 1/3 of its original thickness after 40 h, when syneresis appeared to be finished.

It may be concluded that unequivocal results have not been published to date. Nevertheless, we may gather some trends.

7.2 Results

Acidity. Some results are summarized in Fig. 11. Those of Wurster[98] obviously reflect the rate of syneresis more than the end point, as the others found far weaker trends. Several workers estimated the voluminosity of

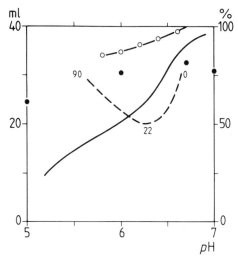

Fig. 11. The effect of pH (varied by adding HCl or NaOH) on the volume of pieces of syneresed curd. Results recalculated from Wurster[98] ——, ml of curd from 100 ml of renneted milk after centrifugation (average of several experiments); Stoll[28] ●, volume as % of original of curd pieces put in whey; Delsing *et al.*[100] ○, volume as % of volume at pH 6·7 of pieces of fresh cheese put in whey. Also given are results (ml) by Wurster (–––) where $CaCl_2$ was added (and which altered the pH); the figures near the curve give the quantity (mM) of added Ca.

casein micelles at various pH values, and found at first a decrease when the pH was reduced from 6·7 but obtained a distinct maximum near pH 5·4 and a shallow minimum near pH 4·5.[101,102,100,103] Such a maximum, that is clearly related to dissolution of casein,[104] has never been observed for curd. Recent results by Van Hooydonk[105] on voluminosity estimated by sedimentation of casein micelles and paracasein micelles as a function of pH gave a slight decrease with a shallow maximum near pH 5·6 for the latter when the pH was lowered; the corresponding casein micelles showed a distinct maximum near pH 5·4.

Calcium. Experiments in which the calcium concentration is varied are very difficult to interpret. Probably, both the calcium ion activity in the solution and the content of colloidal calcium phosphate of the micelles are important variables and they both change with conditions, but the authors determined neither. Moreover, changes in the salt equilibria tend to be sluggish; it may take 72 h before equilibrium is reached. Wurster[98] added $CaCl_2$ to the milk, and his results are shown in Fig. 11. He concluded that the initial decrease in volume was due to the pH change. As stated before, the method employed makes the results questionable. Stoll[28] found a shrinkage of curd particles at 90 mM Ca as compared to the control (no added Ca) while higher additions caused swelling; pH was not stated and there probably was not enough time to establish equilibrium. Delsing *et al.*[100] found for pieces of fresh cheese kept in whey of pH 6·7 at Ca concentrations from 3 to 9 mM, a decrease in water content from 3·0 to 2·3 g/g protein. Geurts *et al.*[99] found for pieces of fresh cheese kept in aqueous solutions at pH 5·1 that adding Ca (9–90 mM) caused swelling, but this may have been due to a mere increase in ionic strength. If an excess of NaCl was present ($\geq 0·7$ M), the same Ca additions caused progressive shrinkage. The voluminosity of casein micelles was found to decrease on adding $CaCl_2$ up to 25 mM without correcting for pH changes.[101] Other experiments at a constant pH of 6·7 also showed a decrease up to 9 mM added Ca.[100,103]

NaCl. Small additions of NaCl (up to about 0·5 mM) caused an increase while larger additions caused a decrease in the swelling of freshly-made cheese at low pH.[99]

Temperature. Wurster[98] found a considerable decrease in curd volume (to 35%) on increasing temperature from 25 to 47°C, but, again, this reflects syneresis rate rather than end point. Darling[102] found values for the voluminosity of paracasein micelles by sedimentation at 20 and 40°C of 2·5 and 2·2 ml/g, respectively. The voluminosity of native casein micelles has been found to depend more strongly on temperature.[103] Incidentally, it is well known by makers of Feta cheese (pH ≈ 4·8), which is kept in brine (about 1·5 M NaCl and 0·08 M Ca) that the cheese swells when kept at low temperatures (e.g. 5°C) and shrinks at high temperatures (e.g. 25°C).

Fat content.   It must be assumed that a high fat content in the curd will hinder shrinking, as may be reflected in the higher water content in the non-fat matter that a high-fat cheese shows in comparison to a low-fat cheese, made in the same way (see, for example, Ref. 86). Also, results on syneresis after prolonged times suggest that a high fat content corresponds to a higher final curd volume.[90]

Heat treatment.   Heating milk to temperatures that cause serum proteins to become associated with the casein micelles leads, of course, to a greater curd volume,[98,107] but whether it affects the final voluminosity of the curd is uncertain.

Proteolysis.   The swelling of cheese in salt solutions was observed to be somewhat smaller if the cheese had undergone pronounced proteolysis,[106] but the correlation was weak. In another study[111] under similar conditions, swelling was found to increase with ageing, hence presumably with proteolysis.

It may be concluded that a lower pH, a higher temperature and a lower fat content coincide with a slightly but significantly lower equilibrium moisture content of the fat-free curd. The effects of various salts and some other factors (heat treatment, proteolysis) are less clear.

8.   THE WATER CONTENT OF CHEESE

The factors affecting syneresis should influence the quantity of moisture remaining in the cheese and the results on syneresis as given in Sections 6 and 7 indeed qualitatively agree with results on the water content of cheese (e.g. Refs 66, 86, 112, 70, 113). Whether there is exact agreement is uncertain. The water content of cheese always shows considerable random variation (e.g. Ref. 114) and this makes exact comparisons difficult. During cheesemaking, conditions usually change, for instance pH, temperature and effective pressure acting on the curd, so that one has to take some, often unknown, kind of average. Moreover, the factors are interrelated; for instance, temperature affects the rate of acidification. The latter is also affected by oxygen content[115] and this may explain why some authors found a negative correlation between stirring rate of the curd–whey mixture and the final water content of the cheese;[57] presumably faster stirring causes a higher oxygen content, hence slower acidification, and consequently less syneresis. It often has been stated, beginning with Sammis *et al.*,[66] that very rapid initial syneresis causes the curd grains to acquire a kind of skin, which leads eventually to a higher water content than would have been obtained otherwise. In this section we discuss some factors that may affect the water content of cheese with little effect on syneresis.

In the manufacture of several types of cheese, after stirring for some time the curd grains are allowed to sediment and form a layer onto which pressure is applied (e.g. 400 Pa); moreover, there is some pressure (mostly < 100 Pa) because of the density difference between curd and whey. In such a submerged curd column, three processes occur that affect the final moisture content of the cheese:

1. Moisture (whey) moves from the curd grains into the surrounding liquid; factors affecting this process have been discussed above.
2. Whey moves through the pores between the curd grains out of the column. The rate of removal primarily depends on the dimensions of the pores.
3. The dimensions of the pores change, i.e. the pores become narrower and may eventually be closed due to deformation and fusion of the curd grains, which in turn determines the rate of process 2. The deformation is mainly viscous and will depend on the external pressure and on the rheological properties of the curd grains, which, in turn, depend on their composition (water content, pH, etc.), on their size and inhomogeneity (presence of a 'skin') and on temperature. Complete fusion of the curd grains will virtually stop moisture loss.

We present here some preliminary results obtained in our laboratory.[63] Curd was made from skim milk, using no starter. After cutting and stirring (and removing some whey) a column of curd and whey, 30 cm high, was taken; the curd sedimented almost immediately to a height of ∼ 20 cm, after which pressure was applied via a perforated disc, and the curd column gradually compressed to a height of, for instance, 5 cm; the compression

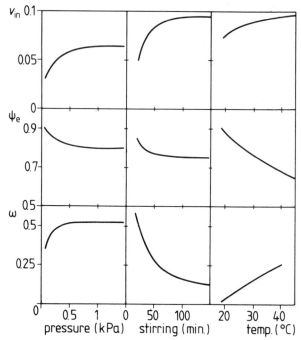

Fig. 12. Effect of some variables on the change in moisture in a column of curd grains in whey. v_{in} is the initial rate of moisture loss after applying pressure $(-\mathrm{d}\ln V/\mathrm{d}t,$ where $V =$ volume and $t =$ time in min); ψ_e is the final fraction of moisture in the column; ω is the fraction of removed moisture that originated in the curd grains. Variables are external pressure applied (stirring time 20 min); time of (cutting and) stirring before applying pressure; temperature of stirring and compressing (stirring time 80 min). Unless indicated otherwise, temperature was 31°C and the external pressure was 0·4 kPa (approximate results after Ref. 63).

was allowed to proceed for 90 min. The final moisture content of the curd column was determined and the earlier values were calculated from the change in height and expressed as the mass fraction of moisture (here, moisture means liquid containing dissolved substances, i.e. whey—in this case). The proportion of moisture between the grains was originally about 40%. Some results are shown in Fig. 12, which partly speaks for itself. Clearly, if the moisture content of the curd grains was high (brief stirring time, low temperature) the initial rate of moisture loss was low; presumably, channels between the curd grains soon became narrow, as the curd grains deformed easily. This difference in v_{in} was partly reflected in the final moisture content, despite the fact that there would have been sufficient time for syneresis to proceed to nearly an equilibrium value. A much more comprehensive study would be needed to draw definite conclusions; in particular, the effect of pH needs to be known. Probably, the deformation of the curd grains and the ensuing narrowing of pores is promoted by conditions where residual syneresis rate is slow, the external pressure high, the deformability of the curd grains considerable and the pH dropping while not yet being very low. The latter factor may particularly promote complete fusion of curd grains.

Often, the curd is taken out of the whey, either by sieving or after letting the grains sediment and form a more or less coherent mass that is taken out. The greater pressure due to gravity now acting on the curd gives a rapid 'burst' of syneresis (Fig. 6; Section 6.3). The rate of moisture loss also depends on the possibility of the moisture flowing away, i.e. the perforation of the vessel in which the curd is kept.[35] But the main variable appears to be, again, the deformability of the curd grains, firm grains permitting faster drainage, as was already observed by Vas.[67] Scott Blair and Coppen[73] made use of this in devising a test method to determine the 'pitching point' of the curd, i.e. the moment at which the grains have lost sufficient moisture and in the opinion of the cheesemaker the curd should now be removed in order to obtain a good cheese. A volume of curd and whey is put into a perforated cylinder and allowed to drain for a fixed time; now the 'superficial density' is determined, i.e. the weight of curd divided by the height of the curd column. They found a fair positive correlation between the water content and the superficial density, indicating that high moisture and thus soft grains deformed rapidly to close the channels between them, thereby greatly hindering further drainage; drainage in narrow pores is also restricted by capillary forces. Firm (i.e. 'dry') grains permitted ongoing drainage, leading to a low superficial density, because the voids between particles now became filled with air. Besides water content, other factors must affect the draining rate since Scott Blair and Coppen found for the same value of superficial density, a range in water content of about 14 percentage units. There was a tendency for rapid initial syneresis, hence presumably the presence of a more or less rigid 'skin' around the curd grains, to lead to a lower superficial density. Likewise, curd at a lower pH (Cheshire as compared to Cheddar) tended to have a lower superficial density. It would be useful to study these and other variables in greater detail.

Finally, the curd is often put into a mould and pressed at pressures of usually 10–100 kPa. If the curd is not yet very dry, this high pressure (as compared to pressures during stirring and shaping) leads to a considerable moisture loss. But it is well known among cheesemakers that pressing at an earlier stage or at a higher pressure causes less loss of moisture than pressing later or at a lower pressure (e.g. Ref. 116); the differences may amount to a few per cent water. Presumably, pressing causes the formation of a closed rind around the loaf of cheese, thereby greatly hindering further drainage. Geurts,[43] who studied this in more detail for Gouda-type cheese, found that loaf size also had some effect. If the water content of the curd grains was normal for Gouda cheese, a larger loaf of cheese lost more moisture (e.g. 2 percentage units) during pressing; this was due to slower cooling, hence higher average temperature and more rapid acidification, both of which cause more syneresis. If the curd was made very dry (water in the unsalted full-cream cheese < 41%), a smaller loaf gave a lower water content (1–2%) than a larger one; this is to be expected because of the shorter transport distance in a smaller loaf. But temperature affected this also, since it was found that such a dry curd lost more water during pressing if the temperature was lower. In this case, the higher deformability of the curd grains at a higher temperature appears to override the greater tendency to synerese.

Incidentally, temperature differences throughout a loaf of cheese cause an uneven moisture distribution: the moisture goes to where the temperature is lowest.[43] Likewise, it goes to where the pressure is lowest, i.e. to the top of a loaf lying for a long time in the same position.[117]

In several types of cheese, the drained mass of curd is allowed to spread laterally for a considerable time ('cheddaring'). Olson and Price[118] found that this led to a higher moisture content (1–2% more water), as compared to curd kept for the same time but which was prevented from spreading. Although the cheddaring may have caused a slightly lower average temperature, the main cause for the differences was presumably that the flow of curd promoted deformation of the curd grains, hence closing of channels between grains and hence hindering drainage of any moisture still leaving the grains due to syneresis.

Washing of the curd, i.e. adding water after part of the whey has been removed, has been reported to enhance syneresis,[84] and to give a slightly, possibly insignificantly, lower water content.[119] However, washing may coincide with a change in temperature and with a difference in the effectiveness of stirring, both of which affect syneresis. In studies in our laboratory,[74] either water or an equal quantity of whey at the same temperature was added at a certain stage during cheesemaking and the water content of the curd determined after various times. The water content of the curd to which water was added was up to 2 percentage units higher, but the difference could be fully explained by taking into account the difference in dry matter content of the moisture (liquid) in the curd. Hence, the osmotic effects of washing are negligible. Salting the cheese may affect its water content. Dry salting of the curd may, in principle, cause water to leave the curd by pseudo-osmosis, but usually it is pressed into a big loaf immediately afterwards, and some of the water is retained. Salting a cheese loaf after pressing, e.g. by brining, causes considerable water loss, as was studied extensively by Geurts *et al.*[120,121] At first approximation, the water loss during brining was proportional to salt uptake: 1·7–3·2 g water/g NaCl. This ratio was higher for a higher cheese pH, a higher temperature, a lower initial water content, and a more concentrated brine.

After pressing and salting, the cheese may lose water. This can be due to ongoing syneresis, but also to evaporation. Anyway, the loss will be greater for a higher surface to mass ratio.

9. ONE-DIMENSIONAL SYNERESIS IN CONSTANT CONDITIONS

Thin layers of milk or skim milk were renneted and the syneresis of the gel obtained was measured by recording its thickness as a function of time.[2] In other experiments, the milk was renneted in long tubes and the permeability of the gel was measured by percolation of whey under a known pressure; in some experiments the gel was deformed prior to measurement.[2] During the experiments, conditions (temperature, pH, etc.) were kept constant. Variables studied included geometrical constraints, pretreatment of milk, amount of rennet added, time elapsed after renneting, pH of milk, addition of $CaCl_2$, temperature, fat content of the milk and concentration of the milk by ultrafiltration.

The results on the permeability coefficient (in the order of $3 \times 10^{-13} \, m^2$) could be explained only by assuming the gel network to be fairly inhomogeneous. Permeability decreased with concentration and fat content (as expected) and increased markedly with time (when the gel was kept at rest and could not shrink) and with deformation history. Syneresis pressure could not be determined but could be derived from a computational model (of the Darcy and the continuity equations, solved by a finite difference method for small increments in time and space), provided that the observed (changes in) permeability and an additional pressure exerted by gravity were introduced.[4] Then it followed that the

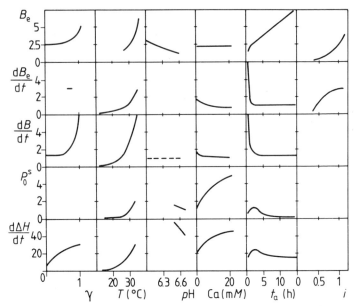

Fig. 13. Effect of some variables on syneresis properties (approximate results). Results on initial permeability (B_e); change in B_e with time (dB_e/dt); change in permeability with time while the curd is deformed (dB/dt); initial endogenous syneresis pressure (P_0^s); rate of syneresis in thin slabs $(d\Delta H/dt)$. Variables are relative deformation of curd (γ); temperature during measurement (T); pH of curd; added $CaCl_2$ (without adjusting pH), time elapsed after renneting without syneresis occurring (t_a); concentration, i.e. volume of curd/original volume of milk (i). Broken lines are less certain.

endogenous syneresis pressure at 30°C and physiological pH was about 1 Pa. The dependence of syneresis pressure and of permeability and its time derivative on the mentioned variables were determined, thereby more or less establishing the causes for the change in syneresis rate commonly observed. Some results are summarized in Fig. 13.

The increase in permeability with time could largely be explained by the occurrence of microsyneresis: rearrangement of the caseinate network, causing a local condensation of the network and the formation of wide pores elsewhere. In agreement with this, the endogenous syneresis pressure was observed to relax, being reduced to about 10% of its peak value (at about 1 h after renneting) after 18 h. A thin gel slab left to shrink under constant conditions (30°C, pH ~ 6·6) did not shrink any more after 24 h, reaching about 1/3 of its original thickness.

The distribution of moisture throughout a syneresing slab could not be determined but calculated; an example of results is shown in Fig. 14.

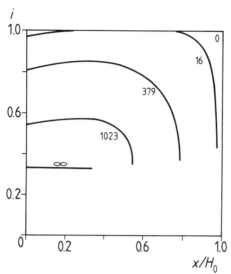

Fig. 14. Shrinkage profile of a slab of rennet curd at various times (indicated in minutes) after starting syneresis. i = concentration factor, x/H_0 = relative distance from the bottom of the slab. Assumptions: thickness of slab 10 mm; endogenous syneresis pressure, 1 Pa. The initial decrease in i near $x = 0$ is caused by gravity. (Kindly computed by H. J. C. M. van den Bijgaart.)

ACKNOWLEDGEMENTS

We are indebted to the Stichting J. Mesdagfonds for financial support; to the then students J. G. van de Grootevheen, P. R. Kwant, B. M. A. Delsing and G. J. Heerink for experimental studies; to the Netherlands Institute for Dairy Research for help in the study described in Ref. 63; to A. C. M. van Hooydonk, T. van Vliet and P. Zoon for letting us use unpublished results; to J. Schenk for help with the computational model; to H. J. C. M. van den Bijgaart for computing Fig. 14; and to H. J. C. M. van den Bijgaart, D. G. Dalgleish, A. C. M. van Hooydonk and T. van Vliet for useful comments on the manuscript.

REFERENCES

1. van Dijk, H. J. M., Walstra, P. and Geurts, T. J., *Neth. Milk Dairy J.*, 1979, **33**, 60.
2. van Dijk, H. J. M., Syneresis of curd, Doctoral thesis, Agricultural University, Wageningen, 1982.

3. Walstra, P. and Jenness, R., *Dairy Chemistry and Physics*, 1984, Wiley, New York.
4. van Dijk, H. J. M., Walstra, P. and Schenk, J., *Chem. Eng. J.*, 1984, **28**, B43.
5. Schmidt, D. G. In: *Developments in Dairy Chemistry—I. Proteins*, P. F. Fox (ed.), 1982, Applied Science, London, pp. 61–86.
6. Payens, T. A. J., *J. Dairy Res.*, 1979, **46**, 291.
7. Walstra, P., Bloomfield, V. A., Wei, G. J. and Jenness, R., *Biochim. Biophys. Acta*, 1981, **669**, 258.
8. Alais, C., *Science du Lait*, 3rd edn, 1974, SEP Editions, Paris.
9. van Hooydonk, A. C. M., Olieman, C. and Hagedoorn, H. G., *Neth. Milk Dairy J.*, 1984, **38**, 207.
10. Dalgleish, D. G. In: *Developments in Dairy Chemistry—I. Proteins*, P. F. Fox (ed.), 1982, Applied Science, London, pp. 157–87.
11. Dalgleish, D. G., *J. Dairy Res.*, 1983, **50**, 331.
12. van Vliet, T. and Zoon, P., unpublished.
13. Mulder, H., de Graaf, J. J. and Walstra, P., *Proc. 17th Intern. Dairy Congr.*, *München*, 1966, Vol. D, p. 413.
14. Henstra, S. and Schmidt, D. G., *Proc. 7th Intern. Congr. Electron Microscopy*, *Grenoble*, 1970, Vol. 1, p. 389.
15. Knoop, A. M. and Peters, K. H., *Kieler Milchw. ForschBer.*, 1975, **27**, 227.
16. Kalab, M. and Harwalkar, V. R., *J. Dairy Sci.*, 1973, **56**, 835.
17. Green, M. L., Hobbs, D. G., Morant, S. V. and Hill, V. A., *J. Dairy Res.*, 1978, **45**, 413.
18. Sutherland, J., *J. Colloid Sci.*, 1967, **22**, 373.
19. Knoop, A. M. and Peters, K. H., *Kieler Milchw. ForschBer.*, 1975, **27**, 315.
20. Roefs, S. P. F. M. and van Vliet, T., *Proc. 9th Intern. Congr. Rheology*, *Acapulco*, 1984, Vol. 4, p. 249.
21. Flory, P. J., *Principles of Polymer Chemistry*, 1953, Cornell University Press, Ithaca.
22. Dušek, K., *J. Polym. Sci.*, 1967, **C16**, 1289.
23. Cheeseman, G. C., *Proc. 16th Intern. Dairy Congr.*, *Copenhagen*, 1962, Vol. B, IV, p. 465.
24. Dimov, N. D. and Mineva, P., *Proc. 16th Intern. Dairy Congr.*, *Copenhagen*, 1962, Vol. B, IV, p. 817.
25. Geurts, T. J., Walstra, P. and Mulder, H., *Neth. Milk Dairy J.*, 1974, **28**, 46.
26. Rüegg, M., Lüscher, M. and Blanc, B., *J. Dairy Sci.*, 1974, **57**, 387.
27. Lelievre, J. and Creamer, L. K., *Milchwissenschaft*, 1978, **33**, 73.
28. Stoll, W. F., Syneresis of rennet-formed milk gels, Doctoral thesis, University of Minnesota, St. Paul, 1966 (Diss. Abstr. 27B(3), 851).
29. Walstra, P. and Oortwijn, H., *Neth. Milk Dairy J.*, 1982, **36**, 103.
30. Treloar, L. R. G., *The Physics of Rubber Elasticity*, 3rd edn, 1975, Clarendon Press, Oxford.
31. Schmidt, D. G., Walstra, P. and Buchheim, W., *Neth. Milk Dairy J.*, 1973, **27**, 128.
32. Scheidegger, A. E., *The Physics of Flow Through Porous Media*, 1960, Sine Nomina, London.
33. van Brakel, J., *Powder Technol.*, 1975, **11**, 205.
34. Kirchmeier, O., *Milchwissenschaft*, 1972, **27**, 99.

35. Weber, F. In: *Le Fromage*, A. Eck (ed.), 1984, Lavoisier, Paris, p. 22.
36. Lawrence, A. J. and Hill, R. D., *Proc. 19th Intern. Dairy Congr.*, New Delhi, 1974, Vol. 1E, p. 204.
37. Beltman, H., Verdikken en Geleren, Doctoral thesis, Agricultural University, Wageningen, 1975.
38. Tarodo de la Fuente, B., Alais, C. and Frentz, R., *Lait*, 1969, **49**, 400.
39. Christ, W., *Milchwissenschaft*, 1956, **11**, 381.
40. Thomé, K. E., Axelsson, I. and Liljegren, G., *Milk Dairy Res. Rep. Alnarp*, 1958, **53**.
41. Berridge, N. J. and Scurlock, P. G., *J. Dairy Res.*, 1970, **37**, 417.
42. Gyr, A., *Ann. Paediatrici*, 1944, **163**, 314.
43. Geurts, T. J., *Neth. Milk Dairy J.*, 1978, **32**, 112.
44. Wurster, K., *Milchw. Forsch.*, 1934, **16**, 200.
45. van der Waarden, M., Onderzoek naar de factoren die invloed hebben op de wei-uittreding uit gestremde melk, Alg. Ned. Zuivelbond FNZ, The Hague, 1947 (unpublished).
46. Aiyar, K. R. and Wallace, G. M., *Proc. 18th Intern. Dairy Congr.*, Sydney, 1970, Vol. 1E, p. 47.
47. Kiermeier, F. and von Wüllerstorf, B., *Milchwissenschaft*, 1963, **18**, 553.
48. Siegenthaler, E. and Flückiger, E., *Schweiz. Milchztg.*, 1964, **90**, 766 (Wissensch. Beilage 96).
49. Schulz, M. E. and Kley, W., *Milchwissenschaft*, 1956, **11**, 116.
50. Lawrence, A. J., *Austr. J. Dairy Technol.*, 1959, **14**, 166.
51. Cheeseman, G. C. and Chapman, H. R., *Dairy Industries*, 1966, **31**, 99.
52. Lelievre, J., *J. Dairy Res.*, 1977, **44**, 611.
53. Marshall, R. J., *J. Dairy Res.*, 1982, **49**, 329.
54. Storry, J. E., Grandison, A. S., Millard, D., Owen, A. J. and Ford, G. D., *J. Dairy Res.*, 1983, **50**, 215.
55. Johnston, D. E., Murphy, R. J. and Whittaker, N. R., *J. Dairy Res.*, 1983, **50**, 231.
56. Lawrence, A. J., *Austr. J. Dairy Technol.*, 1959, **14**, 169.
57. Kiermeier, F. and von Wüllerstorf, B., *Michwissenschaft*, 1963, **18**, 75.
58. Beeby, R., *Austr. J. Dairy Technol.*, 1959, **14**, 77.
59. Voss, E., *Kieler Milchw. ForschBer.*, 1962, **14**, 83.
60. Pulay, G., Csók, J. and Bakos, A., *Proc. 18th Intern. Dairy Congr.*, Sydney, 1970, Vol. 1E, p. 326.
61. Kwant, P. R., Geurts, T. J. and van Dijk, H. J. M., Een methode ter bepaling van het watergehalte van pas gesneden wrongel, Wageningen, 1980 (unpublished).
62. Zviedrans, P. and Graham, E. R. B., *Austr. J. Dairy Technol.*, 1981, **36**, 117.
63. Heerink, G. J. and Geurts, T. J., Comprimeerbaarheid van een wrongelbed onder de wei, Wageningen, 1981 (unpublished).
64. Pearse, M. J., Mackinlay, A. G., Hall, R. J. and Linklater, P. M., *J. Dairy Res.*, 1984, **51**, 131.
65. Patel, M. C., Lund, D. B. and Olson, N. F., *J. Dairy Sci.*, 1972, **55**, 913.
66. Sammis, J. L., Suzuki, S. K. and Laabs, F. W., *Bur. Animal Industry, USDA, Bull.*, 1910, **122**.
67. Vas, K., *Milchw. Forsch.*, 1931, **11**, 519.

68. Koestler, G. and Petermann, R., *Landw. Jahrb. Schweiz*, 1936, **50**, 103.
69. Lodin, L. O. and Buhrgard, A. B., *Svenska Mejeritidn.*, 1952, **44**, 405.
70. Birkkjaer, H. E., Sørensen, E. J., Jørgensen, J. and Sigersted, E., *Beretn. Statens Forsøgsmejeri*, 1961, **128**.
71. Nilsen, K. O. and Abrahamsen, R. K., *J. Dairy Res.*, 1985, **52**, 209.
72. Foley, J., *Proc. 17th Intern. Dairy Congr.*, München, 1966, Vol. D, p. 425.
73. Scott Blair, G. W. and Coppen, F. M. V., *J. Dairy Res.*, 1940, **11**, 187.
74. van de Grootevheen, J. G. and Geurts, T. J., Het instellen van het vochtgehalte van verse ongezouten wrongel, Wageningen, 1977 (unpublished).
75. Hostettler, H. and Stein, J., *Schweiz. Milchztg.*, 1954, **80**, 591.
76. Thomé, K. E. and Liljegren, G., *Proc. 15th Intern. Dairy Congr.*, London, 1959, Vol. 3, p. 1922.
77. Vaikus, V., Lubinskas, V. and Mitskevichus, E., *Proc. 18th Intern. Dairy Congr.*, Sydney, 1970, Vol. 1E, p. 320.
78. Tarodo de la Fuente, B. and Alais, C., *Chimia*, 1975, **29**, 379.
79. Pearse, M. J., Linklater, P. M., Hall, R. J. and Mackinlay, A. G., *J. Dairy Res.*, 1985, **52**, 159.
80. Nilsen, K. O., *Meieriposten*, 1982, **71**, 123, 162.
81. Emmons, D. B., Price, W. V. and Swanson, A. M., *J. Dairy Sci.*, 1959, **42**, 866.
82. Kovalenko, M. S. and Bocharova, S. G., *Dairy Sci. Abstr.*, 1973, **35**, 372.
83. Lelievre, J., Kelso, E. A. and Stewart, D. B., *Proc. 20th Intern. Dairy Congr.*, Paris, 1978, Vol. E, p. 760.
84. Kammerlehner, J., *Deutsche Molkerei-Ztg.*, 1974, **95**, 306, 342, 377.
85. Scott Blair, G. W. and Burnett, J., *J. Dairy Res.*, 1958, **25**, 297.
86. Whitehead, H. R., *J. Dairy Res.*, 1948, **15**, 387.
87. Grandison, A. S., Manning, D. J., Thomson, D. J. and Anderson, M., *J. Dairy Res.*, 1985, **52**, 33.
88. Cheeseman, G. C. and Mabbitt, L. A., *J. Dairy Res.*, 1968, **35**, 135.
89. Mulder, H. and Walstra, P., *The Milk Fat Globule. Emulsion Science as Applied to Milk Products and Comparable Foods*, 1974, Pudoc, Wageningen.
90. Johnston, D. E. and Murphy, R. J., *Milchwissenschaft*, 1984, **39**, 585.
91. Humbert, G., Driou, A., Guerin, J. and Alais, C., *Lait*, 1980, **60**, 574.
92. Green, M. L., Marshall, R. J. and Glover, F. A., *J. Dairy Res.*, 1983, **50**, 341.
93. Harwalkar, V. R. and Kalab, M., *Scanning Electron Microscopy*, 1981, **III**, 503.
94. Walstra, P., *Kolloid-Z.Z. Polymere*, 1973, **251**, 603.
95. Franks, F. In: *Water: a Comprehensive Treatment,* Vol. 7, 1982, F. Franks (ed.), Plenum Press, New York, p. 215.
96. Rüegg, M. and Blanc, B., *J. Dairy Sci.*, 1976, **59**, 1019.
97. Walstra, P., *J. Dairy Res.*, 1979, **46**, 317.
98. Wurster, K., *Milchw. Forsch.*, 1934, **16**, 215.
99. Geurts, T. J., Walstra, P. and Mulder, H., *Neth Milk Dairy J.*, 1972, **26**, 168.
100. Delsing, B. M. A., Geurts, T. J. and Walstra, P., De zwellingstoestand van gesynereerde wrongel, Wageningen, 1981 (unpublished).
101. Tarodo de la Fuente, B. and Alais, C., *J. Dairy Sci.*, 1975, **58**, 293.
102. Darling, D. In: *The Effect of Polymers on Dispersion Properties,* T. F. Tadros (ed.), 1981, Academic Press, New York, p. 285.

103. Snoeren, T. H. M., Klok, H. J., van Hooydonk, A. C. M. and Damman, A. J., *Milchwissenschaft*, 1984, **39**, 461.
104. Roefs, S. P. F. M., Walstra, P., Dalgleish, D. G. and Horne, D. S., *Neth. Milk Dairy J.*, 1985, **39**, 119.
105. van Hooydonk, A. C. M., Hagedoorn, H. G. and Boerrigter, I. J., *Neth. Milk Dairy J.*, 1986, **40**, 281.
106. Koestler, G., *Landw. Jahrb. Schweiz*, 1940, **54**, 605.
107. Harwalkar, V. R. and Kalab, M., *Milchwissenschaft*, 1983, **38**, 517.
108. Modler, H. W., Larmond, M. E., Lin, C. S., Froehlich, D. and Emmons, D. B., *J. Dairy Sci.*, 1983, **66**, 422.
109. Grandison, A. S., Ford, G. D., Owen, A. J. and Millard, D., *J. Dairy Res.*, 1984, **51**, 69.
110. Grandison, A. S., Ford, G. D., Millard, D. and Owen, A. J., *J. Dairy Res.*, 1984, **51**, 407.
111. Pejič, O., *Preradivačka Industrija*, **1952**(4), 129 (cited from: *Dairy Sci. Abstr.*, 1955, **17**, 429).
112. Whitehead, H. R. and Harkness, W. L., *Austr. J. Dairy Technol.*, 1954, **9**, 103.
113. Feagan, J. T., Erwin, L. J. and Dixon, B. D., *Austr. J. Dairy Technol.*, 1965, **20**, 214.
114. Straatsma, J., de Vries, E., Heijnekamp, A. and Kloosterman, L., *Zuivelzicht*, 1984, **76**, 956.
115. Gillies, A. J., *Proc. 15th Intern. Dairy Congr.*, London, 1959, Vol. 2, p. 523.
116. Czulak, J., *Proc. 15th Intern. Dairy Congr.*, London, 1959, Vol. 2, p. 829.
117. Geurts, T. J., *Versl. Landbouwk. Onderz.*, Wageningen, 1972, **777**.
118. Olson, N. F. and Price, W. V., *J. Dairy Sci.*, 1970, **53**, 1676.
119. van den Berg, G. and de Vries, E. *Neth. Milk Dairy J.*, 1975, **29**, 181.
120. Geurts, T. J., Walstra, P. and Mulder, H., *Neth. Milk Dairy J.*, 1974, **28**, 102.
121. Geurts, T. J., Walstra, P. and Mulder, H., *Neth. Milk Dairy J.*, 1980, **34**, 229.
122. Kiermeier, F. and Keis, K., *Milchwissenschaft*, 1964, **19**, 79.
123. Kiermeier, F., Renner, E. and Djafarian, M., *Z. Lebensm. Unters. Forsch.*, 1966/7, **132**, 352.
124. O'Keeffe, A. M., Phelan, J. A., Keogh, K. and Kelly, P. *Ir. J. Food Sci. Technol.*, 1982, **6**, 39.
125. Emmons, D. B., Lister, E. E., Beckett, D. C. and Jenkins, K. J., *J. Dairy Sci.*, 1980, **63**, 417.
126. Nitschmann, H. L. and Lehmann, W., *Helv. Chim. Acta*, 1947, **30**, 804.
127. Meakin, P., *J. Colloid Interf. Sci.*, 1984, **102**, 491, 505.
128. Darling, D. and van Hooydonk, A. C. M., *J. Dairy Res.*, 1981, **48**, 189.
129. van Vliet, T. and Walstra, P., *Neth. Milk Dairy J.*, 1985, **39**, 115.

Chapter 6

Cheese Starter Cultures

T. M. Cogan

*The Agricultural Institute, Moorepark Research Centre,
Fermoy, Co. Cork, Ireland*

and

C. Daly

*Department of Food Microbiology, University College,
Cork, Ireland*

1. INTRODUCTION

The diversity of cheese varieties produced throughout the world is reflected in the variety of traditions and approaches to the supply and preparation of the cultures used in their production. Cultures vary from the unsophisticated use of naturally soured milk or whey to the use of carefully selected mixed or defined strains which are sometimes concentrated for direct inoculation of milk in the cheese vat. While the cheese industry has been somewhat conservative in embracing new developments, a steady change in the preparation and use of cultures has been catalysed by results of continuing research. In addition, the amalgamation of smaller cheesemaking plants into large, highly-mechanized and automated units in many countries during the 1970s put severe pressure on the starter systems then available. The major problem has been the well-documented susceptibility of dairy fermentations to attack by bacteriophage. This has led to new initiatives in the selection of starter strains;[1-3] the use of such strains in recent years has provided a significant degree of process control in cheesemaking.

The use of a 'starter culture' is a *sine qua non* in the manufacture of essentially all cheeses. Its main function is to produce acid at the rate appropriate for the particular cheese being made. The acid produced is mostly lactic acid and hence the fermentation is often called the *lactic acid fermentation* and the bacteria involved, *lactic acid bacteria.* Because of this, starter cultures are often called *lactic starter cultures* or *lactic cultures* or *cheese starter cultures,* all of which are synonymous. The increased acidity, together with heating of the curd/whey mixture to $\sim 35°C$ (for Dutch-type cheeses), $\sim 40°C$ (for Cheddar-type cheeses) or $\sim 53°C$ (for Swiss-type cheeses) and more or less vigorous stirring, causes the curd to synerese and expel moisture (whey) from the coagulum to produce a product—cheese—with a much lower water content (87% down to 35–60%) and a lower pH (reduced from 6·6 to 4·6–5·2) and which has, consequently, a much longer shelf-life than milk.

Acid production affects several aspects of cheese manufacture, besides gel syneresis, e.g.

1. Coagulant activity during coagulation.
2. Denaturation and retention of the coagulant in the curd during manufacture; this affects subsequent proteolysis during ripening and consequently, cheese flavour and texture.
3. Curd strength, which influences cheese yield.
4. The extent of dissolution of colloidal calcium phosphate, which modifies the susceptibility of casein to proteolysis and influences the rheological properties of the cheese, e.g. compare the texture of Emmental, Gouda, Cheddar and Cheshire cheeses.
5. Inhibition of the growth of many species of non-starter bacteria, especially pathogens, food-poisoning and defect-producing microorganisms.

Two types of starter culture are used: mesophilic, with an optimum temperature of 30°C and thermophilic, with an optimum temperature of 45°C. The choice of culture depends on the cheese being made, e.g. mesophilic cultures are used in most common cheeses, such as Cheddar, Gouda, Edam, Blue and Camembert, while thermophilic cultures are used in the production of Swiss and Italian varieties. The choice is related to the method of cheese manufacture since Swiss and Italian cheeses are cooked to much higher temperatures (50–55°C) during manufacture than the other varieties mentioned and, therefore, the bacteria used to produce the necessary acid in the former must withstand the higher temperature.

During the past few years several general reviews and books have been written on cheese starter bacteria.[4–7] In addition, specific aspects of starters have been treated by several authors, e.g. lactose metabolism,[8] phage,[9] genetics,[10,11] citrate metabolism,[12] and the use of phage-containing cheese starters.[3]

In this chapter, we will address ourselves to providing a broad understanding of what starter cultures are, the taxonomy, metabolism and genetics of the lactic acid bacteria in these cultures, the factors affecting them or controlling their growth, their propagation and growth in milk, and the major outstanding problem areas. It is not intended to be an exhaustive review but we would hope to indicate the likely direction of future research. The amount of information available on mesophilic cultures is much greater than that on thermophilic cultures, as will become evident as this chapter is developed.

2. HISTORICAL

The use of starter cultures to initiate or 'start' the cheese manufacturing process was practised long before anything was known about the bacteria they contained or indeed before it was appreciated that bacteria were involved at all. Milk for 'starters' was allowed to stand at room temperature for several hours during which the indigenous lactic acid bacteria multiplied and produced lactic acid. The milk eventually coagulated and was used as inoculum for the cheese milk. If the subsequent cheese was of good quality, the inoculum was transferred for further use. A variation of this is still used in parts of Switzerland, Italy and France (Section 3.2). All starter cultures originated via this practice and were passed from one generation of cheesemakers to the next. Such haphazard methods were used until the end of the 19th century when Storch in Denmark and Conn in the USA showed that a good-flavoured ripened-cream butter could be produced from cream which was soured with pure cultures of *Streptococcus lactis* or *Str. cremoris.* However, the truly fine flavour of traditional butter was lacking for a reason which became apparent in 1919 when three groups of workers—Hammer and Bailey in the USA, Storch in Denmark and de Vries in Holland—independently established that starter cultures capable of producing the best-flavoured butter were mixtures of two different types of bacteria, one of which (*Str. lactis* and/or *Str. cremoris*) was responsible for lactic acid production and the other (*Leuconostoc*) for flavour production. Initially, it was thought that volatile acids were responsible for the flavour but in 1929, van Niel *et al.*[13] showed that diacetyl was *the* important aroma compound; subsequently, in 1938, Michaelian *et al.*[14] showed that citrate was its precursor. Because of this, the flavour producers are often called aroma producers, citrate utilizers or citrate fermenters. The latter term is an unfortunate choice since it implies that citrate is used as an energy source, which is incorrect. Originally, the flavour producers were identified as *Leuconostoc* spp. (*Betacoccus* spp. in some of the older literature) but in 1936, additional flavour organisms were isolated independently in Poland by Matuszewski *et al.*,[15] who called them *Str. diacetylactis*, and in The Netherlands by van Beynum and Pette,[16] who called them *Str. citrophilus*. The organisms were subsequently shown to be similar and named *Str. lactis* subsp. *diacetylactis*.[17] The most significant difference between *Str. lactis* and this organism is the ability of the latter to dissimilate citrate.

3. TYPES OF CULTURES

3.1 Mesophilic Cultures

Mesophilic cultures in the dairy industry are either mixed strains of undefined composition, used mostly in Europe and North America, or defined strains which are used singly, in pairs or in multiples, and have been pioneered mainly in New Zealand. All cultures contain lactic acid producers, *Str. cremoris* (mainly) and *Str. lactis*, but many mixed strain cultures also contain flavour producers. Depending on the nature of the flavour producers, mixed cultures are categorized as:

—B or L type, containing *Leuconostoc* spp. as the sole flavour producers;
—D type, containing *Str. lactis* subsp. *diacetylactis* as the sole flavour producer;
—BD or DL type, containing both *Leuconostoc* spp. and *Str. lactis* subsp. *diacetylactis* as flavour producers;
—O type, containing no flavour producers.

The function of the flavour producers is to metabolize citrate to compounds of which diacetyl and CO_2 are probably the most important. Mixed cultures are used because of their inate phage resistance[3] and in many cases, especially in The Netherlands, carry phage which, however, does not lead to serious problems because when the phage multiply, the number of phage-sensitive organisms is reduced to a minor proportion of the population, leaving a predominantly phage-insensitive flora. Mixed cultures must be handled very carefully during storage and propagation because their sub-culture often leads to 1 or 2 strains dominating the culture due either to the activity of phage present or because some strains outgrow the others. When this happens the cultures are much more susceptible to phage than the original mixed culture. Domination may be related to the incubation temperature used since most strains of Group N streptococci have the same generation time at 27°C but not at higher or lower temperatures.[18] The usual incubation temperature for cheese starters is ~21°C and overgrowth by those strains which grow most rapidly at this temperature may occur. Domination may also be related to the production of bacteriocins by some strains (Section 6.2) which inhibit other susceptible strains in the mixture.[19]

Defined-strain starter cultures were introduced in New Zealand by Whitehead and co-workers in 1934 to avoid starter-associated open-texture defects in Cheddar cheese, apparently caused by the flavour-producing organisms in the mixed cultures then in use (cf. Ref. 20). These defined strains were generally used as pairs in 4 or 5 day rotations with one pair being used each day. The known strain identity facilitated scientific understanding of the component bacteria and their interaction with phage.[21] However, the introduction of large cheesemaking plants in New Zealand in the 1970s put severe pressure on this system and led to new initiatives in the selection of phage-insensitive strains.[1,2] Mixed strain cultures, known to provide good quality cheese, were plated out and the individual colonies isolated and purified. Each strain was rigorously screened for ability to produce acid at different temperatures, sensitivity/insensitivity to all available phage including ability to adsorb phage, ability to act as an indicator of lysogenic phage, compatability with other strains, sensitivity to NaCl and ability to grow and produce a clean acid flavour in pasteurized milk. When a strain was considered acceptable in terms of acid production at 21°C (bulk culture preparation) and at 30–39°C (cheesemaking temperature profile), it was examined for its ability to overcome attack by phage under cheesemaking conditions. This was assessed in the test procedure devised by Heap and Lawrence[22] in which the strain was successfully exposed to all phage available in a manner designed to allow initial low numbers of phage to propagate, to detect any alterations in phage or host and to allow the influence of any temperature-sensitive restriction systems (Section 6.3) to be assessed. Generally, strains that survived seven growth cycles in the presence of phage were useful for inclusion in stable culture blends. The test has been improved further by ensuring that the phage cocktail used to challenge the strain contains representatives of the main types of phage observed in commercial cheese factories.[2]

Since most strains of lactic streptococci are lysogenic (Section 6.3), all potentially useful strains were checked for their ability to act as indicators of induced lysogenic phage, which could affect other strains in a blend. Compatibility between strains was another characteristic that needed to be checked to prevent inhibition of one strain by another; this was best assessed in the deferred antagonism method described by Davey and Pearce[23] and strains showing marked inhibition were avoided. While organoleptic assessment of a strain grown in pasteurized milk is a useful indication of the propensity to undesirable flavours, the ultimate test of the suitability of selected strains is their use in cheesemaking trials. These newer types of defined strain starters are generally used in blends of 3–6 strains without rotation. Since their development, their use has been extended to Australia,[24-26] the USA[27-30] and Ireland,[31-33] where they were used in ~80% of all Cheddar cheese produced in 1985 (Cogan and Daly, unpublished data).

A completely different approach to culture selection has been adopted in The Netherlands. In 1966, Galesloot *et al.*[34] noticed that many mixed-strain starter cultures were much more susceptible to phage when transferred in the laboratory (laboratory or 'L' cultures) than when the same cultures were transferred in the factory (practice or 'P' cultures). They reasoned that since the L-culture had been propagated under aseptic conditions, they had become dominated by phage-sensitive strains. In contrast, the P-starters, propagated under the non-aseptic conditions pertaining in the factory, contained the optimum balance of phage-sensitive and -insensitive strains. The best of these mixed P-starters have been stored at −80°C at The Netherlands Dairy Research Institute, where they are propagated under carefully controlled conditions and distributed, as required, to the cheese factories. Like the new defined strain starters, these mixtures are also used without rotation in large-scale cheese production.[3]

3.2 Thermophilic Cultures

Thermophilic cultures can be classified into 2 types, namely undefined or 'artisan' starters, and defined. Undefined strains are commonly used in the traditional small cheesemaking factories of Switzerland and France in which Gruyère, Emmental and Comté cheese are produced and in Italy, especially for Grana cheese production. The flora are not selected and are composed mainly of *Str. thermophilus* (other streptococci, especially faecal streptococci, may be present also) and several species of *Lactobacillus*, e.g. *Lb. fermentum, Lb. helveticus, Lb. lactis* and to a lesser extent *Lb. bulgaricus* and *Lb. acidophilus*.[35] In Italy, natural whey cultures ('culture naturali in siero') are used;[35] in the past, these were low-acid whey cultures in which *Str. thermophilus* predominated but more recently, high-acid whey cultures, consisting mainly of *Lactobacillus* spp. are used.[36] One of the reasons given for the use of these cultures in Italy is the inherent resistance to change within the Italian Dairy Industry.[36] In Switzerland and France, the artisan starter cultures are produced by macerating air-dried calf vells in whey from the previous day's make. In this process, both the production of rennet and the multiplication of phage-insensitive strains of the *Str. thermophilus* and *Lactobacillus* spp. occur.[35]

Efforts are being made to refine these artisan cultures. In the past, Emmental cheese has been prone to a defect, the secondary fermentation, which is characterized by increased CO_2 production and blowing of the cheese during storage at 10–13°C, i.e. after the propionic acid fermentation. This was thought to be due to the further metabolism of propionic acid bacteria (PAB) but investigations[37] have shown that it is actually due to the use of an excessively proteolytic starter. The more intense proteolysis leads to increased growth of the PAB and further production of CO_2.[37] The problem has been alleviated to some extent by careful selection of cultures. One hundred and eighty six natural raw mixed cultures ('Rohmischkulturen'), were collected from factories making good quality Emmental cheese. At the Swiss Federal Research Institute, these were screened for acid-producing and proteolytic activities, storage stability and cheesemaking performance. Only 8 cultures survived the selection procedure and these were deep frozen. Each week they are propagated under carefully controlled conditions at the Research Institute and distributed to the cheese factories to be used as daily inocula; in 1979, 150 000 inocula were produced.[38]

A completely defined-strain system of *Str. thermophilus* and *Lb. helveticus* has been developed in France.[39,40] The strains are grown individually, concentrated by centrifugation and frozen at −30°C. Since the volume of inoculum used in the manufacture of Gruyère and Emmental cheese is small—only 3–10% of that used for Cheddar or Dutch-type cheeses—these frozen concentrated cultures are used widely in France for the direct inoculation of the cheese milk.[40]

4. TAXONOMY

The distinguishing characteristics and functions of the bacteria found in mesophilic and thermophilic cultures are summarized in Table I. The taxonomy of some of the bacteria found in starter cultures is rather poorly

TABLE I

Distinguishing characteristics and functions of the micro-organisms found in mesophilic and thermophilic lactic starter cultures

Organism	M or T[a]	Function[b]	Sugar fermentation[c]	Isomer of lactate	Litmus milk[d]	% LA[e] in milk	Fermentation of: glu	gal	lac	Citrate metabolism	Acetoin from citrate in milk	NH$_3$ from arginine	Optimum temp. (approx.) °C	Growth at 40°C	% GC[f]
Str. lactis subsp. *lactis*	M	A	GLY	L	RAC	0·8	+	+	+	−	−	+	30	+	38·5
Str. lactis subsp. *cremoris*	M	A	GLY	L	RAC	0·8	+	+	+	−	−	−	30	−	39·0
Str. lactis subsp. *diacetylactis*	M	A+F	GLY	L	RAC	0·4–0·8	+	+	+	+	+	±	30	±	38·5
Leuc. lactis	M	F	PKP	D	A±C	0·4–0·7	+	+	+	+	−	−	30	−	43–44
Leuc. mesenteroides subsp. *mesenteroides*	M	F	PKP	D	NC	0·2	+	+	+	+	−	−	30	−	39–42
Leuc. mesenteroides subsp. *cremoris*	M	F	PKP	D	NC	0·2	+	+	+	+	−	−	30	−	39–42
Str. salivarius subsp. *thermophilus*	T	A	GLY	L	rAC	0·6	+	−	+	−	−	−	45	+	37–40
Lb. delbrueckii subsp. *lactis*	T	A	GLY	D	rAC	1·8	+	−	+	−	−	+	45	+	50·2
Lb. delbrueckii subsp. *bulgaricus*	T	A	GLY	D	rAC	1·8	+	−	+	−	−	+	45	+	50·3
Lb. helveticus	T	A	GLY	DL	rAC	2·0	+	+	+	−	−	−	45	+	39·3

[a] M, mesophilic; T, thermophilic.

[b] A, acid; F, flavour.

[c] GLY, glycolytic pathway; PKP, phosphoketolase pathway.

[d] R, complete reduction; r, incomplete reduction; A, acid; C, clot; NC, no change.

[e] LA, lactic acid.

[f] GC, guanine plus cytosine.

understood, despite the fact that the cultures themselves are fairly well defined. However, taxonomic studies on these bacteria are ongoing.

4.1 Streptococcus

In the older literature, the 3 species of lactic streptococci, *Str. lactis*, *Str. cremoris* and *Str. diacetylactis*, collectively known as Group N streptococci, were considered to be 3 distinct species; however, they are now regarded to be subspecies of *Str. lactis*.[41] Many of the phenotypic properties that distinguish these subspecies are plasmid coded (see Section 7.2), e.g. *Str. lactis* subsp. *diacetylactis* is indistinguishable from *Str. lactis* subsp. *lactis* except for the presence of a plasmid which codes for citrate utilization. For this reason, the former organism is no longer considered a subspecies but *Str. lactis* subsp. *lactis* and *Str. lactis* subsp. *cremoris* are.[42] The official designation of the genus has recently been changed from *Streptococcus* to *Lactococcus* so that these 2 subspecies are now more correctly called *Lactococcus lactis* subsp. *lactis*, and *Lc. lactis* subsp. *cremoris*. In this review, for ease of writing, we will refer to them as *Streptococcus*; and because of the importance of citrate metabolism in some starter bacteria, we will retain the 3 subspecies. *Str. thermophilus* was once considered to be closely related to *Str. lactis* but is now regarded to be a subspecies of *Str. salivarius*.[43]

4.2 Leuconostoc

The taxonomy of the leuconostocs is also quite complicated. Many of the early workers were more interested in what determined flavour development in fermented products than in bacterial taxonomy and two of the most important—Orla-Jensen and Hammer—did not differentiate *Pediococcus* from *Leuconostoc*.[44] Recent studies[45,46] suggest that there are 4 species of *Leuconostoc*: *Leuc. oenos*, *Leuc. lactis*, *Leuc. mesenteroides* and *Leuc. paramesenteroides*; *Leuc. cremoris* and *Leuc. dextranicum* are considered to be sub-species of *Leuc. mesenteroides*. Factual information on the *Leuconostoc* species present in starter cultures is very limited; it is not clear whether *Leuc. lactis* or *Leuc. mesenteroides* subsp. *cremoris* or *Leuc. mesenteroides* subsp. *dextranicum* is the most important: this may be relatively unimportant in practice so long as the culture produces the correct flavour. Galesloot and Hassing[47] and Garvie[45] feel that *Leuc. mesenteroides* subsp. *cremoris* is the principal *Leuconostoc* species while Stadhouders[48] states that both *Leuc. lactis* and *Leuc. mesenteroides* subsp.

cremoris are found in starters. A study[49] of 45 leuconostocs isolated from starter cultures and sour cream showed that 47% were probably *Leuc. mesenteroides* subsp. *cremoris* while 34% were *Leuc. mesenteroides* subsp. *mesenteroides*; the remaining 14% differed from any species of *Leuconostoc* recognized at that time. Galesloot and Hassing[47] also refer to work done on Dutch cultures in 1936 and 1948 which showed that leuconostocs (generally *Leuc. mesenteroides* subsp. *cremoris*) were the sole flavour producers while similar cultures examined in 1954 contained both *Leuconostoc* and *Str. lactis* subsp. *diacetylactis* as flavour producers (BD cultures). This is interesting when one realizes that *Str. lactis* subsp. *diacetylactis* was first isolated in 1936.

4.3 Lactobacillus

Lb. lactis and *Lb. bulgaricus* are considered to be sub-species of *Lb. delbruekii*.[50] *Lb. helveticus* is easily distinguished from *Lb. lactis* and *Lb. bulgaricus* by the lack of metachromatic granules when methylene blue-stained cells are examined microscopically, by its ability to produce both D and L lactate and to produce large amounts of lactate in milk (Table I). *Lb. lactis*, *Lb. bulgaricus* and *Str. thermophilus* do not metabolize galactose (gal⁻); in fact, lactose metabolism by *Str. thermophilus* results in the accumulation of galactose in the medium.[51] Only strains of thermophilic lactobacilli which ferment galactose (gal⁺) should be used as starter cultures for Swiss cheese, since they will use the galactose produced by *Str. thermophilus*.[52] If gal⁻ strains are used, galactose accumulates in the cheese and acts as an energy source for potential off-flavour production by undesirable non-starter bacteria. Turner and Martley[52] suggest that some commercial strains of *Lb. bulgaricus* used commercially in the USA are gal⁺ and are incorrectly classified; they should be reclassified as *Lb. helveticus*. They further suggest that this mistaken identification may explain why *Lb. bulgaricus* is said to be preferred for Swiss cheese manufacture in the USA while *Lb. helveticus* is preferred in Europe. A symbiotic relationship exists between *Str. thermophilus* and *Lb. bulgaricus* and the compounds involved have been identified as CO_2, formate, peptides and amino acids (cf. Ref. 53). Some data have also been published showing that a symbiotic relationship exists between *Str. thermophilus* and *Lb. helvecticus*; stimulation of the streptococcus by the lactobacillus is more pronounced than the converse but the actual compounds involved have not been identified.[54]

4.4 Media for Growth and Differentiation

The lactic acid bacteria found in starter cultures are very fastidious requiring several preformed amino acids, vitamins and other nutritional factors for growth. Because of this, complex media are used that generally include a fermentable carbohydrate, yeast and/or beef extract, one or more enzymatic digests of protein (tryptone, a peptic or tryptic digest of casein, is commonly used), a buffer (usually phosphate) and several inorganic ions (Fe, Mg, Mn). In the past, the most common general-purpose medium used for growing the Group N streptococci was the unbuffered lactic medium of Elliker *et al.*[55] The current medium of choice is M 17 (Ref. 56) which is buffered with β-glycerophosphate. This medium is also very useful for growing *Str. thermophilus*[57,58] and for preparing and assaying phage for both this organism and Group N streptococci.[56] Media containing β-glycerophosphate are unsuitable for thermophilic lactobacilli, especially *Lb. bulgaricus* and *Lb. lactis* and in fact they are used to selectively enumerate *Str. thermophilus* in yoghurt.[59] MRS broth[60] is the most useful general-purpose medium for lactobacilli; streptococci and leuconostocs also grow well in this medium (Cogan, unpublished data).

Numerous differential media have been proposed to distinguish the flavour and acid producers found in mesophilic starter cultures. The KCA medium of Nickels and Leesment[61] was found to be the most useful of several examined.[62] Most media contain insoluble calcium citrate: the flavour producers are detected as colonies surrounded by a clear zone due to metabolism of the insoluble calcium citrate. These media are opaque so that it is difficult to see the acid producers. Addition of 2,3,5-triphenyltetrazolium chloride (0·1 mg/ml) allows the acid producers to be visualized easily (Cogan, unpublished data). Addition of tetracycline (0·15 μg/ml) to a suitable medium has been reported to be selective for *Leuconostoc* spp.[63] Two promising media have been suggested recently, one of which distinguishes the three species of Group N streptococci by virtue of their ability/inability to metabolize citrate and produce NH_3 from arginine.[64] The second medium[65] is very useful for the differential enumeration of *Str. lactis* subsp. *diacetylactis* but its suitability for growth of *Leuconostoc* spp. has not been reported. Potassium ferrocyanide and a mixture of sodium and ferric citrates are added to a milk/tryptone/dextrose agar. The differential property of this medium depends on the precipitation of Fe as 'Prussian blue', which occurs only in the absence of citrate. Colonies unable to utilize citrate are white while those which utilize citrate appear blue because the inhibitor (citrate) of the 'Prussian blue' precipitation reaction is no longer present. Differential/selective media to distinguish *Str. thermophilus* from the thermophilic lactobacilli have been reviewed by Radke-Mitchell and Sandine,[53] who concluded that none of those available works equally well for all strains. More recently, a provisional standard was proposed by the IDF:[66] *Str. thermophilus* is enumerated on M17 agar[56] (after aerobic incubation at 37°C for 48 h) and *Lb. bulgaricus* on MRS agar[60] at pH 5·4 (after anaerobic incubation at 37°C for 72 h).

5. METABOLISM OF STARTER BACTERIA

Despite the fact that lactic acid bacteria are found in almost all fermentations, they have very limited biosynthetic ability and require many amino acids and vitamins for growth. Their major metabolic activity is catabolic and the industrially important functions, which are common to most cheeses, are the metabolism of lactose, citrate and protein.

5.1 Lactose Metabolism

5.1.1 Transport

Almost all lactic acid bacteria, and certainly all those used as cheese starters, need a fermentable carbohydrate for energy production and growth. In milk, this is lactose, a disaccharide composed of galactose and glucose. Several mechanisms of carbohydrate transport are found in bacteria, all of which, except that for glycerol, require energy in some form (cf. Ref. 67). In the lactic acid bacteria found in starter cultures two different mechanisms for lactose transport are used, i.e. the permease and the phosphoenol pyruvate–phosphotransferase (PEP/PTS) systems. The permease system is found in the thermophilic lactic acid bacteria and the leuconostocs (see below) while the PEP/PTS system is found in the Group N streptococci.[68] In the permease system, lactose is transported intact in an energy requiring reaction; inside the cell, it is hydrolysed to glucose and galactose by β-galactosidase (β-gal). The precise form of energy used has not been elucidated but it is likely that it is ATP, as in the case of the galactose permease of *Str. lactis*.[69] In the PEP/PTS system, lactose is transported into the cell via a complex system in which the lactose is phosphorylated to lactose-phosphate as it is transported across the cell

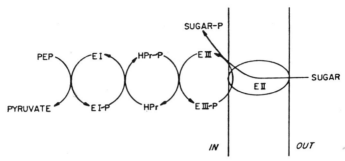

Fig. 1. Phosphoenol pyruvate:phosphotransferase system for sugar metabolism. EI, enzyme 1; EII, enzyme II; EIII, enzyme III; HPr, heat stable phosphocarrier protein; P, phosphorylated compound (from Dills *et al.*,[67] reprinted with permission).

wall; inside the cell, the lactose phosphate is hydrolysed to glucose and galactose-6-P by phospho-β-galactosidase (P-β-gal).

There have been relatively few studies on the transport of lactose by thermophilic cultures. *Str. thermophilus* possesses equal amounts of β-gal and P-β-gal implying that lactose uptake occurs via a permease and a PEP/PTS system.[70] However, another study[58] showed that the activity of β-gal was 3000 times that of P-β-gal, suggesting that the permease is the functional transport system *in vivo*. This contradiction has not been resolved. Galactose transport in *Str. thermophilus* has been studied[71] and occurs via an ATP dependent permease system. *Lb. lactis, Lb. bulgaricus* and *Lb. helveticus* possess much greater amounts of β-gal than of P-β-gal[72,73] again implying that the permease is the more important system *in vivo* for lactose transport. Some evidence for a glucose specific PEP/PTS system has been reported in thermophilic lactobacilli.[73] It is not known which system of lactose transport is used by *Leuconostoc* spp. but it is likely that it is via a permease since PEP/PTS systems are absent from organisms, like leuconostocs, which do not ferment sugars by glycolysis (Ref. 74; Section 5.1.2).

The PEP/PTS is a complex system (Fig. 1) requiring Mg^{2+} and four proteins, two of which, Enzyme II and Enzyme III, are membrane-bound and are sugar-specific, while the other two, Enzyme I and the low-molecular weight, heat-stable protein, HPr, are soluble proteins and are common to all PEP/PTS sugar transport systems (cf. Ref. 67). Enzyme III is peripheral to whereas Enzyme II is an integral component of the cell membrane. Lawrence and Thomas[75] suggested that the PEP/PTS system for transport of lactose and P-β-gal for the hydrolysis of lactose-P are prerequisites for rapid lactose fermentation. This was supported by the

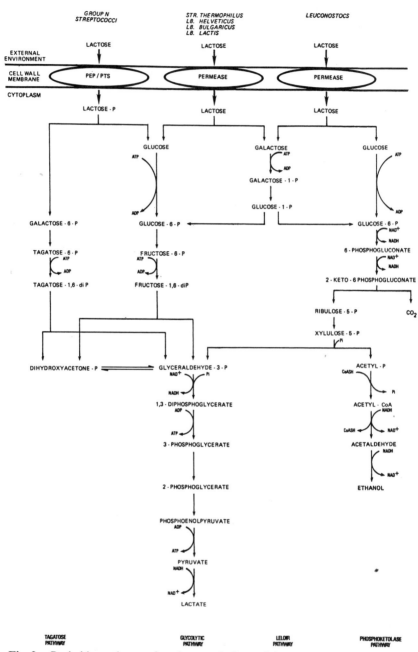

Fig. 2. Probable pathways for the metabolism of lactose in mesophilic and thermophilic lactic acid bacteria.

findings of Farrow[76] who showed that starter strains which fermented lactose rapidly had high P-β-gal and no β-gal activity while non-starter strains (wild-type) which fermented lactose slowly had high levels of β-gal and low levels of P-β-gal. This was further confirmed by Crow and Thomas[77] who showed that *Str. lactis* 7962 transports lactose by the PEP/PTS system but has low P-β-gal activity and consequently, ferments lactose slowly. In some Group N streptococci, glucose is transported by a PEP/PTS system and galactose by two sugar-specific systems—a low affinity PEP/PTS system and a high-affinity permease system.[69,78] This has led to speculation[69,79] that, when growing on low levels of galactose, uptake of the sugar is via the high affinity permease system and further metabolism by the Leloir pathway (Section 5.1.2) and that when growing on high levels of galactose, uptake is via the low affinity PEP/PTS system and further metabolism by the tagatose pathway (Section 5.1.2).

5.1.2 Further metabolism

In the Group N streptococci, lactose-P (from the PEP/PTS transport system) is hydrolysed to glucose and galactose-6-P by P-β-gal. Glucose is fermented via the normal glycolytic pathway (Fig. 2) while galactose-6-P is metabolized through several tagatose derivatives to glyceraldehyde-3-P and dihydroxyacetone-P which then enter the terminal reactions of glycolysis.[80] In *Str. thermophilus* and the thermophilic lactobacilli, lactose (from the permease system) is hydrolysed by β-gal to glucose and galactose; the glucose is further metabolized by glycolysis while galactose, when it is metabolized, is probably transformed to glucose-1-P by the Leloir pathway (Fig. 2). Surprisingly, all of the strains of *Str. thermophilus* examined are gal⁻ probably because of low levels of galactokinase.[51] The galactose formed from lactose as a result of β-gal activity is secreted and accumulates in the medium.[51] This probably occurs also in the gal⁻ thermophilic lactobacilli (e.g. *Lb. lactis* and *Lb. bulgaricus*) and is the reason why gal⁺ lactobacilli (e.g. *Lb. helveticus*) should be used in the starters for Swiss and Italian cheese varieties (Section 4.3).

In the case of leuconostocs, lactose is probably taken up via a permease system[74] and hydrolysed by β-gal to galactose and glucose. However, the further metabolism of these sugars is not via the glycolytic pathway but rather by the phosphoketolase pathway (Fig. 2), resulting initially in one carbon being split off as CO_2 and the remaining 5 carbons being cleaved at the level of xylulose-5-P to glyceraldehyde-P and acetyl-P. It is not known how galactose is metabolized by the leuconostocs but, again, this is probably via the Leloir pathway (Fig. 2).

The overall production of energy via the glycolytic pathway is twice as high as in the phosphoketolase pathway and lactic acid is the sole end product. In the case of the phosphoketolase pathway, other major end products are formed, e.g. ethanol and CO_2.

Glycolytic pathway:

1 lactose $+ 4$ ADP $\rightarrow 4$ lactate $+ 4$ ATP

Phosphoketolase pathway:

1 lactose $+ 2$ ADP $\rightarrow 2$ lactate $+ 2$ ethanol $+ 2$ CO_2 $+ 2$ ATP

These pathways have, traditionally, been referred to as the homofermentative and heterofermentative lactic acid fermentations, respectively. However, in recent years confusion has arisen over the terms 'homo' and 'hetero'. Originally, heterofermentation referred to the phosphoketolase pathway only where CO_2, ethanol and lactate are produced from sugar metabolism but recently the term 'heterofermentation' has also been applied to situations where essentially homofermentative bacteria[81] produce other products (e.g. formate, acetate, ethanol, acetoin) besides lactate from pyruvate. Because of this confusion, it might be better to abandon the use of the terms hetero- and homofermentation and replace them by the names of the actual pathways.

Nearly all of the enzymes required for both pathways of lactose metabolism have been detected in one strain or another of starter bacteria but relatively few have been purified and studied in detail. This is surprising in view of the importance of lactose metabolism in cheese manufacture. The major properties of the enzymes involved in sugar metabolism which have been purified from starter lactic acid bacteria are summarized in Table II. As far as we are aware, no glycolytic enzyme has been purified from the thermophilic lactobacilli and in the case of Str. thermophilus, only β-galactosidase[99a,b,100] and phosphofructose kinase.[101] The purification of a D type LDH from Str. lactis 760 (Ref. 102) is unusual since Str. lactis produces only L lactic acid (Table I). The ratio of L to D isomer produced was 36:1 and only the L LDH required FDP for activity. The results could be explained by assuming that the culture was a mixed culture of Str. lactis, which produces only L lactate, and a leuconostoc contaminant, which produces only D lactate (Table I). This is not an unusual situation since Orberg and Sandine[103] recently showed that Str. lactis 290P was contaminated with a leuconostoc which was detected only when the culture was grown in the presence of high concentrations of valincomycin.

5.1.3 Regulation

Except for the Group N streptococci, very little information is available on the regulation of lactose metabolism in cheese starter culture organisms. In the Group N streptococci, the regulation of lactose metabolism is extremely complicated.[104] The two main regulatory enzymes are pyruvate kinase (PK) and lactate dehydrogenase (LDH). PK is a tetrameric allosteric enzyme[84,85] which is activated by fructose-1,6-di P (FDP) and all of the intermediates of glycolysis from glucose-6-P to glyceraldehyde-3-P and is inhibited by inorganic phosphate (Pi); except for FDP, the concentrations of all these compounds are very low in growing cells.[105-107] The major effectors *in vivo* are thought to be FDP and Pi.[105] In growing (glycolysing) cells, the concentration of FDP is high and that of Pi is low which stimulate PK activity. In starved cells, Pi is high and that of FDP is low; therefore, PK activity ceases and the concentration of PEP increases. This means that starved cells have an immediate source of PEP for sugar transport by the PEP/PTS system as soon as they are exposed to it.[105,107]

LDH is also an important regulatory enzyme in Group N streptococci and is activated by FDP.[104] In cells growing on glucose or lactose, lactate is the only product of sugar metabolism, whereas cells growing on galactose or low concentrations of glucose produce in addition formate, acetate, ethanol and acetoin from pyruvate. This has been correlated with lower levels of both LDH and its activator, FDP, and higher levels of pyruvic–formic lyase and its activators, triose phosphates.[79,81] Both factors stimulate the formation of the other products of pyruvate metabolism.

Str. thermophilus does not metabolize galactose but it metabolizes glucose and lactose simultaneously;[58] lactose is fermented more rapidly than glucose.[77] When galactose-grown cells of *Str. lactis* are resuspended in a medium containing glucose, lactose and galactose, glucose and lactose are metabolized immediately while galactose metabolism does not occur until the other two sugars have been metabolized.[108] Addition of lactose or glucose to galactose-grown cells of *Str. lactis* also causes an immediate cessation of galactose metabolism which resumes once the inhibitory sugar has been metabolized.[108] These results suggest that some product (probably cAMP) of glucose or lactose metabolism inhibits galactose transport since the cells are fully induced.

Lactic acid is produced from pyruvate in an NADH-requiring reaction catalysed by LDH. Two isomers of lactic acid are possible, viz. D and L, and lactic acid bacteria can produce either or both; the isomer(s) produced is useful in species identification (Table I). The production of both isomers by the same organism could be due to the presence of two specific LDHs or to one specific LDH and a racemase which transforms one isomer into

TABLE II

Some of the properties of the enzymes of sugar metabolism which have been purified from the lactic acid bacteria found in starter cultures

Enzyme	Organism	Optimum pH	$MW \times 10^3$	No. sub-units	Substrate	K_m (mM)	V_m (u/mg)	Kinetics[a]	Effectors	Reference
Group N streptococci										
phospho-β-galactosidase	Str. cremoris HP	5·0–8·0	67		ONPGP	0·59	23·8	H	galactose-6-P	82
β-galactosidase	Str. lactis ATCC7962 unusual strain, contains a lactose PEP/PTS system but low p-β-gal[77]	7·0	1000	2	ONPG	1·1	4·0	H		83
Tagatose-1,6-diphosphate aldolase	Str. cremoris E8	7·0–7·3	34·5		TDP / FDP	0·1 / 0·25	44·4 / 22·3	H		84
Fructose-1,6-diphosphate aldolase	Str. cremoris E8	7·8–8·0			TDP / FDP	NA[b] / 1·1	NA[b] / 22·4	H		84
Pyruvate kinase	Str. lactis ML3	6·9–7·5			PEP / ADP	0·17 / 1·0	98·0	S(−FDP) / H(+FDP)	Pi; FDP; SO_4^{2-}	85
	Str. lactis C10	7·5	240	4	PEP / ADP / GDP	0·13 / 1·3 / 0·1	53–80	S(PEP) / H(ADP)	Pi; FDP	86
L(+) Lactate dehydrogenase	Str. lactis C10	7·0			Pyruvate / NADH / Lactate	1·5 / 0·08 / 100·0	1 110 / 1 700	H(Tris/maleate) / S (phosphate)	Pi; FDP	87
	Str. cremoris US3	5·0–7·0	140	2	NAD / Pyruvate / NADH	2·4 / 1·15 / 0·044	290	H(+FDP) / S(−FDP)	Pi; ATP; FDP	88
Leuconostoc spp.										
β-galactosidase	Leuc. citrovorum ATCC 8081, actually Ped. pentosaceus[91]	6·5			ONPG / Lactose	3·3 / 7·8	4·0 / 1·3	H		89
Glucose-6-phosphate dehydrogenase	Leuc. lactis NCDO 546	7·8 (NAD) / 10·0 (NADP)	123		Glu 6P (NAD) / (NADP) / NAD / NADP	0·19 / 0·20 / 0·11 / 0·014		H		91
	Leuc. mesenteroides ATCC12291	7·8	104		Glu 6P (NAD) / (NADP) / NAD / NADP	0·053 / 0·081 / 0·106 / 0·006		H		92

Enzyme	Organism	pH			Substrate	K_m		H/S	Products; Inhibitors	Ref
6-phosphogluconate dehydrogenase	Leuc. mesenteroides BO7	7·5			6P gluc.; NAD	0·2; 0·026		H	ATP; ADP	93
Phosphotransferase	Leuc. mesenteroides IFO 3426	8·1			CoA; Acetyl P	0·025; 2·8		H		94
Aldehyde dehydrogenase	Leuc. mesenteroides IFO 3426				Acetaldehyde; CoA; NAD$^+$	3·7; 0·009; 0·17		H	AMP; ADP; ATP	95
Alcohol dehydrogenase	Leuc. mesenteroides IFO 3426				Acetaldehyde; NADH; Ethanol; NAD	0·69; 0·01; 1·4; 2·5		. H (?)	AMP; ADP	95
Alcohol dehydrogenase NAD dependent	Leuc. mesenteroides		160		Acetaldehyde; NADH; Ethanol; NAD	—; 0·25; 50; 0·5		H	AMP; ADP; ATP	96
Alcohol dehydrogenase NADP dependent	Leuc. mesenteroides		160		Acetaldehyde; NADPH; Ethanol; NAD	0·2; 17; 0·085; —		H		96
D (−) Lactate dehydrogenase	Leuc. lactis NCDO 546	7·6 (pyruvate) 8·0 (lactate)	80		Pyruvate; NADH; lactate; NAD	2·0; 0·22; 50·0; 12·5	160; 77	H		91
	Leuc. lactis NCDO 533	6·6-8·0	77	2	Pyruvate; NADH; lactate; NAD	0·33; 0·15; 20·0; 2·9		H	ADP; ATP	97
	Leuc. mesenteroides ATCC 12291		64		Pyruvate; NADH; lactate; NAD	1·0; 0·067; —; 2·2		H		98
Str. thermophilus β-galactosidase	Str. thermophilus 19258	8·0	105		ONPG	0·69		H (?)	Galactose, galactal, galactose-6-P	99[a]
	Str. thermophilus	7·0	600		ONPG	0·25	83	H		99[b]
	Str. thermophilus B3641	7·0	530		ONPG	0·98	193	H	Galactose	100
Phosphofructokinase	Str. thermophilus	7·0	148	4	lactose; fru-6P; ATP	6·9; 2·15; 0·28	295; 300	H		101

[a] H, hyperbolic; S, sigmoidal; [b] NA, no activity.

the other. Racemases have been found in very few strains of lactic acid bacteria and in none of those present in starter cultures; consequently, it is generally considered that the production of L and D lactate is due to two specific LDHs (cf. Ref. 109). Cheddar cheese contains high concentrations of L and D lactate although the major starter organisms, the Group N streptococci, produce only the L isomer. The production of D lactate in cheese has been attributed to the activity of two specific LDHs in some of the non-starter bacteria (*Lb. casei, Lb. plantarum* and especially *Pediococcus pentosaceus*), which are important in ripening cheese and which are adventitiously present in the milk used for cheese manufacture.[110]

5.2 Citrate Metabolism

Citrate metabolism is important only in mesophilic cultures and has apparently no role in thermophilic cultures. Bottazzi and Dellaglio[111] and Groux[112] reported that several strains of *Str. thermophilus* and yoghurt cultures produced traces of diacetyl in milk; the inference of this finding is that citrate may have been metabolized (see below) but citrate disappearance *per se* was not measured in either study. More recent work has shown that *Lb. bulgaricus*,[113] *Lb. helvecticus*[113] and *Str. thermophilus*[114] do not metabolize citrate. However, pyruvate (an intermediate of citrate and sugar metabolism) is metabolized by *Lb. bulgaricus* and *Str. thermophilus* strains but not by *Lb. helveticus.*

The relatively low concentration of citrate in milk ($\sim 8\,mM$) belies the importance of its metabolism in many cheeses made with mesophilic culture. Citrate metabolism is responsible for eye formation in Dutch-type cheese due to CO_2 production and for aroma formation in Cottage cheese and Quarg-type products due mainly to diacetyl. Aroma formation is also important in many fermented milks, e.g. cultured buttermilk, but this is not a subject of the present review. Diacetyl has also been found in Cheddar cheese and is thought to be involved in flavour.[115] Sometimes, citrate metabolism is undesirable in cheese, e.g. CO_2 produced from it is thought to be responsible for floating curd in Cottage cheese[116] and for openness in Cheddar cheese.[117]

Citrate is not used as an energy source by the flavour-producing bacteria present in cheese cultures although there is some evidence that it is by *Str. faecalis.*[118] However, the flavour-producing bacteria can metabolize it very rapidly in the presence of a fermentable carbohydrate by the pathway outlined in Fig. 3. Citrate is taken into the cell by a permease where it is hydrolysed to acetate and oxalacetate by citrate

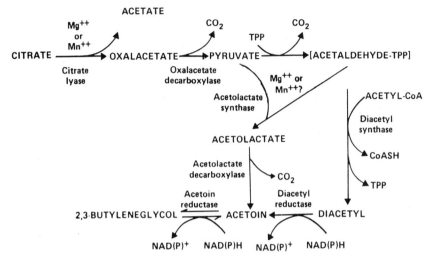

Fig. 3. Pathway for the metabolism of citrate in *Str. lactis* subsp. *diacetylactis* and *Leuconostoc* spp.

lyase.[119a–121]. This enzyme is constitutive in *Str. lactis* subsp. *diacetylactis*[121,122] and inducible in *Leuconostoc* spp.[123] Oxalacetate is decarboxylated in two steps via pyruvate to acetaldehyde–TPP which can condense with acetyl CoA to form diacetyl or with another molecule of pyruvate to form α-acetolactate,[119b,c] which can then be decarboxylated to acetoin. It is not clear if pyruvate decarboxylase is involved in decarboxylating pyruvate to the acetaldehyde–TPP complex or whether, in fact, acetolactate and diacetyl synthases carry out both the decarboxylation and condensation activities. It is also not clear whether divalent cations, e.g. Mn^{2+} and Mg^{2+}, are involved in the acetolactate synthase reaction, as in other micro-organisms.[124] The acetolactate synthase of *Leuc. lactis* does not have a requirement for divalent cations[125] but so much manganese was present in the cell-free extracts used that it may have masked any effect.

Acetolactate is very unstable and is readily decarboxylated in purely chemical reactions, non-oxidatively to acetoin or oxidatively to diacetyl.[126,127] This raises the question as to whether or not diacetyl and acetoin are formed chemically or enzymatically from acetolactate as shown in Fig. 3. This is a contentious issue which has not been resolved satisfactorily. Jonsson and Petersson[128] and Stadhouders[48] have shown that some mixed cultures excrete acetolactate, implying that acetoin and diacetyl can be formed chemically. The two former workers[128] feel that diacetyl is formed enzymatically because the redox potential in starter cultures is very low. This does not preclude non-enzymatic formation of acetoin from acetolactate. The specificity of the method used by Jonsson and Petersson[128] to measure acetolactate should be investigated since a very similar method is used to measure a different but related compound, diacetylmethylcarbinol, in cultures of *Micrococcus ureae*.[132] It is not clear which bacteria in the mixed cultures are responsible for acetolactate production; the likelihood is that it is one or other of the aroma producers, probably *Str. lactis* subsp. *diacetylactis*. However, Speckman and Collins[129] have shown that pure cultures of *Str. lactis* subsp. *diacetylactis* do not excrete acetolactate. The conclusions of this study may be questionable because the strains used produced very little acetoin, which would be expected in large amounts from cells metabolizing citrate.[130] Diacetyl and acetoin levels in cultures are often determined in steam distillates. This complicates the issue further since distillation *per se* can result in decarboxylation of acetolactate to diacetyl and acetone, resulting in erroneously high values.[131] Support for the enzymatic formation of acetoin from acetolactate has come from studies which showed the presence of acetolactate synthase and decarboxylase activities in *Str. lactis* subsp. *diacetylactis*.[120,125] Support for the enzymatic formation of diacetyl from acetyl CoA and not from the chemical decarboxylation of acetolactate has come from studies which showed that ^{14}C-labelled diacetyl was formed from ^{14}C-labelled acetate.[119a] The rationale behind these experiments is that in the absence of lipoic acid, *Str. lactis* subsp. *diacetylactis* can form acetyl CoA (and consequently diacetyl) only from acetate via acetate kinase and phosphotransacetylase.

Acetoin can also be produced from diacetyl and 2,3-butylene glycol from acetoin in NADH-requiring reactions catalysed by diacetyl reductase (more correctly called acetoin dehydrogenase) and acetoin reductase (more correctly called 2,3-butylene glycol dehydrogenase), respectively. These activities are catalysed by two enzymes in *Escherichia coli*[133] and by one enzyme in *Saccharomyces cerevisiae* and *Enterobacter aerogenes*[134,135] (Fig. 3). In the lactic acid bacteria, it is not known how many enzymes are involved. Citrate represses the synthesis of both acetoin dehydrogenase and 2,3-butylene glycol dehydrogenase in *Str. lactis* subsp. *diacetylactis*[122] which may explain the accumulation of diacetyl and acetoin by these cultures.[122,130] Once citrate has been exhausted, increased synthesis of acetoin dehydrogenase and 2,3-butylene glycol dehydrogenase occurs with a consequent reduction in the levels of both diacetyl and acetoin.[122,130] These data suggest that these enzymes are associated with the outside of the cell wall or, alternatively, that their substrates (diacetyl and acetoin) are freely transported across the cell wall.

Str. lactis subsp. *diacetylactis* and *Leuconostoc* spp. behave completely differently in the production of acetoin and diacetyl from citrate. *Str. lactis* subsp. *diacetylactis* produces both compounds as soon as growth begins while *Leuconostoc* spp. produce them only at relatively low pH.[136,137] Much greater amounts of acetoin than diacetyl are produced by *Str. lactis* subsp. *diacetylactis* from citrate; the ratio can be as high as 43:1 (Ref. 130) and this is believed to be due to a limited rate of acetyl CoA synthesis.[119b] Acetoin dehydrogenase activity may be important also since it may reduce diacetyl to acetoin as soon as it is formed. No diacetyl and little acetoin are produced by *Str. lactis* subsp. *diacetylactis* from lactose even though the necessary enzymes and intermediate (pyruvate) are present.[119b,122] This has been attributed to the need of the organism to convert all the pyruvate produced during glycolysis to lactate in order to produce the NAD^+ needed to continue the metabolism of lactose (see Fig. 2). However, NAD^+ can also be produced through the activities of acetoin and 2,3-butylene glycol dehydrogenases (Fig. 3), suggesting that other, as yet unknown, factors are involved in regulating the production of diacetyl and acetoin.

Leuconostoc spp. metabolize citrate but produce no diacetyl or acetoin from it at neutral pH values; however, these compounds are produced from citrate at acidic pH values.[137] The optimum pH for citrate utilization by *Leuc. lactis* is 5·4; production of acetoin shows no optimum but increases directly as the pH decreases within the pH-range tested (Fig. 4). Relatively low concentrations of glucose ($\geq 5\,mM$) stimulate citrate uptake but completely inhibit production of acetoin.[137] This has been ascribed to inhibition of acetolactate synthase (Fig. 3) by many of the intermediates (6-PG, 2-PG, 3-PG, PEP and ATP) of the phosphoketolase pathway.[125] Inhibition by some of the intermediates is relieved at low pH and this allows production of acetoin. This, however, does not explain the lack of diacetyl production during the growth of *Leuconostoc* spp. at neutral pH, again suggesting that other, as yet unknown, factors are involved in regulating diacetyl production by these organisms.

The formation of eyes in Dutch-type cheese is due to CO_2 production by the aroma producers. *Leuconostoc* spp. produce CO_2 during metabolism of lactose (Section 5.1), but both they and *Str. lactis* subsp. *diacetylactis* also produce CO_2 during citrate metabolism by decarboxylation of oxalacetate, pyruvate and acetolactate (Fig. 3).

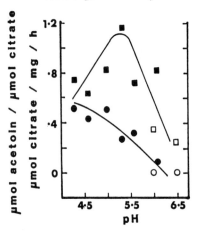

Fig. 4. Effect of pH on citrate uptake (□, ■) and acetoin production (○, ●) in *Leuconostoc lactis* NCW1. Phosphate buffer, open symbols; acetate buffer, closed symbols (from Cogan, unpublished).

5.3 Protein Metabolism

All the lactic acid bacteria used in starter cultures are nutritionally very fastidious, requiring several amino acids and other growth factors for adequate growth. Aseptically-drawn milk contains only 5–20% of the concentration of free amino acids required for maximum growth and so, for good growth in milk, the lactic acid bacteria must hydrolyse milk proteins, at least to small peptides, if not to amino acids.[138] Law and Kolstad[139] have compared the concentration of amino acids required for adequate growth of the Group N streptococci and *Str. thermophilus* with the naturally occurring levels in milk. The Group N streptococci require at least six amino acids (glutamate, valine, methionine, leucine, isoleucine and histidine); many strains have an additional requirement for phenylalanine, tyrosine, lysine and alanine.[140] A detailed study of the amino acid requirements of the *Leuconostoc* spp. has been reported but the requirements vary considerably:[141] all require valine and glutamate; methionine stimulates most of them and none require alanine. The other 14 amino acids tested either stimulated or were required by one strain or another. The amino acid requirements of *Str. thermophilus* are very similar to those of the Group N streptococci; glutamate, valine, leucine, isoleucine (one strain) and histidine are required in addition to cysteine and tryptophan.[142] No information appears to be available on the amino acid requirements of the thermophilic *Lactobacillus* spp. but, in general, lactobacilli are probably more fastidious than streptococci so that one would expect thermophilic lactobacilli to require a wider range of amino acids.

The Group N streptococci have been studied more thoroughly regarding transport of amino acids and peptides than any of the other bacteria found in starter cultures. Peptide transport has been the subject of considerable investigation and is more advantageous to the cell than individual amino acid transport since less energy is expended per amino acid residue. In most bacteria, oligopeptides containing 6 or 7 amino acid residues can be transported but uptake of only di-, tri- and tetrapeptides has been reported for the Group N streptococci.[143-145] One strain which grew poorly on a dipeptide grew relatively better with tripeptides as a source of essential amino acids.[143] Separate transport systems for amino acids and peptides are present.[143,144] In some strains, individual amino acids are more efficacious than peptides in promoting growth but in other strains the reverse is true.[145] The effects of pH, temperature and metabolic inhibitors on the transport of leucine, isoleucine and valine by *Str. thermophilus* have been reported; an excess of many amino acids inhibited growth.[146]

Lactic acid bacteria are only mildly proteolytic compared with other bacteria, e.g. *Bacillus* or *Pseudomonas*, as evident from the lack of visible proteolysis in milk even on prolonged incubation. While several proteinases and peptidases from lactic acid bacteria with different specificities have been purified and their properties studied,[147-163] their cellular location has been contentious in some cases because cell leakage had not been studied simultaneously. In more recent work,[150,151,153,160-163] the association of proteinases and peptidases with the cell surface or cell wall/cell membrane interface has been strongly indicated by data which show that no loss or release of intracellular enzymes occurs when proteinases are assayed in intact cells or protoplasts produced from lysozyme- or phage lysin-treated cells. Intracellular proteinases and peptidases have also been detected in lactic acid bacteria[152,154-156] but their probable role is in intracellular protein turnover and in the termination reactions of newly synthesized proteins. Calcium appears to be involved in attachment of proteinase(s) to the cell wall, e.g. if cells of *Str. cremoris* or *Str. lactis* are suspended in a Ca-free buffer, part of the proteolytic activity is released without lysis;[159,164] this is surpressed by adding calcium[159,164] and is temperature- and pH-dependent.[164] Further information on the proteinases and peptidases in lactic acid bacteria can be found in the recent review by Law and Kolstad.[139] Since then, Hugenholtz et al.[165] have shown that four immunologically distinct proteinases were present in the cell wall of Str. cremoris, only one of which was common to all 10 strains tested. These proteinases can also be distinguished on the basis of their pH and temperature optima into three distinct types—P_1 (optimum pH, 5·8; optimum temperature, 40°C), P_{11} (optimum pH, 6·5; optimum temperature, 30°C) and P_{111} (optimum pH, 5·4; optimum temperature, 30°C).[157]

The location and complexity of the proteinases found in the different starter bacteria make it very difficult to envisage a model which accommodates all the data (cf. Ref. 139). The most popular hypothesis at present is that the free amino acids and peptides in milk are metabolized first, followed by the amino acids and peptides produced from protein by the cell wall-associated proteinase(s). The amino acids are transported into the cell directly while the peptides may be transported directly or further hydrolysed by the cell wall/membrane-associated peptidases to amino acids which are then transported. An outline of the different systems used is shown in Fig. 5. The precise protein which is hydrolysed during growth

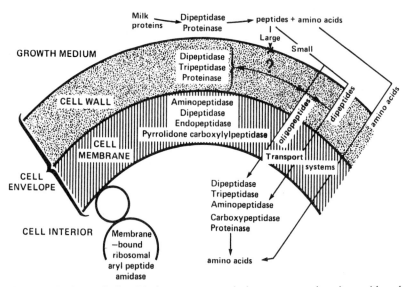

Fig. 5. The interrelationship between proteolytic systems and amino acid and peptide transport systems in lactic acid bacteria (from Davies and Law,[7] p. 80, reprinted with permission).

in milk has not been unequivocally determined but all, including the whey proteins, are available to the cell.[138] One would expect that the more accessible proteins in the casein micelle (e.g. κ- and β-casein) would be hydrolysed before the less accessible α_s-casein. This was found for *Str. cremoris* AM2 and E8;[138] the whey protein, β-lactoglobulin, was also an important nitrogen source. This has been confirmed by Rymaszewski *et al.*[166] for 1 strain each of *Str. lactis*, *Str. cremoris* and *Str. diacetylactis*. Hugenholtz *et al.*[165] cited unpublished data of Exterkate that only β-casein is hydrolysed by *Str. cremoris* except for strain AM1 which can also hydrolyse α-casein. The cell wall-associated proteinase for *Str. cremoris* ACI is specific for β-casein.[161] Regarding the thermophiles, El-Soda and Desmazeaud[167] showed that *Lb. helveticus* does not hydrolyse β-casein and only partially hydrolyses α_s-casein while *Lb. lactis* and *Lb. bulgaricus* can hydrolyse both of these caseins. The data for *Lb. bulgaricus* have been substantiated by Chandan *et al.*[168]

Bitterness is a problem in many cheese varieties, especially those made with mesophilic cultures, and has been associated with the production of bitter peptides, which contain predominantly hydrophobic amino acid residues, by rennet and the starter bacteria. From earlier work, the following hypothesis was developed to explain the occurrence of bitterness:[169-172] apparently all starter strains are potentially capable of causing bitterness but this does not occur if the rate of multiplication during manufacture is controlled (e.g. by higher cooking temperatures or the presence of phage) such that relatively low cell numbers are found in the curd. Bitterness develops when high cell numbers occur due to increased hydrolysis of non-bitter peptides to lower molecular weight bitter peptides.

More recent work[173-175] contradicts this hypothesis to some extent. Only some starter bacteria produce bitter peptides but all can degrade such peptides, if produced.[173] The principal sources of bitter peptides are residues 84–89 and 193–209 of the C-terminal end of β-casein.[175] Salt decreases the permeability of the starter cells and increases the hydrophobic association between the bitter peptides.[174] Both factors result in reduced availability of the substrate for the membrane-associated proteinases and consequently a bitter cheese, if a bitterness producing strain was used as a starter. Very recently, De Vos (personal communication) classified cultures into bitter and non-bitter strains based on their action on the different caseins. The latter hydrolysed both α_s- and β-caseins into low MW products while bitter strains had no effect on α_s- and only limited activity on β-casein (Fig. 6). This difference in specificity may be

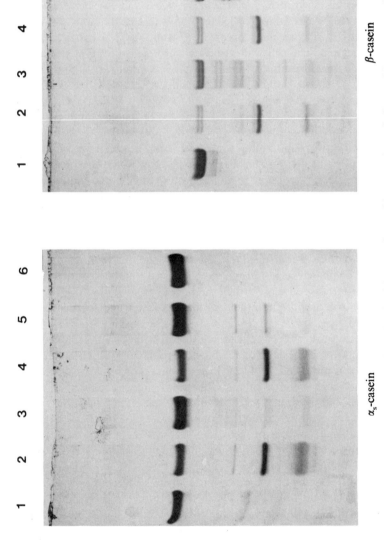

α_s-casein

β-casein

Fig. 6. Degradation of α_s- and β-caseins by bitter and non-bitter strains of Group N streptococci. Analysis was by SDS-PAGE. Lanes 1–6 are control (no proteinase added), strain SK11, strain E8, strain AM1, strain FD27 and strain Wg2, respectively. Strains SK11, E8 and AM1 are non-bitter, while strains FD27 and Wg2 are bitter (from Simons and De Vos, unpublished data).

due to the lack of one or more of the different proteinases in non-bitter starter strains.

5.4 Metabolite Production in Milk and Cheese

Although the optimum temperature of the bacteria found in mesophilic cultures is $\sim 30°C$, most of them will grow over the range 5–40°C. Most Group N streptococci have the same growth rate at 27°C but at other temperatures, especially 21°C, considerable differences occur.[18] This has important practical implications for growth because it means that in mixed cultures, domination by the faster-growing components can occur at the traditional incubation temperature ($\sim 21°C$) and so it would probably be better to incubate cultures at 27°C. Three parameters (rate of inoculation, temperature and time of incubation) determine when a culture is fully grown in milk; this coincides with coagulation. The usual incubation conditions for both mixed and defined strains of lactic starters are 0·5% (v/v) inoculum at 21°C for 16 h. Under these conditions, mixed and defined strains of lactic streptococci will coagulate milk in 16 h during which the pH value falls from $\sim 6·5$ to 4·5; the concentration of lactic acid can reach 0·85% (Table I).

Previously, cheese was made only once a day. The choice of 21°C as the incubation temperature then becomes significant since it meant that a culture could be inoculated at 4 p.m., incubated at room temperature (21°C) and be ready for cheesemaking 16 h later, i.e. 8 a.m. the following morning. At 21°C, the generation time (GT) of both mixed and defined strain starters in milk is 2·2 h while at 30°C, it is 1 h;[176] in complex media, these values are approximately halved. A mathematical basis can also be found for the choice of 21°C as the incubation temperature: if the GT is 2·2 h, 7·2 generations would occur in 16 h and if a 0·5% inoculum is used, a fully grown culture would be equivalent to 7·5 generations. Both calculations give approximately the same value for the number of generations.

Except for *Leuc. lactis*, most species of *Leuconostoc* grow poorly in milk unless a stimulant, e.g. 0·3% (w/v) yeast extract, is added and in some cases, 1·0% (w/v) glucose also;[44] under these conditions and using a 0·1–1% (w/v) inoculum, *Leuconostoc* spp. will coagulate milk in less than 24 h at 30°C and produce $\sim 0·6\%$ lactic acid. The requirements for yeast extract and glucose probably reflect the inability of some strains to produce sufficient proteinase to hydrolyse milk proteins to the amino acids and small peptides required for growth and the inability to use lactose as an energy source, respectively.

Similar quantitative data on generation times do not appear to be available for thermophilic cultures but one can generalize that these cultures grow much more rapidly in milk than mesophilic cultures; incubation periods of 4–5 h at 40–45°C are sufficient for coagulation using a 0·5% (v/v) inoculum. *Str. thermophilus* produces 0·5–0·6% lactic acid in milk[177] while the thermophilic lactobacilli produce ~0·9% in 16 h at 38°C from a 0·1% (v/v) inoculum (C. Steffen, personal communication). It should be noted that the final concentrations of lactate produced by the lactobacilli are much higher than 0·9% (Table I). The optimum temperatures for different strains of *Str. thermophilus, Lb. helveticus* and *Lb. bulgaricus* also show some variation; 39–46°C for *Str. thermophilus* and 42–48°C for the thermophilic lactobacilli.[177,178]

There is relatively little published information on the levels of lactate in cheese. Data for experimental New Zealand Cheddar[179] suggest values of 0·7–1·0% at pressing with the concentration depending on the manufacturing protocol and the % salt-in-moisture; these levels generally increase to a maximum during the first 8 days of ripening as all the lactose is metabolized; the final concentration reached is ~1·5%.[179,180] In young cheese the acid is mainly L lactate but in older cheese (~3 weeks), D lactate may be present also, due to racemization of L lactate (Section 5.1.3); its concentration increases as ripening continues and can reach 0·6% (w/w) in 6 month old cheese.[180] Pediococci are mainly responsible for this L→D transformation.[110] In Swiss cheese, the lactate level varies considerably within the cheese, being lowest at the centre and highest at the surface.[37] The reason for this is that the cheese cools faster on the outside with consequent more rapid growth and metabolism of lactose as the temperature decreases. In addition, the lactate level varies considerably during ripening reaching a maximum of 1·35% after 20 days ripening after which it decreases due to the action of propionic acid bacteria.[37]

As already stated (Section 5.2), *Leuconostoc* spp. and *Str. lactis* subsp. *diacetylactis* behave completely differently in the production of diacetyl and acetoin. *Str. lactis* subsp. *diacetylactis* metabolizes citrate and produces diacetyl and acetoin as soon as growth begins with maximum levels reaching ~3 mM acetoin and 0·1 mM diacetyl, after which the diacetyl, and sometimes the acetoin, level decreases.[130] On the other hand, although *Leuconostoc* spp. metabolize citrate at neutral pH, they do not produce diacetyl or acetoin unless citrate is present at low pH.[136,137] D and BD cultures utilize citrate much more rapidly than B cultures because of the faster rate of growth of *Str. lactis* subsp. *diacetylactis* compared to the *Leuconostoc* spp; generally in the former cultures, citrate is totally utilized in 10 h at 21°C (from a 1%, v/v, inoculum) while in B cultures, some citrate is still present after 18 h of incubation. BD and D cultures metabolize citrate and produce acetoin and diacetyl in a similar way to pure cultures of *Str. lactis* subsp. *diacetylactis* but in B cultures, citrate utilization, and therefore acetoin and diacetyl production, lags acid production slightly.[181] One might ask how diacetyl and acetoin are produced in B cultures since *Leuconostoc* spp. do not produce either compound except at low pH. The main reason appears to be that *Leuconostoc* spp. grow slowly and consequently metabolize citrate slowly in mixed culture in milk. Thus, there is still sufficient citrate present in the milk to act as precursor after the pH has become sufficiently low.[137] A comparison of the production of lactic acid, diacetyl and acetoin and citrate utilization by B and BD cultures is shown in Fig. 7. These are semi-logarithmic plots and it is important to plot the data in this way to show the relationships since bacteria multiply and produce metabolic products exponentially.

There is no information on the accumulation of acetate or 2,3-butylene glycol during the growth of *Str. lactis* subsp. *diacetylactis* or *Leuconostoc* spp. Presumably, acetate production parallels citrate dissimilation. One of the most likely reasons for the lack of information on the accumulation of 2,3-butylene glycol is the difficulty of measuring it colorimetrically[182] as it must be first oxidized to diacetyl and acetoin, with possible losses, and the diacetyl and acetoin already present may interfere. However, diacetyl, acetoin and 2,3-butylene glycol can be resolved by salting out chromatography before their individual colorimetric estimation[183,184] or more simply by gas liquid chromatography;[185] some data on 2,3-butylene glycol production by fully grown cultures have been reported recently.[185]

Diacetyl is thought to contribute to Cheddar cheese flavour but little definitive data have been published.[115] Keen and Walker[186] have shown that about 1 ppm of diacetyl occurs in cheese when made without citrate utilizers. In cheese made with *Str. cremoris* AM2, large amounts (up to 80 ppm) of acetoin were produced initially but the levels decreased to 0 ppm as ripening continued and this was accompanied by a corresponding increase in the 2,3-butylene glycol level to ~80 ppm. In cheese made with *Str. cremoris* HP, a low level (~30 ppm) of acetoin was formed and this decreased very slowly during ripening; no 2,3-butylene glycol was produced.[186] When the cheese was made with *Str. lactis* subsp.

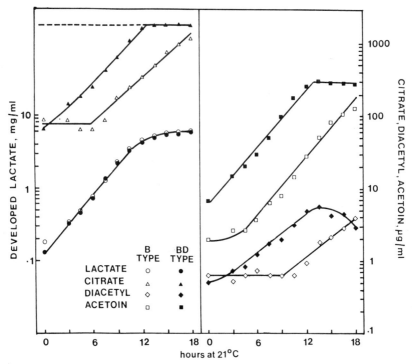

Fig. 7. Comparison of citrate utilization and lactic acid, acetoin and diacetyl production by a B- and a BD-type culture in milk at 21°C.

diacetylactis the level of diacetyl reached 11·3 ppm after 5 days of ripening after which it decreased to ~ 1 ppm after 100 days; the level of acetoin was constant at about 15 ppm throughout ripening while the level of 2,3-butylene glycol varied from 100 to 180 ppm.

6. INHIBITORS OF CULTURE GROWTH

A number of factors may adversely affect the activity of the bulk starter in the starter tank, or, more likely, in the cheese vat. These include variations in milk composition, e.g. due to mastitis and seasonal factors, and in cheese manufacturing conditions, e.g. cooking temperature and/or salt level. In addition, a range of inhibitors may be present in milk, e.g. antibiotics, agglutinins, dissolved oxygen, phage, free fatty acids, inhibitory bacteria, the lactoperoxidase system, residual sanitizers and bacteriocins.[26,48] Adherence to good quality control procedures and good manufacturing practices has helped to minimize the influence of most of these factors in the modern cheese industry. The most important inhibitory factors are antibiotic residues, bacteriocins and phage and these will be considered further.

6.1 Antibiotics

Antibiotics occur in milk primarily because of their use in controlling mastitis in the mammary gland of the cow. Little information is available regarding the levels of antibiotics required to inhibit leuconostocs but among the other starter organisms, considerable inter- and intra-species variations occur in their susceptibility to the antibiotics commonly used in

TABLE III
Concentrations (μg/ml $\pm$ SD) of four antibiotics causing 50% inhibition of various cheese starter organisms, modified from Cogan[187]

Organism	No. of strains	Antibiotic			
		Peni-cillin	Cloxa-cillin	Tetra-cycline	Strepto-mycin
Str. cremoris	4	0.11 ± 0.028	1.69 ± 0.38	0.14 ± 0.02	0.67 ± 0.15
Str. lactis	4	0.12 ± 0.025	2.16 ± 0.41	0.15 ± 0.05	0.53 ± 0.18
Str. thermophilus	3	0.01 ± 0.002	0.42 ± 0.07	0.19 ± 0.06	10.5 ± 0.29
Lb. bulgaricus	2	0.03 ± 0.006	0.29 ± 0.04	0.37 ± 0.04	3.0 ± 2.0
Lb. lactis	1	0.024	0.24	0.60	2.29

mastitis therapy (Table III). Two important practical points are apparent, i.e. mesophilic starters are less susceptible to penicillin and much more susceptible to streptomycin than are thermophilic cultures. Strict penalty schemes have reduced the impact of antibiotics very significantly.

6.2 Bacteriocins

Bacteriocins are proteins of low or high molecular weight (MW) which are secreted by many bacteria and which kill only closely related species (cf. Ref. 188). Thus, a bacteriocin-producing strain of Group N streptococci could cause domination in a mixed culture and for this reason potentially useful defined strain cultures are checked for compatibility (Section 3). Bacteriocins for the Group N streptococci have also been called lactostrepsins[19,189] or diplococcin.[190] Two surveys[190,191] have shown the potential of Group N streptococci to produce bacteriocins; in the first,[190] it was found that 7% of *Str. cremoris* and in the second[191] 9% of *Str. lactis*, 7·5% of *Str. cremoris* and 1% of *Str. lactis* subsp. *diacetylactis*, could produce bacteriocin-like activities. There is some evidence[192] that the production of bacteriocins by Group N streptococci is linked to the presence of plasmids in the producing cells (Section 7). A bacteriocin has been purified from *Str. cremoris* 346 (Ref. 190) and *Str. cremoris* 202 (Ref. 189). That from strain 346 loses 75% of its activity after heating to 100°C for 1 min; it has a MW of 5300. The mechanism of action of bacteriocins has been studied and found to require the presence of cell walls since protoplasts were not susceptible.[189]

6.3 Bacteriophage

6.3.1 Occurrence, taxonomy and structure

In contrast to antibiotics, phage remains a major problem. The term 'disturbing' phage[3,26] is used to describe those phage that attack and destroy the ability of the culture to produce acid during cheese manufacture. This designation is necessary because some phage may be present, from the cheese factory environment or carried by the culture itself, but do not inhibit the fermentation. Contamination of the culture with phage is more serious than contamination of the cheese milk; growth of the phage leads to complete lysis of the culture and loss of its ability to produce acid. Not surprisingly, therefore, lactic streptococcal phage, especially those for mesophilic cultures, have been the subject of intensive research;[9,193,194] only their main properties are described here. Phage for the leuconostocs,[195,196] *Str. thermophilus*,[57,197-199] *Lb. bulgaricus*,[198-200] *Lb. lactis*,[198-200] and *Lb. helveticus*[198-200] have been isolated; morphologically, phage for *Lb. helveticus*, are of Bradley's[201] group A, while phage for *Str. thermophilus*, *Lb. lactis* and generally *Lb. bulgaricus* are of Bradley's group B; phage for leuconostocs can be either group A or B. Phage for thermophilic cultures have not been studied as intensively as those for mesophilic cultures; this may reflect the necessity for much less growth and acid production in Swiss and Italian cheese varieties than in Cheddar and Dutch cheeses. In addition, Kurmann[202] has demonstrated that *Str. thermophilus* and thermophilic lactobacilli are lysogenic (Section 6.3.2).

Since they were first isolated by Whitehead and Cox,[203] a number of approaches to the characterization and classification of phage for Group N streptococci have been described. Indeed many of the problems of

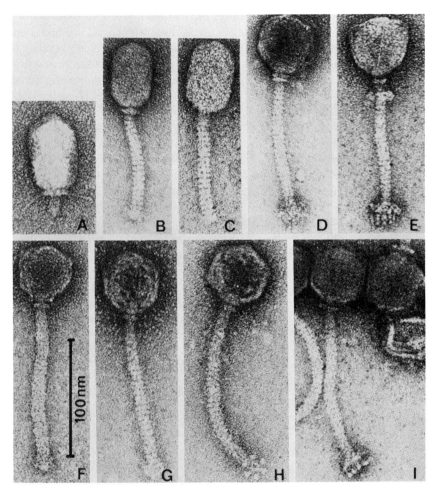

Fig. 8. Electronmicrographs of negatively stained phages active against different strains of Group N streptococci. The magnification (see bar) is the same for all pictures (from Lembke *et al.*,[215] reprinted with permission).

phage taxonomy highlighted by Ackermann[204] are experienced in the case of phage for dairy cultures because much of the data was accumulated for commercial rather than taxonomic considerations; in addition, no attempts have been made to compare phage studied by different groups. Substantial host-range data have been accumulated, establishing a high degree of diversity.[205-208] The detection of low efficiency phage–host interactions has been facilitated by the availability of improved plating media.[56,209,210] Morphologically, most lactic streptococcal phage fit into the Styloviridae family[204] or Group B of Bradley[201] in having hexagonal heads and non-contractile tails. Within this grouping there are three types: prolate and small isometric, both of which are common, and large isometric which are relatively rare.[194,211–218] Individual phage isolates are further differentiated by various ultrastructural features such as collars, baseplates, fibres and whiskers (Fig. 8). Morphological groupings of phage correlate well with serology and DNA homology studies, but not with host range data.[211,213,214,217] There is some evidence, however, that prolate phages may have broader host ranges than isometric ones.[212,214] The percentage GC for different phage varies between 32·0 and 41·0[193] and the genome from 12 to 27 Mdal.[219–223] Restriction endonuclease patterns of phage DNA cannot be used to distinguish phage;[217] DNA from a few phage have been mapped in some detail[220–223] and a map of phage P008, which attacks *Str. lactis* subsp. *diacetylactis* and which is widespread in German cheese factories, is shown in Fig. 9. (A restriction endonuclease (RE) is an enzyme which has the ability to recognize sequences of 4–6 bases in DNA and cleave the DNA only at this point of recognition. The use of REs with different recognition sequences allows one to construct 'maps' of the DNA which show the relative position of the different recognition sites.)

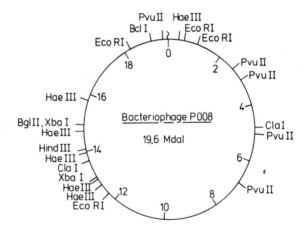

Fig. 9.   Restriction endonuclease map of bacteriophage P008. The numbers denote the molecular weight in Mdal (from Budde-Niekiel *et al.*,[216] reprinted with permission).

6.3.2 Phage–host relationships

Phage can enter two different relationships with their host bacteria—the lytic and lysogenic states. The lytic action of phage is the one of most concern in cheesemaking. In the lytic cycle, the phage adsorbs to specific receptors on the cell surface.[224] Little is known of the detailed molecular events which surround adsorption, injection, replication and lysis of the lactic acid bacterial cell. The lytic cycle is characterized by a latent period of about 45 (range 32–56) min and a burst size of about 34 (range 2–105) particles.[225] Thus, rapid development of phage can quickly generate up to 1×10^{10} phage/ml[226] and destroy the host culture. It should also be remembered that phage-associated lytic enzymes, lysins, may be important; three lysins have been purified and shown to have broad specificities.[227-229] Lysins may be responsible for inhibition in mixed cultures in which one of the component strains has been attacked by a lytic phage since a large amount of lysin may be present and may inactivate other phage-unrelated strains.

In the lysogenic (or temperate) state, the phage DNA integrates into the bacterial chromosome and is inherited by the progeny cells during growth. This makes the cell immune to further infection by this or closely related phage but it may become infected by unrelated phage. Temperate phage (or prophage) can, under certain circumstances, e.g. ultra-violet irradiation, or addition of the antibiotic, mitomycin C, be induced from the lysogenic to the lytic state with consequent replication and release of new phage. Indicator strains are used to detect these induced phage. (An indicator strain is one in which the induced phage can multiply.) Several surveys have shown that essentially all lactic streptococci are lysogenic (cf. Refs. 9, 193) and some are multilysogenic, i.e. release 2 or more distinguishable phage types;[230,231] however, there is a paucity of indicator strains except for the report of Reyrolle *et al.*[232] who found that 25% of those tested could act as indicators. Jarvis[218] found considerable homology in the DNAs of three temperate phage, suggesting that the paucity of indicator strains may be due to the use of closely related lysogenic strains which were consequently immune to infection by the induced phage. This conclusion suggests that Reyrolle *et al.*[232] used a wider range of lysogenically-different strains in their study of lysogeny. The lysogenic nature of most strains has fuelled speculation that such strains are the major source of virulent phage in dairy fermentations. Lawrence *et al.*[2] found that the removal from cheese starters of strains that released phage spontaneously contributed to a reduction in the levels of phage in the environment. An elegant study by Shimizu-Kadota and colleagues[233,234] established that the single-strain lysogenic starter used in the production of Yakult (a type of Japanese fermented milk) was the source of a virulent phage which caused culture failure. The failure was relieved by using a prophage-cured strain. In contrast, Jarvis[218] found no homology between the DNAs of lysogenic and lytic phages of several strains of Group N streptococci, implying that the release of temperate phage is not the source of lytic phage in cheese factories. From these contradictory findings one can only conclude that the ultimate source of phage in cheese manufacture remains to be determined.

There is little quantitative information in the literature concerning the levels of phage which cause problems in cheese manufacture. The kinetics of phage multiplication during cheese manufacture (Fig. 10) have been reported.[226] Contamination of the culture itself is much more important than contamination of the cheese milk. Pearce[235] presented data which showed that between 600 and 6000 phage/ml are necessary to slow down cheese manufacture although in a later paper from the same Institute, Limsowtin and Terzaghi[236] showed that an initial titre of 100 phage/ml and a multiplication factor of 1×10^7 could significantly affect acid production during cheesemaking. Pearce et al.[226] found average phage numbers in wheys at running and at milling of 1×10^5/ml and 2.4×10^8/ml, respectively. These workers calculated that this inferred an initial level of 5–500 phage/ml; at the lower level, this is equivalent to about 0.01 ml of an average milling-whey per 6000 litres of milk. Obviously, this is a very low level of contamination and clearly demonstrates the need for adequate control procedures.

6.3.3 Resistance to bacteriophage

The importance of phage in causing problems in the cheese industry has led inevitably to attempts to isolate phage-resistant strains.[26,236−238] These arise spontaneously in many cultures and are the basis for the replacement of phage sensitive strains in the newly developed defined-strain starter systems (Section 8.3). These can be unstable and quickly revert to phage sensitivity. In this connection it should be noted that in studies on the Group N streptococci the term, phage resistance, is used in a general sense, indicating any insensitivity to phage, and not in its genetic sense of specifically referring to failure of phage to adsorb to its host.

A further important factor in phage resistance is the presence of restriction/modification (R/M) systems within the cell. Restriction is suspected when a phage plaques at a much lower efficiency on a strain other than its homologous host. It is thought to be caused by the presence

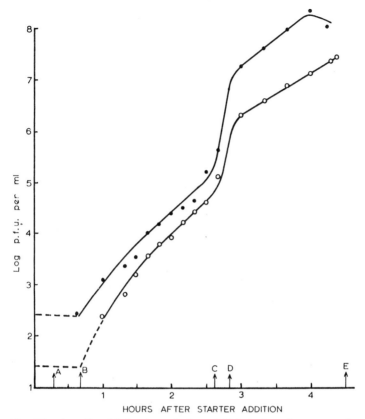

Fig. 10. Kinetics of multiplication of phage ML8 during cheese manufacture. Closed symbols, first fill; open symbols, second fill; A, set; B, cut; C, run; D, dry; E, salt (from Pearce *et al.*,[226] reprinted with permission).

of a restriction enzyme (RE) whose function is to degrade 'foreign' or invading DNA within the cell. Obviously, if an organism has a restriction enzyme, it must also protect its own DNA from destruction. This is accomplished by the presence of another enzyme (a methylase), which has the same sequence specificity as the restriction enzyme and which methylates the adenine or cytosine residues at the same specific sites which the RE recognizes, thus rendering the target sequence of the RE resistant to degradation. R/M systems are now well established in the Group N streptococci[9,206,207,219,239,240] and a restriction endonuclease has been isolated from *Str. cremoris* F.[241] This strain appears to have modification systems also since this enzyme was unable to cleave phage DNA isolated after growth on *Str. cremoris* F although it could cleave DNA from the same phage following replication on *Str. cremoris* KH.

Another factor involved in phage resistance may be the presence of plasmids, which have been implicated in encoding several different phage resistance mechanisms (Section 7.2.4).

6.3.4 Detection and enumeration of bacteriophage

Two different methods are used to detect and enumerate phage for lactic acid bacteria—the plaque method and the inhibition of acid production method. Regardless of the method used, the source of phage must be filter-sterilized (0·45 μm) before being tested. Bulk starters are centrifuged before membrane filtration of the supernatant while cheese wheys are usually filtered directly; such wheys may clog the membrane filters but this can be overcome by centrifuging or prefiltering the whey through a coarse filter before being filter-sterilized.

The plaquing method requires a medium which is nutritious and well buffered because of the large amounts of acid produced by these bacteria. Ca^{2+} are considered important for the attachment of phage to the host cells but precipitate in phosphate-buffered media; because of this, unbuffered media were often used in the past to detect phage. Ca^{2+} precipitation is overcome in glycerophosphate-buffered media which are used for the Group N streptococci,[56,209] and *Str. thermophilus*[57] but are inhibitory to many thermophilic lactobacilli;[59] for these bacteria, MRS broth[60] is recommended.[198,200] Dilutions of the filtered-sterilized source, Ca^{2+} and host organism are added to 'sloppy' agar (M 17[56] or MRS[60] broth containing 0·4% (w/v) agar) which is quickly poured on solidified agar in a petri dish. Some mesophilic phage multiply much better at 21°C (Daly and Cogan, unpublished) and others at 35°C.[242] For this reason, plates should be incubated at 21°C, 30°C and 37°C. At 30 and 37°C, plaques can often be seen after 5 h incubation but plates are generally incubated overnight. Information on the effect of temperature on phage for thermophilic cultures is not available. Incubation of plates for thermophilic phage is generally at 37–40°C[57,198,200] under aerobic conditions for *Str. thermophilus*,[57,198] or aerobic[198] or anaerobic conditions[200] for the lactobacilli. The mesophilic phages which multiply best at 35°C are known as 'raw milk phages' because they multiply better in raw or pasteurized milk than in sterilized milk and only effect acid production during the final stages of cheese manufacture;[242] the reason(s) for the more rapid multiplication in raw milk has not been determined.

In the milk inhibition assay, dilutions of the filter-sterilized source are added to pasteurized and sterilized milks inoculated with the relevant host organism. Again, it is important to incubate at different temperatures for the reasons outlined above; commonly these are: 21°C for 12 h, 30°C for 6 h and over the cheese temperature profile for 6 h (90 min at 30°C followed by an increase over 45 min to 39°C; this temperature is held for the remaining 3 h 45 min) for mesophilic cultures. Thermophilic cultures are incubated at 42°C for 4 h.[57] After incubation, the pH is determined and related to that of a control without phage but treated in the same way. A difference of ≥0·3 pH units from the control is presumptive evidence of phage.

It is possible to detect mesophilic phage by the milk inhibition test and yet see no evidence by plaquing[242] (Daly and Cogan, unpublished data); to determine if such inhibition is due to phage or some other inhibitor membrane-filtered wheys are prepared from the milks showing inhibition, diluted and retested in the milk inhibition test; persistence of the inhibition on retesting is indicative of the presence of phage. Host heterogeneity[243] may be responsible for this phenomenon but this has not been unequivocably shown. For the reasons outlined above and because acid production by the starter in milk is a key reaction in cheese manufacture, it is better to monitor phage by methods involving inhibition of acid production in milk, even though, unlike the plaquing method, it does not give categorical evidence of phage.

6.3.5 Control of bacteriophage
Data on the heat resistance of phage for the lactic streptococci are summarized in Table IV; to our knowledge, there are no data on the heat resistance of phage for thermophilic starters. From these data it can be concluded that heat treatment is not effective unless carried out at high temperatures for a long time. For this and other reasons (Section 8·2), milk for bulk starter culture production is generally heat-treated at 90°C for 20 min. Phage inhibitory media (PIM) are used, especially in the USA. These media attempt to combine adequate nutritional sources for the growth of starter bacteria (e.g. milk supplemented with corn steep liquor and yeast extract) with the inclusion of phosphates and/or citrates to chelate Ca^{2+} which are considered to be essential for phage adsorption. The use of these media has been questioned on the basis of cost,[249] effectiveness,[250] cell damage[251] and inhibition of the *Leuconostoc* component of mixed strain starter cultures.[252] More recently developed media, e.g. the externally-buffered whey-based medium of Wright and Richardson[253] and the internally-buffered Phase 4 medium developed by

TABLE IV
Comparative heat resistances of phage for the Group N streptococci

Species		Com-ponent	Temp., (°C)	D value, (min)	Z value, (°C)	Ref.
Str. cremoris	R1	Fast	65	16·0	3·3	244
		Slow	65	64·0	3·6	
Str. lactis	240		70	14·0	4·9	245
Str. lactis	C10		65	9·9	5·8	246
Str. cremoris	C1		65	1·1	5·8	244
Str. lactis	144F		70	20·0	5·8	245
Str. cremoris	E8	Fast	65	0·6	5·8	247
		Slow	65	1·9	10·2	
Str. lactis	C2	Fast	65	202·0	a	246
		Slow	65	102·0	31·0	
Strain 77		Fast	75	0·5	5·3	248
		Slow	75	1·0	4·8	
Strain 20		Fast	75	0·5	5·6	248
		Slow	75	0·9	5·9	
Strain 8		Fast	75	0·9	5·6	248
		Slow	75	2·6	5·9	
Strain 170		Fast	75	0·7	6·3	248
		Slow	75	2·6	4·6	
Strain 9		Fast	75	1·9	6·3	248
		Slow	75	15·9	4·6	

[a] Could not be calculated since only 1 D value was reported.

Sandine's group (see Ref. 254), are effective inhibitors of phage multi-plication as well as being nutritionally adequate for growth; Phase 4 has also been modified for use in the production of bulk culture for Swiss and Italian cheese varieties.[255]

Aseptic inoculation methods for bulk starter preparation have received particular attention for the prevention of phage contamination. In the Lewis system,[256] used extensively in the UK and to some extent in Ireland, inoculation of the starter milk is performed through a rubber septum using a specially designed needle assembly. Inoculation through a steam 'converger' or flame or through an inverted spring-loaded flap valve has been used also.[20,257] In the latter system, a chlorous bath is placed above the valve; the inoculation flask is pushed quickly through the bath on to the seat of the flap valve which opens and allows the inoculum to enter the tank; on withdrawal, the valve closes automatically. An aseptic inoculation device has been developed in The Netherlands and is in common use in many Dutch cheese factories. It is usually used in combination with High Efficiency Particulate Air (HEPA) filters, for which an efficiency of phage removal of 1 in 2.4×10^9 has been claimed.[258,259]

In factories where cheese vats are filled several times, phage levels can build up. These are very effectively controlled by chlorinating the vats before each fill; a contact time of 10 min with 200 ppm available chlorine is usually recommended.

7. GENETIC STUDIES ON LACTIC ACID BACTERIA

7.1 Background

The phenotypic instability of several key properties of lactic acid bacteria, especially lactic streptococci, has long been recognized, e.g. reduced ability to grow in milk, loss of ability to metabolize citrate and loss of phage resistance. In the early 1970s, biochemical studies on lactic streptococci showed that lactose and/or proteinase-deficient variants were readily isolated and led to speculation that plasmid DNA may be important in these bacteria.[260,261] Plasmids are extra-chromosomal, autonomously replicating DNA molecules which exist independently of the main genetic material of the bacterial cell, the chromosome. They are found in most bacterial species and, usually, are not required for growth.[262] When plasmids are lost, there is simultaneous loss of the phenotypic traits they encode. However, plasmids may contain genes that are essential or confer a selective advantage on cells in certain environments (cf. Refs 10, 11, 263).

The pioneering work of McKay (cf. Refs 11, 264) and Gasson and Davies (cf. Refs 10, 263, 265) confirmed the presence of plasmids in the Group N streptococci and paved the way for detailed genetic studies by many research groups. The focus now is on the molecular characterization of plasmids and genes, the development of DNA vector molecules and efficient gene transfer systems, with the long term objective of improving lactic starter bacteria by recombinant DNA technology. The main developments are outlined here, as are some potential applications of genetically engineered lactic acid bacteria in the cheese industry. Recent texts[266,267] provide a convenient introduction to molecular biology and genetic engineering terminology.

7.2 Plasmids in the Lactic Streptococci

The widespread presence of plasmids in lactic streptococci is now established. While many plasmids are cryptic, i.e. no specific function has been

TABLE V
Industrially important plasmid encoded functions in Group N streptococci[a]

Phenotype	Technological function	Plasmid size (Mdal)
Lactose fermentation	Lactic acid production	20–40
Proteinase activity	Hydrolysis of milk proteins	10–55
Citrate utilization	Production of diacetyl and CO_2	5·5
Bacteriocin production	Inhibition of other streptococci	37–75
Inhibition of phage adsorption	Resistance to bacteriophage	30–35
Restriction of phage DNA	Resistance to bacteriophage	10–30
Inhibition of phage maturation	Resistance to bacteriophage	30–50
Sensitivity to lactoperoxidase–thiocyanate–hydrogen–peroxide	Resistance to milk inhibitors	?
Slime production[b]	Consistency of fermented milks	18·5

[a] See text for references. [b] See Ref. 360. A restriction map of the plasmid, pLP 712, from *Str. lactis* 712 is shown in Fig. 12.

assigned to them, it is ironic that the key industrial metabolic functions of lactic streptococci (e.g. lactose, citrate and protein metabolism) are encoded on plasmids (Table V). Strains typically harbour 4–7 plasmids, but strains with 11 plasmids have been described;[263,264,268] plasmid profiles of strains vary considerably (Fig. 11). It is interesting to note that no naturally occurring plasmid-free strain of lactic streptococci has been identified although such isolates have been 'created' in the laboratory and are very useful for plasmid characterization and gene transfer studies.[192,240,269,270] The role of plasmids in specific metabolic functions and phage resistance is summarized briefly here.

7.2.1 Lactose metabolism

Since the discovery of the plasmid-associated nature of lactose metabolism (Lac) in *Str. lactis* C2 by McKay and co-workers,[271,272] a similar linkage has been demonstrated in many other strains[270] (cf. Refs 11, 263). These

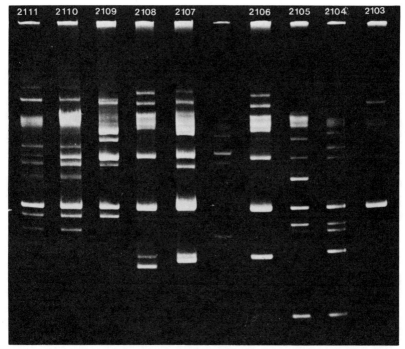

Fig. 11. Plasmid profiles of different strains of *Streptococcus lactis* subsp. *diacetylactis*. The unnumbered track carries marker plasmids (from Gasson, unpublished data).

Lac plasmids are of different sizes but are usually greater than 30 Mdal. Biochemical and genetic studies have shown that the Lac plasmid of *Str. lactis* and *Str. cremoris* strains codes for Enzyme II and Enzyme III of the PEP/PTS system and for phospho-β-galactosidase.[264,272–274] The role of the Lac plasmid of *Str. lactis* in coding for enzymes involved in tagatose metabolism has also been reported.[275] Definitive evidence for the presence of Lac plasmids in some *Str. cremoris* strains has proved difficult to obtain, suggesting that either unusually stable plasmids may be present[276] or that the *lac* genes may have been integrated into the chromosome (cf. Ref. 263).

7.2.2 Proteolytic activity

The association between proteolytic (Prt) activity and plasmid DNA has been demonstrated in many strains of lactic streptococci (cf. Refs 263, 264); initial reports were confusing because this trait is linked to Lac in some strains. Prt plasmids range in size from 9 to 50 Mdal. There is an urgent need to improve the knowledge of the biochemistry and physiology of this important trait and to determine the precise activity encoded by the plasmid(s). The definitive study of the *Str. cremoris* Wg2 proteolytic system[277] is an important advance towards this goal.

7.2.3 Citrate metabolism

The role of plasmid DNA in the ability of *Str. lactis* subsp. *diacetylactis* to metabolize citrate was first demonstrated by Kempler and McKay.[12,278] Citrate-negative variants lacked a 5·5 Mdal plasmid, present in the parent cells, and had lost the ability to transport citrate but retained citrate lyase activity,[278] implying that the plasmid encoded citrate permease. It is now considered that all *Str. lactis* subsp. *diacetylactis* strains contain a 5·5 Mdal plasmid, which are similar, based on their restriction endonuclease patterns.[12,263]

7.2.4 Bacteriophage resistance

Several recent reports have indicated that resistance to phage infection is plasmid-linked in some strains of lactic streptococci. The mechanisms involved may operate at different stages of the phage proliferation cycle. The ability of plasmids of ~30 Mdal to reduce the capacity of phage to adsorb to *Str. lactis* and *Str. cremoris* hosts has been observed.[279,280] Loss of the plasmid led to increased adsorption and, therefore, increased virulence of the infecting phage. Restriction-modification is now well established for the Group N streptococci and is considered to be a factor in phage resistance (cf. Ref. 193). Plasmids coding for restriction-modification activity have been demonstrated in *Str. cremoris* strains.[240,281,282] Plasmid-coded phage resistance systems that operate neither at the level of adsorption nor restriction have been reported recently.[283-286] They confer either total or partial resistance to phage, depending on the phage–host system. Partial resistance is manifested by a decrease in burst size which leads to a reduced plaque diameter without altering the plaque titre. The plasmids involved vary in size from 30 to 50 Mdal and have been found in all three species of Group N streptococci.

7.3 Plasmids in Other Lactic Acid Bacteria

While the mesophilic lactic acid bacteria have received most study, plasmids have been observed also in other lactic acid bacteria. Most *Str. thermophilus* strains are plasmid-free but a few contain plasmids.[263,287,288] In contrast, plasmids are widely distributed in various lactobacilli[289-291] and have been associated with antibiotic resistance[292-294] and lactose utilization.[295-297] Plasmids have also been detected in *Pediococcus*[298,299] and *Leuconostoc*[103,300] species.

7.4 Gene Transfer

The development of gene transfer systems (cf. Refs 11, 263) has been essential to the progress of genetic studies on the lactic acid bacteria, especially the Group N streptococci. The advances in this area have been rapid and have provided interesting information for the molecular biologist as well as fuelling hopes that improved starter strains will be developed by genetic manipulation techniques. Four mechanisms—transduction, conjugation, protoplast fusion and transformation—are presently available for the transfer of genes between strains of streptococci and are described briefly here.

7.4.1 Transduction

Transduction or bacteriophage-mediated transfer of bacterial DNA from one strain to another is a classical method for the movement of DNA between bacterial strains and has been demonstrated in lactic streptococci. Early reports described the transduction of streptomycin resistance and tryptophan independence using virulent phage.[301,302] However, more recently, temperate phage have been used to transfer both plasmid (mainly Lac and Prt) and chromosomal markers (cf. Refs 11, 263). The transducing phage carried only a portion of the Lac plasmid (due to transductional shortening) and some transconjugants behaved as high frequency donors when used in further transfer experiments.[265,303] Although Gasson[270] has exploited the transduction process to generate deleted derivatives of the Lac plasmid of *Str. lactis* 712, the usefulness of transduction as a means of genetic analysis of lactic streptococci is limited by its specificity and indeed much of the work to date has featured the related *Str. lactis* C2, ML3 and 712 phage–host systems (cf. Refs 11, 263). An interesting feature of these studies has been the stabilization of lactose metabolism in *Str. lactis* C2 following transduction. Analysis of transductants revealed that the transducing DNA, harbouring *lac* genes, had integrated into the chromosome.[304] Transduction of Lac to *Str. cremoris* C3 by a lysogenic phage has been reported also.[305]

Although many *Lactobacillus* spp. are lysogenic,[202,306,307] successful transduction of a genetic trait between members of this genus has not been reported. When one considers the contribution of the lambda and P phage

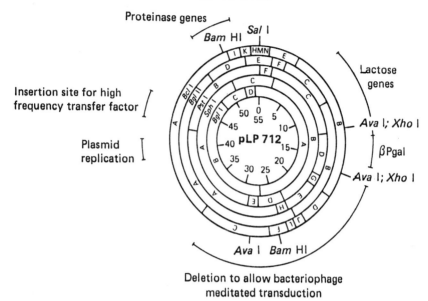

Proteinase genes

Insertion site for high frequency transfer factor

Plasmid replication

Lactose genes

Ava I; Xho I

βPgal

Ava I; Xho I

Ava I   Bam HI

Deletion to allow bacteriophage mediated transduction

Fig. 12. Restriction-endonuclease map of the metabolic plasmid pLP 712, from *Str. lactis* 712. The location of several important genetic determinants is shown (from Gasson, unpublished data).

to *E. coli* genetics, it is likely that the use of transduction as a direct method for the introduction of new genes will be further exploited in the lactic acid bacteria.

7.4.2 Conjugation

Conjugation, i.e. gene transfer requiring cell to cell contact, has been widely reported in the lactic acid bacteria and has contributed most towards the identification of plasmid-coded functions. Conjugation, or mating, is performed on solid surfaces, usually a membrane filter or agar surface, where donor and recipient strains are forced into close physical contact. Since the abundance of plasmid DNA in lactic streptococci and the lack of any natural antibiotic resistance markers causes difficulty in studying individual plasmids, the present availability of a number of plasmid-free strains that can be used as recipients in conjugation experiments is valuable.[192,240,269,270] In addition, single plasmids present in transconjugants can be isolated in quantity and analysed in detail. Kempler and McKay[308] were the first to describe the conjugative transfer of a lactose plasmid from *Str. lactis* subsp. *diacetylactis* 18–16 to a plasmid-free *Str. lactis* C2. Since then, many strains with the ability to transfer the

Lac plasmid by conjugation have been documented (cf. Refs 11, 263). High frequency transfer of this plasmid has been observed when some *Str. lactis* C2 or 712 transconjugants are used as donors.[309,310] These high frequency donors often possess enlarged Lac plasmids, in addition to the ability to aggregate and produce a novel colony morphology.[265,309-311] Other plasmid-coded traits of Group N streptococci transferred by conjugation include: proteinase activity,[309,312] restriction-modification activity,[240] mechanisms that inhibit phage replication,[283-286] bacteriocin production,[192,313,314] sucrose utilization and nisin production[283,315-317] where plasmid DNA was not detected in transconjugants. The wide host-range *Str. faecalis* plasmid, pAMBI, has been transferred by conjugation to various strains of Group N streptococci[318] and has been used to mobilize Lac and Prt plasmids of *Str. cremoris* strains that do not transfer in its absence.[312]

Conjugative transfer of plasmid DNA has also been demonstrated among lactic acid bacteria other than Group N streptococci, e.g. the Lac plasmid of *Lb. casei*.[297] pAMBI has been introduced into *Str. thermophilus*[309] and species of *Lactobacillus*[319] and *Pediococcus*.[298] Hill and co-workers[320] have recently reported the introduction of the conjugative *Str. sanguis* transposon, Tn919, into different species of *Streptococcus*, *Lactobacillus* and *Leuconostoc* and described the potential of transposons for the targeting and cloning of genes of these bacteria. The same workers subsequently improved the delivery system of Tn919 into *Str. lactis* subsp. *diacetylactis* 18–16 and demonstrated insertion in both plasmid and chromosomal DNA in that strain.[321] (A transposon is a piece of DNA which has the ability to move or transpose within or between replicons, i.e. sections of plasmid or chromosomal DNA capable of replication.)

7.4.3 Transformation

Transformation is a process whereby naked bacterial DNA can be taken up by a bacterial cell resulting in the acquisition of a specific phenotype. In the absence of phage vectors, transformation is the best method for the introduction of *in vitro* engineered DNA into an appropriate host. Since natural competence (i.e. ability to take up naked DNA), such as occurs in *Str. sanguis* and *Str. pneumoniae*, is not found in the Group N streptococci, protoplasts must be used in transformation protocols. Protoplasts are generated by the enzymatic digestion of the bacterial cell wall while maintaining an osmotically buffered environment. The exposed cell membrane is then available for DNA uptake, which is promoted by polyethylene glycol (PEG) treatment. Cell wall degradation is usually achieved with lysozyme and/or mutanolysin and sucrose, sorbitol, raffinose or succinate may be used as an osmotic buffer. Kondo and McKay[322] achieved the first transformation of protoplasts of lactic streptococci by introducing plasmid encoded *lac* genes into a Lac⁻ mutant of *Str. lactis* ML3. The frequency of transformation was very low, but refinements of the protocol have improved its efficiency. The most significant changes have been unusually long exposure to PEG,[323] the use of Ca^{2+} in the transformation buffer,[324-326] and the use of liposomes (Kok and Venema, personal communication).

Transfection (the uptake of naked bacteriophage DNA) has been demonstrated in the lactic streptococci.[327] Phage P008 DNA was introduced into *Str. lactis* subsp. *diacetylactis* F7/2 protoplasts at a frequency of 5×10^4 plaque forming units/g DNA by a protocol similar to that used for transformation experiments.

Recent studies have provided encouraging progress toward the development of a transformation system for *Lb. casei*. Methods for the production and regeneration of protoplasts are available[328] and the successful transfection of *Lb. casei* with DNA encapsulated in liposomes has also been reported.[329] In addition, Chassy[330] has described the first transformation of *Lb. casei*; the efficiency was 10^4 transformants per μg of Lac plasmid DNA and the phospho-β-galactosidase gene was integrated into the chromosome during the transformation. Hofer[331] has described transformation of Lac in naturally competent *Lb. lactis*.

7.4.4 Protoplast fusion

Protoplasts can also be used to achieve gene transfer by a fusion process. In this method, total gene pools of different cell types can be mixed following protoplast fusion in the presence of polyethylene glycol. Following regeneration of the fused protoplasts, recombinants can be isolated. Gasson[332] transferred both plasmid and chromosomal markers between derivatives of *Str. lactis* 712 using this technique. Okamoto and co-workers also reported[333] recombination of chromosomal markers from derivatives of *Str. lactis* 527 following protoplast fusion. This technique offers some potential for the construction of improved starter strains but further research is needed.

7.5 Gene Cloning

The accumulated knowledge derived from plasmid biology and gene transfer studies has created a situation where the lactic streptococci may now be manipulated genetically with realistic prospects of creating improved strains for use in the dairy industry. Recombinant DNA technology is the most powerful approach for achieving this end. This requires suitable vectors as well as efficient transformation protocols. A vector is a replicon consisting of plasmid and/or bacteriophage DNA into which passenger DNA can be inserted without affecting the vector's ability to replicate in the appropriate recipient cell. Conventional vectors derived from *E. coli* plasmids (e.g. pACYC184, pAT153) or *Str. sanguis* plasmids (e.g. pDB101 and pGB301) have been used in cloning studies on genes of Group N streptococci and lactobacilli.[274,323,334,335] In addition, shuttle vectors capable of replicating in *Bacillus*, *E. coli* and Group N streptococci, have been constructed recently. These include the pGK series[336] derived from the *Str. cremoris* pWV01 plasmid and the pCK[326] and pNZ series,[337] both derived from the pSH71 cryptic plasmid of *Str. lactis* 712. The pNZ plasmids can replicate in *S. aureus* also.

Restriction fragments of the *Str. lactis* C2 Lac plasmid, pLM2001, have been cloned into the streptococcal cloning vector, pDB101.[335] When transformed into a strain of *Str. sanguis* Challis which was defective in Enzyme II, Enzyme III and phospho-β-galactosidase of the PEP/PTS system, the recombinant plasmid restored the Lac$^+$ phenotype. Significantly, when the same strain was transformed directly with purified restriction fragments of pLM2001, the Lac$^+$ phenotype was also restored although plasmid DNA could not be detected in the transformants. This suggested that the *lac* genes had integrated into and become stabilized in the chromosome. Kondo and McKay[323] also cloned *lac* genes from *Str. lactis* LM0230 using the pGB301 vector. However, in this instance, the recombinant plasmid was returned to a *Str. lactis* Lac$^-$ derivative using protoplast transformation, demonstrating that classical cloning could be applied in full to these bacteria. Maeda and Gasson[274] have cloned the gene for phospho-β-galactosidase from *Str. lactis* 712 into *E. coli* using the pAT153 vector. de Vos and co-workers[337] have reported the cloning and expression of this gene in *E. coli*, *B. subtilis* and *Str. lactis*. Likewise, the gene for D-tagatose-1,6-diphosphate aldolase from *Str. lactis* H1 has been cloned in *E. coli* using the pACYC184 vector.[334] In the case of *Lb. casei* 64H, the gene for phospho-β-galactosidase has also been cloned in *E. coli*.[297]

Considerable effort is being devoted to the cloning of proteinase genes of lactic streptococci. Although difficulties have been experienced, possibly due to the lethality of the enzyme(s) in some hosts, significant progress has been achieved. Kok and co-workers[277] cloned proteinase genes of *Str. cremoris* Wg2 in *B. subtilis* using a pGKV2 shuttle vector. Crossed immunoelectrophoretic analysis of the *Bacillus* transformants showed that the cloned restriction fragment specified two proteins of the *Str. cremoris* Wg2 proteolytic system. Most significantly, when the recombinant plasmid was introduced into a plasmid-free derivative (Prt⁻) of *Str. lactis* 712, the Prt⁺ phenotype was restored to wild-type levels. The P_{111}-proteinase of *Str. cremoris* SK11 has been cloned in *E. coli* using phage lambda vectors,[337] while the proteinase activity of *Str. lactis* 712 has been cloned into *Bacillus* and subsequently transformed into *Str. lactis*.[326]

The citrate plasmid of *Str. lactis* subsp. *diacetylactis* 176 has been studied extensively and cloned both in its entirety and as various segments into *E. coli* (cf. Ref. 263).

Chopin *et al.*[338] have cloned a gene which enhances UV resistance and prophage stability from the *Str. lactis* pIL7 plasmid using the *Bacillus* pHV1301 vector. The recombinant plasmid was transferred to other *Str. lactis* strains by either protoplast transformation or protoplast fusion and expression of the cloned genes detected.

While the cloning experiments just described represent rapid progress towards the genetic manipulation of lactic streptococci, considerable research aimed at understanding molecular processes such as plasmid replication, gene expression and regulation in these bacteria is required. The recent construction of cloning, promoter-screening and terminator-screening shuttle vectors for *Str. lactis* and *B. subtilis*, the first reports of sequences of specific lactic streptococcal genes and the isolation and characterization of lactic streptococcal promoters[337,339] confirm the progress being made in this area.

7.6 Potential Applications of Genetic Studies on Cheese Starters

The intensity of the genetic research effort presently being devoted to the lactic acid bacteria, especially the Group N streptococci, is rapidly changing them from being genetically unknown to genetically well-characterized micro-organisms. Provided that this effort is continued and backed up by biochemical and physiological studies, genetic advances may soon be applied to improve existing starter strains and produce new ones. This represents an exciting challenge for the dairy microbiologist who must preserve the traditional acceptance of starter bacteria by the judicious use of the powerful recombinant DNA techniques now available. It is essential that starter strains used in the dairy industry in the future should contain only DNA from the lactic acid bacteria themselves or from other bacteria approved for use in foods. This means that 'food grade' vectors will have to be constructed.

A major requirement of a cheese starter culture is the ability to produce acid at a predictable rate. It is envisaged that the manipulation of the genes encoding lactose metabolism will allow stabilization and amplification of this trait in useful strains. In addition, available strain banks will be extended by improving lactose utilization in phage-resistant strains and by cloning the *lac* genes into strains isolated from natural sources which are usually Lac$^-$.

Proteinase activity in lactic acid bacteria also has a role in growth in milk. While considerable further research on both the biochemistry and genetics of this trait is essential, stabilization and amplification of this activity would benefit the more rapid production of unripened cultured milk products. In the case of ripened cheeses, manipulation of proteinase activity, either of the existing starter proteolytic system or by the introduction of non-starter proteinases, may have applications in avoiding flavour defects, e.g. bitterness, and in accelerating the ripening of cheeses, with associated savings in storage costs. A related objective would be the production of highly flavoured cheese bases for use in other foods.

Stabilization and amplification of citrate genes in flavour-producing bacteria may have benefits for flavour and eye formation in some cheeses. The possibility of maximizing diacetyl production without concommitant CO_2 production may have potential for cheese flavour improvement, even if it appears unattainable with present biochemical knowledge.

Although empirical selection procedures have provided useful phage-insensitive strains (Section 3.1), there is enormous potential for genetic manipulation in this area. At least three plasmid-encoded phage resistance mechanisms have been discovered (Section 7.2.4) and plasmid transfer and gene cloning strategies will be used to increase and stabilize this property in existing and new strains. More detailed analysis of phage–host interactions may allow the cloning of components of the immune system(s) associated with lysogeny.

The production of inhibitory substances by lactic acid bacteria has potential practical applications that may benefit from genetic studies. Genetically-modified strains capable of producing (and resistant to) high concentrations of nisin would be useful to control undesirable sporeformers in cheeses and other food systems. The concept of cloning other food additives, e.g. lysozyme, in lactic acid bacteria may also be attractive. In this regard, the future use of controlled expression systems (e.g. in response to higher cooking temperatures or to added salt), may offer the starter microbiologist useful options.

The dairy industry also has a need for strains of starter bacteria with enhanced resistance to ions (improved growth in phosphate-containing, phage-inhibitory media) and enhanced tolerance to freeze-drying. The latter would allow extension of the strain bank available for direct addition to milk in the cheese vat. Conceivably, it would be desirable to maximize all the required characteristics in an individual starter strain for a single fermentation. The achievement of these objectives will require a continuation of the present research effort and also a closer interaction between molecular biologists, microbial physiologists and cheese technologists that share an interest in the challenges of the lactic acid bacteria.

8. COMMERCIAL PRODUCTION OF CULTURES

A major technological development in recent years has been the provision of cultures in a diversity of forms by commercial supply companies and dairy research centres. The use of concentrated cultures to inoculate either the bulk culture milk or the cheese milk itself has allowed the cheese industry, when desired, to discontinue in-factory starter propagation with its inherent risk of contamination with undesirable micro-organisms and phage.

8.1 Supply of Culture Inocula

The principles of culture growth, harvesting and storage required to achieve high numbers of cells that retain activity over extended storage periods are now well established.[340,341] Batch fermentation conditions are favoured with the choice of medium dictated by nutritional requirements, ease of harvesting and cost. Milk or whey-based media with additives such as yeast extract, protein digests and corn steep liquor are frequently used. Temperature and pH are usually controlled to provide optimum cell yields; aeration is not used since these are essentially anaerobic bacteria. In the case of mesophilic cultures, 30°C and pH 6·0–6·5 are frequently used, with neutralization by NaOH or NH₄OH. Mixing of the alkali requires gentle agitation of the culture which may lead to accumulation of H_2O_2

(cf. Ref. 342) and consequent inhibition of growth. This may be avoided by using a 'head' of nitrogen over the culture. While yield and activity are important in the growth of cultures, it is also essential to maintain the integrity and homogeneity of the original culture. These may be lost in the case of some strains which accumulate slow-coagulating variants when grown in media containing readily available amino-nitrogen. In the case of mixed cultures, the balance may be upset by growth at controlled pH.[343,344]

Growth of cultures, as described above, gives a 2–8 fold increase in cell density compared to traditionally grown, unneutralized starters; such cultures may be frozen immediately to −40°C for storage and supply to the factories.[345] However, the cells are usually harvested by centrifugation or filtration and resuspended in a medium (e.g. milk) containing cryo-protective agents (e.g. lactose, glycerol) before being frozen or freeze-dried.[346,347] Freeze-dried cultures offer distinct advantages for storage and transport. Depending on the degree of concentration, the culture may be suitable for inoculation of the bulk culture vessel (concentrates with cell density $\sim 10^{10}$/g) or for direct addition to the cheesemilk (super-concentrates with cell density $\sim 10^{13}$/g).

These concepts have also been applied to thermophilic bacteria. Rousseaux *et al.*[40] highlighted the advantages of using concentrated, frozen, mixed thermophilic starters for the direct inoculation of Gruyère cheesemilk, which, with Emmental, has the advantage of a low level of inoculum, 3–10% of that used for many other cheeses. While acknowledging the advantages of freeze-dried cultures, Auclair and Accolas[35] referred to the inability of thermophilic concentrates to withstand this process, with *Lb. bulgaricus* being particularly sensitive to the freeze-drying step.

8.2 Bulk Culture Preparation

Super-concentrates that can be added directly to the cheese milk in the vat are finding increasing industrial use. They would appear to be especially attractive for small factories due to saving of labour and facilities but may be economically uncompetitive for large factories. However, the preparation of active bulk starter culture, free of disturbing phage, at the cheese factory remains a key aspect of cheese production at present. While there is a general concensus that the bulk culture should be protected from phage attack, there are different philosophies as to how this can be best achieved. Some users favour physical protection methods based on the total exclusion of disturbing phage, while others rely on the phage inhibitory properties of the selected culture media. A combination of these concepts may be practised also.

A variety of media may be used to prepare the bulk culture, e.g. phage inhibitory media (PIM), whole milk, skim milk, or skim milk fortified with extra solids.[348] Reconstituted antibiotic-free skim milk powder (10–14% solids) should be the choice. In modern bulk-culture production, the medium (and the head-space of the tank) are heated at $\geq 90°C$ for 20 min. Heating has several effects. It destroys contaminating bacteria which might be present and whose subsequent growth could compete with culture growth or cause problems subsequently in the cheese. It causes more rapid growth of the culture because of the production of more available nitrogen from partial hydrolysis of the milk protein. It destroys natural inhibitors present in the milk and it destroys any phage which might be present in the skim milk powder. To further improve the efficacy of phage destruction in the head space, this may be steamed during the heating period. Cooling of the bulk culture medium represents a possible hazard in terms of phage contamination and therefore either a pressurized tank is used or the air, which is sucked into the tank as it is cooled, is filtered, through a High Efficiency Particulate Air filter.[258,259] For simplicity, some cheese manufacturers prefer to heat-treat the bulk culture medium in a plate heater ($90°C \times 20\,s$) before addition to the pre-sterilized bulk starter tank.[348] Such a treatment would not inactivate all phage (Table IV) and would generate little additional growth stimulatory compounds. The latter could be advantageous since the low heat-treated medium simulates cheese milk more closely than does more severely heated milk. Culture inoculation is another critical step in bulk culture preparation and several systems for aseptic inoculation have been described (Section 6.3.5). The inoculum volume and the time and temperature of incubation of the bulk culture must be carefully controlled to avoid over-ripe cultures with consequent loss of activity during storage.

The use of PIM to control phage is common in the USA and to a lesser extent in Europe.[250] The cost and lack of effectiveness of available PIM led Richardson and co-workers[253,349] to combine the concepts of pH control, lactose limitation and relatively low concentrations of phosphate in the development of a PIM for bulk culture preparation at cheese factories. This system uses diluted factory whey with added yeast extract and phosphates; the pH is controlled by added NH_4OH. The culture is incubated until the lactose is exhausted. The control of pH increases cell number (4-fold greater than conventional cultures) and the absence of làctose prevents the pH from decreasing after growth, thus minimizing injury by acid during storage. This system has also been used for thermophilic cultures.[350] Another approach to pH control, which avoids the need to attach pH electrodes, recorders and alkali injectors to bulk tanks, is the development of PIM with internal buffers;[254,255] these provide a high density of active cells with protection from phage and enhanced storage characteristics. Attractive features of these systems are reduced cheese vat inoculation rates, extended storage life of cultures, reduction in the bulk culture volumes and reduced labour requirements, especially at weekends. Manipulation of the pH of bulk cultures to provide a more active bulk culture has also been recommended by New Zealand researchers[351] who used a one or two shot neutralization to double cell yield.

8.3 Practical Use of Cultures

As mentioned already (Section 1), the different traditions observed in cheesemaking have been accompanied by a variety of approaches to the use of cultures. Current developments in the use of mesophilic cultures emphasize the desire to maximize process control so as to ensure products of consistent composition and quality. In The Netherlands, this has been achieved by maintaining the proper strain balance in 'P' (practice) starters by careful attention to the conditions of storage and propagation. These starters can be used in large-scale cheesemaking without rotation, provided they are protected from disturbing phage.[3] While this report describes a fascinating study of the interactions of phage and starter strains in mixed cultures, it also highlights the complexity of using mixtures of unknown composition.

In contrast, many mixed-strain mesophilic cultures used in countries other than The Netherlands are quite sensitive to phage attack and can be used only in rotations.[29,348] The basis of this practice is that phage remaining from the use of one culture should have cleared by the time a phage-related starter is used again. It is difficult to anticipate problems with this system due to lack of precise information on the phage-relationships of the mixtures. This makes process control difficult and leads to variations in manufacturing schedules. The use of numerous strains contributes to an increase in the number and diversity of phage in the factory.[3,29]

The use of defined strains of mesophilic cultures was pioneered in New Zealand where there is close interaction between the Dairy Research

Institute and the cheese industry. The demands of large-scale cheese production have necessitated the fine-tuning of this system so that now only a small number (often a pair) of phage-insensitive strains are used daily without rotation. Indeed, the strains presently available are remarkably phage resistant and have been used for years without replacement.[2,352] The known identity of the strains facilitates phage monitoring and trouble-shooting in the factory and ensures maximum information on culture performance. It is noteworthy that it is not necessary to have a phage-free system. Indeed, it is very likely that phage are always present but do not interfere with manufacturing schedules.[352] These are slow-replicating phage and were observed as early as 1951[353] but have received little detailed research attention.

Carefully selected defined strains are very stable when used in combination with protective measures at the bulk culture stage and good manufacturing practices, e.g. chlorination of vats between fills and careful disposal of whey. The occasional appearance of fast-replicating virulent phage can necessitate the use of a replacement strain. This may be a phage-unrelated strain with established cheesemaking characteristics[2] or a bacteriophage-insensitive mutant (BIM) of the strain which succumbed to phage in the factory. Based on the observations of Galesloot et al.[34] and Thomas and Lowrie[354] on starter growth in the presence of phage, several groups of workers (Refs 25–27, 236–238, 355, 356) have isolated BIMs of defined strains. In practice, the strain is incubated in sterile milk in the presence of phage or factory whey until coagulation is achieved (24–36 h). This culture is then plated on a medium which facilitates the selection of variants with good acid-producing ability.[357,358] Isolates are then characterized for suitability for cheesemaking by the criteria outlined earlier (Section 3.1). Although this approach to strain replacement is widespread in Australia[25,26] and in the USA,[355] it should be noted that for unknown reasons, BIMs have been isolated only from some strains.[238,356] In addition, some BIMs demonstrate properties different from the parent strains and may produce undesirable flavours in cheese.[359] Further studies are needed to clarify the potential of BIMs as replacement strains in starter cultures. However, their successful use could be facilitated by closer interaction between culture suppliers and the cheese industry.

Disturbing phage levels in cheese factories can be reduced greatly when only a small number of strains, whether mixtures or defined blends, are used. Thus, the more widespread use of these strains is essential for the achievement of maximum process control. The use of defined strains by the cheese industry will facilitate the commercialization of benefits provided by studies on the genetic manipulation of starter bacteria. However, mixtures are still favoured by many users and there is a challenge to the starter microbiologist to establish the biochemical characteristics that are required in strains to ensure the desired flavour and other attributes in a variety of cheese products.

9. CONCLUDING COMMENTS

In this chapter, we have reviewed the considerable progress that has been made on the microbiology and technology of cheese starter cultures during the past few decades. The diversity of this topic is evident from the contrast between the widespread use of totally undefined mixed starters (artisan starters) in cheesemaking, on the one hand, and the potential use of genetically engineered strains on the other. Bridging the gap between these two extremes is a major challenge to the dairy microbiologist at present. While most starters of unknown microbiological composition are capable of yielding a good quality cheese, they can be unpredictable, resulting in partial or total failure to produce acid; this cannot be tolerated in modern-day mechanized and, perhaps, automated cheese plants. Exceptions to this general statement are the P-starters used in The Netherlands (Section 3.1). Defined strain blends, capable of the consistent acidification of Cheddar and some 'thermophilic cheeses' (e.g. Emmental), have been developed. Further research is needed to extend the use of similar blends to the manufacture of a wider range of cheeses. This may involve a detailed study of the associative growth interactions of individual strains and of their contributions to flavour and textural changes during cheese ripening. The extension of the use of defined strain systems should help to maximize the benefits of genetically manipulated strains in the future.

Inhibition of acid production by phage remains a major problem in cheesemaking and is, of course, a major factor in the acceptability of either mixed or defined strain cultures. The lack of detailed information on the molecular level events associated with phage attack, i.e. phage adsorption, DNA injection and phage replication is surprising and is to be regretted. A concerted effort in this area is necessary to ensure maximum return from studies aimed at providing phage-resistant strains. In addition, there is a need to clarify aspects of bacteriophage insensitive mutants (BIMs), e.g.

the nature of their ¦phage¦resistance, their reversion to phage sensitivity and, indeed, the failure to isolate BIMs from many strains. Recent advances in techniques available to characterize and compare phage should allow the relationship between temperate and lytic phage (and the source of the latter in cheese factories) to be clarified. There is also a need to develop improved methods for phage monitoring and modern techniques based on recombinant DNA technology may find application in this regard.

With a few notable exceptions, little detailed research has been devoted to the industrially-important traits of starter bacteria. Studies are needed to bring cohesion to the complex proteinase systems to extend some of the excellent results already achieved in this area (Section 5.3). The factors that affect and regulate the transport and metabolism of sugars, especially lactose, have been greatly clarified, yet, in view of the importance of lactic acid production from lactose in cheesemaking, it is surprising that so few of the enzymes of the various pathways of lactose metabolism have been purified and characterized at the molecular level (Section 5.1). Our knowledge of citrate metabolism is even less detailed as none of the enzymes involved have been purified. Such 'classical' biochemical information is needed to complement the progress that has and is being made in the role of plasmids in starter cultures and the application of recombinant DNA technology in constructing and improving strains. Research in this area has received a timely impetus from the recent upsurge in genetic studies on these bacteria; some examples of the anticipated benefits of this work were given in Section 7.6. Success will depend on a continued research commitment and on an interdisciplinary approach to solving the problems encountered. For example, improved understanding of the biochemistry of the cell wall and membrane is central to improvements, including genetic manipulation, in aspects of sugar metabolism, proteinase activity, phage–host interactions and tolerance to freeze-drying. Indeed, there is an urgent need to extend the range of mesophilic and thermophilic strains available as freeze-dried concentrates.

It is likely that maximum progress on the application of dairy culture research has been impeded by the conservative nature of the cheese industry and by the lack, in many instances, of an effective interaction between researchers, culture suppliers and cheese manufacturers. It is important that improved dialogue is achieved to maximize the benefits of the present major genetic research effort. Finally, there is a need to devote comparatively more research effort to all aspects of thermophilic starter cultures.

REFERENCES

1. Limsowtin, G. K. Y., Heap, H. A. and Lawrence, R. C., *N.Z. J. Dairy Sci. Technol.*, 1977, **12**, 101.
2. Lawrence, R. C., Heap, H. A., Limsowtin, G. K. Y. and Jarvis, A. W., *J. Dairy Sci.*, 1978, **61**, 1181.
3. Stadhouders, J. and Leenders, G. J. M., *Neth. Milk Dairy J.*, 1984, **38**, 157.
4. Proceedings of Conference of The Society for General Microbiology (Irish Branch), Cork, Ireland, 1982, *Ir. J. Food Sci. Technol.*, 1983, **7**, 1–82.
5. Symposium: Lactic Acid Bacteria in Foods, Wageningen, The Netherlands, *Ant. v. Leeuwenhoek*, 1983, **49**, 209–352.
6. Gilliland, S. E., *Bacterial Starter Cultures*, 1985, CRC Press, Florida.
7. Davies, F. L. and Law, B. A., *Advances in the Microbiology and Biochemistry of Cheese and Fermented Milk*, 1984, Elsevier Applied Science Publishers, London.
8. McKay, L. L. In: *Developments in Food Microbiology, Vol. 1*, R. Davies (ed.), 1982, Applied Science Publishers, London, p. 153.
9. Klaenhammer, T. R. In: *Advances in Applied Microbiology, Vol 30*, A. I. Laskin (ed.), 1984, Academic Press, New York, p. 1.
10. Davies, F. L. and Gasson, M. J., *J. Dairy Res.*, 1981, **48**, 363.
11. Kondo, G. and McKay, L. L., *J. Dairy Sci.*, 1985, **68**, 2143.
12. Kempler, G. M. and McKay, L. L., *J. Dairy Sci.*, 1981, **64**, 1527.
13. Van Niel, C. B., Kluyver, A. J. and Deux, H. G., *Biochem. Z.*, 1929, **210**, 234.
14. Michaelian, M. B., Hoecker, W. H. and Hammer, B. W., *J. Dairy Sci.*, 1938, **21**, 213.
15. Matuszewski, T., Pijanowski, E. and Supinska, J., *Polish Agric. Forest Ann.*, 1936, **36**, 1.
16. Van Beynum, J. and Pette, J. W., *Verslag. handbouk. Onderzoek*, 1936, **42**, 360.
17. Swartling, P. F., *J. Dairy Res.*, 1951, **18**, 256.
18. Lee, D. A. and Collins, E. B., *J. Dairy Sci.*, 1976, **59**, 405.
19. Kozak, W., Bardowski, J. and Dobrzanski, W. T., *J. Dairy Res.*, 1978, **45**, 247.
20. Whitehead, H. R., *Bacteriol. Rev.*, 1953, **17**, 109.
21. Lawrence, R. C. and Pearce, L. E., *Dairy Industries Int.*, 1972, **37**, 73.
22. Heap, H. A. and Lawrence, R. C., *N.Z. J. Dairy Sci. Technol.*, 1976, **11**, 16.
23. Davey, G. P. and Pearce, L. E., *N.Z. J. Dairy Sci. Technol.*, 1980, **15**, 51.
24. Hull, R. R., *Aust. J. Dairy Technol.*, 1977, **32**, 65.
25. Czulak, J., Bant, D. J., Blyth, S. C. and Crace, J. B., *Dairy Industries Int.*, 1979, **44**(2), 17.
26. Hull, R. R., *Aust. J. Dairy Technol.*, 1983, **38**, 149.
27. Richardson, G. H., Hong, G. L. and Ernstrom, C. A., *J. Dairy Sci.*, 1980, **63**, 1981.
28. Danielle, S. D. and Sandine, W. E., *J. Dairy Sci.*, 1981, **64**, 407.
29. Thunell, R. K., Sandine, W. E. and Bodyfelt, F. W., *J. Dairy Sci.*, 1981, **64**, 2270.
30. Huggins, A. R. and Sandine, W. E., *J. Dairy Sci.*, 1979, **62**, 70.
31. Hurley, M., Timmons, P., Drinan, F., Cogan, T. M. and Daly, C., *Ir. J. Food Sci. Technol.*, 1982, **6**, 210.
32. Daly, C., *Ir. J. Food Sci. Technol.*, 1983, **7**, 39.

33. Daly, C., *Ant. v. Leeuwenhoek*, 1983, **49**, 297.
34. Galesloot, Th. E., Hassing, F. and Stadhouders, J., *17th Intern. Dairy Congr.*, 1966, Vol. D, p. 492.
35. Auclair, J. and Accolas, J-P., *Ir. J. Food Sci. Technol.*, 1983, **7**, 27.
36. Wood, N. J., *Dairy Industries Int.*, 1981, **46**(12), 14.
37. Steffen, C., IDF Doc 126, 1980, **16**.
38. Steffen, C., *Deutsche Molkerei-Zeitung*, 1980, **101**, 1186.
39. Valles, E. and Mocquot, G., *Le Lait*, 1968, **48**, 631.
40. Rousseaux, P., Vassal, L., Valles, E., Auclair, J. and Mocquot, G., *Le Lait*, 1968, **48**, 241.
41. Garvie, E. I. and Farrow, J. A. E., *Intern. J. Syst. Bacteriol.*, 1982, **32**, 453.
42. Schleifer, K. H., Kraus, J., Dvorak, C., Klipper-Bälz, R., Collins, M. D. and Fischer, W., *System. Appl. Microbiol.*, 1985, **6**, 183.
43. Farrow, J. A. E. and Collins, M. D., *J. gen. Microbiol.*, 1984, **130**, 357.
44. Garvie, E. I., *J. Dairy Res.*, 1960, **23**, 283.
45. Garvie, E. I., *Intern. J. Syst. Bacteriol.*, 1983, **33**, 118.
46. Hontebeyrie, M. and Gasser, F., *Intern. J. Syst. Bacteriol.*, 1977, **27**, 9.
47. Galesloot, Th. E. and Hassing, F., *Neth. Milk Dairy J.*, 1961, **15**, 225.
48. Stadhouders, J., *Milchwissenschaft*, 1974, **29**, 329.
49. Schlegel, J. A. and Babel, F. J. In: *Developments in Industrial Microbiol.*, *Vol.* 7, 1966, American Institute of Biological Sciences, p. 247.
50. Weiss, N., Schillinger, U. and Kandler, O., *System appl. Microbiol.*, 1983, **4**, 552.
51. Thomas, T. D. and Crow, V. L., *Appl. Environ. Microbiol.*, 1984, **48**, 186.
52. Turner, K. W. and Martley, F. G., *Appl. Environ. Microbiol.*, 1983, **45**, 1932.
53. Radke-Mitchell, L. and Sandine, W. E., *J. Food Protect.*, 1984, **47**, 245.
54. Accolas, J-P., Veaux, M. and Auclair, J., *Le Lait*, 1971, **51**, 249.
55. Elliker, P. R., Anderson, A. W. and Hannesson, G., *J. Dairy Sci.*, 1956, **39**, 1611.
56. Terzaghi, B. E. and Sandine, W. E., *Appl. Environ. Microbiol.*, 1975, **29**, 807.
57. Accolas, J-P. and Spillmann, H., *J. appl. Bacteriol.*, 1979, **47**, 135.
58. Tinson, W., Hillier, A. J. and Jago, G. R., *Aust. J. Dairy Sci. Technol.*, 1982, **37**, 8.
59. Shankar, P. A. and Davies, F. L., *J. Soc. Dairy Tech.*, 1977, **30**, 28.
60. De Man, J. C., Rogosa, M. and Sharpe, M. E., *J. appl. Bacteriol.*, 1960, **23**, 130.
61. Nickels, C. and Leesment, H., *Milchwissenschaft*, 1964, **19**, 374.
62. Waes, G., *Neth. Milk Dairy J.*, 1968, **22**, 29.
63. McDonough, F. E., Hargrove, R. E. and Tittsler, R. P., *J. Dairy Sci.*, 1963, **46**, 386.
64. Reddy, M. S., Vedamuthu, E. R., Washam, C. J. and Reinbold, G. W., *Appl. Microbiol.*, 1972, **24**, 947.
65. Kempler, G. M. and McKay, L. L., *Appl. Environ. Microbiol.*, 1980, **39**, 926.
66. IDF Standard, 117: 1983.
67. Dills, S. S., Apperson, A., Schmidt, M. R. and Saier, Jr., M. H., *Microbiol. Rev.*, 1980, **44**, 385.
68. McKay, L. L., Miller, A., III, Sandine, W. E. and Elliker, P. R., *J. Bacteriol.*, 1970, **102**, 804.
69. Thompson, J., *J. Bacteriol.*, 1980, **144**, 683.
70. Hemme, D., Nardi, M. and Jette, D., *Le Lait*, 1980, **60**, 595.

71. Hutkins, R., Morris, H. A. and McKay, L. L., *Appl. Environ. Microbiol.*, 1985, **50**, 772.
72. Premi, L., Sandine, W. E. and Elliker, P. R., *Appl. Microbiol.*, 1972, **24**, 51.
73. Hickey, M. W., Hillier, A. J. and Jago, G. R., *Appl. Environ. Microbiol.*, 1986, **51**, 825.
74. Romano, A. H., Trifone, J. D. and Brustolon, M., *J. Bacteriol.*, 1979, **139**, 93.
75. Lawrence, R. C. and Thomas, T. D. In: *Microbial Technology*, A. T. Ball, D. C. Ellwood and C. Ratledge (eds), Society of General Microbiology, Symposium, 1979, Vol. 24, p. 187.
76. Farrow, J. A. E., *J. appl. Bacteriol.*, 1980, **49**, 493.
77. Crow, V. L. and Thomas, T. D., *J. Bacteriol.*, 1984, **157**, 28.
78. Park, Y. H. and McKay, L. L., *J. Bacteriol.*, 1982, **149**, 420.
79. Thomas, T. D., Turner, K. W. and Crow, V. L., *J. Bacteriol.*, 1980, **144**, 672.
80. Bissett, H. D. L. and Anderson, R. L., *J. Bacteriol.*, 1974, **117**, 318.
81. Thomas, T. D., Ellwood, D. C. and Longyear, V. M. C., *J. Bacteriol.*, 1979, **138**, 109.
82. Johnson, K. G. and McDonald, J. J., *J. Bacteriol.*, 1974, **117**, 667.
83. McFeters, G. A., Sandine, W. E. and Elliker, P. R., *J. Bacteriol.*, 1967, **93**, 914.
84. Crow, V. L. and Thomas, T. D., *J. Bacteriol.*, 1982, **151**, 600.
85. Collins, L. B. and Thomas, T. D., *J. Bacteriol.*, 1974, **120**, 52.
86. Crow, V. L. and Pritchard, G. G., *Biochim. Biophys. Acta*, 1976, **438**, 90.
87. Crow, V. L. and Pritchard, G. G., *J. Bacteriol.*, 1977, **131**, 82.
88. Jonas, H. A., Anders, R. F. and Jago, G. R., *J. Bacteriol.*, 1972, **111**, 397.
89. Singh, H. P., Rao, M. V. R. and Dutta, S. M., *Milchwissenschaft*, 1979, **34**, 475.
90. Felton, E. A. and Niven, C. F., *J. Bacteriol.*, 1953, **65**, 482.
91. Hontebeyrie, M. and Gasser, F., *Biochimie*, 1973, **55**, 1047.
92. Olive, C., Geroch, M. E. and Levy, H. R., *J. Biol. Chem.*, 1971, **246**, 2047.
93. Yashima, S. and Kitahara, K., *J. gen. appl. Microbiol.*, 1968, **14**, 359.
94. Yashima, S., Kawai, K., Kazahaya, T., Okami, Y. and Sasaki, Y., *J. gen. appl. Microbiol.*, 1971, **17**, 173.
95. Kazahaya, T., Kawai, K., Yashima, S. and Sasaki, Y., *J. gen. appl. Microbiol.*, 1972, **18**, 43.
96. Hatanaka, A., Adachi, O., Chiyonobu, T. and Ameyama, M., *Agric. Biol. Chem.*, 1971, **35**, 1304.
97. Gordon, G. L. and Doelle, H. W., *Microbios*, 1974, **9**, 199.
98. Garland, R. C., *Arch. Biochem. Biophys.*, 1973, **157**, 36.
99a. Somkuti, G. A. and Steinberg, D. H., *J. Appl. Biochem.*, 1979, **1**, 357.
99b. Ramana Rao, M. V. and Dutta, S. M., *J. Food Sci.*, 1981, **46**, 1419.
100. Greenberg, N. A. and Mahoney, R. R., *J. Food Sci.*, 1982, **47**, 1824.
101. Simon, W. A. and Hofer, H. W., *Biochim. Biophys. Acta*, 1981, **661**, 158.
102. Mou, L., Mulvena, D. P., Jonas, H. A. and Jago, G. R., *J. Bacteriol.*, 1972, **111**, 392.
103. Orberg, P. K. and Sandine, W. E., *Appl. Environ. Microbiol.*, 1984, **48**, 1129.
104. Thomas, T. D., *Appl. Environ. Microbiol.*, 1976, **32**, 474.
105. Thompson, J., *J. Bacteriol.*, 1978, **136**, 465.
106. Thompson, J. and Thomas, T. D., *J. Bacteriol.*, 1977, **130**, 583.
107. Mason, P. W., Carbone, D. P., Cushman, R. A. and Waggoner, A. S., *J. Biol. Chem.*, 1981, **256**, 1861.

108. Thompson, J., Turner, K. W. and Thomas, T. D., *J. Bacteriol.*, 1978, **133**, 1163.
109. Garvie, E. I., *Microbiol. Rev.*, 1980, **44**, 106.
110. Thomas, T. D., McKay, L. L. and Morris, H. A., *Appl. Environ. Microbiol.*, 1985, **49**, 908.
111. Bottazzi, V. and Dellaglio, F., *J. Dairy Res.*, 1967, **34**, 109.
112. Groux, M., *Le Lait*, 1973, **53**, 147.
113. Hickey, M. W., Hillier, A. J. and Jago, G. R., *Aust. J. Biol. Sci.*, 1983, **36**, 487.
114. Tinson, W., Hillier, A. J. and Jago, G. R., *Aust. J. Dairy Technol.*, 1982, **37**, 22.
115. Manning, D. J. and Robinson, H. M., *J. Dairy Res.*, 1973, **40**, 63.
116. Sandine, W. E., Elliker, P. R. and Anderson, A. W., *J. Dairy Sci.*, 1959, **42**, 799.
117. Sherwood, I. R., *J. Dairy Res.*, 1939, **10**, 326.
118. Campbell, J. J. R. and Gunsalus, I. C., *J. Bacteriol.*, 1944, **48**, 71.
119a. Harvey, R. J. and Collins, E. B., *J. Biol. Chem.*, 1963, **238**, 2648.
119b. Speckman, R. A. and Collins, E. B., *J. Bacteriol.*, 1968, **95**, 174.
119c. Speckman, R. A. and Collins, E. B., *Appl. Microbiol.*, 1973, **26**, 744.
120. Seitz, E. W., Sandine, W. E., Elliker, P. R. and Day, E. A., *Canad. J. Microbiol.*, 1963, **9**, 431.
121. Kummel, A., Behrens, G. and Gottschalk, G., *Arch. Microbiol.*, 1975, **102**, 111.
122. Cogan, T. M., *J. Dairy Res.*, 1981, **48**, 489.
123. Mellerick, D. and Cogan, T. M., *J. Dairy Res.*, 1981, **48**, 497.
124. Malthe-Sorenssen, D. and Stormer, F. C., *Eur. J. Biochem.*, 1970, **14**, 127.
125. Cogan, T. M., Fitzgerald, R. J. and Doonan, S., *J. Dairy Res.*, 1984, **51**, 597.
126. De Man, J. C., *Recueil trav. chem.*, 1959, **78**, 480.
127. De Man, J. C. and Pette, J. W., *14th Intern. Dairy Congr.*, 1956, Vol. 2(1), p. 89.
128. Jonsson, H. and Petersson, H. E., *Milchwissenschaft*, 1977, **32**, 513.
129. Speckman, R. A. and Collins, E. B., *Canad. J. Microbiol.*, 1974, **20**, 805.
130. Cogan, T. M., *Ir. J. Food Sci. Technol.*, 1982, **6**, 69.
131. Veringa, H. A., Verburg, E. H. and Stadhouders, J., *Neth. Milk Dairy J.*, 1984, **38**, 251.
132. Juni, E. and Heym, G. A., *Arch. Biochem. Biophys.*, 1957, **67**, 410.
133. Silber, P., Chung, H., Gargiulo, P. and Schulz, H., *J. Bacteriol.*, 1974, **118**, 919.
134. Louis-Eugene, S., Ratomahenina, R. and Galzy, P., *Z. allg. Mikrobiol.*, 1984, **24**, 151.
135. Bryn, K., Hetland, O. and Stormer, F. C., *Eur. J. Biochem.*, 1971, **18**, 116.
136. Drinan, D. F., Tobin, S. and Cogan, T. M., *Appl. Environ. Microbiol.*, 1976, **31**, 481.
137. Cogan, T. M., O'Dowd, M. and Mellerick, D., *Appl. Environ. Microbiol.*, 1981, **41**, 1.
138. Thomas, T. D. and Mills, O. E., *N.Z. J. Dairy Sci. Technol.*, 1981, **16**, 43.
139. Law, B. A. and Kolstad, J., *Ant. v. Leewenhoek*, 1983, **49**, 225.
140. Reiter, B. and Oram, J. D., *J. Dairy Res.*, 1962, **29**, 63.
141. Garvie, E. I., *J. gen. Microbiol.*, 1967, **48**, 439.
142. Bracquart, P. and Lorient, D., *Milchwissenschaft*, 1979, **34**, 676.
143. Rice, G. H., Stewart, F. H. C., Hillier, A. J. and Jago, G. R., *J. Dairy Res.*, 1978, **45**, 93.
144. Law, B. A., *J. gen. Microbiol.*, 1978, **105**, 113.
145. Law, B. A., *J. Dairy Res.*, 1977, **44**, 309.

146. Akpemado, K. M. and Bracquart, P. A., *Appl. Environ. Microbiol.*, 1983, **45**, 136.
147. Williamson, W. T., Tove, S. B. and Speck, M. L., *J. Bacteriol.*, 1964, **87**, 49.
148. Cowman, R. A., Swaisgood, H. A. and Speck, M. L., *Appl. Microbiol.*, 1967, **15**, 851.
149. Westhoff, D. C., Cowman, R. A. and Speck, M. L., *J. Dairy Sci.*, 1971, **54**, 1253.
150. Thomas, T. D., Jarvis, B. D. W. and Skipper, N. A., *J. Bacteriol.*, 1974, **118**, 329.
151. Pearce, L. E., Skipper, N. A. and Jarvis, B. D. W., *Appl. Microbiol.*, 1974, **27**, 933.
152. Ohmiya, K. and Sato, Y., *Appl. Microbiol.*, 1975, **30**, 738.
153. Law, B. A., *J. appl. Microbiol.*, 1979, **46**, 455.
154. Desmazeaud, M. J. and Zevaco, C., *Ann. Biol. Anim. Bioch. Biophys.*, 1976, **16**, 851.
155. Zevaco, C. and Desmazeaud, M. J., *J. Dairy Sci.*, 1980, **63**, 15.
156. Desmazeaud, M. J. and Zevaco, C., *Milchwissenschaft*, 1979, **34**, 606.
157. Exterkate, F. A., *Neth. Milk Dairy J.*, 1976, **30**, 95.
158. Exterkate, F. A., *FEMS Microbiol. Lett.*, 1979, **5**, 111.
159. Exterkate, F. A., *Arch. Mikrobiol.*, 1979, **120**, 247.
160. Exterkate, F. A., *Appl. Environ. Microbiol.*, 1984, **47**, 177.
161. Geis, A., Bockelmann, W. and Teuber, M., *Appl. Microbiol. Biotech.*, 1985, **23**, 79.
162. Argyle, P. J., Mathison, G. E. and Chandan, R. C., *J. appl. Bacteriol.*, 1976, **41**, 175.
163. Eggimann, B. and Bachmann, M., *Appl. Environ. Microbiol.*, 1980, **40**, 876.
164. Mills, O. E. and Thomas, T. D., *N.Z. J. Dairy Sci. Technol.*, 1978, **13**, 209.
165. Hugenholtz, J., Exterkate, F. and Konings, W. N., *Appl. Environ. Microbiol.*, 1984, **48**, 1105.
166. Rymaszewski, J., Poznanski, S. and Markowicz-Robaczewska, M., *Le Lait*, 1972, **52**, 571.
167. El-Soda, M. and Desmazeaud, M. J., *Canad. J. Microbiol.*, 1982, **28**, 1181.
168. Chandan, R. C., Argyle, P. J. and Mathison, G. E., *J. Dairy Sci.*, 1982, **65**, 1408.
169. Lowrie, R. J., Lawrence, R. C., Pearce, L. E. and Richards, E. L., *N.Z. J. Dairy Sci. Technol.*, 1972, **7**, 44.
170. Lowrie, R. J., Lawrence, R. C. and Peberdy, M. F., *N.Z. J. Dairy Sci. Technol.*, 1974, **9**, 116.
171. Sullivan, J. J., Mou, L., Rood, J. I. and Jago, G. R., *Aust. J. Dairy Technol.*, 1973, **28**, 20.
172. Mills, O. E. and Thomas, T. D., *N.Z. J. Dairy Sci. Technol.*, 1980, **15**, 131.
173. Stadhouders, J., Hup, G., Exterkate, F. A. and Visser, S., *Neth. Milk Dairy J.*, 1983, **37**, 157.
174. Visser, S., Hup, G., Exterkate, F. A. and Stadhouders, J., *Neth. Milk Dairy J.*, 1983, **37**, 169.
175. Visser, S., Slangen, K. J., Hup, G. and Stadhouders, J., *Neth. Milk Dairy J.*, 1983, **37**, 187.
176. Cogan, T. M., *Ir. J. Food Sci. Technol.*, 1978, **2**, 105.

177. Accolas, J-P., Bloquel, R., Didienne, R. and Reguier, J., *Le Lait*, 1977, **57**, 1.
178. Martley, F. G., *N.Z. J. Dairy Sci. Technol.*, 1983, **18**, 191.
179. Turner, K. W. and Thomas, T. D., *N.Z. J. Dairy Sci. Technol.*, 1980, **15**, 265.
180. Thomas, T. D. and Pearce, K. N., *N.Z. J. Dairy Sci. Technol.*, 1981, **16**, 253.
181. Walsh, B. and Cogan, T. M., *Appl. Microbiol.*, 1973, **26**, 820.
182. Speckman, R. A. and Collins, E. B., *Anal. Chem.*, 1982, **54**, 1449.
183. Speckman, R. A. and Collins, E. B., *Anal. Biochem.*, 1968, **22**, 154.
184. Keen, A. R. and Walker, N. J., *Anal. Biochem.*, 1973, **52**, 475.
185. Thornhill, P. and Cogan, T. M., *Appl. Environ. Microbiol.*, 1984, **47**, 1250.
186. Keen, A. R. and Walker, N. J., *J. Dairy Res.*, 1974, **41**, 65.
187. Cogan, T. M., *Appl. Microbiol.*, 1972, **23**, 960.
188. Tagg, J. R., Danjani, A. S. and Wannamaker, L. W., *Bacteriol. Rev.*, 1976, **40**, 722.
189. Zajdel, J., Geglowski, P. and Dobrzanski, W. T., *Appl. Environ. Microbiol.*, 1985, **49**, 969.
190. Davey, G. P. and Richardson, B. C., *Appl. Environ. Microbiol.*, 1981, **41**, 84.
191. Geis, A., Singh, J. and Teuber, M., *Appl. Environ. Microbiol.*, 1983, **45**, 205.
192. Neve, H., Geis, A. and Teuber, M., *J. Bacteriol.*, 1984, **157**, 833.
193. Davies, F. L. and Gasson, M. J. In: *Advances in the Microbiology and Biochemistry of Cheese and Fermented Milk*, F. L. Davies and B. A. Law (eds), 1984, Elsevier Applied Science Publishers, London.
194. Teuber, M. and Lembke, J., *Ant. v. Leeuwenhoek*, 1983, **49**, 283.
195. Sozzi, T., Poulin, J. M., Meret, R. and Pousaz, R., *J. appl. Bacteriol.*, 1978, **44**, 159.
196. Shin, C. and Sato, Y., *Jap. J. Zootech. Sci.*, 1981, **52**, 639.
197. Sozzi, T. and Maret, R., *Le Lait*, 1975, **55**, 269.
198. Sozzi, T., Maret, R. and Poulin, J. M., *Appl. Environ. Microbiol.*, 1976, **32**, 131.
199. Reinbold, G. W., Reddy, M. S. and Hammond, E. G., *J. Food Prot.*, 1982, **45**, 119.
200. Accolas, J-P. and Spillman, H., *J. appl. Bacteriol.*, 1979, **47**, 309.
201. Bradley, D. E., *Bacteriol. Rev.*, 1967, **31**, 230.
202. Kurmann, J. L., *Schweiz. Milchwirtsch. Forsch.*, 1979, **8**, 71.
203. Whitehead, H. R. and Cox, G. A., *N.Z. J. Sci. Technol.*, 1935, **16**, 319.
204. Ackermann, H-W. In: *A Critical Appraisal of Viral Taxonomy*, R. E. F. Mathews (ed.), 1983, CRC Press, Florida, p. 105.
205. Henning, D. R., Black, C. H., Sandine, W. E. and Elliker, P. R., *J. Dairy Sci.*, 1966, **51**, 16.
206. Chopin, M-C., Chopin, A. and Roux, C., *Appl. Environ. Microbiol.*, 1976, **32**, 741.
207. Boussemaer, J. P., Schrauwen, P. P., Sourroville, J. L. and Guy, P., *J. Dairy Res.*, 1980, **47**, 401.
208. Sanders, M. E. and Klaenhammer, T. R., *Appl. Environ. Microbiol.*, 1980, **40**, 500.
209. Douglas, J., Qanber-Agha, A. and Phillips, V., *Lab. Pract.*, 1974, **23**, 3.
210. Keogh, B. P., *Appl. Environ. Microbiol.*, 1980, **40**, 798.
211. Keogh, B. P. and Shimmin, P. D., *Appl. Microbiol.*, 1974, **27**, 411.
212. Terzaghi, B. E., *N.Z. J. Dairy Sci. Technol.*, 1976, **11**, 155.
213. Tsaneva, K. P., *Appl. Environ. Microbiol.*, 1976, **31**, 590.

214. Heap, H. A. and Jarvis, A. W., *N.Z. J. Dairy Sci. Technol.*, 1980, **15**, 75.
215. Lembke, J., Krusch, U., Lompe, A. and Teuber, M., *Zbl. Bakt. I. Abt. Orig.*, 1980, CI, 79.
216. Budde-Niekiel, A., Muller, V., Lembke, J. and Teuber, M., *Milchwissenschaft*, 1985, **40**, 477.
217. Jarvis, A. W., *Appl. Environ. Microbiol.*, 1984, **47**, 343.
218. Jarvis, A. W., *Appl. Environ. Microbiol.*, 1984, **47**, 1031.
219. Daly, C. and Fitzgerald, G. F. In: *Microbiology*—1982, D. Schlessinger (ed.), 1982, American Society for Microbiology, p. 213.
220. Loof, M., Lembke, J. and Teuber, M., *System. appl. Microbiol.*, 1983, **4**, 413.
221. Lyttle, D. J. and Peterson, G. B., *Appl. Environ. Microbiol.*, 1984, **48**, 242.
222. Powell, I. B. and Davison, B. E., *J. gen. Virol.*, 1985, **66**, 2737.
223. Jarvis, A. W. and Meyer, J., *Appl. Environ. Microbiol.*, 1986, **51**, 556.
224. Oram, J. D., *J. gen. Virol.*, 1971, **13**, 59.
225. Keogh, B. P., *J. Dairy Res.*, 1973, **40**, 303.
226. Pearce, L. E., Limsowtin, G. K. Y. and Crawford, A. M., *N.Z. J. Dairy Sci. Technol.*, 1970, **5**, 145.
227. Oram, J. and Reiter, B., *J. gen. Microbiol.*, 1965, **40**, 57.
228. Tourville, D. R. and Tokuda, S., *J. Dairy Sci.*, 1967, **50**, 1019.
229. Mullan, W. M. A. and Crawford, R. J. M., *J. Dairy Res.*, 1985, **52**, 123.
230. Jarvis, A. W., *21st Intern. Dairy Congr.*, Vol. 1, Book 2, Mir Publishers, Moscow, p. 314.
231. Chopin, M-C. and Rousseau, M., *Le Lait*, 1983, **63**, 102.
232. Reyrolle, J., Chopin, M-C., Letellier, F. and Novel, G., *Appl. Environ. Microbiol.*, 1982, **43**, 349.
233. Shimizu-Kadota, M. and Sakurai, T., *Appl. Environ. Microbiol.*, 1982, **43**, 1284.
234. Shimizu-Kadota, M., Sakurai, T. and Tsuehida, N., *Appl. Environ. Microbiol.*, 1983, **45**, 669.
235. Pearce, L. E., *19th Intern. Dairy Congr.*, 1974, Vol. IE, p. 411.
236. Limsowtin, G. K. Y. and Terzaghi, B. E., *N.Z. J. Dairy Sci. Technol.*, 1976, **11**, 251.
237. Marshall, R. J. and Berridge, N.J., *J. Dairy Res.*, 1976, **43**, 449.
238. King, W. P., Collins, E. B. and Barrett, E. L., *Appl. Environ. Microbiol.*, 1983, **45**, 1481.
239. Pearce, L. E., *N.Z. J. Dairy Sci. Technol.*, 1978, **13**, 166.
240. Chopin, A., Chopin, M-C., Moillo-Batt, A. and Langella, P., *Plasmid*, 1984, **11**, 260.
241. Fitzgerald, G. F., Daly, C., Browne, L. R. and Gingeras, T. R., *Nucleic Acids Res.*, 1982, **10**, 8171.
242. Hull, R. R. and Brooke, A. R., *Aust. J. Dairy Technol.*, 1982, **37**, 143.
243. Limsowtin, G. K. Y., Heap, H. A. and Lawrence, R. C., *N.Z. J. Dairy Sci. Technol.*, 1978, **13**, 1.
244. Koka, M. and Mikolajcik, E. M., *J. Dairy Sci.*, 1967, **50**, 1025.
245. Zottola, E. A. and Marth, E. H., *J. Dairy Sci.*, 1966, **49**, 1338.
246. Koka, M. and Mikolajcik, E. M., *J. Dairy Sci.*, 1970, **53**, 853.
247. Daoust, D. R., El-Bisi, H. and Litsky, W., *Appl. Microbiol.*, 1965, **13**, 478.
248. Chopin, M-C., *J. Dairy Res.*, 1980, **47**, 131.

249. Le Grange, W. S. and Reinbold, G. W., *J. Dairy Sci.*, 1968, **51**, 1985.
250. Gulstrom, T. J., Pearce, L. E., Sandine, W. E. and Elliker, P. R., *J. Dairy Sci.*, 1979, **62**, 208.
251. Ledford, R. A. and Speck, M. L., *J. Dairy Sci.*, 1979, **62**, 781.
252. Henning, D. R., Sandine, W. E., Elliker, P. R. and Hays, H. A., *J. Milk Food Technol.*, 1965, **28**, 273.
253. Wright, S. L. and Richardson, G. H., *J. Dairy Sci.*, 1982, **65**, 1882.
254. Mermelstein, N. H., *Food Technol.*, 1982, **36**(8), 69.
255. Willrett, D. L., Sandine, W. E. and Ayres, J. W., *Cult. Dairy Products J.*, 1982, **17**, 5.
256. Lewis, J. E., *J. Soc. Dairy Technol.*, 1956, **9**, 123.
257. Robertson, P. S., *Dairy Industries Int.*, 1966, **31**(10), 805.
258. Leenders, G. J. M., Bolle, A. C. and Stadhouders, J., Rapport R119, Netherlands Dairy Research Institute, 1983.
259. Bolle, A. C., Leenders, G. J. M. and Stadhouders, J., Rapport R121, Netherlands Dairy Research Institute, 1985.
260. McKay, L. L., Baldwin, K. A. and Zottola, E. A., *Appl. Microbiol.*, 1972, **23**, 1090.
261. Pearce, L. E., *18th Int. Dairy Congr.*, Sydney, 1970, Vol. IE, p. 118.
262. Novick, R. P., Clowes, R. C., Cohen, S. N., Curtiss, R., III, Datta, N. and Falkow, S., *Bacteriol. Rev.*, 1976, **40**, 168.
263. Gasson, M. J. and Davies, F. L. In: *Advances in the Microbiology and Biochemistry of Cheese and Fermented Milk*, 1984, F. L. Davies and B. A. Law (eds), 1984, Elsevier Applied Science Publishers, London, p. 99.
264. McKay, L. L., *Antoine v. Leeuwenhoek*, 1983, **49**, 259.
265. Gasson, M. J., *Antoine v. Leeuwenhoek*, 1983, **49**, 275.
266. Perbal, B., *A Practical Guide to Molecular Cloning*, 1984, John Wiley, New York.
267. Old, R. W. and Primrose, S. B., *Principles of Gene Manipulation*, 3rd edn, 1985, Blackwell Scientific Publications, Oxford.
268. Andresen, A., Geis, A., Drusch, U. and Teuber, M., *Milchwissenschaft*, 1984, **39**, 140.
269. Efstathiou, J. D. and McKay, L. L., *J. Bacteriol.*, 1977, **130**, 257.
270. Gasson, M. J., *J. Bacteriol.*, 1983, **154**, 1.
271. McKay, L. L. and Baldwin, K. A., *Appl. Microbiol.*, 1974, **28**, 342.
272. Anderson, D. G. and McKay, L. L., *J. Bacteriol.*, 1977, **129**, 367.
273. St Martin, E. J., Lee, L. N. and Le Blanc, D. J. In: *Microbiology—1982*, D. Schlessinger (ed.) American Society for Microbiology, Washington D.C., p. 232.
274. Maeda, S. and Gasson, M. J., *J. gen. Microbiol.*, 1986, **132**, 331.
275. Crow, V. L., Davey, G. P., Pearce, L. E. and Thomas, T. D., *J. Bacteriol.*, 1983, **153**, 76.
276. Snook, R. J. and McKay, L. L., *Appl. Environ. Microbiol.*, 1981, **42**, 904.
277. Kok, J., Van Dijl, J. M., Van der Vossen, J. M. B. M. and Venema, G., *Appl. Environ. Microbiol.*, 1985, **50**, 94.
278. Kempler, G. M. and McKay, L. L., *Appl. Environ. Microbiol.*, 1979, **37**, 316.
279. Sanders, M. E. and Klaenhammer, T. R., *Appl. Environ. Microbiol.*, 1983, **46**, 1125.

280. De Vos, W. M., Underwood, H. M. and Davies, F. L., *FEMS Microbiol. Lett.*, 1984, **23**, 175.
281. Sanders, M. E. and Klaenhammer, T. R., *Appl. Environ. Microbiol.*, 1981, **42**, 944.
282. Sanders, M. E. and Klaenhammer, T. R., *Appl. Environ. Microbiol.*, 1984, **47**, 979.
283. McKay, L. L. and Baldwin, K. A., *Appl. Environ. Microbiol.*, 1984, **47**, 68.
284. Klaenhammer, T. R. and Sanozky, R. B., *J. gen. Microbiol.*, 1985, **131**, 1531.
285. Steenson, L. R. and Klaenhammer, T. R., *Appl. Environ. Microbiol.*, 1985, **50**, 851.
286. Baumgartner, A., Murphy, M., Daly, C. and Fitzgerald, G. F., *FEMS Microbiol. Lett.*, 1986, **35**, 233.
287. Somkuti, G. A. and Steinberg, D. H., *J. Dairy Sci.*, 1981, **64**, Suppl. 1, 66.
288. Herman, R. W. and McKay, L. L., *Appl. Environ. Microbiol.*, 1985, **50**, 1103.
289. Klaenhammer, T. R. and Sutherland, S. M., *Appl. Environ. Microbiol.*, 1980, **35**, 592.
290. Vescovo, M., Bottazzi, V., Sarra, P. G. and Dellagio, F., *Microbiologica*, 1981, **4**, 413.
291. Lin, J. H. C. and Savage, D., *Appl. Environ. Microbiol.*, 1985, **49**, 1004.
292. Ishiwa, H. and Iwata, S., *J. gen. appl. Microbiol.*, 1980, **26**, 71.
293. Vescovo, M., Morelli, L. and Bottazzi, V., *Appl. Environ. Microbiol.*, 1982, **43**, 50.
294. Morelli, L., Vescovo, M. and Bottazzi, V., *Microbiologica*, 1983, **6**, 145.
295. Chassy, B. M., Gibson, E. M. and Giuffrida, A., *Curr. Microbiol.*, 1978, **1**, 141.
296. Smiley, M. B. and Fryder, V., *Appl. Environ. Microbiol.*, 1978, **35**, 777.
297. Lee, L. J., Hansen, J. B., Jagusztyn-Krynicka, K. and Chassy, B. M., *J. Bacteriol.*, 1982, **152**, 1138.
298. Gonzalez, C. F. and Kunka, B. S., *Appl. Environ. Microbiol.*, 1983, **46**, 81.
299. Graham, D. C. and McKay, L. L., *Appl. Environ. Microbiol.*, 1985, **50**, 532.
300. O'Sullivan, T. and Daly, C., *Ir. J. Food Sci. Technol.*, 1982, **6**, 206.
301. Allen, L. K., Sandine, W. E. and Elliker, P. R., *J. Dairy Res.*, 1962, **30**, 351.
302. Sandine, W. E., Elliker, P. R., Allen, L. K. and Brown, W. C., *J. Dairy Sci.*, 1962, **45**, 1266.
303. McKay, L. L., Baldwin, K. A. and Efstathiou, J. D., *Appl. Environ. Microbiol.*, 1976, **32**, 45.
304. McKay, L. L. and Baldwin, K. A., *Appl. Environ. Microbiol.*, 1978, **36**, 360.
305. Snook, R. J., McKay, L. L. and Ahlstrand, G. G., *Appl. Environ. Microbiol.*, 1981, **42**, 897.
306. Stetter, K. O., *J. Virol.*, 1977, **24**, 685.
307. Shimizu-Kadota, M. and Tsuchida, N., *J. gen. Microbiol.*, 1984, **130**, 423.
308. Kempler, G. M. and McKay, L. L., *Appl. Environ. Microbiol.*, 1979, **37**, 1041.
309. Gasson, M. J. and Davies, F. L., *J. Bacteriol.*, 1980, **143**, 1260.
310. Walsh, P. M. and McKay, L. L., *J. Bacteriol.*, 1981, **146**, 937.
311. Anderson, D. G. and McKay, L. L., *Appl. Environ. Microbiol.*, 1984, **47**, 245.
312. Hayes, F., Fitzgerald, G. F. and Daly, C., *Ir. J. Food Sci. Technol.*, 1985, **9**, 77.
313. Davey, G. P., *Appl. Environ. Microbiol.*, 1984, **48**, 895.
314. Scherwitz, K. M., Baldwin, K. A. and McKay, L. L., *Appl. Environ. Microbiol.*, 1983, **45**, 1506.

315. Gasson, M. J., *FEMS Microbiol. Lett.*, 1984, **21**, 7.
316. Gonzalez, C. F. and Kunka, B. S., *Appl. Environ. Microbiol.*, 1985, **49**, 627.
317. Steele, J. L. and McKay, L. L., *Appl. Environ. Microbiol.*, 1986, **51**, 57.
318. Gasson, M. J. and Davies, F. L., *FEMS Microbiol. Lett.*, 1980, **7**, 51.
319. Vescovo, M., Morelli, L., Bottazzi, V. and Gasson, M. J., *Appl. Environ. Microbiol.*, 1983, **46**, 753.
320. Hill, C., Daly, C. and Fitzgerald, G. F., *FEMS Microbiol. Lett.*, 1985, **30**, 115.
321. Hill, C., Daly, C. and Fitzgerald, G. F., *Appl. Environ. Microbiol.*, 1987, **53**, in press.
322. Kondo, J. K. and McKay, L. L., *Appl. Environ. Microbiol.*, 1982, **43**, 1213.
323. Kondo, J. K. and McKay, L. L., *Appl. Environ. Microbiol.*, 1984, **48**, 252.
324. Von Wright, A., Taimisto, A-M. and Sivela, S., *Appl. Environ. Microbiol.*, 1985, **50**, 1100.
325. Simon, D., Rouault, A. and Chopin, M-C., *FEMS Microbiol. Lett.*, 1985, **26**, 239.
326. Gasson, M. J. and Anderson, P. H., *FEMS Microbiol. Lett.*, 1985, **30**, 193.
327. Geis, A., *FEMS Microbiol. Lett.*, 1982, **15**, 119.
328. Lee-Wickner, L.-J. and Chassy, B. M., *Appl. Environ. Microbiol.*, 1984, **48**, 994.
329. Shimizu-Kadota, M. and Kudo, S., *Agric. Biol. Chem.*, 1984, **48**, 1105.
330. Chassy, B. In: *Biotechnology in Food Processing*, S. K. Harlander and T. P. Labuza (eds.), 1986, Voyez Publications, New York, p. 197.
331. Hofer, F., *N.Z. J. Dairy Sci. Technol.*, 1985, **20**, 179.
332. Gasson, M. J., *FEMS Microbiol. Lett.*, 1980, **9**, 99.
333. Okamoto, T., Fujita, Y. and Irie, R., *Agric. Biol. Chem.*, 1983, **47**, 2675.
334. Limsowtin, G. K. Y., *FEMS Microbiol. Lett.*, 1986, **33**, 79.
335. Harlander, S. K., McKay, L. L. and Schachtele, C. F., *Appl. Environ. Microbiol.*, 1984, **48**, 347.
336. Kok, J., van der Vossen, J. M. B. M. and Venema, G., *Appl. Environ. Microbiol.*, 1984, **48**, 726.
337. De Vos, W. M., *Neth. Milk Dairy J.*, 1986, **40**, 141.
338. Chopin, M-C., Chopin, A., Rouault, A. and Simon, D., *Appl. Environ. Microbiol.*, 1986, **51**, 233.
339. Van der Vossen, J. M. B. M., Kok, J. and Venema, G., *Appl. Environ. Microbiol.*, 1985, **50**, 540.
340. Porubcan, R. S. and Sellars, R. L. In: *Microbial Technology*, M. J. Pepplar and D. Perlman (eds), Vol. 1, 1979, Academic Press, New York, p. 59.
341. Gilliland, S. E., *J. Dairy Sci.*, 1977, **60**, 805.
342. Condon, S., *Ir. J. Food Sci. Technol.*, 1983, **7**, 15.
343. Gilliland, S. E., *J. Dairy Sci.*, 1968, **54**, 1129.
344. Pettersson, H. E., *Appl. Microbiol.*, 1975, **29**, 133.
345. Turner, K. W., Davey, G. P., Richardson, G. H. and Pearse, L. E., *N.Z. J. Dairy Sci. Technol.*, 1979, **14**, 16.
346. Tamime, A. Y. In: *Dairy Microbiology, Vol. 2*, Robinson, R. K. (ed.), 1981, Applied Science Publishers, London, p. 113.
347. Anonymous, *Dairy Industries Int.*, 1983, **48**, 19.
348. Walker, A. L., Mullan, W. M. A. and Muir, M. E., *J. Soc. Dairy Technol.*, 1981, **34**, 78.

349. Ausavanodom, N., White, R. S., Young, G. and Richardson, G. H., *J. Dairy Sci.*, 1977, **60**, 1245.
350. Reddy, K. D. and Richardson, G. H., *J. Dairy Sci.*, 1977, **60**, 1527.
351. Limsowtin, G. K. Y., Heap, H. A. and Lawrence, R. C., *N.Z. J. Dairy Sci. Technol.*, 1980, **15**, 219.
352. Lawrence, R. C., Heap, H. A. and Gilles, J., *J. Dairy Sci.*, 1984, 67, 1632.
353. Collins, E. B., *J. Dairy Sci.*, 1951, **34**, 894.
354. Thomas, T. D. and Lowrie, R. J., *J. Milk Food Technol.*, 1975, **38**, 275.
355. Thunell, R. K., Sandine, W. E. and Bodyfelt, F. W., *J. Dairy Sci.*, 1984, **67**, 1175.
356. Jarvis, A. W., *N.Z. J. Dairy Sci. Technol.*, 1981, **16**, 25.
357. Pearce, L. E., *N.Z. J. Dairy Sci. Technol.*, 1984, **19**, 129.
358. Huggins, A. R. and Sandine, W. E., *J. Dairy Sci.*, 1984, **67**, 1674.
359. Coventry, M. J., Hillier, A. J. and Jago, G. R., *Aust. J. Dairy Technol.*, 1984, **39**, 154.
360. Vedamuthu, E. R. and Neville, J. M., *Appl. Environ. Microbiol.*, 1986, **51**, 677.

Chapter 7

Salt in Cheese: Physical, Chemical and Biological Aspects

T. P. Guinee and P. F. Fox

Department of Dairy and Food Chemistry,
University College, Cork, Ireland

1. INTRODUCTION

The use of salt (NaCl) as a food preservative dates from pre-historic times and together with fermentation and dehydration (air/sun) is one of the classical methods of food preservation. So useful and widespread was the use of salt as a food preservative in Classical and Medieval times that it was a major item of trade and was used as a form of currency in exchange for goods and labour. It is perhaps a little surprising that Man discovered the application of salt in food preservation so early in civilization since, in contrast to fermentation and dehydration, salting is not a 'natural event' in foods but requires a conscious act. It is interesting that the three classical methods of food preservation, i.e. fermentation, dehydration and salting, are all exploited in cheese manufacture and in fact are interdependent. The fourth common method of food preservation, i.e. use of high and/or low temperatures, was less widespread than the others because the exploitation of low temperatures was confined to relatively few areas until the development of mechanical refrigeration about 1870 and, although heating was probably used to extend the shelf-life of foods throughout civilization, its controlled use dates from the work of Nicolas Apert (1794) and Louis Pasteur ($\sim$1840). In modern cheese technology, temperature control complements the other three methods of food preservation.

In addition to its preservative effect, NaCl plays two other important roles in foods. Man requires $\sim$4 g Na per day and although this

251

requirement can be met through the indigenous Na content in foods, added NaCl is a major source in modern western diets. In fact, western diets contain, on average, 3–5 times more Na than is necessary and excessive intakes of Na have toxic, or at least undesirable, physiological effects, the most significant of which are hypertension and increased calcium excretion which may lead to osteoporosis (for reviews on the dietary significance of Na, see Refs 1–4).

Cheese, even when consumed in large amounts, as in France and Switzerland, makes a relatively small contribution to dietary Na intake (see Chapter 10) although it may be a major contributor in individual cases where large amounts of high-salt cheeses, e.g. Blue, Feta, Domiati, are consumed. Nevertheless, there is interest in many western countries in the production of low-Na cheese, for at least certain sectors of the population, but, as discussed below, this has significant repercussions in cheese manufacture. The most common approach at present is to replace some or all of the NaCl by KCl, but apart from cost, this practice affects the flavour of cheese since the flavour of KCl is distinctly different from that of NaCl and a bitter flavour (not due to abnormal proteolysis) is detectable in cheese containing >1% KCl (see Refs 5–8 for some recent work on the production of low-Na cheese). Excellent quality Cheddar containing 1% of NaCl may be produced from milk concentrated by ultrafiltration, apparently because of increased buffering capacity which maintains a normal pH.[6]

The third major feature of the use of NaCl in foods is its direct contribution to flavour. The taste of salt is highly appreciated by many and saltiness is regarded as one of the four basic flavours. Presumably, the characteristic flavour of NaCl resides in the Na moiety since KCl has a distinctly different flavour sensation. At least part of the desirability of salt flavour is acquired but while one can easily adjust to the flavour of foods without added salt, the flavour of salt-free cheese is insipid and 'watery', even to somebody not 'addicted' to salt; the use of 0·8% NaCl is probably sufficient to overcome the insipid taste.[8]

In this chapter, we will concentrate on the role of NaCl in controlling cheese ripening rather than on its dietary and direct flavour effects. NaCl influences cheese ripening principally through its effect on water activity but it probably has some more specific effects also which appear to be only partly due to water activity. Among the principal effects of salt are:

1.   Control of microbial growth and activity.
2.   Control of the various enzyme activities in cheese.

3. Syneresis of the curd resulting in whey expulsion and thus in a reduction of cheese moisture, which also influence 1 and 2 above.
4. Physical changes in cheese proteins which influence cheese texture, protein solubility and probably protein conformation.

2. CONTROL OF MICROBIAL GROWTH

Probably the most extreme example of the use of NaCl for this purpose is in the manufacture of Domiati-type cheeses where 12–15% of NaCl is added to cheesemilk to inhibit bacterial growth and thus maintain milk quality (see Chapter 9, Volume 2). In all other major varieties, NaCl is added after curd formation but nevertheless it plays a major role in regulating and controlling cheese microflora. The simplest example of this is the regulation of the pH of cheese, which in turn influences cheese ripening and texture.

The pH of cheese may be regulated by:

1. Reducing the amount of residual lactose in the curd which is accomplished by washing the curd with water, as practised in Dutch-type cheeses, Tallegio and Cottage.
2. The natural buffering capacity of the cheese and the toxic effect of the lactate anion which establishes a natural lower limit to pH ($\sim 4 \cdot 5$), e.g. Blue, hard Italian varieties.
3. Salt addition.

The use of salt to regulate final pH appears to be almost exclusively confined to British-type cheeses. The curd for most, if not all, non-British cheeses is placed in moulds while the pH is still high ($> 6 \cdot 0$) and acid development continues during pressing. Since levels of NaCl $> \sim 1 \cdot 5\%$ inhibit starter activity, such cheeses are salted by immersion in brine or by surface application of dry salt. In British cheeses, e.g. Cheddar-types and Stilton, the pH has reached its final, desired level at hooping and salt is added to maintain the pH at that (desired) level. One could probably argue that the method of salting cheese that predominates in a certain region reflects the form of salt available in that region: in regions where salt deposits occur, dry salt was readily available and thus permitted the manufacture of cheeses in which dry salt was added to the curd or to the surface of the cheese; in regions where salt was prepared by evaporation of sea water, it would have been more convenient to salt the cheese by immersion in concentrated brine rather than wait for crystallization.

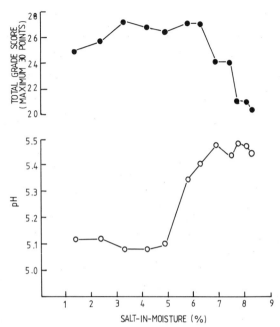

Fig. 1. The correlation between the salt-in-moisture (S/M) levels and the pH (○) at eight weeks, and between the S/M and the total grade score (maximum 30) (●) of batches of curd from the same vats, salted at different rates (from Ref. 95).

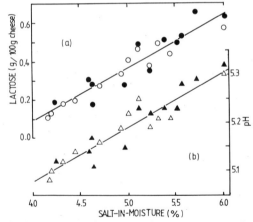

Fig. 2. Effect of S/M concentration on (a) lactose concentration and (b) pH, within single Cheddar cheese blocks. From each of two cheese blocks (open and closed symbols), manufactured at the same time, 12 plugs were removed 14 days after manufacture. Each plug was analysed for S/M, lactose (○, ●) and pH (△, ▲) (from Ref. 15).

Curd for Cheddar, and similar varieties, contains ~0·6% lactose at hooping; this is fermented during the early stages of ripening by continued starter activity but this depends strongly on the salt-in-moisture (S/M) level in the curd and the salt tolerance of the starter. Commercial lactic acid cultures are stimulated by low levels of NaCl but are very strongly inhibited >2·5% NaCl.[9] Thus, the activity of the starter and its ability to ferment residual lactose is strongly dependent on the S/M level in the curd. This is clearly evident from the data of O'Connor,[10] Fig. 1: the pH decreased after salting, presumably due to the action of starter, at S/M levels <5% but at higher values of S/M, starter activity decreased abruptly and the pH remained high. The grade assigned to the cheese also decreased sharply at S/M levels >5%.

Inhibition of starter occurs within quite a narrow pH range (Fig. 1), emphasizing the importance of precise control of % S/M. However, since the sensitivity of starter cultures to salt varies, the influence of NaCl concentration on post-salting acid production in cheese obviously depends on the starter used and a general value for S/M cannot be definitely stated. *S. lactis* starters are generally more salt-tolerant than strains of *S. cremoris*[11] but there is also considerable variation in salt sensitivity between strains of *S. cremoris.*[12,13] If starter activity is inhibited after manufacture, residual lactose will be metabolized by non-starter lactic acid bacteria but the number of these present, which is influenced by level of contamination at salting, % S/M, rapidity with which pressed curd is cooled and ripening temperature,[14] is usually insufficient to cause significant lactose metabolism for several days and consequently the pH falls slowly.

In the study by Turner and Thomas,[13] non-starter bacteria, mainly *Pediococci*, were more salt-tolerant than starter bacteria and metabolized the lactose with the production of DL-lactate and the racemization of L-lactate. Non-starter bacteria grew in all cheeses but their growth was markedly dependent on temperature and they had little influence on lactose or lactate concentration until numbers exceeded 10^6–10^7 cfu/ml.

The control of lactose metabolism by S/M concentration within a single cheese was clearly demonstrated by Thomas and Pearce[15] (Fig. 2). In this study also, the greater salt-tolerance of non-starter bacteria was clearly apparent with the fermentation of lactose to D-lactate relatively late in ripening and the racemization of L-lactate to D-lactate.

Although acid production can be uncoupled from cell growth, it is likely that acid production at low salt levels will be accompanied by high cell numbers which tend to lead to bitterness.[16] Not surprisingly, bitterness in

Cheddar cheese is markedly influenced by % S/M over a very narrow range: *S. cremoris* HP generally yielded bitter cheese at S/M levels <4·3% but rarely >4·9% (Ref. 17).

In the foregoing discussion on the influence of NaCl on the fermentation of residual lactose in cheese curd by starter micro-organisms, it has been assumed that the NaCl is distributed throughout the cheese within a very short period after salting. However, this is not so. Cheddar cheese is usually milled into quite large particles of cross section 2 cm × 2 cm or larger. Obviously, dry salt applied to the surface of such particles requires a considerable period of time to diffuse to the centre of the curd chips and to attain an inhibitory level throughout. Consequently, starter will continue to grow and produce acid at the centre of a chip for a considerable period after growth at the surface has ceased.

Experimental support for this is provided by the experiments of Hoecker and Hammer[18] who measured the salt and moisture contents and pH at the surface and centre of individual chips, pried from a block of Cheddar cheese, over a 72 h period after pressing. Their data showed that the pH fell faster and to a greater extent at the centre where NaCl concentration was lower than at the surface. In one experiment, the difference in pH persisted for 72 h but in a duplicate experiment the difference in pH had essentially disappeared after 48 h. Turner and Thomas[13] showed that a higher level of salt addition is required to inhibit lactose metabolism when the curd is milled into large chips than for smaller ones.

In surface-salted Meshanger cheese, Noomen[19] showed considerable zonal variations in the changes in carbohydrate, lactate and pH throughout the cheese in response to variations in S/M concentration.

S. thermophilus is considerably less salt-tolerant than *S. lactis*;[20] its critical NaCl concentration is 0·4 M (2·34%), corresponding to an A_w of 0·984, compared with 1·10 M NaCl ($A_w = 0.965$) for *S. lactis*. *Lactobacillus helveticus* and *L. lactis* were also less salt tolerant, being inhibited by 0·95 M and 0·90 M NaCl, respectively.

Data on the sensitivity of *Propionibacteria* to NaCl appear to be variable: Orla-Jensen[21] reported that concentrations of NaCl as low as 0·5% are sufficient to reduce the growth of *Propionibacteria* in a medium containing calcium lactate. However, Antilla[22] reported that 3% NaCl is necessary to reduce growth. In fact, salt tolerance appears to be strain and pH-dependent:[23] in a lactate medium, 6% NaCl was required to inhibit the growth of a fast-growing strain of *Propionibacteria* at pH 7·0 and 3% at pH 5·2 whereas a slow-growing strain was more salt-tolerant at pH 5·2 than at pH 7·0. The data reported by Ruegg and Blanc[20] show that *P. shermanii* was the most salt tolerant of the starter species investigated: its critical NaCl concentration was 1·15 M (~6·7%; $A_w = 0·955$). However, Emmental cheese, with NaCl concentrations of ~0·7%, is the least heavily salted among major cheese varieties.

Blue cheeses are among the most heavily salted varieties with 3–5% NaCl (Stilton <3%). Ripening in these varieties is dominated by the enzymes of *P. roqueforti* and consequently good growth of this mould is paramount. Germination of *P. roqueforti* spores is stimulated by 1% NaCl but inhibited by >3–6% NaCl, depending on strain; however, the growth of germinated spores on malt extract agar or cheese curd is less dependent of NaCl concentration than is germination and some strains grow in cheese curd containing 10% NaCl, although growth is retarded compared to that in curd containing lower levels of NaCl.[24,25] Morris[26] reports that it is fairly common commercial practice to add 1% NaCl directly to Blue cheese curd before hooping, possibly to stimulate spore germination, although it also serves to give the cheese a more open structure which facilitates mould growth. Since most Blue cheeses are surface-salted, a salt gradient from the surface to the centre exists for a considerable period after manufacture; a high initial level of salt in the outside zone of the cheese will inhibit spore germination at a critical time and a mould-free zone at the outside is a common defect in Blue cheeses.[25]

Growth of *P. camemberti* is also stimulated by low levels of NaCl; < 0·8% NaCl, mould growth on Camembert cheese is poor and patchy (O'Nulain, M. and Fox, P. F., unpublished data).

3. INFLUENCE OF NaCl ON ENZYME ACTIVITY IN CHEESE

3.1 Coagulant

With the exception of Emmental, Mozzarella and similar high-cooked cheeses, the initial proteolysis in cheese is catalysed by residual coagulant. Application of polyacrylamide gel electrophoresis to cheese ripening[27] has shown that in hard and semi-hard, bacterially ripened cheeses, α_{s1}-casein undergoes considerable proteolysis during ripening but β-casein remains unchanged until an advanced stage of ripening. A similar pattern is evident during the early phases of mould-ripening cheeses, when the coagulant is the principal ripening agent[28,29] but fungal proteinases dominate in these cheeses during the later phases of ripening (see Chapter 9, Volume 2).

The proteolytic activity of chymosin and pepsins on α_{s1}-casein is stimulated by NaCl concentrations up to an optimum at $\sim 5\%$ and although activity is inhibited at higher NaCl levels, proteolysis of α_{s1}-casein occurs up to 20% NaCl.[30] In contrast, proteolysis of β-casein is strongly inhibited by 5% NaCl and completely inhibited by 10% NaCl.[30] Sucrose[31] and glycerol[32] also selectively inhibit proteolysis of β-casein. KCl, LiCl, NH_4Cl and $CaCl_2$ are as effective as NaCl in inhibiting the proteolysis of β-casein (O'Nulain, M. and Fox, P. F., unpublished data). Since the inhibitory effect of solutes is substrate- rather than enzyme-specific, it appears that NaCl and similar solutes cause some conformational change in β-casein which renders its chymosin (pepsin)-susceptible bonds less accessible to the enzyme. The nature of these conformational changes does not appear to have been investigated but may arise from the strongly hydrophobic nature of β-casein. The resistance of β-casein in cheese to proteolysis is not dependent solely on the salt concentration since it is also very resistant to proteolysis in salt-free cheeses,[33] suggesting that a high protein concentration is sufficient to induce the necessary conformational change(s). However, a certain level of NaCl ($> 4.9\%$ S/M) is necessary to prevent the development of bitterness in cheese.[17]

The inhibitory effect of NaCl on proteolysis is pH-dependent, and at low pH NaCl also alters the proteolytic specificity of chymosin and pepsins: NaCl (2·5%) inhibits the formation of β-III and promotes the formation of β-IV and β-V.[34] The formation of the α_{s1}-casein peptides, α_{s1}-VII and α_{s1}-VIII, in solution is at least stimulated by and perhaps dependent on, the presence of NaCl (5%) and these peptides are also formed in cheese.[35]

The proteolytic activity of *Mucor miehei* rennet on β-casein is less strongly inhibited by NaCl than is that of chymosin or pepsins and stimulation of the proteolysis of α_{s1}-casein by *M. miehei* rennet is very pronounced.[36]

3.2 Milk Proteinase

Milk contains several indigenous proteinases,[37-40] the most significant of which, alkaline milk proteinase (plasmin), is almost exclusively associated with the casein micelles at the normal pH of milk[37] but dissociates from the micelles as the pH is reduced.[41] Richardson and Elston[41] indicate that the dissociation of plasmin from the casein micelles is pH- and time-dependent and that it occurs at pH 5·7 and possibly higher. However, Grufferty and Fox (unpublished data) found no dissociation at >pH 4·9. If the latter observation is confirmed, then essentially all the plasmin in milk should accompany the curd in most cheese varieties. However, the concentration of plasmin in Swiss-type cheese is 2–3 times that in Cheddar[42,43] while the plasmin activity in Cheshire cheese is very low,[43] suggesting that the plasmin content of cheese may be influenced by the pH at hooping.[43] The role of plasmin in cheese ripening has not been extensively studied but the presence of γ-caseins in most cheeses suggests at least some activity; it appears to make a significant contribution to the maturation of Gouda[44,45] and of Swiss[42,46] in which the coagulant is extensively denatured by the high cooking temperature[47] but it has only a limited role in the ripening of Cheddar[44,48] and soft Meshanger-type cheese.[49] Noomen[49] suggested that plasmin may make a significant contribution to proteolysis in soft cheeses with a surface flora in which the pH rises markedly during ripening to a value more favourable to the activity of plasmin.

Milk also contains an acid proteinase which apparently has a specificity similar to milk coagulants[50,51] (which are also acid proteinases) and consequently its significance to cheese ripening may be underestimated.

Noomen[49] showed that the activity of alkaline milk proteinase in simulated cheese was stimulated by low concentrations of NaCl up to a maximum at 2% but was inhibited by higher concentrations of NaCl although some activity remained at 8% NaCl. To our knowledge, the influence of NaCl on the activity of acid milk proteinase has not been investigated.

3.3 Microbial Enzymes

There appears to be relatively little information on the influence of NaCl on microbial enzymes in cheese; indirect evidence, e.g. in relation to bitterness in cheese[15,17,52,53] suggests that the activity of starter proteinase is inhibited by moderately high levels of NaCl. *P. roqueforti* lipases[54] and proteinases[55] are inhibited by NaCl concentrations >6%.

4. INFLUENCE OF NaCl ON THE WATER ACTIVITY (A_w) OF CHEESE

In addition to reducing the moisture content of cheese via syneresis, NaCl also reduces the water activity, A_w, of cheese, which in the case of young cheese, especially those containing $>40\%$ H_2O, is determined almost entirely by NaCl content according to the equation, $A_w = 1 - 0.033\,m$, where m = molality of NaCl in cheese moisture.[56] In hard and semi-hard cheeses, the contributions of lactate and ash (other than NaCl) to reducing A_w must be considered and as cheese matures, the formation of low molecular compounds, notably peptides and amino acids, also influence A_w; these compositional factors have been included in the formulae developed by Ruegg and Blanc[20,57,58] for the calculation of A_w. The inhibitory effect of NaCl on the activity of starter is undoubtedly due to its influence on A_w, the inhibitory effect of which is species- and strain-specific.[20,59] Presumably, the activity of the various enzyme systems in cheese is also inhibited at reduced values of A_w but detailed studies are lacking.

5. OVERALL INFLUENCE OF NaCl ON CHEESE RIPENING AND QUALITY

5.1 Cheddar Cheese

The influence of % salt-in-cheese moisture (% S/M) on lactose metabolism in young Cheddar cheese has already been discussed. There appears to be little information available on the influence of % S/M on lipolysis in Cheddar cheese. However, Thakur *et al.*[5] have compared lipolysis in salted (3 lots, 1·48–1·79% NaCl) and unsalted Cheddar: the concentration of volatile acids was significantly higher in the unsalted than in the salted cheeses due mainly to acetic acid which is presumably a product of lactose metabolism. The concentrations of all individual fatty acids, except linoleic and linolenic (at certain ages), were also higher in the unsalted cheese compared to the control; the authors did not comment on the markedly lower level of linoleic acid in the unsalted cheese. However, Lindsay *et al.*[7] found little difference between the levels of free fatty acids in cheeses with low (3·5%) or intermediate (4·2%) S/M levels except for myristic and palmitic acids which were considerably higher in the higher salt cheese.

Proteolysis is considerably more extensive in unsalted than in salted cheese and consequently the body of the former is less firm.[5] A linear relationship between the extent of degradation of both α_{s1}- and β-caseins in young (1 month) cheese and % S/M is apparent from the data of Thomas and Pearce.[15] During the normal ripening of Cheddar cheese, α_{s1}-

casein is the principal substrate for proteolysis with little degradation of β-casein;[27] proteolysis of β-casein is more extensive at low salt levels.[33] However, Thomas and Pearce[15] noted that while the normal products of β-casein degradation (β-I, β-II produced by rennets, and γ-casein by milk proteinase) were not apparent in their studies, the concentration of unhydrolysed β-casein decreased, suggesting that proteolysis of β-casein in low-salt cheese may be due to bacterial proteinases.

At least 5 studies[60-64] have attempted to relate the quality of Cheddar cheese to its composition. While these authors agree that the moisture content, % S/M and pH are the key determinants of cheese quality, they disagree as to the relative importance of these three parameters.

In a study of 300 Scottish Cheddar cheeses, O'Connor[60] found that flavour and aroma, texture and total score were not correlated with moisture content but were significantly correlated with % NaCl and particularly with pH. Salt content and pH were themselves strongly correlated, as were salt and moisture; a very wide variation in composition was noted. Gilles and Lawrence[61] proposed a grading scheme for young (14 day) Cheddar cheese, based on analysis of cheese made at the New Zealand Dairy Research Institute over many years and also by commercial cheese factories in New Zealand. The influence of cheese composition on quality and compositional grading of Cheddar cheese will be discussed in Chapter 1, Volume 2; suffice it to record here that the S/M specified for Premium and First Grade Cheddar in New Zealand are 4·0–6·0 and 2·5–6·0, respectively.

Fox[62] assessed the influence of moisture, salt and pH on the grade of 123, 10-week-old Irish Cheddar cheeses (70 high quality and 53 'rejects') from 6 factories and 27 extra-mature, high-quality Cheddars. The composition of the cheeses varied widely and while the correlations between grade and any of the compositional factors were poor, a high percentage of cheeses with compositional extremes were downgraded, especially those with low salt ($< 1\cdot4\%$), high moisture ($> 39\%$) or high pH ($> pH\ 5\cdot4$). In the samples studied, salt concentration seemed to exercise the strongest influence on cheese quality and the lowest percentage of down-graded cheeses can be expected in the salt range 1·6–1·8% or in the S/M range, 4·0–4·9%. The composition of high quality extra-mature cheeses also varied widely but less than that of the young cheeses. Although the mean salt levels are identical for both groups of cheese, the spread was much narrower for the mature cheeses and only 3 had $< 1\cdot7\%$ NaCl. The mean moisture content of the mature cheeses was 1% lower than that of the regular cheeses.

The grading ratio (ratio of high to low grading cheeses) for 486 14-day-old cheeses produced at the New Zealand Dairy Research Institute was most highly correlated with the % moisture in fat-free substances and second best with % salt.[63] The optimum compositional ranges were: moisture-in-non-fat substances: 52–54%; % S/M: 4·2–5·2%; pH: 4·95–5·15. Cheese with a S/M of 3·1% gave highest grade cheese in a study by Knox[65] although there was little difference in grade in the S/M range 3·1–5·2; quality declined markedly at % S/M > 6·4.

A very extensive study of the relationship of the grade and composition of nearly 10 000 cheeses produced in 5 commercial New Zealand factories was made by Lelievre and Gilles.[64] As in previous studies, considerable compositional variation was evident but the variation was considerably less for some factories than others. While the precise relationship between grade and composition varied from plant to plant, certain generalizations emerged: (1) within the compositional range suggested by Gilles and Lawrence[61] for 'premium' quality cheese, composition does not have a decisive influence on grade, which falls off outside this range; (2) composition alone does not provide a basis for grading as currently acceptable to the dairy industry (New Zealand); (3) moisture-in-non-fat substances was again found to be the dominant factor influencing quality; (4) within the recommended compositional bands, grades declined marginally as moisture-in-non-fat solids (MNFS) increased from 51% to 55%, increased slightly as S/M decreased from 6% to 4% while pH had no consistent effect within the range 4·9–5·2 and FDM had no influence in the range 50–57%. The authors stress that since specific inter-plant relationships exist between grade and composition, each plant should determine the optimum compositional parameters pertinent to that plant.

Apart from the acid flavour associated with low-salt cheese, bitterness has been reported consistently as a flavour defect in such cheeses. A complex correlation exists between the propensity of a cheese to develop bitterness and starter culture, pH, rate of acid development and % salt-in-moisture. There is still some controversy on the development of bitterness (cf. Refs 16, 66–68) but the subject will not be reviewed here.

From the compositional viewpoint, % S/M appears to be the most important factor influencing bitterness.[17] The probability of bitterness developing is greatly increased at % S/M < 4·9 and pH is a significant factor only between 4·3 and 4·9% S/M. The bitterness of peptides is strongly correlated with hydrophobicity.[69,70] The bitter peptides in cheese appear to arise primarily from β-casein[71] which might be expected since β-casein is the most hydrophobic casein. The effectiveness of NaCl in preventing bitterness is very likely due to the selective inhibition by NaCl of β-casein hydrolysis.[30,33,68]

The protein matrix in young cheese appears to consist of α_{s1}-casein molecules linked through hydrophobic interactions between their amino terminal regions; the primary site for rennet action on α_{s1}-casein is Phe$_{23}$–Phe$_{24}$ (Ref. 72) or Phe$_{24}$–Val$_{25}$ (Ref. 73), hydrolysis of which leads to the formation of α_{s1}-I-casein and rupture of the matrix. This specific cleavage is considered to be primarily responsible for the loss of firmness of cheese during the early stages of ripening.[74,75] The influence of NaCl on the proteolysis of α_{s1}-casein (see above) partly explains its influence on cheese texture: a weak, pasty body at low salt concentrations and an excessively firm body at high salt levels. The influence of NaCl on cheese moisture levels and possibly on protein conformation probably also influence cheese texture.

5.2 Blue Cheese

The influence of NaCl concentration on the principal ripening events in Blue cheese was studied by Godinho and Fox.[24,25,28,76] Proteolysis as measured by polyacrylamide gel electrophoresis and the formation of 12% TCA-soluble N was invariably lower in the outer (high salt) region than in the middle or centre (lower salt levels) zones; the differences were apparent both before visible mould growth (during the first 2 weeks when coagulant is the principal proteolytic agent) and during the mould phase (after 2 weeks).[28,29] There was a strong negative correlation between salt concentration and TCA-soluble N. Unfortunately, formation of amino acid N (e.g. PTA soluble N) or other more detailed characterizations of proteolysis were not investigated. With a few exceptions the pH increased faster at the centre than in the outer region of the cheese, indicating that amino acid catabolism was also influenced by NaCl concentration.

Lipolysis in Blue cheese was also influenced by salt concentration with maximum activity occurring at 4–6% NaCl.[76] However, the concentrations of methyl ketones was relatively independent of salt concentration.

5.3 Camembert Cheese

The ripening of the surface mould-ripened cheeses, Camembert and Brie, is characterized by a very marked softening, almost liquefaction, of the body from the surface to the centre due mainly to the production of ammonia by the surface mould, *P. camemberti* and its inward diffusion;

TABLE I

Influence of NaCl on proteolysis in Camembert cheese (4 weeks old)

NaCl (%)	Zone	pH	WSN as % TN	pH 4·6 soluble N as % TN	70% ethanol soluble N	5% PTA soluble N
0·20	I	5·5	36·1	43·4	23·7	16·8
	O	6·4	100	54·4	35·7	18·9
0·70	I	5·3	28·7	29·1	15·8	10·4
	O	6·1	100	39·2	28·7	15·5
0·93	I	5·2	17·9	17·3	13·3	12·1
	O	6·0	100	49·5	32·8	15·2
1·14	I	5·2	22·5	23·8	15·8	8·1
	O	6·2	93·7	43·4	28·4	10·4
1·73	I	5·1	26·6	28·3	15·8	8·8
	O	6·45	85·3	37·1	22·7	10·1
2·49	I	5·15	22·2	23·1	18·0	8·3
	O	6·3	63·2	29·8	26·1	9·3

I = inner portions of cheese; TN = total nitrogen; PTA = phosphotungstic acid; O = outer portions of cheese; WSN = water soluble N.

however, proteolysis by coagulant and starter proteinases is also important and although the proteinases excreted by *P. camemberti* undergo only very limited diffusion in the cheese, peptides produced by them do, apparently, diffuse into the cheese (see Chapter 4, Volume 2).

In this variety also, NaCl concentration has a major influence on proteolysis and pH changes, as well as on surface mould growth (Table I).

6. SALT ABSORPTION AND DIFFUSION INTO CHEESE

6.1 Methods of Salting

There are three principal methods of salting cheese curd:

1. Direct addition and mixing of dry salt crystals to broken or milled curd pieces at the end of manufacture, e.g. Cheddar and Cottage.
2. Rubbing of dry salt or a salt slurry to the surface of the moulded curds, e.g. in Blue-type cheeses.
3. Immersion of moulded cheese curds in brine solution, e.g. Edam, Gouda, Saint Paulin and Provolone. Sometimes, a combination of

the above methods is used, e.g. Emmental, Parmesan, Romano and Brick.

6.2 Mechanism of Salt Absorption and Diffusion in Cheese

6.2.1 Brine-salted cheeses

When cheese is placed in brine there is a net movement of NaCl molecules from the brine into the cheese as a consequence of the osmotic pressure difference between the cheese moisture and the brine. Consequently, the water in the cheese diffuses out through the cheese matrix so as to restore osmotic pressure equilibrium. Gels, including cheese, consist of a ramified framework of long-chain polymers which gives the mass its structure and a certain degree of rigidity and elasticity; the properties of the interpenetrating fluid are generally not appreciably different from those of corresponding solutions. It would appear, therefore, that NaCl molecules diffusing in cheese moisture, while having a longer distance to travel than in solution (diffusing molecules/ions must travel a circuitous route to by-pass obstructing protein strands and fat globules through which they can not penetrate) would not be appreciably affected otherwise. However, based on the mobilities of NaCl and H_2O in Gouda-type cheeses brine-salted under model conditions to obey Fick's law for unidimensional brine flow, Geurts *et al.*[77] concluded that the penetration of salt into cheese and the concomitant outward migration of water could be described as an impeded diffusion process, i.e. NaCl and H_2O molecules move in response to their respective concentration gradients but their diffusion rates are much lower than those in pure solution due to a variety of impeding factors. The diffusion coefficient (D) for NaCl in cheese moisture is $\sim 0.2 \, cm^2/d$, though it varies from ~ 0.1 to $0.3 \, cm^2/d$ with cheese composition and brining conditions,[77,78] compared to $1.0 \, cm^2/d$ for NaCl in pure H_2O at 12.5°C.

Geurts *et al.*[77] used the term 'pseudo-diffusion coefficient' in relation to the movement of NaCl in cheese moisture since the value of the observed coefficient depended on the net effect of many interfering factors on true diffusion. The discrepancies between the true- and pseudo-diffusion coefficients, i.e. D and D^*, respectively, were explained by a simplified model of cheese structure consisting of moisture and discrete spherical fat globules dispersed in a protein matrix comprised of discrete spherical protein particles and 15% (w/v) bound water. Based on theoretical considerations, the impedance of various compositional and structural features intrinsic to the model structure were formulated and their effects on D quantified. The principal factors responsible for impedance of NaCl diffusion in cheese, as postulated by Geurts et al.[77] are:

1. The effect of the protein matrix on the mass ratios of salt and water migrating in opposite directions. The pores (estimated to be 2·5 nm wide) of the protein matrix exert a sieving effect on both the inward-diffusing NaCl molecules and outward-moving H_2O molecules but the effect is more pronounced on the former because of their greater effective diffusion radii, which are approximately twice that of the H_2O molecules. Hence, during brining, the H_2O flux is approximately twice the NaCl flux. The net outflow of H_2O during brining causes the plane of zero mass transfer (a plane where the average flux of all diffusing species is zero) to move away from the cheese/brine interface into the brine and hence reduces the apparent rate of NaCl diffusion due to the additional path length through which the NaCl molecules must migrate. The interference, which is most pronounced when moisture loss is high, e.g. when using concentrated brines or high brining temperatures, was estimated to reduce the pseudo-diffusion coefficient by a factor of ~ 0.2, hence $D^* = 0.8\,D$.

2. When the NaCl molecules do enter the cheese, the relatively narrow pore width of the protein matrix exerts a frictional effect on the diffusing NaCl and H_2O molecules and reduces their relative diffusion rates from 1 in true solution to 0·5 and 0·75, respectively, in cheese. As the effective pore restriction on the diffusion of NaCl in cheese moisture is determined by its effect on the larger-sized molecule, i.e. NaCl, the pseudo-diffusion coefficient was estimated to be reduced by a factor of 0·5.

3. Frictional effects of protein-bound water. Water binding in cheese (0·1 to 0·15 g H_2O/g para-casein[79]) makes $\sim 10\%$ of the total cheese moisture unavailable for salt uptake and hence reduces the apparent diffusion coefficient. Furthermore, the protein-bound water reduces the relative pore-width of the protein matrix, thus retarding further the movement of NaCl and H_2O molecules.

4. The high relative viscosity of cheese moisture. The viscosity of cheese moisture is about 1·27 times that of pure water at 12·5°C due to the presence of dissolved materials, e.g. acids, salts and nitrogenous substances. NaCl molecules diffusing through the cheese moisture encounter an increased collision frequency with

the dissolved substances, and are also affected by the charge fields of these substances; both these factors reduce NaCl mobility and the pseudo-diffusion coefficient is thus reduced by a factor of $1/\eta_{rel}$.

5. Obstructions of fat globules and globular protein particles. On proceeding from one parallel plane to another within the cheese, the diffusing molecules must travel by a circuitous route to by-pass obstructing particles. The ratio of the real to the apparent distance travelled is a measure of the obstructions caused by fat globules (λ_f) and protein particles (λ_p). Theoretically, λ_f can vary from $\pi/2$ for a close-pack arrangement to 1 for a very low fat system, e.g. skim milk cheese. In experimental Gouda cheeses, λ_f and λ_p were found to vary with composition which altered the volume fractions of the fat and protein phases and reduced the pseudo-diffusion coefficient by a factor of $1/(\lambda_f\lambda_p)$. Typical values of λ_f and λ_p were 1·32 and 1·35, respectively, for a Gouda cheese containing 29% fat and 43% moisture.[77] Beginning from a simplified model of cheese structure and considering the relative effects of the interfering factors discussed, Geurts *et al.*[77] postulated a theoretical 'pseudo-diffusion' coefficient, $D^* = (0\cdot8 \times 0\cdot5\,D)/(\lambda_f\lambda_p\eta_{rel})$.

While the model cheese structure adopted by Geurts *et al.*[77] may appear oversimplified in view of the results of electronmicroscopic examinations of cheese structure,[80,81] the calculated impedance derived therefrom was sufficient to explain the very low diffusion coefficient of NaCl in cheese moisture and the variations of D^* with variations in cheese composition and brining conditions.

6.2.2 Direct mixing of salt with milled curd

When dry salt is distributed over the surface of milled curd or curd granules, some NaCl dissolves in the surface moisture and diffuses slowly inwards a short distance.[82,83] This causes a counterflow of whey from the curd to the surface which dissolves the remaining salt crystals and, in effect, creates a brine solution around each particle, provided mixing of curd and salt is adequate. However, because of the relatively large surface area to volume ratio of the curd as a whole, salt uptake occurs from many surfaces simultaneously and less time is required for uptake of an adequate amount of salt in dry-salting milled curd (10–20 min) than in brining whole cheeses (3–5 days). Some of the 'brine' on the surface of curd particles drains away through the curd mass while more is physically expelled from the curd particles during pressing and is lost in the 'press whey'. As the salt/surface area ratio is usually low, and the period of contact of the curd surface with the concentrated brine layer is relatively short, little localized surface protein contraction occurs compared to that in dry-salted, moulded curds.[83]

6.2.3 Dry surface salting of moulded pressed cheese curd

A block of curd can be regarded as a very large particle and solution of dry salt in the surface moisture layer is a prerequisite for salt absorption in this method also. The counterflow of water from the cheese creates a concentrated brine layer on the cheese surface and salt uptake then occurs by an impeded diffusion process. Because the surface is in contact with a concentrated brine for a long time (several days), there is considerable contraction of the curd surface (salting-out of protein) and this probably leads to relatively high moisture losses from the surface region and hence a reduction in the inward mobility of NaCl which accounts for the lower rate of salt uptake in this method than in brining.[25]

6.3 Factors Influencing Salt Absorption by Cheese

The only prerequisite for salt absorption by cheese is the existence of a salt-in-moisture gradient between the cheese and the salting medium. However, the quantity of salt absorbed depends on the intrinsic properties of the cheese, the conditions of salting and the duration of salting. As the different procedures of salting all involve salt absorption via an impeded diffusion process, the general factors affecting salt uptake by cheese apply equally to granules or milled curd pieces on mixing with dry salt and moulded cheeses which are brined and/or dry salted. Certain peculiarities of the salting of milled curd pieces, as in Cheddar, which affect salt absorption will be discussed separately.

6.3.1 Concentration gradient

It is generally accepted that an increase in brine concentration results in higher rates of salt absorption and increased salt-in-moisture levels in the cheese.[77,82,84] However, while the rate of NaCl diffusion is scarcely affected by brine concentration in the range 5–20%,[77,78] the rate of salt uptake increases at a diminishing rate with increasing brine concentration.[82,84] In model brining experiments, in which cheese slices of different thickness were completely submerged in brine, there was a sharp decrease in the rate of salt absorption as the difference between the NaCl concentration in the cheese moisture and the brine decreased, especially when the initial difference was large.[84] A somewhat similar situation applies to dry-salted cheeses: the increase in salt-in-moisture level in Cheddar curd is not proportional to the increase in the level of dry salt added to the milled curd.[10,85] This was attributed to increased salt losses with increased salting rates, which reflects the decreasing effect of the driving force (concentration gradient) in raising the quantity of salt absorbed as the salt-in-moisture level in the cheese approaches that of the brine.

6.3.2 Cheese geometry

It is generally agreed that the rate of salt absorption increases with increasing surface area to volume ratio of the cheese.[82,84,85] This is most readily observed on comparing the rate of salt uptake by milled curd (e.g. Cheddar) and whole moulded cheeses (Brick, Emmental, Romano and Blue-type cheeses) in brine: in the former, salt absorption occurs from many surfaces simultaneously and the time required to attain a fixed level of salt is very much less than in brined moulded cheeses.[77,82,84,86-91] While at first sight it may appear that smaller cheeses would have a higher mean salt content than larger ones after brining for equal intervals, this applies only to cheeses of the same shape and relative dimensions as salt uptake is linearly related to the surface area to volume ratio of the cheese.[77,78]

In addition to its influence on the surface area to volume ratio, cheese shape also affects the rate of salt absorption via its effect on: (i) the number of directions of salt penetration from the salting medium into the cheese[78] and (ii) the ratio of planar to curved surface area of the cheese.[84,88] Geurts *et al.*[88] found that on brining Edam-type cheese, the quantity of NaCl absorbed per cm^2 cheese surface was greater for an infinite slab than for a sphere and the relative reduction in salt uptake through curved surfaces increased with brining time and with degree of curvature. In Romano-type cheeses with approximately equal surface area to volume ratios, the rate of salt absorption by rectangular-shaped cheeses (volume: $4000 \, cm^3$; three effective directions of salt penetration) was higher than that by cylindrical cheeses (volume: $3400 \, cm^3$; two effective directions of salt concentration) at any time during a 9-day brining period (Fig. 3).[78]

6.3.3 Salting time

It is well established that the quantity of salt absorbed increases with salting time (Refs 18, 25, 82, 92, 93) but that the rate of salt absorption decreases with time due to a decrease in the NaCl concentration

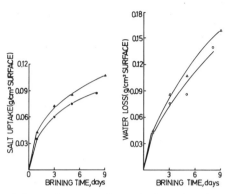

Fig. 3. Influence of cheese shape on salt uptake (▲, ●) and moisture loss (△, ○) by Romano-type cheese during salting in 19·5% NaCl brine at 23°C. Rectangular cheeses (▲, △), cylindrical cheeses (●, ○) (from Ref. 78).

differential between the cheese moisture and the brine.[84] Indeed, the quantity of salt taken up by a cheese is proportional to the square root of brining time [$\sqrt{t}$].[84,88] However, as the curvature of the cheese surface increases, the proportionality of salt uptake with $\sqrt{t}$ is lost and the relative reduction in salt uptake per unit area of cheese surface increases with increasing degree of curvature, and with time.[88] This implies that for cheeses with equal surface area to volume ratios, volumes and compositions, brined under the same conditions, the rate of salt absorption per unit surface area (and hence the cheese as a whole) would be in the order: rectangular > cylindrical > spherical[78] (however, other aspects of cheese geometry affect the mean salt level, as discussed above).

Geurts et al.[88] derived a theoretical relationship for the quantity of salt absorbed from a flat surface as a function of brining time:

$$Mt = 2(C - C_o)(D^*t/\pi)^{1/2}V_w$$

where Mt = quantity of salt absorbed over time, g NaCl/cm^2
C = salt content of brine, g NaCl/ml
C_o = original salt content of the cheese, g/ml
t = duration of the salting period, days
D^* = pseudo-diffusion coefficient, cm^2/day
V_w = average water content throughout the cheese at time t, g/g.

Applying this theoretical relationship to their model brining experiments on cylindrical Gouda cheeses brine-salted by unidimensional diffusion through one of the planar surfaces in contact with the brine,[77] Geurts et *al.*[88] found that the predicted values for the quantity of salt absorbed per cm^2 planar surface (M_p) were in close agreement with the experimental values (M_t) over a three day brining period: $M_t = 0.98 M_p$.

6.3.4 Temperature of curd and brine

In brining experiments with milled Cheddar chips, Breene *et al.*[82] found that for curd tempered to any temperature in the range 26.7–43.3°C, salt uptake increased with increasing brine temperature in the same range. However, curd tempered to 32°C absorbed salt less readily than curd tempered at lower or higher temperatures before brining. This was attributed to a layer of exuded fat on the surfaces of the curd particles at 32°C which impeded salt uptake; less fat was exuded at lower temperatures while at higher temperatures exuded fat was liquid and dispersed in the brine. Geurts *et al.*[77,79] showed that increasing brine temperatures resulted in higher mobility of NaCl and higher salt absorption in Gouda cheese due partly to an increase in true diffusion and partly to an increase in the effective pore width of the protein matrix as non-solvent water decreases with increasing temperature.[79]

6.3.5 Curd pH

While the effect of pH on the rate of salt absorption by whole cheeses has not been investigated, a number of studies have investigated the effect of titratable acidity at salting on salt retention by Cheddar cheese curd. Curd salted at low acidity retains more salt than more acidic cheeses (Fig. 4);[17,84,85,95] since low acid curd normally contains more moisture than high acid curd one might expect more syneresis and higher salt losses in the former. Lawrence and Gilles[17] suggest that the observed difference in salt retention may be due to the higher solubility of the curd at the higher pH values, which may effect a higher retention of salt by the curd structure *per se.*[94]

6.3.6 Moisture content of the curd

Geurts *et al.*[77,79] showed that the diffusion coefficient and the quantity of salt absorbed by experimental Edam and Gouda-type cheeses during brine-salting generally increased as the moisture content of the curd increased. Similar results were obtained by Byers and Price[92] for brine-salted Brick cheese. Undoubtedly, the higher salt uptake which accompanies increased moisture levels is a consequence of the concomitant increase in the rate (and depth) of penetration into the cheese which has been attributed[77] to an increase in the relative pore width of the protein matrix (volume

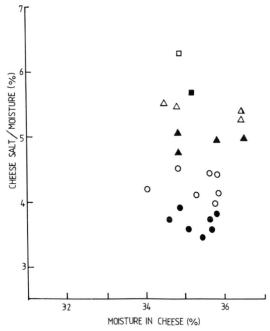

Fig. 4. The effect of salting acidity on salt/moisture in Cheddar cheese: open symbols, curd TA at salting, 0·50%; closed symbols, curd TA at salting, 0·75%. Salting rate 1·8% (w/w): ○ ●; salting rate 2·5%: △ ▲; salting rate 2·75%: □ ■ (from Ref. 85).

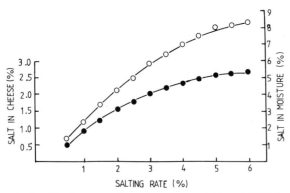

Fig. 5. The relationship between the salt contents (●) and S/M levels (○) of batches of curd from the same vats, salted at different rates (from Ref. 95).

fraction of protein phase decreases as moisture content increases), which reduces the frictional effect on the inward-diffusing NaCl molecules.

On dry-salting milled Cheddar curd, the reverse situation occurs: as the initial moisture level increases, the rate of salt absorption decreases giving lower salt and salt-in-moisture values in the cheese for a fixed salting rate.[83,85] Such decreases were attributed to greater whey and salt losses from the high-moisture curds; an increase in curd moisture content from 39·1 to 43·4% caused a 30% increase in the amount of whey drainage and a decrease in salt retention from 59% to 43% of the amount applied.[83] Thus, while the extent of salt penetration within each granule increases, there is less salt available for uptake as the initial curd moisture increases (salt causes loss of moisture from the curd and at the same time is itself removed).

6.4 Factors Affecting Salt Uptake in Cheddar Curd

6.4.1 Method of salting

Breene *et al.*[82] showed that salting of milled Cheddar curd by brining gives a higher rate of salt absorption and a higher level of salt-in-moisture in the pressed curd than dry salting. Differences in absorption rates were explained on the basis of availability of salt at the surfaces of the curd. When dry salt is placed on freshly milled curd, a portion dissolves in the surface moisture, creating a very thin layer of super-saturated brine. The salt-in-moisture gradient between the brine and the cheese moisture results in mutual movements of salt and water in opposite directions in response to their respective concentration gradients. Some water is also 'squeezed out' of the curd due to localized surface contraction (salting-out of the protein matrix) as a result of contact with the super-saturated brine. The moisture level in the curd, which influences whey release, affects the rate of solution of surface salt. When curd is placed in brine, salt absorption begins immediately through all surfaces. Release of whey occurs, as in dry salting, but its extent is not a limiting factor.[83]

6.4.2 Salting rate

As expected, an increase in salting rate increases the rate of salt absorption by, and whey drainage from, cheese thus giving higher levels of salt and salt-in-moisture and lower levels of moisture in the cheese after salting for a fixed time (Refs 10, 60, 78, 83, 85, 96, 97). However, the relationship is curvilinear (Fig. 5), i.e. the increase in the salt and salt-in-moisture levels in the cheese is not proportional to the level of salt added, especially at the higher salting rates, because of higher salt losses at increased salting rates. Although these principles are probably generally applicable, the precise relationship between salt losses and retention depends on the pH and moisture content of the curd and the period of time allowed for salt diffusion into the curd. These interrelationships have been studied by Sutherland[83] and Gilles.[85]

Sutherland[83] showed that the volume of whey released from the curd and the percentage of added salt lost increased linearly with the level of salt added (over a narrower range than that used by O'Connor[10]) while the % moisture, % salt, % salt-in-moisture and pH of the cheeses increased in a curvilinear fashion as the level of added salt was increased. The level of salt addition had no significant effect on fat losses (~ 0.25 kg/100 kg curd). The percentage of added salt lost increased slightly with increasing salting temperature but the proportion of salt lost during the holding, pre-pressing, period increased markedly. The pH and % moisture in the finished cheese were essentially unaffected by salting temperature but % salt and % S/M decreased and % fat lost increased markedly. Increasing the duration of mixing salt into the curd had little effect on the volume of whey released but decreased the percentage of salt lost and hence increased the salt and S/M contents of the cheese; fat losses were markedly increased. Salt losses were substantially reduced and consequently % salt and % S/M were substantially increased by extending the pre-pressing holding period. Not surprisingly, salt losses increased with increasing moisture content in the curd.

As well as confirming the work of Sutherland,[83] Gilles[85] confirmed that greater salt losses occurred at high than at low acidity, that salt particle size has little effect on salt retention but milling the curd to smaller particles gives higher salt retention. Indeed, Gilles[85] maintains that while the best way to regulate the salt content of cheese is to control its moisture content (which can be best done by dry stirring), it is also possible to do so by varying the level of added salt though this is less desirable because of the influence of several factors on salt retention.

Degree of mixing of salt and curd
Extending the stirring time of salted Cheddar curd from 20 s to 6 min caused a significant increase in salt and S/M levels, i.e. from 1·53 to 1·97%, and 4·41 and 5·71%, respectively.[83] Undoubtedly, better mixing leads to salt absorption from more faces and hence there is less 'free' salt to be lost in the press whey. In relation to this, mechanical salting procedures give

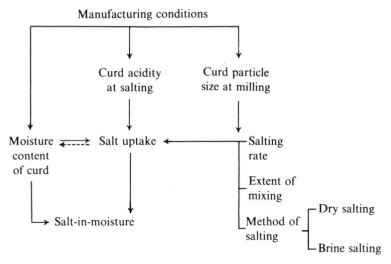

Fig. 6. Principal factors that affect the uptake of salt by Cheddar curd.

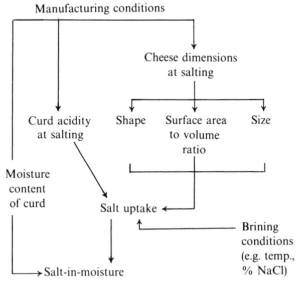

Fig. 7. Principal factors that affect salt uptake by brine-salted cheeses.

more uniform distribution of salt in Cheddar cheese than hand or semi-automated salting systems.[65,98,99]

Time between salting and pressing
Extending the holding time between salting and pressing increases the salt and S/M levels of the pressed (Cheddar) cheese.[82,83,85] The increase was attributed to a higher total absorption and hence a reduction in the physical loss of salt.

Curd depth during holding
When the depth of salted Cheddar curd during holding was increased from 12·7 to 68·0 cm, the moisture, salt and S/M levels decreased from 35·1 to 34·9%, 1·81 to 1·68%, and 5·1 to 4·8%, respectively.[83]
   The interaction of some factors influencing salt uptake in Cheddar-type curd and brine- or dry-salted cheeses are summarized in Figs. 6 and 7, respectively.

6.5 Factors Influencing Salt Diffusion in Cheese During Salting

There is relatively little information on the factors which influence the movement of NaCl in cheese during salting. The first such study was made by Georgakis[100] who related the diffusion of NaCl in Greek Feta cheese to cheese surface area, duration of salting, brine concentration and the fat and moisture contents of the cheese. In model brining experiments, Geurts *et al.*[77] quantified the influence of variations in cheese composition and brining conditions on the pseudo-diffusion coefficient (D^*) of NaCl in the moisture phase of Gouda cheese. As the pseudo-diffusion coefficient is an intrinsic property of a given cheese, obviously the factors which affect the movement of salt in cheese during brining presumably also apply to the cheese after brining and hence have a decisive effect on the rate of attainment of salt-in-moisture equilibrium, and hence moisture equilibrium since moisture transport is a direct consequence of salt transport.[77] Although continuing physico-chemical changes during ripening may alter the situation somewhat, it is worth noting that the diffusion coefficient for NaCl in the moisture phase of a dry-salted, 12-week old Cheddar (50% FDM, 37·9% H_2O) corresponded well[101] with that found by Geurts *et al.*[77] for brine-salted Gouda cheese of similar composition.
   The effects of the various factors on NaCl diffusion in Gouda cheese have been studied by Geurts *et al.*[77] and Guinee.[78]

TABLE II

Influence of cheese composition on salt diffusion in cheese moisture (Ref. 78)

Cheese code	Properties of unsalted cheese								Obstructing factors		Diffusion coefficients	
	Fat (%)	Moisture (%)	Solids not-fat (%)	Fat-in-dry matter (%)	Moisture in-fat-free cheese (%)	Volume fraction of fat phase (ϕ_f)	Volume fraction of protein matrix (ϕ_p)	Relative pore width of protein matrix (v/d_p)	Fat tortuosity (λ_f)	Protein tortuosity (λ_p)	D^* (cm^2/day)	$D^*\lambda_f$ (cm^2/day)
1	00·00	53·00	47·00	0·00	53·00	0·00	0·466	0·132	1·00	1·425	0·136	0·136
2	10·88	49·00	40·12	21·33	54·98	0·127	0·442	0·152	1·117	1·409	0·153	0·171
3	19·88	45·93	34·19	36·77	57·33	0·227	0·413	0·178	1·229	1·389	0·203	0·249
4	26·25	43·48	30·27	46·44	58·96	0·297	0·394	0·198	1·296	1·378	0·227	0·294
5	0·00	52·90	47·10	0·00	52·90	0·00	0·467	0·132	1·00	1·425	0·140	0·140
6	10·00	48·93	41·07	19·58	54·37	0·117	0·449	0·146	1·105	1·414	0·202	0·223
7	18·25	44·90	36·85	33·12	54·92	0·207	0·442	0·152	1·208	1·409	0·205	0·248
8	30·28	40·50	29·22	50·89	58·09	0·340	0·404	0·187	1·333	1·383	0·236	0·315
9	18·18	49·20	32·62	37·59	60·13	0·207	0·380	0·213	1·208	1·365	0·295	0·356
10	20·00	47·94	32·06	38·42	59·93	0·227	0·382	0·211	1·229	1·366	0·263	0·323
11	21·00	45·02	37·98	38·20	56·99	0·240	0·417	0·174	1·242	1·392	0·207	0·257
12	21·00	44·44	34·60	37·77	56·25	0·240	0·427	0·165	1·242	1·400	0·176	0·218
13	29·00	41·11	28·89	49·24	57·90	0·326	0·406	0·185	1·322	1·384	0·216	0·285
14	27·66	44·02	28·32	49·41	60·85	0·310	0·371	0·223	1·308	1·358	0·247	0·324

For calculation of ϕ_f and ϕ_p, it was assumed that: (a) cheese moisture contained 5% dissolved solids, density = 1 g/ml; (b) the protein matrix consisted of protein + 15% water bound and had a specific gravity of 1·25; (c) the specific gravity of fat = 0·93. Cheeses were from four trials, i.e. cheese 1–4, from trial 1; 5–8, from trial 2; 9–12, from trial 3; and 13, 14 from trial 4. All cheeses were salted in 18·5% NaCl at 20°C for 3–4 days.

TABLE III

Experimentally determined diffusion coefficient (D*) of salt in moisture in cheeses varying in properties and brined under different conditions. Calculation of diffusion coefficient in moisture ($D^*\lambda_v$) and of relative pore width of the protein matrix (y/d)$_e$ in fat-free cheese (Ref. 77)

Brine (g NaCl/100 g H_2O)	Properties of non-salted cheese				Calculation of factors				Diffusion coefficient (cm^2/day)	
	Type g fat in 100 g DM	pH	Fat content (%)	Moisture content (%)	ϕ_v	λ_v	ϕ_e	$(y/d)_e$	D^*	$D^*\lambda_v$
19·7	12	5·00	5·3	53·0	0·06	1·04	0·42	0·171	0·164	0·170
19·0	12	5·01	4·9	54·0	0·06	1·04	0·41	0·181	0·185	0·192
19·5	12	4·99	5·0	55·0	0·06	1·04	0·40	0·191	0·162	0·168
20·2	22	5·00	10·9	50·2	0·13	1·12	0·42	0·171	0·152	0·171
19·8	50	5·10	33·0	36·2	0·37	1·36	0·44	0·153	0·100	0·136
20·5	50	4·79	31·2	41·1	0·35	1·34	0·37	0·225	0·160	0·215
20·0	50	5·42	30·9	41·5	0·34	1·33	0·37	0·225	0·160	0·213
19·6	50	5·09	30·4	42·2	0·34	1·33	0·37	0·225	0·172	0·229
20·4	50	5·02	29·9	42·5	0·33	1·32	0·36	0·238	0·185	0·245
34·8	50	5·09	29·9	42·5	0·33	1·32	0·36	0·238	0·148	0·196
14·0	50	5·10	30·2	42·5	0·34	1·33	0·37	0·225	0·194	0·258
19·7	50	5·07	29·2	42·9	0·33	1·32	0·36	0·238	0·187	0·248
13·8	50	5·18	29·5	43·0	0·33	1·32	0·36	0·238	0·177	0·234
20·0	50	5·64	28·9	43·4	0·32	1·32	0·36	0·238	0·168	0·221
13·8	50	4·92	26·9	48·0	0·30	1·30	0·31	0·312	0·235	0·305
20·1	50	4·92	26·6	49·0	0·29	1·29	0·30	0·330	0·258	0·333
19·4	50	5·09	25·8	50·1	0·29	1·29	0·29	0·349	0·239	0·309
20·0	62	5·00	39·1	38·5	0·43	1·40	0·34	0·265	0·179	0·251
20·1	62	4·98	37·1	40·8	0·41	1·39	0·32	0·295	0·224	0·311

ϕ_v = volume fraction of fat in cheese, calculated from fat content.

λ_v = tortuosity factor of fat, a function of ϕ_v.

ϕ_e = volume fraction of protein matrix in fat-free cheese.

$(y/d)_e$ = relative pore width of this matrix.

D^* = pseudo-diffusion coefficient in moisture in cheese.

In calculating ϕ_v and ϕ_e it is assumed that cheese moisture contains 5% dissolved substances (density of solution = 1), that the protein matrix consists of protein + 15% water (density 1·25), and that the density of the fat is 0·93. All experiments were carried out at about 12·5°C.

6.5.1 Moisture

It is generally accepted that the moisture content of cheese affects the rates of salt absorption and/or diffusion.[86,92,100] However, from calculations of diffusion coefficients it has been shown[77,78] that for two cheeses of the same variety, the rate of diffusion is not necessarily higher in the higher moisture cheese; the diffusion coefficient depends on the ratios of fat to solids-not-fat (SNF) and moisture to SNF (the structure of the cheese, which determines the impedance to the diffusing molecules (as discussed above), is dependent on its composition). The results in Table II indicate the importance of cheese composition, and hence structure, in salt diffusion. The diffusion coefficient for NaCl in the cheese moisture (D^*) increased with increasing FDM when the % SNF (and hence protein tortuosity, λ_p) decreased and the relative pore width of the protein matrix (γ/d_p) increased (e.g. cheeses 1–8) but decreased when both the FDM and SNF levels increased (cheeses 9–10). In some instances (e.g. cheeses 2, 6 and 9 had $\sim 49\%$ H_2O and cheeses 12 and 14 had $\sim 44\%$ H_2O) the moisture contents were approximately equal but the D^*-values differed considerably due to differences in fat (and hence fat tortuosity, λ_f) and protein (SNF), while in other cheeses (e.g. 11 and 13), D^* was almost equal while the moisture levels differed appreciably. Similar results, Table III, were obtained by Geurts *et al.*[77] Therefore, while it is not feasible to study the effect of moisture, or indeed any one compositional parameter separately, on salt flux, it will be attempted to deduce the quantitative effect of moisture separately.

Within a series of cheeses of the same variety with equal FDM, D increases curvilinearly with moisture content, Fig. 8.[77] Considering cheeses 9–12, Table II, it is apparent that the contribution of the decreasing fat tortuosity (λ_f) (with increasing moisture content) to the increase in D^* was small (D^* and $D^*\lambda_f$ increased by a factor of 1·7 and 1·6, respectively, when the moisture content increased from 44·5 to 49·2%). The principal factor affecting the increase in salt flux was the reduced frictional effect on the diffusing molecules as the volume fraction of the protein matrix decreased; hence the relative pore width increased concomitantly with increasing moisture content (cf. Tables II and III).

The relationship between the diffusion coefficient in the fat-free cheese, $D^*\lambda_f$, ($D^*\lambda_f$ can be considered as the 'theoretical' value of D^* for a system with the same structural features of cheese but from which the impedance to salt diffusion, due to the physical presence of fat globules, has been eliminated) and the relative pore width of the protein matrix is seen in Fig. 9.[77] While the decrease in the protein tortuosity (λ_p) contributes to the

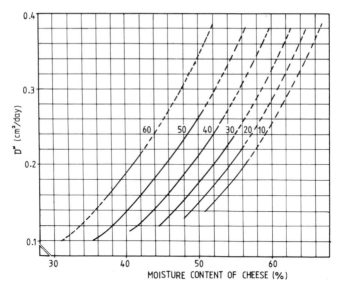

Fig. 8. Diffusion coefficient of NaCl in cheese moisture (D^*) as a function of initial moisture content of the cheese. Parameter is g fat/100 g DM in unsalted cheese. The solid lines are experimental values, broken lines are extrapolations (from Ref. 77).

increase in D^* associated with increasing moisture content (cheeses 9–12, Table II), its effect is small as it varies little within the range of values for protein volume fraction, ϕ_p, encountered.

The role of moisture as the preponderant compositional factor affecting salt flux has been confirmed by Morris et al.[102] who found that the values of D^* for different commercial cheese varieties ($\sim 37 \cdot 3$–49% H_2O; $\sim 23 \cdot 5$–27·5% fat; $\sim 40 \cdot 5$–49·5% FDM; ~ 28–35% SNF) were directly related to the moisture content of the unsalted cheeses (Fig. 10). Of the variation in D^* which could be attributed to compositional parameters ($\sim 70\%$ of total variation), ~ 49, 29 and 22% could be attributed to variations in the relative pore width of the protein matrix, the protein tortuosity and fat tortuosity, respectively.[78]

Perhaps rather surprisingly, it was found that while D^* was strongly dependent on the composition and structure of the unsalted cheese, especially the moisture content, it was scarcely affected by variations in composition along the different planes of a cheese resulting from salt uptake as reflected by: (i) the consistency of D^* over the region of salt and

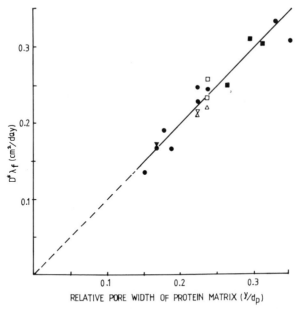

Fig. 9. Diffusion coefficient of NaCl in the moisture in fat-free cheese ($D^*\lambda_f$) as a function of the relative pore width of the protein matrix (y/d_p). Brine concentration, 19–20 g NaCl/100 g H$_2$O; temperature, 12·5°C; 50% fat in DM; pH 5, unless stated otherwise. g fat/100 g DM: ● 12, ▼ 22, ■ 62; ▽ pH 4·79, △ pH 5·50; brine concentration, 14 g NaCl/100 g H$_2$O (from Ref. 77).

water movement and with time,[77,78,90] and (ii) the almost-constant D^* values for brine concentrations in the range of 5–20% NaCl.[77,78] Indeed, pre-salting cheese to different levels (by mixing dry salt with the curd at the end of manufacture) scarcely affected the penetration depth of the salt over a given brining period during subsequent brine-salting, confirming that compositional changes accompanying salt uptake do not influence D^* significantly.[78] Consideration of the physico-chemical changes in cheese associated with the physical presence of salt *per se* and ageing may provide a tentative explanation (cf. Ref. 77). Salting and ageing of cheese are paralleled by a considerable reduction in the amount of protein-bound water and a decrease in the mean diameter of the protein particles[77] and hence an increase in the effective moisture concentration and relative pore width of the protein network. Such changes possibly offset the impeding effects of moisture loss during brining on salt flux and hence D^* remains constant.

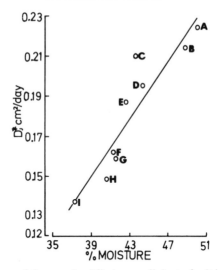

Fig. 10. Dependence of the pseudo-diffusion coefficient of salt in cheese moisture (D^*) on the initial moisture content of cheese salted in $\sim 20\%$ NaCl brine at 15–16°C. Blue cheese (A,B), Gouda (C,D), Romano (E), Jarlsberg (F), Emmental (G,I), unsalted milled Cheddar (H) (from Ref. 102).

6.5.2 Fat content

As discussed previously, the diffusion coefficient for NaCl in cheese moisture is much lower than that in pure solution (i.e. $\sim 0.2\,\text{cm}^2/\text{day}$ as compared to $\sim 1.0\,\text{cm}^2/\text{day}$). This is because salt diffusion in cheese takes place in moisture held in a protein matrix which also occludes fat. Hence, both the sieving effect of the protein matrix and the obstructions of the fat globules and protein strands (through which NaCl can not penetrate and which increase the real distance travelled by a salt molecule on proceeding from one parallel plane to another), reduce the apparent diffusion rate relative to that in pure H_2O. Therefore, the physical presence of fat *per se* reduces the apparent D-value due to its tortuosity factor, λ_f.

However, D^* increases with fat content in cheeses with equal moisture content (Fig. 8). In unidimensional brine salting experiments, Geurts *et al.*[77] observed that for Gouda cheese with 50% moisture, but with 11 or 26% fat, the D^* values were 0·15 and 0·25 cm^2/day, respectively. While the fat tortuosity factor increased with fat level, i.e. 1·12 and 1·29 at 11 and 26% fat, respectively, the relative pore width of the protein matrix also increased (i.e. 0·17 and 0·35 at 11 and 26% fat, respectively). Hence, the increase in D^* with fat content is not due to fat *per se* (which actually reduces D^* by a factor of λ_f) but rather to the concomitant decrease in the protein volume fraction and hence the increase in the relative pore width of the protein matrix; the reduction in the sieve-effect of the protein matrix on the salt molecules overrides the increased obstruction caused by increasing fat levels and hence D^* increases. Indeed, for cheeses of equal moisture content in the fat-free cheese (i.e. cheeses with equal protein volume fractions), D^* is always higher in the cheese with the lower fat content.[77]

From the foregoing it is apparent that the effect of varying any cheese compositional parameter on salt mobility depends on the concomitant changes it causes in the cheese structure (i.e. the ratios of fat to solids-not-fat, and solids-to-moisture). Since increasing fat levels in cheese reduce syneresis,[103,104] D^* should generally increase with increasing fat levels due to the concomitant decrease in the protein volume fraction.

6.5.3 Temperature
Increasing brine (and curd) temperatures are paralleled by increasing diffusion mobilities of NaCl and H_2O in cheese; an increase of $\sim 0.008 \, cm^2/day/°C$ was found for commercial Gouda and Romano-type cheeses in the brine temperature range 5–25°C.[78] Part ($\sim 50\%$) of this increase is attributed[77] to an increase in true diffusion and the remainder to some effect on diffusion-interfering factors, i.e. possible decreases in the relative viscosity of cheese moisture and the amount of protein-bound water which effects an increase in the relative pore width of the protein matrix (in cheese, water non-solvent for sugars decreases with increasing temperature[79]); both of the latter effects would contribute to decreases in the frictional effect on the diffusing species and the protein tortuosity and thus increases in the relative diffusion rate. Extrapolating the effect of temperature on D^* to salted-cheese in which there is large zonal variation of salt and moisture, the higher the storage temperature the shorter should be the time required for equilibration of salt-in-moisture within the cheese mass after salting.

6.5.4 Concentration gradient
While the concentration gradient is a major determinant of the rate of salt absorption by a cheese during salting, it scarcely affects the mobilities of the diffusing species except during brining in supersaturated salt solutions.[77,78] Although the value of the apparent diffusion coefficient decreases on using saturated brines ($\sim 18\%$ lower than that with 5–20% (w/w) NaCl brines at 20°C for Gouda-type cheese[78]) the true value would

be somewhat higher on allowing for the relatively high water loss which in effect causes the plane of zero mass transfer of all diffusing species to recede further into the brine. However, since the salt-in-moisture level in salted cheese scarcely ever reaches saturation point, the inter-zonal variations in salt-in-moisture (S/M) levels do not significantly alter the rate of attainment of S/M equilibrium between different cheeses of the same variety.

6.5.5 Cheese geometry

Cheese geometry influences the rate of attainment of salt-in-moisture equilibrium via its effect on the relative dimensions of the cheese; Guinee,[78] working with commercial Romano-type cheeses of different shapes, showed that at any time during storage, the net difference in S/M concentration along layers of the cheeses increased with layer length. It is worth noting that the depth of salt penetration during brining is proportional to the square root of brining time.[77,78]

Preliminary studies by Guinee[78] using differently shaped cheeses showed that the rate of attainment of S/M equilibrium is not necessarily directly proportional to the volumes when comparing cheeses of the same variety.

Though not investigated to date, conditions of relative humidity and rates of air circulation during storage possibly alter the rate of attainment of salt and moisture equilibria as a result of alterations in cheese moisture.

6.6 Attainment of Salt and Moisture Equilibria after Salting

While salt absorption is a relatively rapid event (~ 15–30 min for salt uptake by Cheddar-type curd;[101,105] and ~ 0.75 h (Camembert) to ~ 15 days (e.g. Parmesan) for brine salting), diffusion of salt post-salting, and hence the rate of attainment of S/M equilibrium throughout the cheese mass, is a slow process, e.g. 10–12 days for Limburger,[86,93] 8–12 weeks for Gouda,[106] Brick,[92] Blue[25] and Romano-type cheeses,[91] ~ 40 days for Feta[100] and ~ 10 months for Parmesan.[89] Salt is fairly uniformly distributed in Cheddar-type cheeses initially, as salt is mixed with the milled curd; however, complete equilibrium is slow and rarely, if ever, reached, giving rise to significant intra- and inter-block variations in the mature cheese (Refs 15, 62, 86, 96–98, 101, 102, 106). In contrast, in cheeses which are salted by immersion in brine and/or by surface application of dry salt there is a large decreasing salt gradient from the surface to the

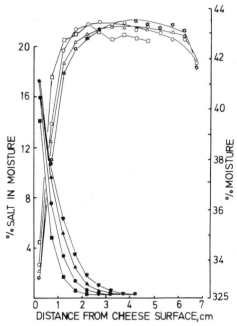

Fig. 11. Moisture content (open symbols) and salt-in-moisture (g NaCl/ 100 g H$_2$O) (closed symbols) in Gouda cheese (fat-in-dry matter 49·1%; moisture, 43·64%; pH, 5·26) as a function of distance from the salting surface after uni-dimensional brine salting (20·3% NaCl) for 1 (□, ■), 2 (○, ●), 3 (△, ▲) and 4 (☆, ★) days at 15°C (from Ref. 78).

centre and a decreasing moisture gradient in the opposite direction at the completion of salting (cf. Fig. 11).[78] Due to the slow diffusion of salt from the rind inwards, these gradients disappear slowly and equilibrium of S/M is practically reached at some stage of ripening, depending on size of cheese and curing conditions (cf. Fig. 12).[78]

Though the importance of the mean, and the uniformity of, S/M levels in cheese in relation to quality have received much attention (Refs 10, 15, 33, 62, 64, 107), the factors that affect the diffusion of NaCl and moisture in cheese after salting and hence the rate of attainment of equilibrium have received little study.

6.7 Diffusion of NaCl in Cheddar Cheese

As cited earlier, significant intra- and inter-block variations in salt concentration occur in mature commercial Cheddar cheese, giving rise to

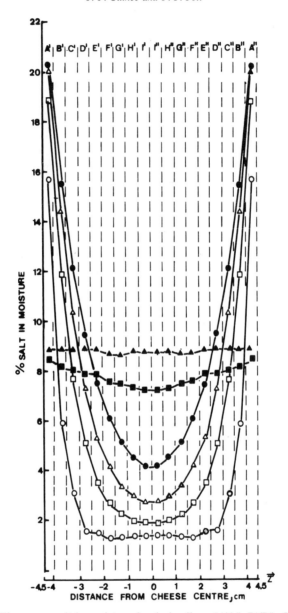

Fig. 12. The mean salt-in-moisture levels in discs A'/A″, B'/B″, C'/C″ etc. (as indicated) of cylindrical Romano-type cheese salted in 19·5% NaCl brine at 23°C for 1 (○), 3 (□), 5 (△) or 8 (●) days or salted for 5 days and stored wrapped at 10°C for 30 (■) and 83 (▲) days (from Ref. 78).

considerable variation in the rate of ripening and quality (Refs 5, 10, 13, 15, 60, 62–64, 102, 108). The method of salt application used in Cheddar cheese manufacture would appear to be particularly amenable to ensuring accurate control of salt concentration with respect to both level and uniformity. However, in commercial practice, this does not appear to be so,[86,99,106] possibly because of the many factors which influence salt uptake (Fig. 6) and the difficulty of obtaining equal salt distribution in all regions of the vat. A preliminary investigation of brine-salting Cheddar curd chips[82] showed that adequate uptake of salt could be accomplished by holding chips ($\frac{3}{8}$ in × $\frac{3}{8}$ in × 2 in) in 25% brine for 5 min and holding for 15 min after removal from the brine before pressing. Considering the problems encountered in controlling salt uniformity using the present mixing procedures, brine-salting of Cheddar appears to warrant further investigation.

O'Connor[98] assessed the uniformity of salt distribution in cheeses salted by hand, semi-automatic or fully-automatic systems; 1 plug from every 10th cheese per vat was analysed. While the range of mean salt contents was relatively narrow, there was very considerable intra-vat and inter-vat variation in salt content with greatest variation in the hand-salted cheese and least with the fully automated system; an inverse correlation between salt and moisture contents was apparent. Further evidence of poor within-vat variation in salt distribution is provided by O'Connor.[109]

The findings of O'Connor[98,108] were confirmed and extended by Fox[99] who showed that, in general, mechanical salting systems gave more uniform salt distribution than hand-salting systems or a semi-automatic system. Considerable within-block variability (12 samples per 20 kg block) in salt concentration was also demonstrated. Morris[106] also found very large differences in the salt content of blocks from the same vat (spread of 0·6% on a mean of 1·38%).

All the foregoing investigators stress the importance of inter- and intra-block variations in salt content, which is inversely related to moisture content; since it is generally agreed that the quality of cheese is strongly dependent on moisture, salt-in-moisture and pH (which was not reported in any of the above studies), it might reasonably be expected that the quality of cheese also varies between blocks from the same vat and even within the same block. It is normal cheese-grading practice to grade a vat of cheese on the basis of a single plug taken from a single cheese per vat; obviously, the quality of this sample may not be representative of the entire vat. For similar reasons, calculation of mass balances in cheese factories on the basis of a single plug sample per vat may be very inaccurate.

Thus, although salt is fairly well distributed in Cheddar cheese during the initial salting, in contrast to brine and/or dry salted cheese, full equilibrium is approached slowly. Sutherland,[101] who prepared Cheddar cheeses (9·5 kg) with regions of high and low salt, found that equilibrium of salt, moisture and, hence, S/M, were not established after 25 weeks ripening at 13°C. Samples situated 7·6 cm apart, which showed an initial difference in S/M concentrations of 4·27%, still showed a difference of 1·56% at the end of the 25-week ripening period. As zones of high and low salt within commercial cheese blocks (∼20 kg, ripened at 4–7°C) are likely to be more widely separated, it was concluded that equilibrium of S/M within such cheeses is unlikely. A similar study by Thomas and Pearce[15] showed that there was only a very slight equilibration of S/M during a 6-month ripening period in Cheddar cheeses prepared with an approximately linear S/M gradient diagonally across the blocks. Equilibration of NaCl in Cheddar cheese intentionally prepared with poor salt distribution was studied by Morris et al.:[102] salt and moisture analyses were performed on samples taken from 32 selected locations in 20 kg blocks (stored at 10°C) over a 24-week ripening period (a similar sampling pattern was used on each of 6 occasions); the results indicated that there was only a slight equilibration of salt over the 24-week period.

Hoecker and Hammer,[18] who measured the salt and moisture levels at the surface and centre of individual chips, pried from a block of Cheddar, over a 72-h period after pressing, found that salt and moisture equilibria were established within individual chips 48 and 24 h after hooping, respectively (a comparable study by Morris et al.[102] gave almost identical results). However, analysis of two 4-month-old cheeses showed significant intra- and inter-block variation in both variables. Hence, while salt and moisture equilibria are attained relatively rapidly within chips because of the short distance over which NaCl molecules have to diffuse from the surface to the centre, the variations throughout the block, as a result of the different quantities of salt absorbed by individual chips, do not disappear during normal ripening. The foregoing observations suggest that the contracted protein layers (salting-out of protein at chip surfaces possibly occurs because of the high initial S/M concentration before equilibrium is established) at the surface of individual chips and/or microspaces between chips which break the continuity of the interpenetrating gel fluid/moisture (in which salt is dissolved), inhibit movement of salt and water across the chip boundaries and hence the cheese mass as a whole, even where a concentration gradient exists. (Indeed, milling per se results in the development of a 'skin' which has fewer fat globules and hence a denser

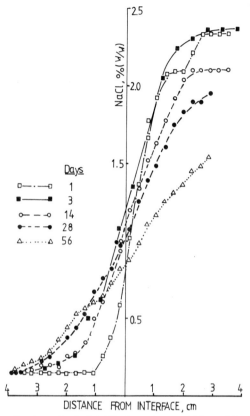

Fig. 13. Distribution of salt (NaCl) throughout a 7·5-cm 'cheese' prepared from half-salted curd and half-unsalted curd at 1, 3, 14, 28 and 56 days after manufacture (from Ref. 102).

protein matrix than the enclosed curd (cf. Ref. 110); moveover, light microscopical studies[111–113] show that the 'skin' at milled curd junctions appears much thicker than those of the enclosed granules.) Observations by Morris[106] on salt diffusion in Cheddar cheese lend support to the view that the milled curd pieces 'trap' absorbed salt: the spread in salt levels within individual cheeses at 3 weeks equalled that observed immediately after hooping.

Morris *et al.*,[102] who also studied salt diffusion in model Cheddar cheese systems, found that equilibrium was established rapidly in cheeses prepared from alternate layers (2 cm thick) of salted and unsalted curd (unmilled) but not in model cheeses prepared from alternate layers (2 cm thick) of salted and unsalted chips. NaCl diffusion across the interface formed between the salted and non-salted layers (from chips) was very slow (Fig. 13) which is in agreement with the results of a similar experiment by McDowall and Whelan.[86] Morris et al.[102] suggested that the fragmented structure of Cheddar cheese (due to its construction from chips) may retard salt diffusion but a further experiment, the results of which showed that the diffusion coefficient for NaCl in the moisture phase of a brine-salted block of Cheddar prepared from unsalted chips at $0.15\,cm^2/day$ was as expected from its moisture content (cf. Fig. 10), could not verify this. Thus it appears that the contracted protein layers between salted chips, which possibly offer a very tight screening effect on the diffusing molecules, overrides the effect of low discontinuous gradients in various directions in commercial Cheddar or even at interfaces between salted and unsalted regions where the concentration gradient is high. In unsalted, milled Cheddar the surfaces of chips would not be as dense as those in dry-salted milled Cheddar due to their higher moisture and fat contents and hence the sieve-effect of the matrix on the diffusing molecules would be much lower than in the latter; indeed the impedance on the salt molecules penetrating the surface layers of milled Cheddar chips during brining is possibly similar to that encountered on penetrating the surface of curd granules *per se* (no light microscopic studies have been reported on unsalted, milled Cheddar curd).

7. EFFECT OF SALT ON CHEESE COMPOSITION

In the light of the findings of O'Connor,[10,60,97] Sutherland[83] and Morris et al.[102] which showed that varying salting rates in Cheddar cheese manufacture were associated with large compositional variations in the cheese, the effect of salt on the gross composition of cheese merits brief discussion.

The moisture content of cheese curd is influenced primarily by syneresis of the cheese curd during manufacture which is, in turn, influenced by the composition of the cheese milk, i.e. fat, protein and calcium levels, the level of rennet used, the curd tension at cutting, and curd treatments during manufacture, i.e. size of curd cut, degree of curd agitation, cooking temperature, rate of acid development, extent of dry-stirring of curd and depth of curd during cheddaring and size of pressed cheese.[103,104,114-119] Further syneresis occurs on addition of salt after milling (e.g. for Cheddar and Cheshire), during pressing and brine and/or dry salting.

It is generally accepted that there is an inverse relationship between the levels of salt and moisture in cheese. This is most readily observed in brine and/or dry salted moulded cheeses during, or immediately after, salting, where a decreasing salt gradient from surface to the centre is accompanied by a decreasing moisture gradient in the opposite direction (cf. Fig. 11) (Refs 77, 86, 87, 90–92). O'Connor[60] found that a negative correlation existed between the salt and moisture concentrations in commercial Scottish Cheddar cheeses. Although there was considerable scatter, the data of Fox[62] show an inverse correlation between the % moisture and % NaCl in 123 commercial Irish Cheddar cheeses. Direct evidence of this relationship is also apparent from the work of O'Connor[96,97] for cheeses from the same batch of curd salted at different rates.

An inverse correlation between % moisture and % NaCl in Cheddar cheese is not surprising since a considerable volume of whey is released from Cheddar curd following salting and during pressing.[83] The amount of whey released is directly related to the amount of salt added to the curd; roughly half of the whey was released during holding following salting and the other half on pressing. Although other factors, e.g. curd temperature, stirring time after salting, depth of curd and duration of holding time after salting and before pressing influence the ratio of whey released during holding after salting to that released on pressing, the overall release of whey was not significantly influenced by these factors.[83] The moisture content of the cheese was inversely related to salting rate.[83]

Geurts *et al.*[77] expressed the relative fluxes of NaCl and H_2O during the unidimensional brine-salting of Gouda-type cheese in terms of the flux ratio, p:

$$-\Delta W_x \sim p\Delta S_x$$

where ΔW and ΔS are the changes (from the non-salted cheese) in the $g\,H_2O$ and $g\,NaCl$, respectively, per $100\,g$ cheese solids-not-salt in planes of cheese x cm from the cheese/brine interface. Experimental values for W and S are shown in Fig. 14 together with theoretical curves calculated for various values of p. The experimental curve for W approximated the theoretical curve for $p = 2$ (i.e. when the amount of H_2O leaving the cheese is twice that of the NaCl entering) but varied from 1·5 at the salt front to 2·34 at the brine/cheese interface and was always > 1. While a similar trend in p values was observed by Guinee and Fox[90] for commercial Romano-type cheese (salted for 9 days in 19·3% NaCl brine), the value of p varied more, i.e. from 3·75 at the rind to < 1 in a region between the rind and the salt front. Guinee[78] concluded that the value of p at a particular

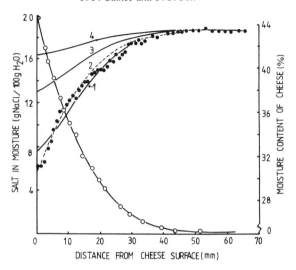

Fig. 14. Moisture (●) and salt (○) content of a full-cream cheese after 8·1 days of brining, as a function of penetration depth. pH 5·64, brine concentration 20·5 g NaCl/100 g H₂O, temperature 12·6°C. Salt contents were calculated from chloride estimations, experimental results (●); (1) moisture content calculated from salt content and a flux ratio (g water:g salt) $p = 2·5$; (2) the same, but p varies from 1·7 at the 'salt front' to 2·9 in the cheese surface; (3) the same, but $p = 1$; (4) the same, but $p = 0$ (from Ref. 77).

location within the region of salt and water movement depends upon the concentrations of NaCl and H₂O at the location—indeed this is possibly the reason why p decreases in the direction from the rind inwards[77,90] along which significant variations of salt and moisture occur as a result of salt uptake *per se*. Indeed, changes in cheese texture and appearance corresponding to changes in p which occur in the region of high salt and moisture movement, are visible when a brined cheese is cut perpendicular to the planar surfaces, during or shortly after brining. In the outermost region (0·3–1·3 cm depending on the duration of the brining period) bordering upon the brine, where the S/M levels were high, i.e. ∼ >12%, the cheese was hard, brittle, dry and white (indicative of salting-out), whereas further removed from the interface where % S/M > 3% and < 10%, the cheese was soft, yellowish and somewhat waxy (indicative of swelling); between the 'waxy' layer and the salt front, the cheese had a uniform appearance and resembled the unsalted cheese.

Since the average flux ratio over the region of salt and water movement

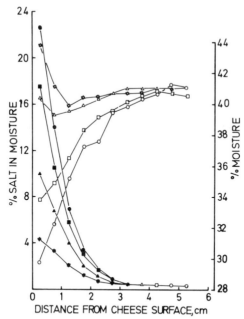

Fig. 15. Moisture content (open symbols) and salt-in-moisture concentration (closed symbols) in Gouda cheese as a function of distance from the salting surface after brine salting for 4 days at 20°C in 5 (☆, ★), 12 (△, ▲), 20 (□, ■) and 24·8 (○, ●) % NaCl solution (without calcium) (from Ref. 78).

is >1 there is a net outflow of water which accounts for the commonly-observed volume reduction in cheese during brining and/or dry salting.

Perhaps, unexpectedly salt uptake during brining is sometimes accompanied by an increase in moisture content in the vicinity of the cheese–brine interface,[86,87,120] especially in weak brines (<10%, w/v, NaCl solution) without calcium (cf. Fig. 15).[78] Such an effect is associated with the 'soft rind' defect and swelling in cheese and is attributed to a salting-in of the protein matrix in low % NaCl solutions which results in increased protein solubility.[87]

7.1 Fat Content

O'Connor[10,60] showed that higher salt levels (especially >2%) in Cheddar cheese are associated with increased fat content, probably due entirely to the decrease in cheese weight as a result of the preponderance of water over salt flux during salting; it is worth noting that O'Connor[60] found a significant inverse relationship between fat and moisture levels ($r = -0.768$) in mature Cheddar cheese. However, on considering the findings of Breene *et al.*,[82] the fat content may decrease, especially at high salting rates if the curd temperature at salting exceeds 32°C.

7.2 Lactose Content and pH

As discussed in an earlier section the lactose content and pH of cheese are strongly influenced by the level and time of salt application.

8. CONCLUSION

Clearly, salt plays a multi-faceted role in cheese ripening with an influence on the physical, chemical and biological attributes of the mature cheese. While a considerable amount of information is currently available on many aspects of the significance of salt in cheese and on salt diffusion in cheese curd, many gaps persist.

REFERENCES

1. Anon, *Food Technology*, 1980, **34**, 85.
2. Joossens, J. V. and Geboers, J., *Acta Cardiologia*, 1983, **1**, 1.
3. Anon, *Dairy Council Digest*, 1984, **55**(6), 33 (National Dairy Council, Ill., USA).
4. Moses, C. (ed.), *Sodium in Medicine and Health: A Monograph,* 1980, Salt Institute, USA, pp. 1–126.
5. Thakur, M. K., Kirk, J. R. and Hedrick, T. I., *J. Dairy Sci.*, 1975, **58**, 175.
6. Kosikowski, F. V., *J. Dairy Sci.*, 1982, **66**, 2494.
7. Lindsay, R. C., Hargett, S. M. and Bush, S. C., *J. Dairy Sci.*, 1982, **65**, 360.
8. Schrveder, C. L., Bodyfelt, F. W., Wyett, C. J. and McDaniel, M. R., *J. Dairy Sci.*, 1985, **68**, Suppl. 1, 66.
9. Irvine, D. M. and Price, W. V., *J. Dairy Sci.*, 1961, **44**, 243.
10. O'Connor, C. B., *Irish Agric. Creamery Rev.*, 1974, **27**(1), 11.
11. Dawson, D. J. and Feagen, J. T., *J. Dairy Res.*, 1957, **24**, 210.
12. Martley, F. G. and Lawrence, R. C., *N.Z. J. Dairy Sci. Technol.*, 1972, **7**, 38.
13. Turner, K. W. and Thomas, D. T., *N.Z. J. Dairy Sci. Technol.*, 1980, **15**, 265.
14. Fryer, R. F., *Proc. 21st Intern. Dairy Congr. (Moscow)*, Vol. 1 (Book 1), p. 485.
15. Thomas, T. D. and Pearce, K. N., *N.Z. J. Dairy Sci. Technol.*, 1981, **16**, 253.
16. Lowrie, R. J. and Lawrence, R. C., *N.Z. J. Dairy Sci. Technol.*, 1972, **7**, 51.
17. Lawrence, R. C. and Gilles, J., *N.Z. J. Dairy Sci. Technol.*, 1969, **4**, 189.
18. Hoecker, W. H. and Hammer, B. W., *Food Res.*, 1943, **9**, 278.

19. Noomen, A., *Neth. Milk Dairy J.*, 1977, **31**, 75.
20. Ruegg, M. and Blanc, B. In: *Water Activity: Influence on Food Quality*, L. B. Rockland and G. F. Stewart (eds), 1981, Academic Press, New York, p. 791.
21. Orla-Jensen, S., *Landw. J. Ahnb.*, 1926, **20**, 437. (Cited from Langsrud, T. and Reinbold, G. W., *Milk Food Technol.*, 1974, **37**, 26.)
22. Antilla, M., *Meijerit. Aikausk.*, 1955, **16**, 7. (Cited from Langsrud, T. and Reinbold, G. W., *Milk Food Technol.*, 1974, **37**, 26.)
23. Rollman, N. O. and Sjostrom, G., *Svenska Mejeritidningen*, 1946, **38**, 199, 209. (Cited from *Dairy Sci. Abstr.*, 1948–50, **11**, 33.)
24. Godinho, M. and Fox, P. F., *Milchwissenschaft*, 1981, **36**, 205.
25. Godinho, M. and Fox, P. F., *Milchwissenschaft*, 1981, **36**, 329.
26. Morris, H. A., *Blue-Veined Cheeses*, Pfizer Cheese Monographs, Vol. 7, 1981, Pfizer Inc., New York.
27. Ledford, R. A., O'Sullivan, A. C. and Nath, K. R., *J. Dairy Sci.*, 1966, **49**, 1098.
28. Godinho, M. and Fox, P. F., *Milchwissenschaft*, 1982, **37**, 72.
29. Hewedi, M. and Fox, P. F., *Milchwissenschaft*, 1984, **39**, 198.
30. Fox, P. F. and Walley, B. F., *J. Dairy Res.*, 1971, **38**, 165.
31. Creamer, L. K., *N.Z. J. Dairy Sci. Technol.*, 1971, **6**, 91.
32. Al-Mzaien, K., Ph.D. thesis, National University of Ireland, 1985.
33. Phelan, J. A., Guinee, T. and Fox, P. F., *J. Dairy Res.*, 1973, **40**, 105.
34. Mulvihill, D. M. and Fox, P. F., *Ir. J. Food Sci. Technol.*, 1978, **2**, 135.
35. Mulvihill, D. M. and Fox, P. F., *Ir. J. Food Sci. Technol.*, 1980, **4**, 13.
36. Phelan, J. A., Ph.D. thesis, National University of Ireland, 1985.
37. Humbert, G. and Alais, C., *J. Dairy Res.*, 1979, **46**, 559.
38. Fox, P. F., *Neth. Milk Dairy J.*, 1981, **35**, 233.
39. Visser, S., *Neth. Milk Dairy J.*, 1981, **35**, 65.
40. Reimerdes, E. H. In: *Developments in Dairy Chemistry—1—Proteins*, P. F. Fox (ed.), 1982, Applied Science Publishers, London, p. 271.
41. Richardson, B. C. and Elston, P. D., *N.Z. J. Dairy Sci. Technol.*, 1984, **19**, 63.
42. Richardson, B. C. and Pearce, K. N., *N.Z. J. Dairy Sci. Technol.*, 1981, **16**, 209.
43. Lawrence, R. C., Gilles, J. and Creamer, L. K., *N.Z. J. Dairy Sci. Technol.*, 1983, **18**, 175.
44. Creamer, L. K., *J. Dairy Sci.*, 1975, **58**, 287.
45. Visser, F. M. W. and Groot-Mostert, A. E. A., *Neth. Milk Dairy J.*, 1977, **31**, 247.
46. Sweeney, K., M.Sc. thesis, National University of Ireland, 1984.
47. Matheson, A. R., *N.Z. J. Dairy Sci. Technol.*, 1981, **16**, 33.
48. Green, M. L. and Foster, P. M. D., *J. Dairy Res.*, 1974, **41**, 269.
49. Noomen, A., *Neth. Milk Dairy J.*, 1978, **32**, 26.
50. Kaminogawa, S. and Yamauchi, K., *Agric. Biol. Chem.*, 1972, **36**, 2351.
51. Kaminogawa, S., Yamauchi, K., Miyazawa, S. and Koga, Y., *J. Dairy Sci.*, 1980, **63**, 701.
52. Sullivan, J. J. and Jago, G. R., *Aust. J. Dairy Technol.*, 1972, **27**, 98.
53. Stadhouders, J. and Hup, G., *Neth. Milk Dairy J.*, 1975, **29**, 335.
54. Morris, H. A. and Jezeski, J. J., *J. Dairy Sci.*, 1953, **36**, 1285.
55. Madkor, S., Studies on Stilton Cheese, Ph.D. thesis, Mania University, Egypt, 1985.

56. Marcos, A., Alcala, M., Leon, F., Fernandez-Salguero, J. and Esteban, M. A., *J. Dairy Sci.*, 1981, **64**, 622.
57. Ruegg, M. and Blanc, B., *Milchwissenschaft*, 1977, **32**, 193.
58. Ruegg, M. In: *Properties of Water in Foods*, D. Simatos and J. L. Multon (eds), 1985, Martinus Nijhoff Publishers, Dordrecht, pp. 603–25.
59. Streit, K., Ruegg, M. and Blanc, B., *Milchwissenschaft*, 1979, **34**, 459.
60. O'Connor, C. B., *Irish Agric. Creamery Rev.*, 1971, **24**(6), 5.
61. Gilles, J. and Lawrence, R. C., *N.Z. J. Dairy Sci. Technol.*, 1973, **8**, 148.
62. Fox, P. F., *Ir. J. Agric. Res.*, 1975, **14**, 33.
63. Pearce, K. N. and Gilles, J., *N.Z. J. Dairy Sci. Technol.*, 1979, **14**, 63.
64. Lelievre, J. and Gilles, J., *N.Z. J. Dairy Sci. Technol.*, 1982, **17**, 69.
65. Knox, J., *Dairy Ind. Intern.*, 1978, **43**(4) 31, 34.
66. Mills, O. E. and Thomas, T. D., *N.Z. J. Dairy Sci. Technol.*, 1980, **15**, 131.
67. Stadhouders, J., *Proc. 20th Intern. Dairy Congr. (Paris)*, 1978, 39ST.
68. Stadhouders, J., Hup, G., Exterkate, F. A. and Visser, S., *Neth. Milk Dairy J.*, 1983, **37**, 157.
69. Ney, K. H., *Lebensmittel. u. Forsch.*, 1971, **147**, 64.
70. Guigoz, Y. and Solms, J., *Chemical Senses and Flavour*, 1976, **2**, 71.
71. Visser, S., Slangen, K. J., Hup, G. and Stadhouders, J., *Neth. Milk Dairy J.*, 1983, **37**, 181.
72. Hill, R. D., Lahav, E. and Givol, D., *J. Dairy Res.*, 1974, **41**, 147.
73. Creamer, L. K. and Richardson, B. C., *N.Z. J. Dairy Sci. Technol.*, 1974, **9**, 9.
74. De Jong, L., *Neth. Milk Dairy J.*, 1976, **30**, 242.
75. Creamer, L. K. and Olson, N. F., *J. Food Sci.*, 1982, **47**, 631.
76. Godinho, M. and Fox, P. F., *Milchwissenschaft*, 1981, **36**, 476.
77. Geurts, T. J., Walstra, P. and Mulder, P., *Neth. Milk Dairy J.*, 1974, **28**, 102.
78. Guinee, T. P., Ph.D. thesis, National University of Ireland, 1985.
79. Geurts, T. J., Walstra, P. and Mulder, P., *Neth. Milk Dairy J.*, 1974, **28**, 46.
80. Kimber, A. M., Brooker, B. E., Hobbs, D. G. and Prentice, J. H., *J. Dairy Res.*, 1974, **41**, 389.
81. Kalab, M., *Scanning Electron Microscopy*, 1979, **III**, 261.
82. Breene, W. M., Olson, N. F. and Price, W. V., *J. Dairy Sci.*, 1965, **48**, 621.
83. Sutherland, B. J., *Aust. J. Dairy Technol.*, 1974, **29**, 86.
84. Guinee, T. P. and Fox, P. F., *Food Chemistry*, 1985, **19**, 49.
85. Gilles, J., *N.Z. J. Dairy Sci. Technol.*, 1976, **11**, 219.
86. McDowall, F. H. and Whelan, L. A., *J. Dairy Res.*, 1933, **4**, 147.
87. Geurts, T. J., Walstra, P. and Mulder, H., *Neth. Milk Dairy J.*, 1972, **26**, 168.
88. Geurts, T. J., Walstra, P. and Mulder, H., *Neth. Milk Dairy J.*, 1980, **34**, 229.
89. Resmini, P., Volonterio, G., Annibaldi, S. and Ferri, G., *Scienza e Tecnica Lattiero-Casearia*, 1974, **25**, 149.
90. Guinee, T. P. and Fox, P. F., *J. Dairy Res.*, 1983, **50**, 511.
91. Guinee, T. P. and Fox, P. F., *Ir. J. Food Sci. Technol.*, 1983, **7**, 119.
92. Byers, E. L. and Price, W. V., *J. Dairy Sci.*, 1937, **20**, 307.
93. Kelly, C. D. and Marqurdt, J. C., *J. Dairy Sci.*, 1939, **22**, 309.
94. Dolby, R. M., *N.Z. J. Dairy Sci. Technol.*, 1941, **22**, 289A.
95. Lawrence, R. C. and Gilles, J., *N.Z. J. Dairy Sci. Technol.*, 1982, **17**, 1.
96. O'Connor, C. B., *IFST Proc.*, 1970, **3**(3), 116.
97. O'Connor, C. B., *Irish Agric. Creamery Rev.*, 1973, **26**(11), 19.

98. O'Connor, C. B., *Dairy Ind. Int.*, 1968, **33**, 625.
99. Fox, P. F., *Irish J. Agric. Res.*, 1974, **13**, 129.
100. Georgakis, S. A., *Milchwissenschaft*, 1973, **28**, 500.
101. Sutherland, B. J., *Aust. J. Dairy Technol.*, 1977, **32**, 17.
102. Morris, H. A., Guinee, T. P. and Fox, P. F., *J. Dairy Sci.*, 1985, **68**, 1851.
103. Whitehead, H. R., *J. Dairy Res.*, 1948, **15**, 387.
104. Marshall, R. J., *J. Dairy Res.*, 1982, **49**, 329.
105. O'Keeffe, A. M. and Phelan, J. A., *Cheese Varieties*, 1979, An Foras Taluntais, Dairy Technology Department, Moorepark, Co. Cork.
106. Morris, T. A., *Aust. J. Dairy Technol.*, 1961, **16**, 31.
107. Lawrence, R. C. and Gilles, J., *N.Z. J. Dairy Sci. Technol.*, 1980, **15**, 1.
108. Lawrence, R. C., Heap, H. A. and Gilles, J., *J. Dairy Sci.*, 1984, **67**, 1632.
109. O'Connor, C. B., *Irish Agric. Creamery Rev.*, 1973, **26**(10), 5.
110. Brooker, B. E., Milk and Its Products. In: *Food Microscopy*, J. G. Vaughan (ed.), 1979, Academic Press, London, p. 273.
111. Rammell, C. G., *J. Dairy Res.*, 1960, **27**, 341.
112. Kalab, M., Lowrie, R. J. and Nichols, D., *J. Dairy Sci.*, 1982, **65**, 1117.
113. Lowrie, R. J., Kalab, M. and Nichols, D., *J. Dairy Sci.*, 1982, **65**, 1122.
114. Emmons, D. B., Price, W. V. and Swanson, A. M., *J. Dairy Sci.*, 1959, **42**, 866.
115. Lawrence, A. J., *Aust. J. Dairy Technol.*, 1959, **14**, 166.
116. Lawrence, A. J., *Aust. J. Dairy Technol.*, 1959, **14**, 169.
117. Aigar, K. and Wallace, G. M., *Proc. 18th Intern. Dairy Congr. (Sydney)*, 1970, Vol. **1E**, p. 47.
118. Lelievre, J., *J. Dairy Res.*, 1977, **44**, 611.
119. Geurts, T. J., *Neth. Milk Dairy J.*, 1978, **32**, 112.
120. Van der Berg, G., Stadhouders, J., Smale, E. J. W. L., De Vries, E. and Hup, G., *Nordeuropaeisk Mejeri-Tidsskrift*, 1976, **43**, 363.

Chapter 8

Cheese Rheology

J. H. Prentice*

Formerly the National Institute for Research in Dairying
(now Food Research Institute),
Shinfield, Reading, UK

1. INTRODUCTION

Rheology, a word coined to denote the study of flow, is formally defined as the study of flow and deformation of matter. It is not immediately evident that all samples of cheese may flow except in the case of some of the softer cheeses of which Brie and Camembert may be cited as typical examples. However, it will be shown later that under many conditions even the hard cheeses may be caused to flow. Nevertheless it is the second part of the definition, the study of deformation, which is more obviously applicable when describing the properties of any cheese since deformation may embrace all aspects of the change of position or the shape of a sample.

Before proceeding to any detailed discussion of the application of rheological methods to the examination of cheese it is pertinent to consider a few of the basic principles. As rheology is a branch of physics, these will all be very familiar to those who have been brought up in the ways of classical physics, but may appear somewhat less esoteric to those who approach the study of cheese from other angles. The layman would probably describe cheese as a solid, certainly the hard cheeses would be so classified and many of the soft ones partake rather more of the nature of a solid than of a liquid. The characteristic which to the layman distinguishes a solid is its rigidity, that is, its ability to maintain, indefinitely, its particular shape. In fact, the precise physical property which describes a solid is known as its rigidity. Without entering into a formal definition at this stage, this is a measure of the relation between the effort which has to

* Present address: Rivendell, 3 Millbrook Dale, Axminster, Devon EX13 7TF, UK.

be applied to a sample of the solid and the deformation which results. It will be understood that if the material is a true solid in the strict physical sense then this relation will be invariant for the material. Furthermore, if the material is a true solid the sample will recover spontaneously once the source of the effort is withdrawn. The physicist will describe such a sample as an elastic solid.

By contrast, the characteristic by which the layman distinguishes a liquid is its fluidity, that is, its ability to flow into and take up the shape of any container which may hold it. With a certain perverseness, actually more apparent than real, the physicist uses the inverse concept for his characteristic property of a liquid, which is called the viscosity. This is, when defined in the same way as before, the relation between the effort applied to the sample and the rate of flow which ensues. Again, if the sample is a true liquid, the viscosity will be invariant for the material and upon cessation of the effort the *rate* of flow will spontaneously return to the status quo, i.e. it will cease. The physicist describes the material as a viscous liquid. If we now replace the word 'flow' in the previous paragraph by the word 'deformation' it can be seen that an elastic solid is characterized by the amount of effort required to produce a certain extent of deformation whilst the viscous liquid is characterized by the effort required to produce a given rate of deformation. The dimension of time does not enter into the measurement of the characteristic property of a solid whereas time is equally important with the spatial dimensions in the measurement of the characteristic physical properties of a liquid.

Solid and liquid may be regarded as the 'black' and 'white' of classical physics. The rheologist is seldom concerned with these except as reference points, but is concerned with the whole spread of that grey area in between, where the material exhibits some of the characteristics of a solid and simultaneously some of the characteristics of a liquid.

It is now possible to define a third category of material. Any material which falls within this grey area, exhibiting both elastic and viscous properties, is known as a viscoelastic material. It may be remarked here that purists reserve the term for materials which appear more nearly to resemble solids, whilst those which flow readily but nevertheless show some kind of elastic behaviour are called elasticoviscous. The distinction is not really necessary though it will be later shown that the two correspond to two different models of behaviour. Both euphony and usage have established the term viscoelastic for general use for describing materials with these intermediate properties unless there is some very compelling reason for making the distinction.

Cheese then fits neatly into the category of viscoelastic materials, as indeed do almost all foodstuffs which are destined to be eaten.

2. DEFINITIONS

Before proceeding further to discuss the rheological properties of cheese or their measurement it is pertinent to give more precise definitions of the terms commonly used by rheologists. What has been loosely described in the foregoing paragraphs as the effort, using a vernacular term, is more precisely known as the *stress*. This is denoted by the greek letter, σ. If this is applied, for example, by means of a weight placed on top of the sample, as in Fig. 1a, the downward force, using SI units is given by the weight in kg, multiplied by the acceleration due to gravity (about $9 \cdot 81\ m/s^2$). This is then given in Newtons. If this is divided by the area of the surface to which it is applied this gives the stress on the sample and is measured in Pascals. Of course, the force could equally well be applied tangentially as in Fig. 1b. It is still the force per unit area of the surface to which it is applied and measured in Pascals. Those familiar with dimensional analysis will see that a stress has the dimensions $ML^{-1}T^{-2}$.

If, as a result of the application of the stress as in Fig. 1a, the height of

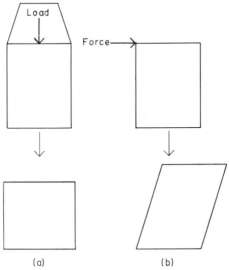

Fig. 1. Application of stress to a sample, (a) compressive strain, (b) shear.

the sample, which may originally be denoted by h_o is changed by an amount Δh, then the fractional change $\Delta h/h_o$ defines the *strain*. This is denoted by the Greek letter, ε. As this is a length divided by a length it is a dimensionless number. Whilst the ratio $\Delta h/h_o$ is the formal definition of the strain, it will be obvious that except when Δh is infinitesimal, the height of the sample changes as the deformation proceeds. It is arguable that for finite, and particularly for large values of strain, this change should be allowed for. This leads to a mathematical definition of the strain as

$$\varepsilon = \ln(h_0/h_1) \tag{1}$$

where h_0 and h_1 are the original and final height of the sample, respectively. Again, this is a dimensionless number. Which definition of strain an author uses depends largely upon his own individual preferences. In the present work, the second (logarithmic) form will be used and the fractional change in a situation such as in Fig. 1, will be described as the compression. In accordance with common usage, this will be given as a percentage to distinguish it from the strain given in decimal form.

When the stress is applied tangentially as in Fig. 1b, the strain which results is described as a *shear*. This is defined as the relative distance through which two parallel planes in the sample travel, divided by the distance separating them and is given by the symbol γ. As before, it is a length divided by a length and is a dimensionless number.

The physical property *rigidity* can now be defined precisely. If the layman's terms, effort and deformation, are replaced by the physical entities, stress and shear, the modulus of *rigidity* is now defined as the stress divided by the shear and this is given the symbol n. $n = \sigma/\gamma$. The dimensions are the same as those of stress and in SI units, rigidity will be measured in Newtons/sq. metre. Although this is dimensionally the same as Pascals, it is convenient to preserve a distinction and reserve the use of Pascals for stresses only.

Returning to the compression of a sample as in Fig. 1a, there is another ratio to be calculated. This is the ratio of the stress to the strain and is termed the *modulus of elasticity* (sometimes known as Young's modulus), and is denoted by the capital letter E. It will be obvious that, if the material composing the sample is incompressible, i.e. its volume is unchanged as a result of any external stresses acting upon it, as the sample is compressed in the vertical direction it will expand in the two other directions. Part of the stress will be used in producing the vertical strain and part in producing horizontal strains. If the material is isotropic, i.e., its properties are the same in any direction, it will follow that the stress is divided equally between the three orthogonal directions and the proper definition of the modulus of elasticity becomes:

$$E = \sigma/3\varepsilon \tag{2}$$

It can easily be shown that as long as the material is incompressible, the modulus of elasticity is 3 times the modulus of rigidity. If, on the other hand, the material is compressible, some of the stress will be expended in compressing the sample and the factor 3 falls to 2 in the extreme case in which no lateral expansion accompanies the vertical compression. The significance of this in the present context is that some research workers quote the results of their measurements on cheese in terms of a rigidity modulus and some in terms of an elasticity modulus. As a rough approximation, cheese may be taken as only slightly compressible so that the factor relating the two is generally nearer to 3 than to 2, but an exact comparison is only possible if the compressibility, and hence this factor, is known precisely.

Turning now to liquid properties, the *rate of deformation* is simply given by the strain divided by the time taken to reach it if the rate is constant or in the more general case by the time derivative of the strain $\dot{\varepsilon}$. This being a pure number divided by a time it has the dimensions of the inverse of time, T^{-1} and is usually measured in reciprocal seconds. In the case of a true liquid it is the tangential forces which give rise to flow, whence the *shear rate* $\dot{\gamma}$ is the relevant rate of deformation. The *viscosity*, denoted by η, is defined as the ratio of the applied stress to the induced shear rate $\eta = \sigma/\dot{\gamma}$, and this is measured in the SI system in Pascal-seconds.

In passing, it may be remarked that the logic of using viscosity instead of fluidity for the characteristic property of a liquid now becomes evident. Both rigidity and viscosity vary in the same sense; in each case a greater numerical value of the property denotes a greater stress being required to achieve the deformation.

The rheological properties of cheese may be studied in two very different ways. The quality of a cheese has long been assessed by graders by feel and by mouth. Apart from those aspects associated with flavour, these graders' judgements are largely rheological in character. In the early days they were the only rheological tests known and much of the early literature attempted to describe rheological properties in terms such as those used by graders. There are severe semantic difficulties in understanding completely some of the earliest research. Graders, whose skill is largely a craft skill, often find it difficult to define precisely the terms they use and other research workers tended to give them their own interpretation, so that confusion arose when trying to distinguish between such terms as consistency and body, hardness and firmness, chewiness and meatiness.

The difficulty was further compounded by the fact that these words do not translate precisely into other languages. Even English and American usage may differ. In more recent years this subjective approach has been much more highly organized,[1-3] and has become a distinct branch of rheology under the name 'Texture studies', the word 'texture' having been adopted for this purpose with a rather different connotation from its OED definition to mean the rheological properties as appraised by the senses and in the case of cheese, amongst other foodstuffs, largely by mouth.

Alongside textural studies, rheological properties may be measured instrumentally and this purely physical approach is that which will be principally considered here. Instrumental measurements may be made on cheese with one of two principal objectives in mind. The more obvious one to the practical cheesemaker is to seek physical measurements which may assist him by providing him with a means of quality control, or to assist the grader in carrying out his assessment, or even to displace him ultimately with a fully automated system that works independently of the human factor. The other aim is the more fundamental one of studying the structure of the cheese itself. It was the first of these two aims which motivated almost all the early work. It is a measure of the complexity of the problem of trying to equate tests made by sensory methods with physical measurements that fifty years later solutions to the problem are still being sought.

It may well be that in endeavouring to seek parity between instrumental measurements and subjective judgements of rheological properties one is asking the wrong question and one to which there is no sensible answer. The real question which should then be asked is what can instrumental measurements tell us about the properties and in particular about the structure of the material, on which the properties depend, and how can this information be useful to the manufacturer and the consumer. It is not the purpose of this chapter to attempt to answer the philosophical question: to do so would be to invoke a discussion of the whole ethos of that branch of rheology—Psychorheology—which is devoted to just that end. Nor is it possible to give a categorical answer to the alternative question. Nevertheless, much of the remainder of this chapter will be devoted to a discussion of the types of instrumental measurements which can be made and to some of the results which have so far been achieved.

3. EMPIRICAL MEASUREMENTS

The instrumentation of cheese rheology may be sub-divided into two more or less separate categories. The first of these historically is that of instruments of an ad hoc nature,[4] which were designed to give some indication of firmness or springiness or similar qualities which the grader or the consumer attributes to the cheese. These are generally unpretentious and hence usually inexpensive and empirical in their mode of action. Because of this, measurements made by them cannot be directly analysed and expressed in terms of basic rheological parameters. Notwithstanding this limitation, they may have a useful place in the cheese scientist's repertoire and much of the earlier work on the rheology of cheese was carried out using them.

The grader, in the course of his examination of a cheese, presses into the surface with the ball of his thumb or finger. One of the most successful of the earlier instruments attempted to simulate this action of the thumb. A hemisphere placed on the upper surface of a cheese was allowed to sink into the cheese under the action of a load and the depth of indentation after a given time was measured. Further, this load could be removed and the recovery of the cheese observed. This instrument, which is depicted diagrammatically in Fig. 2, became known as the Ball Compressor.[5]

It is possible, by making a number of simplifying assumptions, to convert the reading obtained by means of the Ball Compressor into a modulus,[6,7] analogous to the modulus of rigidity, using the formula:

$$G = \frac{3M}{16(RD^3)^{1/2}} \tag{3}$$

where M is the applied force, R the radius of the indentation and D the depth of the indentation. In arriving at this formula it has been assumed that the load is static, that the sample is a homogeneous, isotropic, elastic, incompressible solid and that there is no friction between the surface of the indentor and the surface of the sample. It is fairly evident that every one of these assumptions is violated when cheese is being tested. A cheese is far from homogeneous, its properties vary from the surface to the centre, particularly if it has a rind. Cheddar cheese, especially, because of the process of manufacture, is not isotropic, and other varieties are unlikely to be completely isotropic. Nor is cheese an elastic solid but a viscoelastic material. The indentation is not instantaneous and if the load is removed there is only partial recovery, showing that some flow has taken place. Notwithstanding the limitations, if the test is allowed to

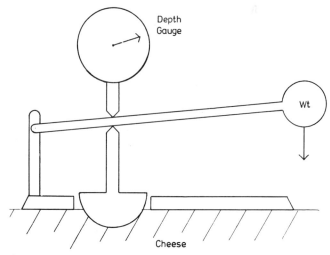

Fig. 2. The Ball Compressor (diagrammatic).

proceed until the indentation becomes slow so that the static condition is very nearly approximated, the use of this formula gives an idea of the magnitude of the firmness of the cheese and enables the reader to relate any measurements quoted in the earlier literature to those made recently using more sophisticated equipment.

The Ball Compressor has been discussed at some length because it has the merit of being a non-destructive test and can be carried out on the whole cheese whereas almost every other rheological test requires a sample to be cut from the whole. Using the Ball Compressor it has been possible to show that in a whole cheese such as Cheddar or Cheshire weighing some 25 kg there are considerable variations in the firmness over the surface of the cheese and that the firmness differs between the upper and the lower side and that this is influenced by the frequency with which the cheese is turned in the store during the maturing period, and the time which has elapsed since it was last turned.[8,9] The implication of this is that whatever instrumental measurement is made it is not possible to assign a single number to any property of the cheese nor is it possible to assess the properties of the cheese by means of a measurement made at a local point in that cheese.

Clearly there is a need for some form of non-destructive testing and for many purposes there is no reason why it should not be empirical, provided that the implications are understood. The Ball Compressor has the merit of cheapness and simplicity, but the time taken to obtain a representative reading militates against its use outside the research laboratory. The problem of devising a suitable test is as yet unsolved. It is unfortunate that the application of ultrasonic techniques which have proved so useful in the non-destructive testing of many engineering materials have so far proved unrewarding with cheese.[10,11] This is because the dimensions of the cracks and other inhomogeneities in cheese are commensurate with or sometimes larger than the wavelength of the ultrasound and large scale scattering takes place. It is difficult for a pulse to penetrate the body of the cheese and both velocity of propagation and the attenuation are more influenced by the scattering than by the properties of the bulk.

One other empirical test deserves to be mentioned. This is the penetrometer.[12-14] It is not quite non-destructive, but almost so as it only requires a needle to be driven into the body of the cheese; no separate sampling is required. The penetrometer test may take several forms. As an example, a needle may be allowed to penetrate under the action of a fixed load,[12,13] or it may be forced into the cheese at a predetermined rate[14] and the force required measured. Whichever mode of operation is used, let the actual action be considered. As the needle penetrates the cheese, that part of the cheese immediately ahead of it is ruptured and forced apart. If the needle is thin, the actual deformation normal to its axis is small, so that the force required to accomplish this may be neglected. On the other hand, the progress of the needle is retarded by the adhesion of its surface to the cheese through which it passes. This may be expected to increase with the progress of the penetration until a point is reached at which the restraining force matches the applied load and further penetration ceases. If a suitable diameter for the needle and a suitable weight have been chosen, this test may be completed in a few seconds. This test will be more useful for cheeses whose body is reasonably homogeneous on the macroscopic scale, such as the Dutch and some Swiss cheeses. With cheeses such as Cheddar or Cheshire, the heterogeneities are generally on too large a scale and the penetration becomes irregular. The needle may pass through weaknesses in the structure, or even cracks and so give rise to the impression of a cheese less firm than it really is, or the point of the needle may attempt to follow a line of weakness, not necessarily vertical. As a result, there will be additional lateral forces acting on the needle and its penetration may be arrested prematurely.

The measurements made with a penetrometer cannot be converted to a well-defined physical constant. Both the cohesive forces within the cheese and the adhesive forces between the cheese and the surface of the needle

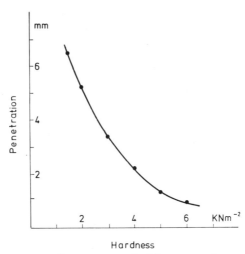

Fig. 3. Penetrometer readings compared with compression modulus (based on data in Ref. 13).

are a consequence of the forces binding the structure together. By inference, these are related to its viscoelastic properties but there is no simple theory which attempts to establish these relations. It has been shown experimentally[15] that there is a statistically significant correlation between firmness as measured by the Ball Compressor and by penetration, but also that this differs between different types of cheese.[16] It has also been shown experimentally[13] that a curvilinear relation exists between the resistance to penetration and an elastic modulus of some Swiss cheese calculated from the results of a compression experiment. This is shown in Fig. 3. A curve such as this has only a limited usefulness since it only relates to one type of cheese, but it does at least give some idea of the magnitude of the forces involved. Except where some such experimental relation is available, penetrometer measurements can only be regarded as purely empirical.

4. PHYSICAL MEASUREMENTS—INTRODUCTORY

The alternative to making purely empirical measurements is to attempt to make objective measurements of recognized physical properties. It has already been remarked that the rheological properties of any material involve both deformation and flow. A complete description of the behaviour of any sample may be said to be given by the dependence of the strain on both the applied stress and the time, i.e. $\varepsilon = f(\sigma, t)$. Graphically, this may be represented by a surface in a three-dimensional diagram. If, for any value of t, the strain is linearly related to the stress, the material is said to be linear viscoelastic. Many substances come within this category for small values of stress and strain; cheeses vary in this respect. For a linear viscoelastic substance a two-dimensional graph of the strain versus time gives a sufficient description; even when there is some departure from this linearity, the graph for any fixed stress gives a useful insight into this behaviour.

The simplest rheological experiment which can be conceived[17] is to apply a known stress to a sample of known dimensions and to observe the progress of the strain with time. When drawn as a graph, this is known as a creep curve. This may be continued indefinitely and eventually some equilibrium will be established. Either the strain will become constant, which occurs when the sample is more akin to a solid, or a constant strain rate will be established if the sample is more akin to a liquid. Instead of allowing the experiment to continue indefinitely, the stress may be removed when a predetermined strain has been reached, or alternatively after a predetermined time. Should the sample possess any elastic characteristics, some energy will have been stored up within it and the strain will decrease again. This part of the graphical representation is known as a recovery curve. The creep and recovery curves between them contain all the information about the rheological behaviour of the sample under that particular stress.

The experiment could be carried out in a different way. Instead of applying a known fixed stress and observing the strain, the sample could be constrained to deform at a known rate and the stress required to maintain this rate of deformation measured. Again, the action may be stopped at any point. If, at this point, the strain is held constant the stress may be followed as it relaxes. Again, the complete cycle contains all the available information about the rheological properties of the sample.

The foregoing is, admittedly, somewhat of an oversimplification. It applies strictly only to those materials which are linear viscoelastic and only to those whose properties are not altered by the action of the strain itself. In the case of cheese, subjecting it to a strain, other than a very small one, certainly modifies its properties and a repetition of the simple rheological experiment will give a different response curve. Indeed, both the extent and the duration of the strain need to be taken into account. A complete rheological description of any sample of cheese will therefore need not only a creep and recovery curve or a compression and relaxation curve, but also a statement of the history of the straining of the sample up to the moment of commencing the measurement. Notwithstanding these caveats, a single rheological experiment on a sample of cheese will yield much useful information. It is pertinent to consider the shape of these response curves and how they may be analysed in terms of easily recognizable physical parameters.

4.1 Models

Returning for the moment to the Ball Compressor. If, after the indentation has become static, or at least so slow as to be nearly so, the load is removed, the cheese begins to recover but the recovery is only partial and eventually the ball comes to rest in such a position that there is a permanent depression in the surface of the cheese. In other words, during the time that the ball had been loaded some flow had taken place. Furthermore, experiments have shown that the longer the time during which the ball was loaded, the greater the permanent depression. This is characteristic viscous behaviour. On the other hand, the fact that some recovery took place is characteristic of an elastic solid.

One convenient way of describing rheological behaviour is by the use of simple models.[18] As the archetype of the elastic solid, one may consider the simple spring. The strain is always proportional to the compression of the spring. In a similar manner, an infinitely long dashpot may be taken as the archetype of a viscous liquid. The rate of displacement is always inversely proportional to the viscosity of the dashpot fluid. These two may be considered to be the essential components of any viscoelastic model.

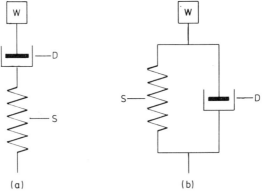

(a)   (b)

Fig. 4.   Viscoelastic models, (a) Maxwell body, (b) Kelvin body.

Starting with just these two units, it is possible to combine them in two different ways to make two new models. If they are placed end to end, as in Fig. 4a, the total displacement (i.e. the strain), is the sum of the displacements of the two units. The mathematical expression of this is:

$$\varepsilon = \frac{\sigma}{G} + \frac{\sigma}{\eta} t \qquad (4)$$

The first term on the right-hand side expresses the elastic component of the strain and this is independent of the time during which the stress is applied, whilst the second term expresses the viscous component, which is proportional to the duration of the stress. If the stress is removed after some given time, t, the spring, no longer constrained, returns to its original length immediately, but that part of the displacement due to the dashpot remains. A complete creep and recovery curve for this type of behaviour is given in Fig. 5a. This model is commonly known as the Maxwell body. Already it may be seen that the Maxwell body model gives a better representation of the rheological behaviour of cheese than one gets by assuming that it is a simple solid or liquid.

If the two units are combined in the other possible way, i.e. in parallel, so that they each have the same compression but they share the stress between them as in Fig. 4b, the equation expressing this is:

$$\sigma = G\varepsilon + \eta\dot{\varepsilon}$$

Solving this equation so that it may be compared with Eqn (4) above gives:

$$\varepsilon = \frac{\sigma}{\eta} \left(1 - \exp\left(-\frac{G}{\eta} t \right) \right) \qquad (5)$$

This is the equation for the Kelvin body. The characteristic curve for the complete rheological experiment now becomes that shown in Fig. 5b. Once again there may be some resemblance between this curve and the behaviour experienced with cheese. The reaction to the application of a

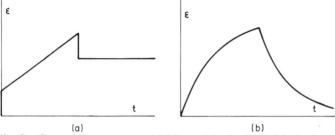

Fig. 5. Creep–recovery curve, (a) Maxwell body, (b) Kelvin body.

load or its removal is not instantaneous, but takes place gradually and only eventually reaches an equilibrium situation.

More sophisticated models may be constructed using the Maxwell and Kelvin bodies themselves as the basic building blocks and combining them in parallel or tandem. The mathematical expressions for the response are readily obtainable. This process may be repeated indefinitely, but the expressions become more cumbersome as the complexity increases. From the practical point of view, little purpose is served by making very complex models; the main use of a model is to give a simple representation, albeit not necessarily exact, of any particular pattern of behaviour. Moreover, the smaller the number of parameters that are introduced, the more likely it is to be useful and comprehensible. Furthermore, there is a very practical consideration that as the complexity of the model increases so it rapidly becomes more difficult to analyse the experimental data. Indeed, the precision of the data may well be insufficient to allow more than a small number of parameters to be identified with any pretentions of accuracy. A simple model, probably with only two or three elements, inexact though it may be, is often the most generally useful in describing the behaviour of cheese.

4.2 Practical Instrumentation

In terms of practical instrument engineering it is easier to apply a deformation and to observe the resulting stress in the sample than to apply a stress smoothly without any jerking at the moment of application. The most popular measurements currently make use of an instrument in which a sample cut from the bulk of the cheese is compressed between two parallel plates, one of which is fixed and the other driven at a constant rate. The total thrust resulting from this is measured or recorded. The plotted curve, or the recorder trace, now has, as one axis, time, which is proportional to the deformation, since the motion is linear, and the other axis is the total thrust. It may be used directly in this form. Cheeses give a characteristic pattern in which certain prominent features may be identified, but this is a semi-empirical use of the instrument.

Before discussing their application in any further detail, two other tests which have had considerable popularity must be mentioned. Both of these derive from the penetrometer. The first is the 'puncture' test,[19] in which a rod is driven into the sample and the resistance to motion measured. There are at least three principal factors affecting this. One is the compression of the sample ahead of the rod, the second is the force required to cut through the sample at the leading edge of the rod and the third is the frictional resistance between the surface of the rod and the surrounding sample. If the sample is semi-infinite so that any compression in a direction perpendicular to the motion may be ignored, the first two factors will be constant once an equilibrium has been established whilst the third will increase linearly with the penetration. By using rods of different cross-sectional shape,[20,21] such that the perimeter remains constant but the cross-sectional area differs, it is possible to separate the effects, and theory exists for this mode of operation.

More usually, the test has been used on small samples of cheese contained within a rigid box.[22–25] In this manner of use, further forces come into play, of which the lateral force on the rod is the most important. At the same time the compressive forces ahead of the rod may no longer be considered constant as the distance between the leading face of the rod and the bottom of the sample diminishes. Some workers[23,25,26] have treated this as the principal force and have calculated a quasi-modulus by dividing the measured stress by the compressive strain. It will be evident that a quasi-modulus so calculated will be greater, by an arbitrary and unknown amount, than any true modulus which could be obtained from a simple unrestrained compression test. Nevertheless, it has proved to be a useful semi-quantitative test.

The other test is the use of a cone[27] to penetrate the sample. A loaded cone penetrates the sample until equilibrium is reached, normally within a matter of a few seconds. This assumes a different model for the sample which is presumed to be plastic, i.e. it behaves as a solid when acted upon by small stresses but once a certain critical stress is exceeded it flows as a viscous liquid. This critical stress is known as the yield stress. From the point of view of the cone penetrometer falling under a constant load, the stress, which is equal to the load divided by the area of contact, is infinite at the commencement when only the apex of the cone touches the surface. As penetration proceeds the cross-sectional area increases in proportion to the square of the depth of penetration of the apex below the surface and the rate of penetration is controlled by the rate at which the sample flows laterally. Equilibrium is rapidly approached when the applied stress no longer exceeds the yield stress. The vertical stress may then be calculated from the penetration distance and the angle of the cone:

$$Y = \frac{Mg}{\pi h^2} \cot^2 \alpha/2 \qquad (6)$$

where α is the apical angle of the cone, h the penetration and M the applied load. This stress is greater than the yield stress of the sample since it does not take into account the stresses involved in causing the sample to flow in a lateral direction. An estimate of the yield stress, σ_y, may be obtained by multiplying the stress Y by $\frac{1}{2}\sin\alpha$,[28] so that:

$$\sigma_y = \frac{Mg}{2\pi h^2}\sin\alpha\cot^2\alpha/2 \tag{7}$$

4.3 Force–Compression Tests

In order to relate instrumental measurements to models as described above and hence to obtain elastic and viscous constants relating to the samples, it is necessary to consider the way in which operation of an instrument differs from the basic rheological experiment proposed.[29] In a compression instrument it is usually the rate at which the plates approach one another which is constant and not the rate of strain. Also, it is the total force which is measured and not the stress, which is the force per unit area. Variations in cross-section were ignored in the simple theory. As a result one cannot obtain true stress–strain curves directly from the instrument; the force–time curves distort the relation between stress and strain.

Consider first the observed stress. As the sample is compressed in a vertical direction its lateral dimensions change. In an ideal situation, if the material is incompressible there is no change in its volume during compression so that the cross-sectional area increases inversely as the height decreases. Assuming that the plates are perfectly smooth so that there is no lateral friction between them and the end surfaces of the sample, a purely viscous sample would deform uniformly as is shown diagrammatically in Fig. 6a. The true stress at any compression may be obtained directly by multiplying the force per original unit area by the fractional height of the sample. However, a viscoelastic sample does not deform so simply,[30–32] but in such a way that the lateral movement near the ends is greater than near the middle, resulting in a concave shape as in Fig. 6b. In this case, the stresses at any instant are not uniform throughout the sample and the simple correction only gives an average value. When the sample is linear viscoelastic this is unimportant, but when there are serious departures from linearity an average tends to 'blur' the result by distorting the shape of the stress–strain curve. A further complication arises when there is some friction between the plates and the sample.[30] The lateral movement of the sample layers near the ends is restricted and further internal stresses develop within the sample. The result is barrel-

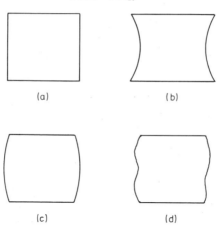

(a)   (b)

(c)   (d)

Fig. 6. Compression of a cylinder, (a) ideal, (b) concave distortion, (c) barrel distortion, (d) complex.

shaped distortion as in Fig. 6c. This may be sufficient to obscure any tendency to concavity, but sometimes a more complex shape develops as in Fig. 6d. The actual shape will depend upon the degree of lubrication of the plates, and a combination of the rate of compression and the rheological properties of the sample. Whatever the shape, the simple correction only gives an average value.

If the sample is compressible, the correction will over-correct. A more accurate correction can only be applied if the compressibility is known, or if the cross-section is actually measured. Most cheeses are only slightly compressible. Moreover, there is usually some moisture or free fat expressed from the surface layers of the cheese during compression so that the plates are at least partially lubricated. Taking also into account the fact that there is considerable variability in cheese, both within and between samples, the simple correction is probably quite adequate for practical purposes. The effect of non-linearity in the strain rate is more serious. Writing:

$$\varepsilon = \ln (h_o/h_1) \tag{1}$$

and:

$$h_1 = h_o(1 - at) \tag{8}$$

where a is a constant defining the rate at which the plates approach, gives:

$$\dot{\varepsilon} = ah_o/h_1 = a\,e^{\varepsilon} \tag{9}$$

The strain rate is not constant but increases exponentially as the sample is compressed, becoming infinite at the point where the plates would come into contact were the experiment to be carried so far. As a result, the stress–strain curve is progressively distorted the further the compression proceeds. If the values of ε and $\dot{\varepsilon}$ are inserted in the constitutive equations for the basic viscoelastic models and the new equations solved the relations between stress and strain for the force–compression test are obtained.

Taking the Kelvin body first, the solution is straightforward:

$$\sigma = G\varepsilon + a\eta\dot{\varepsilon} \tag{10}$$

This is the equation of a curve with a finite intercept on the stress axis proportional to the rate of deformation and to the viscous component and an initial slope proportional to the elastic term. It is concave upwards throughout.

The solution for the Maxwell body is less simple. Making the same substitutions leads to a solution in the form of an infinite series:

$$\sigma = G\exp\left(\frac{G}{a\eta}e^{-\varepsilon}\right)\left[\varepsilon + \sum_{1}^{\infty}\frac{\left(-\dfrac{G}{a\eta}\right)^{i}(1-e^{-\varepsilon i})}{ii!}\right] \tag{11}$$

At the commencement of the compression the stress is zero and the initial slope is proportional to the elastic component. At first, the curve is convex upwards, but as the compression proceeds a point of inflexion is reached depending upon the ratio of the viscous to elastic component and on the rate of compression. Ultimately, the curve becomes asymptotic to a line through the origin and with a slope given by the elastic constant.

If the rheological behaviour of the sample conforms to that of a simple viscoelastic model an inspection of the stress–strain curve obtained in a force–compression test is sufficient to decide which model is appropriate. In general it is unlikely that any simple two-element model would accurately fit the pattern of behaviour for a material so heterogeneous as cheese. More sophisticated models may give a better representation, but as the theory becomes more complex, so the analysis becomes more difficult. Furthermore, the greater number of constants required frustrates the aim of simplicity.

Compression tests on cheese are usually carried on until the strain reached is far greater than that at which any simple theory might be reasonably expected to apply, often reaching a compression to as little as

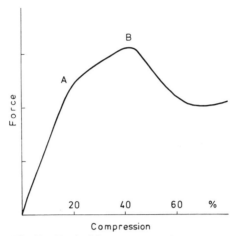

Fig. 7. Typical force–compression curve.

one-fifth of the original height. Such drastic treatment may result in destruction of any structure which may have been present in the original. A typical compression curve is shown in Fig. 7. At the outset it is sometimes difficult to decide whether there is an intercept on the stress axis or whether the stress rises smoothly and steeply from zero as the sample is strained. This is particularly so if the rate of response of the recorder is commensurate with the rate of build-up of the stress.[34] There is also another practical difficulty. It is not easy to prepare a sample of cheese in which the opposing end faces are exactly parallel. If there is a slight angle between the two faces, in the initial stages the take-up of the strain on the sample as a whole may be gradual rather than instantaneous. As the compression proceeds there is a smooth increase of stress with strain, and this portion of the curve may be analysed along the lines suggested above. If the compression is stopped during this stage, the cheese would recover either completely or at least partially and a repeat of the curve could be obtained having the same general shape, showing that the structure still remained intact, though perhaps somewhat modified. Eventually, a point is reached, point A in the figure, at which the slope becomes noticeably less, as the structure commences to break down. This point is usually believed to be that at which cracks begin to develop within the structure and to spread spontaneously.[13,35] The more homogeneous the cheese within the sample the more likely this is to occur at all points within the structure at the same time and the change of slope will be clearly defined. If the cheese is very heterogeneous the change in slope may be very diffuse.

Once this point has been passed the cracks continue to spread at an increasing rate until a point B is reached at which the rate of breakdown of the structure overtakes the rate of build up of stress through further compression and a peak in the curve is reached. This peak value, though it is obviously dependent on a nice balance between spontaneous disintegration of the structure and the rate of deformation applied by means of the instrument, is the most easily determined parameter and may be used as a measure of the firmness[13] (or hardness). Thereafter, there may be a fall in the stress as the breakdown becomes more or less catastrophic until eventually the fragmented particles become reorganized in a new, compacted, arrangement and once again take up the stress which then rises further.

There is an alternative explanation which may be advanced for the shape of the curve before the point A is reached. Often this shape is convex upwards. This is characteristic of a Maxwell body type of model. It is conceivable, however, that the basic structure is a solid one, but that under even comparatively small stresses some minute cracks appear within the bulk,[36] though these are not evident to the eye. As the strain increases, the number of these cracks increases. If, then, cheese is looked at from the engineering aspect as a study in the strength of materials,[37] a material which possesses an extended range of breaking strains would break down progressively as the strain increases. The stress–strain curve for such a material would be indistinguishable from that of a Maxwell body, except that a small initial stress (yield stress), might be expected to be required to overcome any minimum breaking strength. It has already been pointed out, however, that the true curve in the vicinity of the origin is the least easy to determine with any precision and a small yield value (an intercept), could easily be obscured because of the inertia of the instrument as explained above.

On this hypothesis the point A is reached when these minute cracks begin to join up to form larger macroscopic cracks. As before, when the cheese is homogeneous these larger cracks will begin to appear more or less simultaneously and the point A will be well defined. If the cheese is very heterogeneous the onset of macroscopic cracks may appear over a range of stresses and the point A will be poorly defined.

In the semi-empirical use of the compressibility test, two parameters which have been most commonly used are the point B in Fig. 7 and the stress required to reach a given degree of compression, usually 80%, i.e. the stress required to reduce the height to one-fifth of the original. The stress at point B is often referred to as the 'yield value'. It should not be

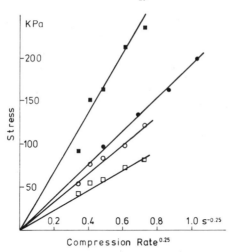

Fig. 8. Effect of rate of compression on stress at yield point: ● Double Gloucester, ■ Cheddar, ○ Leicester, □ Cheshire (based on data from Refs 35 and 38).

confused with the yield stress as determined for instance by a cone penetrometer, which is a constant associated with the model for a plastic material. The yield value at point B is not a material constant defining the breaking strength of the sample. Breakdown has already been occurring at least since the inflexion point A, and maybe earlier. The peak value at B only indicates that at that point the rate of collapse of the stress-supporting structure overtakes the build-up of stress due to compression.

It is to be expected that the yield value obtained in a compression test is dependent upon the rate at which the compression is carried out. Measurements which have been carried out on four cheese types, Cheddar, Cheshire, Leicester[38] and Double Gloucester,[35] all confirm this. The results are shown in Fig. 8 in which the yield stress has been plotted against the fourth root of a (Eqn (8)). Straight lines through the origin have been drawn through each set of points. Bearing in mind that this is a destructive test wherein each measurement has to be made on a different sample, the fit of the lines to the experimental points is acceptable. There is no theoretical significance in this fit: the result is quite empirical. There is a fortuitous practical benefit: it is possible, using this finding, to make plausible reductions of measurements made at different rates to a common rate, so that the results of workers in different laboratories may be compared.

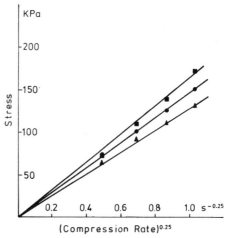

Fig. 9. Effect of rate of compression on stress at various compressions. ● 10%, ■ 40%, ▲ 70% (based on data from Ref. 35).

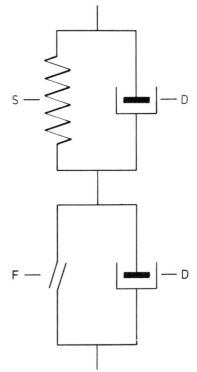

Fig. 10. Viscoelastic model including a fracture element.

Pursuing this variation a little further, the measurements made on Double Gloucester cheese[35] showed that this relationship between stress and rate of deformation held good not only at the peak but throughout the compression. The results for three compressions, 10%, 40% and 70% are shown in Fig. 9. The fact that the relation between rate of deformation and stress is more or less constant before, at and beyond the yield point lends some support to the idea that there is no significant change in the processes taking place within the cheese. The stress at any point results from a balance between the rate of collapse of the structure, i.e. the spread of the cracks, and the build up of stress due to compression and not to any pronounced viscoelastic flow followed by a sudden breakdown. It is possible to construct models which would portray this type of behaviour. A simple example is given in Fig. 10 in which a Kelvin body is shown as representing the structure before any breakdown occurs, but with the addition of a dashpot representing progressive breakdown once the critical stress has been exceeded. Such models help in describing the rheological behaviour: however, they are unlikely to have any predictive value[39] as the 'constants' would differ not only for every variety of cheese but almost certainly for every batch.[40]

4.4 Relaxation

When the simple model is evidently insufficient to describe a relaxation or recovery curve, it may be difficult to carry out an analysis of the experimental curve. This is particularly the case if there is any doubt about the precision of the data. In this case an empirical treatment may sometimes be useful.[41,42] If one writes Y for the decaying parameter, where $Y = (F_o - F_t)F_o$, F_t being the measured value of the stress at time t, Y is the fractional recovery of that stress or strain. It has been found that for many complex viscoelastic materials the decay may be represented to a fair degree of approximation by an expression of the form $1/Y = k_1/t + k_2$. The constants k_1 and k_2 can readily be found by rearranging this equation in the form:

$$t/Y = k_1 + k_2 t \qquad (12)$$

$1/k_2$ is the extent to which the parameter ultimately decays. It is zero for an elastic or a Kelvin body and unity for a liquid or a Maxwell body. For more complex models it lies somewhere in between. The ratio k_2/k_1 is a measure of the rate of decay.

5.   RHEOLOGY AND STRUCTURE

All cheeses contain three major constituents—casein, fat and water—which each contribute to the structure and therefore to the rheological properties in their own specific way. The casein forms an open, mesh-like structure.[43–48] In this is entrapped the fat, originally the fat globules of the milk. The water, usually containing dissolved salt which has been added in the course of manufacture, is partly bound to the protein and the remainder fills the interstices between the casein matrix and the fat. So far, this structure is common to all types of cheese. It is the variations in it which are produced by the particular processes of manufacture which give rise to the differences between cheeses. Variations may be between varieties and characteristic of the different treatments afforded to cheese during manufacture, or they may be adventitious differences between cheeses of the same type reflecting differences in the original milk or in the conditions during the manufacturing and maturing processes.

The solid nature of cheese is mainly determined by the casein. The primary structure is in the form of a three-dimensional cage, whose sides consist of chains of casein molecules. Such a structure has considerable inherent rigidity. The chains are not linear but have a structure somewhat reminiscent of an irregular helical spring.[46] This imparts some elasticity to them which in turn modifies the rigidity of the cage.

During the clotting process these chains have been formed in the serum around the fat globules in the milk so each cage may initially be expected to encase at least one fat globule. The size, and the distribution of the sizes, of these cells will be controlled by the fat globules. For instance, cheese made from homogenized milk[47] will have a more uniform distribution of the cells than cheese made from natural milk. The complete cheese then consists of an aggregate of these cells of casein cages plus fat, the whole being pervaded by brine.

If a force is applied to such a matrix structure, the rigidity of the cage and the elasticity of its structural members will, in the first instance, control the deformation. In the absence of the fat and brine, this would be expected to behave more or less simply as any other open structure, i.e. as a relatively soft solid, and its deformation would be characterized by a single modulus of rigidity or elasticity. However, the presence of the fat limits the deformation. At very low temperatures, the fat, being mainly solid, would merely add to the rigidity. However, at the temperatures at which the cheese is matured and used, the fat has its own peculiar rheological properties, behaving as a plastic material. Any deformation of the casein matrix would require the fat to deform also. At the same time, the movement of the casein relative to the fat is lubricated by the presence of the brine. As a result, the rigidity of the fat is added to that of the casein in a complex manner so that the whole displays viscoelastic characteristics.

The body of the whole cheese does not, however, consist just of a continuous agglomeration of cells just described. During manufacture, the curd is cut into pieces at least once and excess serum may drain away allowing the casein matrix to shrink onto the fat globules. The granules so formed may then be further distorted,[48,49] as in the cheddaring process, or just take up a more or less random orientation as in the maturing of Cheshire cheese. The whole cheese mass consists of an aggregation of these granules. This forms a secondary structure having its own set of rheological properties. This may be further modified by milling, giving rise to a tertiary structure. The whole is subsequently distorted during the process of pressing.

This rudimentary account of the factors contributing to the rheological properties applies to any cheese. During the course of manufacture and subsequently during ripening this basic structure may be modified both by the treatment, mechanical and thermal,[50,51] and by the action of bacteria and any residual enzymes.[52] As a result of these agencies the organization of the protein structure may be changed, contiguous fat globules may coalesce[53] and water may be lost by evaporation from the surface.

Before discussing the effect of cheese structure on its rheological properties it is pertinent to consider the differences which may occur within a single cheese, or between cheeses nominally alike, from the same batch. A cheese with a pronounced rind, i.e. one which matures in contact with air, may show considerable variation throughout its body. The layers near the surface lose moisture more rapidly than the inner portions; as a result, not only is the composition of those layers different but also the actual maturation of the cheese in those layers may be affected. Another source of variation which is encountered particularly in the case of large cheeses such as Cheddar or Cheshire which are turned at intervals during a long period of maturation, the top and bottom layers are subjected to alternating high and low compressive stresses under their own weight, whilst the portions nearer the centre are subject to much less variation. This again may affect the maturation process. There results, even in an otherwise uniform cheese, a distribution of firmness as is shown in Fig. 11. It follows then that the measurements made on the surface or on layers near the surface do not necessarily represent the main body of the cheese.

Differences between cheeses may be considerably greater and the

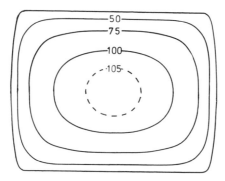

Fig. 11. Typical distribution of firmness throughout a mature cheese.

magnitude of the variations depends to some extent upon the method of measurement. As would be expected, penetration methods, where the instrument only acts locally on a limited quantity of sample, give greater differences than compression methods in which a larger volume of sample is tested. Variations of the order of $\pm 10\%$ of the mean value of a parameter have been found on different samples from the same batch in compression testing: this probably indicates the limit of reproducibility which one may reasonably expect when making measurements on cheese. Using penetrometer methods the variation may go up to as much as 25–30%. Differences between batches may be considerably larger. As an extreme example, one experimenter measuring eight different lots of cream cheese obtained readings which ranged from 54 to 251 units.[54]

It is not possible to consider in isolation the contribution of each constituent to the rheological properties of the whole cheese: it is their interaction which gives rise to its viscoelasticity. Nevertheless, it is possible to examine some of the features associated with each of the major constituents.

First, consider the casein. It is this which gives cheese its solid appearance. By reason of the fact that the casein chains form within the spaces between the fat globules in the original milk, there must necessarily be a minimum amount of casein below which any continuous network cannot exist. This will depend upon the size and size distribution of the fat globules and on the size and size distribution of the casein micelles themselves. Once a sufficient quantity of casein to form a minimum structure has been exceeded any additional casein included will only serve to strengthen the branches and junctions. It is to be expected then that, irrespective of the type of cheese, there will be a general relation between

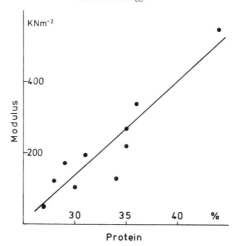

Fig. 12. Relation between firmness of cheeses and total protein content (based on data from Ref. 22).

the amount of casein present in the cheese and its firmness. Figure 12 shows this relation for some ten different types of hard cheese.[22] The scatter about the regression line which has been drawn is quite considerable, as is only to be expected since it relates to cheese of very different origins. Nevertheless, it indicates that in hard cheese, around 25% by weight must be protein in order to provide a rigid framework throughout. Above this critical value, any further protein serves only to strengthen this framework.

As an example of the effect of the protein content within a single cheese variety it is necessary to look at a soft cheese.[55] Figure 13 shows the firmness, measured on an arbitrary scale, of some Meshanger cheeses plotted against the amount of protein, expressed as the volume fraction of protein in fat-free cheese. It is clear that in this case unless sufficient protein were present to occupy almost 40% of the volume, excluding fat, there is little rigidity and the cheese is effectively a soft paste. Above this critical value the rigidity builds up rapidly.

Although it has been claimed that the casein matrix gives rigidity to the cheese there is still a theoretical question which has not been answered. Is the matrix continuous throughout the whole cheese so that it may be treated as a solid body, or does cheese flow, albeit imperceptibly, however small the stress, because of discontinuities in the structure? The evidence is inconclusive. In theory, an examination of the shape of stress–strain curves

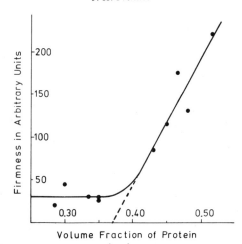

Fig. 13.   Relation between firmness and protein content in a single cheese variety
(based on data from Ref. 55).

(page 316) at very low strains should reveal this information. If there is a
continuous structure there will be a finite stress before any flow is initiated,
though there may be some elastic deformation. Force–compression curves
obtained on commercially available instruments are generally not precise
enough in this region, for they are not designed for this purpose. However,
some measurements have been made at rather higher than usual room

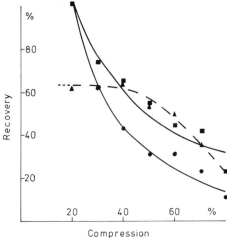

Fig. 14.   Relation between recovery of cheese and previous compression:
● Cheddar, ■ Muenster, ▲ Mozzarella (based on data from Ref. 56).

temperatures, and hence requiring somewhat lower overall stresses, in which cheeses were allowed to recover after being compressed to various strains[56] (Fig. 14). These showed that one Cheddar and a Muenster cheese recovered completely, within the limits of measurement, whilst a Mozzarella certainly did not.

Cheddar cheese has also been studied by means of a relaxation experiment.[42] Samples were compressed to a constant deformation though under different stresses and the subsequent relaxation of the stress followed. Referring to the empirical treatment on page 326 (Eqn (12)), it was found that the value of $1/k_2$ was not independent of the stress applied. The greater the stress, and hence the faster the deformation to reach the fixed strain, the less the internal stresses developed within the cheese were able to relax during the compression and the structure was broken down to a greater extent. Figure 15 shows that the relation between $1/k_2$ and stress was curvilinear, particularly at the low stress end of the experimental range. It is unfortunate that these experiments were not extended to much lower stresses so that it might have been possible to extrapolate the curve with greater confidence to zero stress. Nevertheless it appears likely that an extrapolation would lead to a finite value of $1/k_2$. If this were so it would indicate that there was no continuous structure throughout the cheese.

To establish this with confidence requires measurements to be carried out at very small strains. One way of carrying these out is to apply a small

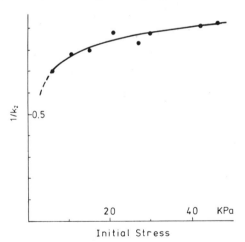

Fig. 15. Amount of relaxation after previous stress (see text) (based on data from Ref. 42).

sinusoidal vibration to one surface of a sample and observe the stress transmitted through it.[57] It is customary to analyse the results of such an experiment in the first instance as if the sample were a Kelvin body. A total modulus is calculated which is the resultant of an elastic component, in phase with the applied strain, and a viscous component out of phase. Measurements made at a single frequency cannot serve to distinguish one viscoelastic model from another. However, if the sample is truly a Kelvin body, the moduli determined are independent of frequency. Neither Cheddar nor Gouda cheese have constant moduli even when the strain is as low as $\varepsilon = 0.04$. One must infer that this small strain is sufficient to cause internal cracks or slip planes to develop within the cheese.

Summarizing the foregoing paragraphs it appears that the rheological role of the casein in cheese is to provide a continuous elastic framework for the individual granules. Where casein chains lying on the surface of neighbouring granules are contiguous they may be bonded together either by physical bonds or by chemical bonds which develop during the ripening of the cheese, giving some rigidity to the agglomeration of granules.[44] If these bonds exist, some at least must be very weak, since the whole cheese mass may be readily constrained to deform inelastically at quite low stresses. There is still a clear need for further definitive research into the relation between the casein structure and the rheological properties of the finished cheese, embracing microscopic examination, chemical analyses and the whole range of rheological techniques available.

By contrast with the casein, the role of the other major constituents is more clearly documented. Fat, derived from the original milk, is roughly one-third of the total mass. It is rheologically very sensitive to temperature changes and so may be expected to impart its temperature sensitivity to the whole cheese. At temperatures around 5°C (normal refrigeration temperatures), many of the glycerides in the milk fat are solid. As the temperature rises, the proportion of solid fat decreases, this decrease being particularly sharp in the region 12–15°C, which is roughly the temperature at which hard cheeses are matured and stored. Above this temperature the proportion of solid glyceride decreases until at about 35°C it is virtually all liquid. This is the temperature which a portion will rapidly attain when placed in the mouth and chewed. The ratio of solid to liquid is the principal factor which determines the rheological properties of the fat.[58] The actual ratio at any temperature depends on a number of factors, which include such features as the breed of the cow or other animal, the pasture and herd management, but the temperature itself is the most important.

Fats are also very prone to supercooling effects, so that not only does the temperature itself affect their properties but also they are affected by their thermal history. This has an impact on the properties of cheese. During ripening, cheese is normally kept at a lower temperature than that at which it has been processed. During this time some of the glycerides will slowly solidify. Although this is most rapid at first, so that most of the change has taken place within the first day or two, it continues progressively as long as the temperature remains low.

Measurements of firmness which have been made on Cheddar, Cheshire,[38] Emmental,[59,60] Gouda and Russian[62] cheeses, by whatever method, all show similar variations. Figure 16 has been drawn to show the average variation, all reduced to the same scale. Individual cheese varieties and cheeses made from milk of different fat composition will naturally show some divergencies from the actual curves shown in the figure. Nevertheless, bearing in mind the limitations in accuracy of individual measurements already discussed, this average is a sufficient guide to what may be expected. It may be mentioned here that different methods give rise to somewhat different results. For example, penetrometers appear to be more influenced by the fat phase in the cheese than do compression tests and so tend to emphasize the temperature variations.

Differences in the glyceride composition of the original milk give rise to differences in the firmness of the final cheese. Taking the iodine number as

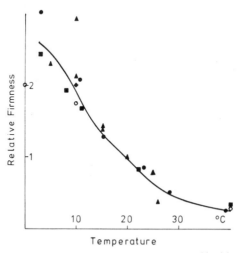

Fig. 16. Variation of firmness with temperature: ● Cheddar, ■ Cheshire, ▲ Emmental, ◆ Gouda, ○ Russian (based on data from Refs 34, 59, 60 and 62).

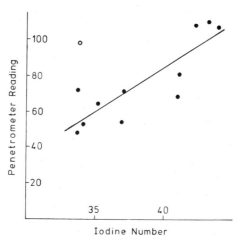

Fig. 17. Variation of firmness with saturation of glycerides (based on data from Ref. 63).

an indicator of the proportion of liquid fat at any one temperature—a low iodine number which indicates a high degree of saturation will indicate a high proportion of solid fat—the firmness of cheese has been shown to vary seasonally in line with the iodine number.[63] In these particular experiments cheeses produced in December appeared anomalous, a fat with a high content of saturated glycerides giving soft cheese, demonstrating that other, unrecorded, influences may overshadow the one being sought. Nevertheless, even including the December result a statistically significant correlation was obtained. Figure 17 shows these results with a regression line drawn ignoring the December result.

The water, or more strictly the brine content of the cheese, also tends to influence the firmness. It has already been stated that the aqueous phase occupies that space not taken up by the casein matrix and the fat, and provided that the water is present in sufficient quantity, it takes up all that space. One of the roles of the water, in the rheological sense, is to act as a low viscosity lubricant between the surfaces of the fat and the casein. One would expect that the greater the water content, and by implication the wider the spaces which are available for it to flow through, the less restraint there should be to the movement of the casein cage around the enclosed fat. This freer movement would be manifest as both a lesser overall resistance to any deformation, and to a greater ease with which it may recover after being deformed.

Considering the latter point first, Fig. 18 shows for some ten varieties of

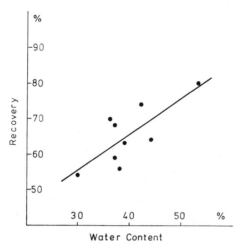

Fig. 18. Relation between elastic recovery and moisture content (based on data from Ref. 22).

cheese, the elastic recovery after a sample had been compressed, but without any visible damage to the structure.[22] In this figure, the recovery has been plotted against the moisture content. Parmesan, which contained only 30% water showed the least recovery whilst at the other extreme, the Mozzarella with over 50% moisture showed the greatest recovery. With these samples there was also a general tendency for the drier cheeses to be firmer, but other factors obscured the issue and the relationship was not so clearly defined.

Within a single variety and again within a single cheese the relation between water content and the firmness has been more clearly demonstrated. In a freshly made cheese the water is distributed more or less evenly throughout the cheese mass. During the maturation period, with the exception of those cheeses which are coated with an impervious layer of wax or other packaging material before ripening, some water evaporates from the surface and although there is a migration of water from the centre to replace this, the replacement is incomplete and a moisture gradient is set up within the cheese. If the firmness and moisture content in successive zones from the surface to the interior are measured and the results plotted, a figure such as Fig. 19 is obtained.[60] In this figure, the firmness and moisture are clearly seen to be highly correlated. Further evidence may be seen in the ripening of Edam cheese. In Fig. 20, a quasi-modulus has been plotted against the overall moisture content of the

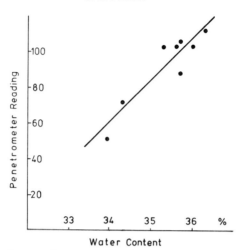

Fig. 19. Relation between firmness and moisture content in a single cheese (based on data from Ref. 60).

cheese in an experiment in which two different batches of cheeses were matured for up to 16 months.[64] One half of the cheeses was matured at low temperatures (around 9°C), indicated by the solid symbols, and the other half at higher temperature (around 16°C), indicated by the open symbols.

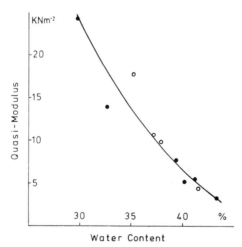

Fig. 20. Relation between quasi-modulus and moisture content in a single cheese variety (Edam) (based on data from Ref. 64).

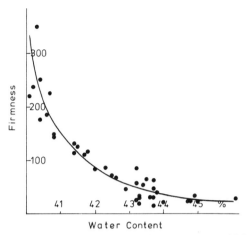

Fig. 21. Relation between firmness and moisture content of Meshanger cheese (based on data from Ref. 55).

The foregoing paragraphs do not give a complete account of the role of water in its effect on the rheological properties of cheese. Besides being a space-filler, it is also a vehicle for carrying enzymes and bacteria. This aspect may be most clearly illustrated by reference to the ripening of Meshanger cheese.[55] This cheese, when it is freshly formed, has a well-organized structure of micellar casein which steadily breaks down during the ripening to become ultimately a loose mass of casein sub-units without any visible organization. The firmness measured on an arbitrary scale, has been shown to be closely related to the moisture content, irrespective of the amount of protein breakdown which has occurred (Fig. 21). The maturation period is short enough for there to be little loss of water during it, so that any change in rheological properties during maturation is unlikely to be due to a change in the physical presence of the water. The rate at which the casein broke down was also closely related to the amount of water available, as shown in Fig. 22, in which the rate coefficients have been calculated assuming a first-order reaction. Combining the two findings leads to the conclusion that in this cheese the amount of water present influences the firmness indirectly through its presence in sufficient quantity to facilitate the breakdown of the protein matrix.

Although the protein, fat and water constitute by far the greatest part of any cheese mass, other components should not be overlooked. Salt, when added dry before pressing, may sometimes appear as crystals embedded in the protein–fat mass; but then it is usually present in such small quantities

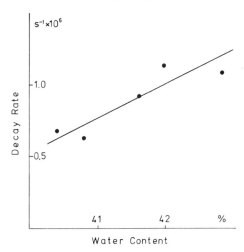

Fig. 22.   Relation between rate of casein breakdown and moisture content (based
on data from Ref. 55).

as to make a negligible contribution to the rheological properties of the
whole. Most of the salt, particularly in cheeses where it has been added by
brining, is present only in solution in the water. The only direct rheological
influence of the presence of salt in the water is to modify its viscosity: the
effect of this on the properties of the whole cheese is minimal.

The only significant contribution of the salt to the rheological
properties is by indirect action. A high concentration of salt increases the
osmotic pressure, diverting a significant quantity of water from the
structural bonds of the protein network.[65,66] This may be seen in its effect
on the ripening of some samples of Mozzarella cheese.[67] When the salt
content was low (0·27%) protein degradation during ripening resulted in
a decrease of modulus from 120 to 45 N/m² in 5 weeks. In other samples of
the cheese with salt content in excess of 1% no change was observed in the
same period.

In cheese to which the salt is added by immersion in brine there is a
further consideration. The inward diffusion of the brine results in a
concentration gradient being set up within the cheese. The effect of this is
twofold. In the first place, the presence of the salt results in the simple
exclusion of some of the water and this in turn reinforces the moisture
gradient simultaneously arising from the evaporation of the water from
the surface layers.[60] Secondly, and probably the more important, the
diffusion of salt into the cheese is a slow process.[68–70] In the early stages

of ripening the salt concentration in the inner regions is unlikely to be sufficient to limit the protein degradation, as described in the previous paragraph. The presence of a higher moisture content and an enhanced proteolytic activity affect the rheological properties in the same sense, giving rise to a weaker structure and hence a less firm cheese. It is probable that the variation of firmness within a single cheese, which is so closely related to moisture distribution as described earlier (page 331), is accentuated by the method of brining.

Some cheeses also contain a significant quantity of gas. In hard and crumbly cheese this may simply be air which has infiltrated any cracks which have developed in the mass. In others gas may exist in discrete pockets having developed *in situ* as the cheese matured. The significance of the presence of either cracks or holes is that rheological measurements made on a whole cheese or on the surface will not fairly represent the properties of the main body of the cheese. From the practical point of view, hidden cracks or holes will give rise to irregularities in the behaviour of any penetration instrument and probably account for a substantial amount of the scatter observed. They also account for the difficulties encountered when attempting to measure the rheological properties of any cheese by studying ultrasonic propagation through it. The velocity of propagation is more influenced by the scattering at the interfaces than by the properties of the cheese mass.

6. SOME EXPERIMENTAL RESULTS

Most of the rheological methods described earlier have been used at one time or another for the study of cheese. Although the most satisfactory of these for routine measurements is the force–compression test, there has been no consensus of opinion regarding the most suitable operating conditions. Sample size, rate of compression and temperature have all varied. Yet, perhaps the most interesting feature is that, in spite of the differences and the different varieties of cheese which have been examined, the general shape of the curve is so similar. This underlines its general usefulness.

There are several important considerations to be taken into account when deciding upon the operating conditions. The sample should be as large as possible to be representative[71] and to avoid local inhomogeneities. On the other hand, it should be small enough to ensure that it does not include hidden cracks. As a compromise, most workers have used samples with dimensions from 10 mm to 25 mm. Cylindrical samples have usually been preferred to rectangular ones[61] because their symmetry tends to minimize irregular crack development. On the other hand it is easier to prepare rectangular samples having exactly known dimensions.

A wide range of compression rates have been used, from 2 mm/min up to 100 mm/min and of course the strain rate depends both on this and on the sample height. The instrument produces curves of total force against linear travel. The rheologist wishes to study a stress–strain curve. As already indicated (page 314) the conversion is readily effected if it be assumed that the volume remains constant, so that the cross-sectional area varies inversely as the height. This is not a justifiable assumption if severe distortion of the cylindrical shape takes place, but it must be accepted in the absence of a better one.

TABLE I
Rheological measurements on cheese by force–compression tests

	Initial slope (kN/m^2)	Yield Value (kPa)	Yield Strain	Stress at 80% (kPa)	Ref.
Appenzell	22	7	0·63	6·1	72
Caerphilly	c7·50	64	0·17	46	35
Cheddar				12	73
				14	73
	48	8	0·20	11	55
		44	0·21		38
	180	23	0·21	22	52
		108			38
Cheshire		44	0·33		38
Double Gloucester	c1 000	94	0·24	54	35
Edam	c500	146	0·63	71	35
Emmental				19	73
	18	12	1·05	9	72
Gouda	405	69	0·37	69	60
	390	68	0·72	36	35
Gruyère	77	15	0·51	9	72
Lancashire	c1 250	87	0·20	95	35
Leicester		50			38
		48	0·30	37	30
Mozzarella	15	2·5	0·55	10	55
Muenster	6	2·8	0·10	10	55
Sbrinz	195	22	0·41	16	72
Tilsit	30	7	0·70	8	72

Table I summarizes the principal measurements which have been made on hard cheeses using the force–compression test. In order to produce this table, the original data from the references cited were used to draw the stress–strain curves and the appropriate values read from these curves. To make it possible to compare various results, these values were then 'corrected' for the rate of compression and temperature, so that the table refers to an initial strain rate of $\dot{\varepsilon} = 0.05$ and a temperature of 20°C. Recalling the treatment on page 315, all the curves showed a tendency to be convex upward at first and showed no intercept on the stress axis. This is consistent with the use of a Maxwell body type of model as a first approximation to cheese behaviour. In this (page 316), the initial slope is a measure of the elastic modulus.

The most striking feature of the results tabulated is the wide variation which occurs within a single variety of cheese (Cheddar). The origin and history of the different samples was not generally documented; it is not possible therefore to draw any conclusions.

TABLE II
Rheological measurements on cheese by various methods

	Modulus (kN/m^2)	Method	Ref.
Brie	1·3	Extruder	74
Sbrinz	41	Extruder	74
Chanakh	58	Cone	66
Emmental	40	Cone	66
	3·5	Cone	27
Gouda	44	Cone	66
Kostroma	54	Cone	66
Lori	40	Cone	66
Cheddar	195	Punch	22
Edam	340	Punch	22
Emmental	220	Punch	22
Gouda	270	Punch	22
Kashkaval	120	Punch	49
Mozzarella	170	Punch	22
	22	Punch	75
Muenster	120	Punch	22
Parmesan	550	Punch	22
Provolone	130	Punch	22
Cheddar	270–400	Compression	76
Mozzarella	80	Compression	67
Kashkaval	60–100	Ball compression	77

Table II summarizes a number of results which have been obtained by other methods, where it has been possible to calculate a modulus from the data. As far as a comparison of the figures in the two tables is possible, it may be recalled that the initial slope of the force–compression curve is determined by the modulus of the elastic element, so that this must be most nearly comparable with any quasi-modulus determined by the punch test or by simple compression. The yield stress measured by a cone penetrometer is more likely to be comparable with the yield value in the force–compression test since both are influenced by the breakdown of the structure. As before, the lack of adequate documentation makes it difficult to make any meaningful comparisons between the results obtained in different laboratories at different times.

7. VARIATION WITH AGE

One aspect of the rheological properties of cheese which has been fairly extensively researched is the development of firmness during ripening. During this process all three principal constituents will undergo change. Moisture evaporates from the surface of the cheese so that during the course of time, a moisture gradient is set up and even the centre is considerably drier than it was originally. The protein in its matrix, as the

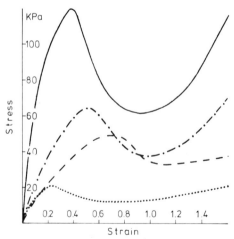

Fig. 23. Force–compression curves for young and mature cheeses: · —— Gouda (mature), —·— Gouda (young), ···· Cheddar (mature), ——— Cheddar (young) (adapted from Refs 44 and 61).

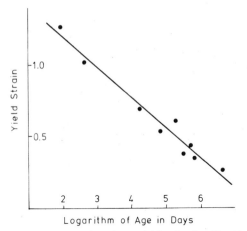

Fig. 24. Relation between age and strain at yield point for Cheddar cheese (based on data from Ref. 44).

available water is reduced and as residual bacteria and enzymes continue to act, undergoes a progressive change.[44,45,50,52,78] Some of the glycerides in the fat slowly crystallize resulting in a more solid mass of fat. These changes are reflected in the change which takes place in the cheese.

The force–compression curves for mature cheese may be considerably

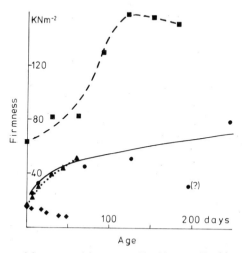

Fig. 25. Variation of firmness with age: ● Cheddar, ■ Kashkaval, ▲ Tamismi and Russian, ◆ unspecified French cheese (based on data from Refs 44, 60, 79 and 80).

different from those for green cheese, as may be seen from Fig. 23 which shows some curves for Cheddar[44] and Gouda[61] cheeses. During ageing the strain which the cheese could sustain before breaking down (at the yield point) progressively decreased more or less exponentially. Figure 24 shows this for a batch of Cheddar cheese.[44] On the other hand, whilst the stress at this point decreased somewhat in these Cheddar cheeses, in the Gouda cheese the ultimate strength of the matrix increased. As the actual balance between the different mechanisms varies from one cheese type to another, so will the paths of the change in firmness vary. Figure 25 shows some of the results which have been reported.[44,50,79,80]

In addition to changes in firmness, changes also take place in the springiness of cheese during ripening. Degradation of the protein, reduction of the free water and the firming up of the fat all tend to reduce the springiness. This does not show directly in single force–compression curves but it has been consistently observed empirically[63,80–83] on a number of varieties of cheese.

8. SUBJECTIVE JUDGEMENTS

Finally, it remains to consider briefly how the rheological properties measured by means of instruments, as just described, relate to the grader's or the consumer's assessment of the cheese. Throughout this chapter the emphasis has been on the measurement of firmness of the cheese which arises from its structure. It should be stressed that for any meaningful comparisons to be made between subjective and instrumental methods it is just as important that the subjective terminology is unambiguously defined as it is that the instrumental measurements are precise. Early experiments on single varieties of cheese showed that the subjective assessment of firmness, which is a fairly simple concept, correlated very highly with measurements made on simple instruments such as the Ball Compressor.[16,84] The simple correlation by itself does not, however, indicate to what extent the instrumental measurements could be used to predict a typical user's appraisal of firmness. Nor can the result on a single variety be extrapolated to all types of cheese without reservation. Nevertheless, the success was encouraging.

Some authors have, on the basis of their own experience, arbitrarily assigned a specific significance in terms of user appraisal to a particular instrumental reading. For instance, a quasi-modulus obtained in a simple compression test,[25] a yield value obtained by a cone penetrometer,[27] and

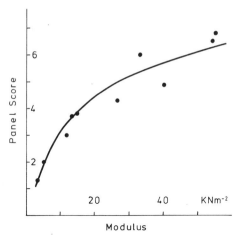

Fig. 26. Comparison of subjective and objective measurements of firmness (based on data from Ref. 73).

the stress at 80% compression[73] in a force–compression test have all been proposed as measurements of firmness. Recovery after a limited compression has been used as an indication of springiness.[22,25,69,83,85] These intuitive opinions are probably quite adequate for the purpose of making comparisons within a particular course of investigation.

The force–compression test provides a number of possibly useful parameters and two of these merit a little consideration. Figure 26 shows an example wherein the assessment of the hardness of a number of different cheeses made by a panel has been plotted against the stress at 80% compression,[73] and a logarithmic regression line has been drawn through the points. The standard deviation about the regression line is less than the scatter of any of the individual subjective assessments arising from differences among the panel. It is clear that within this laboratory this instrumental parameter could be used to predict the panel's assessment. In the same series of experiments the instrumental measurement was carried further: the compression was reversed and the recovered height after the first compression observed. At the same time the springiness was assessed subjectively. This is a less well-defined concept and it proved that there was much poorer agreement between panel members. Nevertheless a highly significant correlation was obtained between the measured recovery and the springiness.

These examples show that rheological measurements can successfully predict users' assessments. What remains is to establish a consensus on instrumental practice and on the definitions of the subjective terms. International co-operation is already fostering the first.[86] The semantic problem is not too difficult.[1-3]

REFERENCES

1. Szczesniak, A. S., *J. Food Sci.*, 1963, **28**, 385.
2. Szczesniak, A. S. and Bourne, M. C., *J. Texture Studies*, 1969, **1**, 52.
3. Jowitt, R., *J. Texture Studies*, 1974, **5**, 351.
4. Baron, M., *The Mechanical Properties of Cheese and Butter*, 1952, Dairy Industries Ltd., London, p. 29.
5. Caffyn, J. E. and Baron, M., *The Dairyman*, 1947, **64**, 345.
6. Mohsenin, N. N., *Physical Properties of Plant and Animal Materials*, 1970, Gordon and Breach, New York, p. 288.
7. Mohsenin, N. N., Morrow, C. T. and Young, Y. M., *Proc. 5th Int. Congr. on Rheology*, 1970, Vol. **2**, p. 647.
8. Wearmouth, W. G., *Dairy Ind.*, 1953, **20**, 726.
9. Cox, C. P. and Baron, M., *J. Dairy Res.*, 1955, **22**, 386.
10. Konoplev, A. D., Krashenin, P. F. and Tabachnikov, V. P., *Trudy vses. nauchno-issled. Inst. masl. i syr. Prom.*, 1974, **17**, 40, 101, 106.
11. Poulard, S., Roucou, J., Durrange, G. and Manry, J., *Rheol. Acta*, 1974, **13**, 761.
12. Baron, M., *Dairy Ind.*, 1949, **14**, 146.
13. Eberhard, P. and Fluckiger, E., *Schw. Milch Ztg.*, 1978, **104**, 24.
14. Tabachnikov, V. P., Borkov, V. Ya., Ilyushkin, V. B. and Tetereva, I. I., *Trudy vses. nauchno-issled. Inst. masl. i syr. Prom.*, 1979, **27**, 61, 118.
15. Baron, M. and Harper, R., *Dairy Ind.*, 1951, **16**, 45.
16. Wearmouth, W. G., *Dairy Ind.*, 1954, **19**, 213.
17. Prentice, J. H., *Measurements in the Rheology of Foodstuffs*, 1984, Elsevier Applied Science Publishers, London, p. 9.
18. Prentice, J. H., *Measurements in the Rheology of Foodstuffs*, 1984, Elsevier Applied Science Publishers, London, p. 12.
19. Bourne, M. C., In: *Food Texture and Rheology*, P. Sherman (ed.), 1979, Academic Press, London, p. 95.
20. De Man, J. M., *J. Texture Studies*, 1969, **1**, 114.
21. Kamel, B. S. and de Man, J. M., *Lebensm. Wiss. u. Technl.*, 1975, **8**, 123.
22. Chen, A. H., Larkin, J. W., Clark, C. J. and Irvine, W. E., *J. Dairy Sci.*, 1979, **62**, 901.
23. Tabachnikov, V. P., *Proc. 19th Int. Dairy Congr.*, 1974, Vol. **1E**, p. 511.
24. Tabachnikov, V. P., *Trudy vses. nauchno-issled. Inst. masl. i. syr Prom.*, 1974, **17**, 84, 104, 109.
25. Davidov, R. and Barabanshchikov, N., *Moloch. Prom.*, 1950, **9**(4), 27.
26. Ramanauskas, R., Urbene, S., Galginaitye, L. and Matulis, P., *Trudy Lit. Fil. vses nauchno-issled Inst. masl. i. syr. Prom.*, 1979, **13**, 64.
27. Fluckiger, E. and Siegenthaler, E., *Schw. Milch Ztg. (Wiss. Beil.)*, 1963, **89**, 707.
28. Mottram, F. J., *Lab. Practice*, 1961, **10**, 767.

29. Sheth, B. B., *J. Texture Studies*, 1976, **7**, 157.
30. Carter, E. J. V. and Sherman, P., *J. Texture Studies*, 1978, **9**, 311.
31. Boyd, J. and Sherman, P., *J. Texture Studies*, 1975, **6**, 507.
32. Hammerle, J. R. and McClure, W. F., *J. Texture Studies*, 1971, **2**, 31.
33. Peleg, M. and Normand, D., *J. Food Sci.*, 1982, **47**, 1572.
34. Voisey, P. W. and Kloek, M., *J. Texture Studies*, 1975, **6**, 489.
35. Shama, F. and Sherman, P., *J. Texture Studies*, 1973, **4**, 344.
36. Polak, M. V., *Diss. Abstr. Int.*, 1982, **B42**, 3178.
37. Jowitt, R. In: *Food Texture and Rheology*, P. Sherman (ed.), 1979, Academic Press, London, p. 146.
38. Dickinson, E. and Goulding, I. C., *J. Texture Studies*, 1980, **11**, 51.
39. Peleg, M., *J. Texture Studies*, 1976, **7**, 243.
40. Groman, A., *Rocz. Inst. przem. mlecz.*, 1978, **20**, 37.
41. Peleg, M., *J. Food Sci.*, 1979, **44**, 277.
42. Peleg, M., *J. Rheol.*, 1980, **24**, 451.
43. Taranto, M. V., Wan, P. J., Chen, S. L. and Rhee, K. C. In: *Scanning Electron Microscopy*, 1979, SEM Inc., O'Hare, p. 273.
44. Creamer, L. K. and Olson, N. F., *J. Food Sci.*, 1982, **47**, 631.
45. Kimber, A. M., Brooker, B. E., Hobbs, D. G. and Prentice, J. H., *J. Dairy Res.*, 1974, **41**, 389.
46. Prentice, J. H., *Measurements in the Rheology of Foodstuffs*, 1984, Elsevier Applied Science, London, p. 157.
47. Emmons, D. B., Kalab, M., Larmond, E. and Lowne, K. J., *J. Texture Studies*, 1980, **11**, 15.
48. Belousov, A., *Moloch. Prom.*, 1949, **10**(2), 32.
49. Kalab, M., *Milchwissenschaft*, 1977, **32**, 449.
50. Stefanovic, R., *Dechema Monograph*, 1973, **77**, 211.
51. Creamer, L. K. and Olson, N. F., *Proc. 21st Dairy Congr.*, 1982, Vol. 1 Book 1, p. 474.
52. Creamer, L. K., Zoerb, H. F., Olson, N. F. and Richardson, T., *J. Dairy Sci.*, 1982, **65**, 902.
53. Hall, D. M. and Creamer, L. K., *N.Z. J. Dairy Sci. Technol.*, 1972, **7**, 95.
54. Roundy, Z. D. and Price, W. V., *J. Dairy Sci.*, 1941, **24**, 135.
55. De Jong, L., *Neth. Milk Dairy J.*, 1978, **32**, 1.
56. Imoto, E. M., Lee, C-H. and Rha, C. K., *J. Food Sci.*, 1979, **44**, 343.
57. Taneya, S., Izutsu, T. and Sone, T. In: *Food Texture and Rheology* , P. Sherman (ed.), 1979, Academic Press, London, p. 367.
58. Jonsson, H. and Andersson, K., *Milchwissenschaft*, 1976, **31**, 593.
59. Fluckiger, E. and Walser, F., *Schw. Milch Ztg.*, 1976, **102,** 571.
60. Steffen, C., *Schw. Milch Forsch.*, 1976, **5**, 43.
61. Culioli, J. and Sherman, P., *J. Texture Studies*, 1976, **7**, 353.
62. Dykalo, N. Ya. and Tabachnikov, V. P., *Trudy vses. naucho-issled. Inst. masl. i syr. Prom.*, 1979, **27**, 55, 118.
63. Fluckiger, E., Walser, F. and Hanni, H., *Dte. Molkereiztg*, 1975, **96**, 1524.
64. Raadsveld, C. W. and Mulder, H., *Neth. Milk Dairy J.*, 1949, **3**, 117.
65. Ramanauskas, R., *Proc. 20th Int. Dairy Congr.*, 1978, Vol. E, p. 265.
66. Khachatryan, G. G., Dilanyan, K. Zh., Tabachnikov, V. P. and Tetereva, I. I., *Proc. 19th Int. Dairy Congr.*, 1974, Vol. 1E, p. 717.

67. Cervantes, M. A., Lund, D. B. and Olson, N. F., *J. Dairy Sci.*, 1983, **66**, 204.
68. Geurts, T. J., Walstra, P. and Mulder, H., *Neth. Milk Dairy J.*, 1980, **34**, 229.
69. Guinee, T. P. and Fox, P. F., *J. Dairy Res.*, 1983, **50**, 511.
70. Guinee, T. P. and Fox, P. F., *Ir. J. Food Sci. Technol.*, 1983, **7**, 119.
71. Peleg, M., *J. Food Sci.*, 1977, **42**, 649, 659.
72. Eberhard, P. and Fluckiger, E., *Schw. Milch Ztg.*, 1981, **107**, 23.
73. Lee, C-H., Imoto, E. M. and Rha, C. K., *J. Food Sci.*, 1978, **43**, 1600.
74. Ruegg, M., Eberhard, P., Moor, U., Fluckiger, E. and Blanc, B., *Schw. Milch Forsch.*, 1980, **9**, 3.
75. Yang, C. S. T. and Taranto, M. V., *J. Food Sci.*, 1982, **42**, 906.
76. Weaver, J. C. and Kroger, M., *J. Food Sci.*, 1978, **43**, 579.
77. Szabo, G., *Proc. 19th Int. Dairy Congr.*, 1974, Vol. 1E, p. 505.
78. Sakharov, S. D., Tabachnikov, V. P., Nebert, V. K. and Krasheninin, P. F., *Trudy vses nauchno-issled Inst. masl. i syr Prom.*, 1975, **18**, 29, 121, 128.
79. Ostojic, M., Miocinovic, D. and Niketic, G., *Mljekarstvo*, 1982, **32**, 139.
80. Le Bars, D. and Bergere, J. L., *Lait*, 1976, **56**, 485.
81. Green, M. L., Turvey, A. and Hobbs, D. G., *J. Dairy Res.*, 1981, **48**, 343.
82. Kunakhov, I. M., *Trudy Vologod. moloch. Inst.*, 1967, **55**, 70.
83. Nikolaev, B. A. and Abdullina, R. M., *Moloch Prom.*, 1969, **30**(7), 27.
84. Baron, M. and Harper, R., *Dairy Ind.*, 1950, **15**, 407.
85. Kasparova, Zh., *Trudy Vologod. moloch. Inst.*, 1972, **64**, 50.
86. COST—*European Cooperation in the Field of Scientific and Technical Research*, COST Secretariat, Brussels, November 1981.

Chapter 9

Nutritional Aspects of Cheese

E. Renner

Justus-Liebig-Universität, Giessen, Federal Republic of Germany

1. CHEESE CONSUMPTION

Although the consumption of liquid milk and of most dairy products is decreasing, there has been a steady increase in the consumption of cheese in most countries; worldwide, the annual growth rate in cheese consumption is about 3%. In the Federal Republic of Germany, cheese consumption has risen since 1962 from 8 to 14·7 kg per capita per annum. Per capita cheese consumption is highest in France while consumption is very low in most South American, African and Asian countries (Fig. 1).

2. NUTRIENTS OF CHEESE

2.1 Milk fat

By adjusting the fat content of cheese milk to different values, cheeses of widely different fat contents (usually expressed as % fat-in-dry matter) are produced. Fresh cheeses have an absolute fat content of up to 12%, while ripened cheeses, in general, contain between 20 and 30% fat (Table I). Consumers generally prefer high-fat cheeses because a high fat content contributes significantly to flavour quality. The typical aroma of some types of cheese, for instance Cheddar, develops only when the fat-in-dry matter content is at least 40–50%, because the aroma is due mainly to the breakdown products of fat formed during cheese ripening.

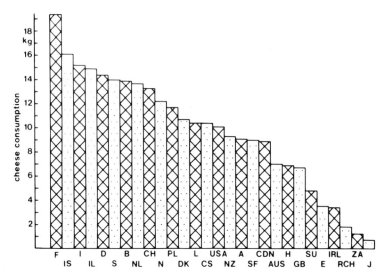

Fig. 1. Consumption (kg per capita per annum) of cheese in some countries (1982).[1]

Lipolysis during cheese ripening is caused primarily by microbial lipases because the native lipase in milk is largely inactivated by pasteurization (except in cheeses in which rennet paste or pregastric esterase is used). As a result of lipolysis, the concentration of free fatty acids in cheese is usually 1–5 g/kg. There is a close link between the content of free volatile fatty acids in a number of cheese varieties and their flavour.[5]

In Germany, cheese contributes only 4·7% of total fat intake (128 g per capita per day). As to the cholesterol content of cheese it has to be emphasized that:

—The cholesterol content of cheese is rather low (0–100 mg/100 g, depending on the fat content).[2]
—Therefore, cheese contributes only 3–4% of total cholesterol intake.
—The cholesterol in the diet has only a limited effect on the level of blood cholesterol. The body has a control mechanism which ensures that the synthesis of cholesterol by the body is reduced when the amount of cholesterol consumed increases.[3,4]

The coefficient of digestibility of the fat of different varieties of cheese is reported to be 88–94%.[2]

TABLE I

Average content of fat, protein, calcium and phosphorus of a number of cheese varieties[2]

Cheese variety	Fat content		Protein content (%)	Ca content (g/kg)	P content (g/kg)
	Fat-in-dry matter (%)	Absolute (%)			
Parmesan	35	26·0	36·5	13·0	8·5
Emmentaler	45	29·0	27·9	10·8	8·6
Tilsiter	45	27·7	26·0	8·0	5·3
Cheddar	50	32·4	25·4	8·0	5·0
Edam	45	26·0	25·5	7·5	4·5
Gouda	45	29·0	25·4	8·2	4·4
Butter cheese	50	28·8	21·1	6·9	4·2
Blue cheese	50	29·0	22·4	7·0	4·9
Brie	50	23·0	22·4	4·0	4·0
Camembert	45	22·3	22·0	4·0	4·0
Limburger	40	19·7	22·4	5·7	3·0
Romadur	30	14·1	23·2	5·1	3·0
Feta	40	18·8	17·8	6·5	4·0
Cottage cheese	20	4·6	14·7	0·8	1·6
Fresh cheese	40	11·8	11·8	0·7	1·5
	skimmed	0·2	16·3	0·9	1·9

2.2 Protein

The nutritional importance of cheese arises from its high content of biologically valuable proteins. Table I shows that the protein content of different varieties of cheese varies between 20 and 35%. Within any one type of cheese, the protein content varies inversely with the fat content. The nutrient density (based on the energy content) for the protein content of different types of cheese is 2·9–6·2. A 100 g portion of soft cheese will provide 30–40% of the daily protein requirements of an adult and 100 g of a hard cheese will supply 40–50%.

In cheese manufacture, the casein of milk is incorporated into the cheese while most of the biologically valuable whey proteins pass into the whey. Thus, 75–80% of the total protein and about 95% of the casein are transferred from the milk to the fresh cheese.[6,7] Since the whey proteins are nutritionally superior to casein, which is somewhat deficient in sulphur amino acids, the biological value of the proteins in cheese is somewhat lower than that of the total milk protein, but is still higher than that of casein alone. If the essential amino acid index of total milk protein is given a value of 100, then the corresponding values of the proteins in a number of cheese varieties range from 91 to 97. The biological value of the proteins is not impaired by the action of rennet or of other enzymes active during cheese ripening, nor is it affected by acid formation. The Maillard reaction does not occur during cheese manufacture so that the availability of lysine in cheese is almost the same as in milk. Ripening periods of 16–20 weeks produce no significant changes in the NPU and PER values of the proteins of Tilsiter and Gouda cheeses; in fact, in some cases the NPR and PER values of cheese proteins are higher even than those of milk proteins.[8-10]

When ultrafiltration is used to concentrate cheese milk up to the dry matter content of cheese so that no whey is produced, the whey proteins are also incorporated into the cheese, thereby improving the nutritive value of the protein. While the whey proteins of a normal cheese account for only 2–3% of the total protein, in such a cheese they represent 15% of the protein.

Cheese can contribute significantly to the supply of essential amino acids. In Table II, where the amino acid composition of milk and cheese proteins are compared to the reference protein, which indicates the ideal concentration of essential amino acids in a dietary protein, it can be seen that cheese protein meets the requirements to the same extent as milk protein, except those for methionine plus cystine.

TABLE II

Concentration of essential amino acids in milk and cheese protein, compared to the reference protein

Essential amino acid	Content (g/100 g protein)		
	Reference protein FAO/WHO	Milk protein	Cheese protein
Tryptophan	1·0	1·4	1·4
Phenylalanine + tyrosine	6·0	10·5	10·9
Leucine	7·0	10·4	10·4
Isoleucine	4·0	6·4	5·8
Threonine	4·0	5·1	4·8
Methionine + cystine	3·5	3·6	3·2
Lysine	5·5	8·3	8·3
Valine	5·0	6·8	6·8
Total	36·0	52·5	51·6

During cheese ripening, part of the water-insoluble casein is converted into water-soluble nitrogenous compounds which include the intermediate products of protein hydrolysis as well as free amino acids. Cheese ripening can be looked upon as a sort of predigestion whereby the digestibility of the proteins is increased. The true digestibility of a number of cheese varieties is almost 100%.[11] Small peptides can pass through the walls of the intestine and it is possible that they penetrate even cell membranes so that they become directly available to the cell. An experiment with rats demonstrated that the rate of utilization of cheese protein was higher than the rate for casein. The mean degree of utilization of the essential amino acids in cheese protein is 89·1%, i.e. greater than the corresponding value for milk protein (which is 85·7%) and almost equal to the value for egg protein, which is 89·6%. The free amino acids of cheese, particularly aspartic and glutamic acids, are said to promote the secretion of gastric juices. It should be noted that a food allergy to cheese protein has never been described.[11]

The decarboxylation of free amino acids during cheese ripening produces amines. The principal amines found in cheese are histamine, tyramine, tryptamine, putrescine, cadaverine, and phenylethylamine. The concentrations of individual amines in cheese show great variations and depend on the ripening period, on the intensity of flavour development and on the microbial flora. Average values for the contents of tyramine and histamine in different types of cheese have been determined and are shown in Table III. It is evident that Cheddar cheese contains an astonishingly high concentration of tyramine, that blue cheeses have high concentrations of amines, tyramine and especially histamine and, that there is little difference between hard, semi-hard and soft cheeses.[12−14,57]

TABLE III

Average tyramine and histamine contents of some cheese varieties[2]

Cheese variety	Content of	
	Tyramine (μg/g)	Histamine (μg/g)
Cheddar	910	110
Emmentaler, Gruyère	190	100
Blue cheese	440	400
Edam, Gouda	210	35
Camembert, Brie	140	30
Cottage cheese	5	5

Physiologically active amines can affect the blood pressure, with tyramine and phenylethylamine having a hypertensive and histamine a hypotensive effect. However, mono- and diamine oxidases convert the biogenic amines that are consumed in foods relatively quickly into aldehydes and finally into carboxylic acids by oxidative deamination. Although opinions on the toxicity threshold values of amines vary widely (for tyramine they are 10–80 mg, for histamine, 70–1000 mg), it is concluded that healthy persons are able to metabolize the biogenic amines ingested, even when large amounts of cheese are consumed, without adverse physiological reactions.[15,16]

Some sensitive people may be subject to attacks of migraine as a result of eating cheese. It is possible that such persons suffer from a genetically-determined lack of monoamine oxidase. The consumption of 100 mg of tyramine produces severe headaches in a large number of these patients. Also, when patients suffering from high blood pressure or similar disorders are treated with drugs containing a monoamine oxidase inhibitor, the normal breakdown of amines in the body is prevented. Cases have been reported in which the consumption of cheese by such patients has led, within 30 min to 2 h, to hypertensive reactions which are therefore called the 'cheese syndrome'. However, such drugs are rarely used nowadays. In those cases where drugs containing monoamine oxidase inhibitors are prescribed, the patient should be warned not to eat cheese or other tyramine-containing foods during the period of treatment, although the great variation in the tyramine content of different types of cheese does not make an adverse reaction inevitable.[17,18]

2.3 Lactose and Lactic Acid

There is no lactose in many cheeses or only a very low concentration (1–3 g/100 g) because most of the lactose of the milk passes into the whey and that retained in the cheese curd is partly or fully converted to lactic acid during cheese ripening. Therefore, cheese is suitable for the diets of persons suffering from lactose malabsorption and of diabetics.[19]

The average lactic acid content of a number of cheeses is as follows: Parmesan, 0·7%; Cheddar, 1·3%; Tilsiter, 1·0%; Quarg (curd cheese), 0·7%; Blue cheese, 0·6%; Emmentaler, 0·4%; Cottage cheese, 0·3%; Camembert, 0·2%. Cheese usually contains both lactic acid isomers, L(+) and D(−), the relative proportion of the D-isomer depending on the type of starter culture used and on some other ripening factors. The content of D(−) lactic acid in different types of cheese can be very different (fresh cheese 4–14%; ripened cheeses, 10–50%).[20–22]. The human organism has only a limited capacity to metabolize D(−) lactic acid but from the data available in the literature, a toxic effect of D(−) lactic acid cannot be derived for the adolescent or the adult. As a logical conclusion, the WHO, in a revised statement, has not limited the admissible intake for adults, while for infants (up to 1 year of age), a D(−) lactic acid-free diet is recommended.[23,24]

2.4 Minerals and Trace Elements

The calcium and phosphorus contents of cheese are as important as those of milk, since 100 g of soft cheese will supply 30–40% of the daily Ca requirement and 12–20% of the daily P requirement and 100 g of a hard cheese will meet the daily Ca requirement completely and contribute 40–50% of the P requirement. In Germany and France, adults ingest about 150 mg Ca per capita per day from cheese, i.e. about 20% of the daily Ca intake. The average concentrations of Ca and P in a number of cheese varieties are shown in Table I. It should be noted that where one variety of cheese is made with different fat contents, the higher fat cheese contains less Ca and P. The nutrient density for Ca in different types of cheese is 1·3–7·0 and for P, 2·6–5·7. Cheeses produced by rennet coagulation usually have higher calcium contents than those made from acid-coagulated milk.[25] About 60–65% of the calcium and 50–55% of the phosphorus of milk are retained in Tilsiter and Trappist cheeses. The calcium, phosphorus and magnesium in cheese are as well utilized by the body as those in milk.[26] The ratio of calcium to phosphorus in cheese is also thought to be desirable nutritionally. Cheese is one of the foods that is not cariogenic.[27]

The contents (g/kg) of some other minerals in various types of cheese are: Na, 0·3–18·5; K, 0·5–3·8; Mg, 0·1–0·7. The wide range of the Na contents is due to the different amounts of NaCl added to cheeses; the following are average values for the NaCl content (%) of different cheeses:[2,28,29]

Fresh cheese, Cottage cheese	0·4–0·8
Emmentaler	0·6
Tilsiter, Camembert, Cheddar	1·3–1·7
Gruyère, Parmesan, Gouda, Edam, Brie	2·1
Roquefort, Feta	4·3–4·6

A minimum intake of less than 500 mg and a maximum of 4 g sodium per capita per day is suggested by the German Society of Nutrition. Since a high sodium intake can induce hypertension, a restricted sodium intake is recommended to accommodate the diets of consumers under medical management for hypertension. Although even in countries with a high consumption, cheese contributes only about 5–8% to the total sodium intake, the manufacture of low-sodium cheese is recommended by using a brine containing mainly KCl.[30,31] Taste panel results show that cheeses prepared to contain up to 75% less sodium than traditional cheese are acceptable to consumers.[32,33] It should be considered also that hypertension may be due to a deficiency of dietary calcium rather than to an excessive intake of sodium, since it has been observed that patients suffering from hypertension consume about 25% less Ca than normotensive persons, because of a low consumption of milk and dairy products.[34]

The range of values for the concentrations (mg/kg) of some trace elements in cheese is listed below:

Fe	0·3–12·0
Cu	0·2–3·6
Mn	0·3–5·3
Mo	0·05–0·5
Zn	2·7–120
F	0·1–3·0
I	0·05–1·0
Co	0·004–0·038

Cottage cheese made from iron-enriched milk retains 58% of the iron of the milk so that 100 g of such a cheese will supply one-third of the recommended daily iron intake for a female adult.

2.5 Vitamins

The concentration of fat-soluble vitamins in cheese depends on its fat content. Most (80–85%) of the vitamin A contained in milk passes into the cheese. The figure is naturally lower for the water-soluble vitamins. The values for thiamine, nicotinic acid, folic acid and ascorbic acid are 10–20%, for riboflavin and biotin, 20–30%, for pyridoxine and pantothenic acid, 25–45% and for cobalamin, 30–60%; the rest remains in the whey.[36,37] However, milk contains such high concentrations of some B vitamins that cheese still contributes significantly to the supply of these vitamins. This is especially true of vitamin B_{12}.

Table IV lists the average concentrations of vitamins in a number of cheese types. Some mould-ripened cheeses contain more of the B vitamins

TABLE IV
Average vitamin content of some cheese varieties[2]

Vitamin	Vitamin content (mg/kg)						
	Emmentaler	Cheddar	Edam	Blue cheese	Camembert	Cottage cheese	Fresh cheese
Vitamin A	3·3	3·6	2·5	3·6	3·0	0·4	0–1
Thiamine	0·5	0·4	0·5	0·3	0·4	0·3	0·3
Riboflavin	3·5	4·7	3·5	2·9	5·8	2·9	2·8
Pyridoxine	0·9	0·7	0·6		2·0	0·25	
Cobalamin	0·02	0·01	0·02	0·02		0·02	0·02
Nicotinic acid	1·0	1·0	1·0	1·0	12	1·0	1·0
Folic acid	0·2	0·15		0·4		0·3	
Tocopherol	3	10		6	3	2·4	

than other types of cheese. Examples are the high contents of vitamins B_2, B_6 and nicotinic acid in Camembert. The concentrations of B vitamins change during ripening since these vitamins are both used and synthesized by the cheese microflora. The concentrations of several of the B vitamins depend on the type of starter culture used and increase with time of storage. After a long ripening period, the concentrations of these vitamins in cheese are therefore increased.[11,38] By isolating individual micro-organisms from cheese it could be shown that they are able to synthesize nicotinic acid, folic acid, biotin and pantothenic acid. The synthesis of vitamin B_{12} by propionic acid bacteria in hard cheese, especially in Emmentaler, has aroused great interest. Propionic acid bacteria have, therefore, been added experimentally to cheese milk in the manufacture of Edam, Tilsiter and a number of other types of cheese with the result that in some cases, especially with *Propionibacterium freudenreichii*, the cobalamin content was doubled (Fig. 2). Most of the ascorbic acid, on the other hand, is broken down during cheese ripening.

3. FRESH CHEESE (QUARG)

Tables I and IV include values for the concentrations of protein, minerals and vitamins in Quarg (fresh cheese). Milk destined for Quarg production is nowadays often strongly heat treated (at 95°C for 10 min). This leads to complex formation between casein and whey proteins so that a large part of the whey proteins is precipitated with the casein on acidification and passes into the Quarg. The percentage of the total nitrogen coagulated

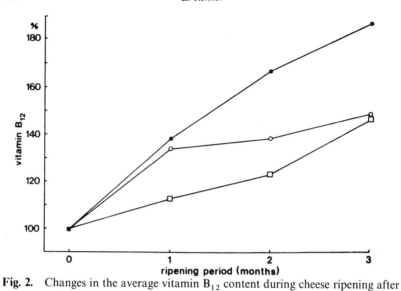

Fig. 2. Changes in the average vitamin B_{12} content during cheese ripening after adding propionic acid bacteria to the cheese milk.[40] ●—● Edam with *P. freudenreichii*; ○—○ Edam with *P. shermanii*; □—□ Tilsiter with *P. shermanii*.

increases from 77–79% to 88–89%. This product has, therefore, a higher content of essential amino acids and a higher biological protein value.[41,42] The complete transfer of the whey proteins into the fresh cheese can be achieved by ultrafiltering the cheese milk.[43]

From the point of view of nutrition, Quarg, which is usually produced by means of a lactic acid culture, is similar to other cultured milk products. Because low-fat Quarg is rich in biologically valuable proteins, calcium and phosphorus, and because its calorie content is relatively low, it is recommended for all sections of the population, but particularly for older people and as part of slimming diets. Quarg is also easily digestible and this makes it valuable in therapeutic diets, especially in cases of liver disease.[44]

4. PROCESSED CHEESE

In the production of processed cheese, the casein is hydrated and peptized by the action of the emulsifying salts and the proportion of water-soluble protein therefore increases considerably. Polyphosphates have the widest range of application as emulsifying salts, but citrates and lactates are used also. During the storage of the processed cheese, the polyphosphates are converted, either partly or wholly, into di- and monophosphates. Processed cheeses contain roughly the same proportions of nutrients as the cheeses from which they were made. The fat content varies between 9 and 31% and the protein content between 8 and 24%. Except for the Na and K content, which are higher, the mineral concentrations are also similar to those in the original cheeses. The addition of polyphosphate does not increase the phosphate content significantly; the natural variation in the phosphate content of cheese is 0·4–2·7% and of processed cheese 0·8–2·7%. Some losses of vitamin B_1, B_2, nicotinic acid, pantothenic acid and vitamin B_{12} occur during the manufacture of processed cheese. The free amino acid content of the cheese and the in vitro digestibility of the proteins are increased by processing and the utilization of the proteins of processed cheese is thought to be better than that of the proteins of natural cheese. No change in the availability of lysine could be detected.[45,46]

Polyphosphates ingested with food do not exert a physiological effect because they are quickly broken down by enzymes to monophosphates which are then absorbed. They are therefore no danger to health. Experiments with rats have shown that polyphosphates are well tolerated, even when administered over long periods of time. The phosphate ingested as part of processed cheese has to be considered in the context of the total phosphorus intake which consists of the natural phosphorus content of the diet plus any additional mono- and polyphosphates. The phosphate contained in processed cheese might even contribute to meeting the P requirement. Because the recommended long-term daily intake of polyphosphate is 40 mg/kg of body weight, on average, there is no danger that the consumption of processed cheese could lead to an overdose of polyphosphates. It has been calculated that the amount of additional phosphorus ingested through the consumption of processed cheese and other phosphate-enriched foods is about 1·2 g/day and this is well within the range of variation of the normal phosphate intake. Processed cheese may be regarded as a valuable food because phosphates are said to inhibit the formation of dental caries. There are no objections to the use of citrates as emulsifying salts because citric acid and its salts occur in many foods and are normal metabolic products of the human body.[47,48]

5. ADDITION OF NITRATE

5.1 Nitrite

In most cheese varieties which undergo a long ripening period there is the danger that anaerobic spore-forming clostridia, particularly *Clostridium tyrobutyricum*, which are not destroyed by pasteurization, may produce considerable butyric acid fermentation resulting in bloating of the cheese, which would make it unfit for consumption. The addition of a maximum of 20 g of $NaNO_3$ or KNO_3 per 100 litres of cheese milk is therefore permitted in the manufacture of some types of cheese (semi-hard cheese), because during the ripening period the nitrates are reduced to nitrites which inhibit the growth of clostridia and thus prevent the so-called late bloating of cheese. Nitrites have no effect on the growth of lactic acid bacteria. No nitrate, or only very little of it, is used during the manufacture of Emmentaler cheese because otherwise the propionic acid fermentation may be disturbed.

Nitrite is a toxic compound and cheese should therefore not contain any harmful amounts of it at the end of its ripening period. This is actually the case, because the nitrite formed during cheese ripening is destroyed rapidly so that the finished product contains only traces of nitrite. When 20 g of nitrate are added per 100 litres of cheese milk, generally no nitrite is detectable.[49,50] The majority of cheeses do not need the addition of nitrate during their manufacture and they are free of nitrite. In Holland, the maximum permitted amount of nitrite in cheese is 2 ppm but the actual values found in an extensive investigation were always lower.[62] Figure 3 shows the change in the nitrite content of Gouda cheese made from milk to which 20 g of nitrate per 100 litres of milk had been added. The nitrite content of the cheese increases to a maximum of 0·7 mg/kg and then falls considerably during ripening. The interaction of lipids with nitrite is considered to cause a considerable reduction in the nitrite content of cheese.[51] The Dutch regulations also include a value for the residual nitrate in cheese which must not exceed 50 mg/kg of cheese. This value is only very rarely exceeded. The usual nitrate concentrations found range from 1 to 40 mg/kg.[62] The small amounts of nitrate found in types of cheese made without the addition of nitrate are probably due to nitrate contained in the water used during processing. Most of the nitrate added to milk passes into the whey. The nitrate content of cheese falls progressively during ripening.

On the basis of the results obtained from animal experiments and including a safety factor of 1:1000, the maximum safe daily dose of nitrite for humans has been worked out to be 46 μg/kg body weight. Preliminary ADI (acceptable daily intake) values suggested by WHO are 5 mg of nitrate or 0·2 mg of nitrite/kg body weight/day. The low concentrations of nitrate and nitrite in cheese do not in any way present a health hazard for the consumer. The average daily intake of nitrate with the diet in different countries varies between 50 and 100 mg, to which vegetables contribute

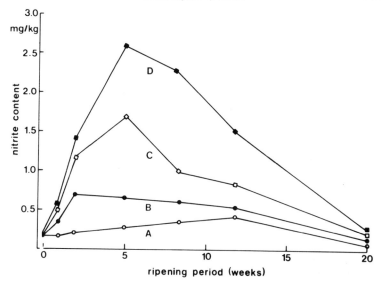

Fig. 3. Changes in the nitrite content of Gouda cheese made from milk to which various amounts of nitrate had been added (A = 10 g, B = 20 g, C = 40 g, D = 60 g per 100 litre).[52]

70–80% and milk and milk products, including cheese, only 0·2–0·9%.[53–55] The amount of nitrite ingested with milk and milk products is even less.[56]

5.2 Nitrosamines

Nitrosamines can be produced by a reaction between secondary amines and nitrite. Sixty different nitrosamines are known and the majority of them have been found to be relatively strongly carcinogenic in rats. The formation of nitrosamines depends on the amount of nitrite present, but is unrelated to the amine concentration.[58] Histamine and tyramine, which are the chief amines occurring in cheese, are not amongst those that can be converted to nitrosamines. The reaction is pH dependent, taking place preferentially in the pH range of 2–4·5. Cheese has a higher pH value and this prevents the reaction leading to the formation of nitrosamines. Some moulds such as *Penicillium camemberti* are able to synthesize nitrosamines in the pH range of cheese. However, those cheese varieties usually made from nitrated milk do not contain this mould culture. Nitrosamines can be formed in the stomach of animals and humans from nitrites and secondary amines; the low pH value of the gastric juices favours the reaction. However, the kinetics of the reaction make it improbable that it should occur either in cheese or in the stomach. This is why only trace amounts of nitrosamines are found in the stomach. Moreover, the reaction can be completely inhibited by ascorbic acid.[59] It is also thought possible that nitroso compounds in cheese might be degraded by enzymes.[60]

These are the reasons why nitrosamines are found only rarely and then in very low concentrations in cheeses that have been made with the addition of the permitted amounts of nitrates.[61–64] Values of $1–5\,\mu g/kg$ have been reported and in many investigations the concentrations found were consistently below $0.2\,\mu g/kg$. The nitrosamine content of most cheese samples examined was below the detectable limit, which is very low, namely $0.01\,\mu g/kg$. The compound most often found in cheese is dimethyl nitrosamine. There is no correlation between the nitrate content of a cheese and its nitrosamine content. It has been pointed out that cheeses made without the addition of nitrate often contain nitrosamines. For instance, when nitrite derived either from nitrite-containing cheese or from meat products is present during the manufacture of processed cheese or of products based on processed cheese, nitrosamines may be formed. This can, however, be prevented by the addition of ascorbic acid. No nitrosamines could be detected in dishes made in the home from nitrite-containing cheeses or meats (e.g. ham and cheese on toast).

Nitrosamines belong to a class of compounds which are highly carcinogenic for animals. It is not known for certain, but strongly suspected, that they are also carcinogenic for man. The 'maximum acceptable dose' of these compounds for humans is at present under discussion. On the basis of toxicity studies on animals, a value of $5–10\,\mu g/kg$ of foodstuff has been proposed. This includes a certain safety factor. It is concluded from relevant studies that individuals ingest less than $50\,\mu g$ of nitrosamines/year with their food. The average daily intake in the United Kingdom is said to be about $1\,\mu g$, of which cheese contributes 4%.[64] The small amounts of nitrosamines sometimes found in cheese can therefore be regarded as quite unimportant. In view of the fact that the body itself produces nitrites and that there is therefore an endogenous nitrosamine synthesis, these small amounts derived from cheese can be neglected.[65,66]

6. MICROBIOLOGICAL TOXINS

Because moulds, particularly strains of *Penicillium*, are used in the manufacture of blue cheeses as well as of cheeses with a surface mould, the question arises whether mycotoxins could be formed. The following substances are degradation products formed by the action of *Penicillium roqueforti*:

1. The alkaloid, roquefortin, is a degradation product typical of *P. roqueforti* and 0·05–6·8 ppm of it have been detected in blue cheese. According to the currently available toxicity data these concentrations are too low to be toxic. The consumption of blue cheese is therefore not a health hazard.[67]

2. The so-called PR-toxin is formed only by a few *P. roqueforti* strains and then only on artificial nutrient media; cheese is an unsuitable medium for the formation of PR-toxin. Moreover, PR-toxin is unstable, and even if present in cheese it would react with amino groups and be converted very quickly into non-toxic substances. This toxin has therefore never been found in cheese, not even when the cheese was made with PR-toxin producing organisms.[68,69]

3. The toxic mould product, patulin, which is carcinogenic for mice, is not produced by those strains of *P. roqueforti* used in cheesemaking. Moreover, the formation of patulin in cheese is strongly inhibited, probably by a reaction with sulphydryl groups, so that this substance would disappear rapidly from the cheese even if it had been present at the beginning. No patulin was detected in Tilsiter cheese which had been deliberately infected with the patulin-producing organisms.[70,71]

None of the mycotoxins under investigation could be detected in cultures of *P. caseicolum* or *P. camemberti*. Cyclopiazonic acid, which is formed by some *P. camemberti* strains, does not have a mutagenic potential.[74]

When mould cultures used in cheesemaking were fed to animals or when crude extracts of these moulds were injected, no harmful effects could be observed.[75,76] Taking into consideration all the results on the occurrence and biological activity of mycotoxins, occurring naturally in mould-ripened cheeses, a health hazard for man can be excluded, even with a considerable intake of cheese.[77]

7. PRESERVATION OF CHEESE

Sorbic acid and its calcium, sodium and potassium salts are very effective in preventing the growth of yeasts and moulds. Sorbic acid therefore might be used for the surface treatment of hard and semi-hard cheeses to prevent the growth of moulds during ripening and storing and thus to preserve the quality of the cheese. This method of preservation derives a special importance from the fact that it also prevents the growth of aflatoxin-producing moulds: for instance, a sorbate concentration of 200–400 ppm inhibits the growth of mycotoxin-producing moulds.[78] Sorbate also greatly reduces or prevents the production of patulin by *P. patulum*.[79]

Sorbic acid is quite harmless because the body uses it as it uses any other dietary fatty acid. It is metabolized like other fatty acids with the same number of C-atoms such as, for example, caproic acid. Experimental animals suffered no ill effects when their diet contained 5% of sorbic acid. In a number of countries, the use of sorbic acid and its salts is, therefore, permitted for the treatment of a range of foods, especially of cheese. Sorbic acid is one of the most commonly used preservatives because it is harmless and very effective.[80,81]

Natamycin (Pimaricin) is an antibiotic produced by *Streptomyces natalensis*. Like sorbic acid, it suppresses the growth of yeasts and moulds, but has very little effect on bacteria; *Aspergillus flavus*, in particular, is very sensitive to natamycin. It has been suggested that natamycin should be used in the same way as sorbic acid for the surface treatment of cheeses. Natamycin remains on the cheese surface for a relatively long time and penetrates only into the outermost layer of the cheese rind. Because the depth of penetration is so small, cheeses treated with natamycin are protected against mould infection for about 8 weeks. Aflatoxin formation is also prevented.[82,83] Although natamycin has now been used for several years, yeasts and moulds have not developed resistance against this antibiotic. Natamycin has no physiological effects and is non-toxic. Doubts have been expressed whether it is advisable to permit the use of an antibiotic that has been used successfully in medicine for the preservation of foods, although investigations have shown that the development of resistant organisms can be practically ruled out. Neither are allergic reactions expected to occur. The acceptable daily intake of natamycin is said to be 0·25 mg per kg body weight.[84]

REFERENCES

1. International Dairy Federation, *IDF Bull.*, 1984, **173**.
2. Renner, E., *Milk and Dairy Products in Human Nutrition*, 1983, Volksw. Verlag, Munich.

3. Finegan, A., Hickey, N., Maurer, B. and Mulcahy, R., *Am. J. Clin. Nutr.*, 1968, **21**, 143.
4. Flaim, E., Ferreri, L. F., Thye, F. W., Hill, J. E. and Ritchey, S. J., *Am. J. Clin. Nutr.*, 1981, **34**, 1103.
5. Biede, S. L., Paulsen, P. V., Hammond, E. G. and Glatz, B. A., *Dev. Industr. Microb.*, 1979, **20**, 203.
6. Antila, V., Hakkarainen, H. and Lappalainen, R., *Milchwissenschaft*, 1982, **37**, 321.
7. Rommel, G., Ph.D. thesis, University of Giessen, 1983.
8. Korolczuk, D., Cieslak, D., Luczynska, A. and Bijok, F., *Proc. 20th Intern. Dairy Congress, Paris*, 1978, Vol. E, p. 1073.
9. Staub, H. W., *Food Technol.*, 1978, **32**(12), 57.
10. Blanc, B. and Sieber, R., *Alimenta*, 1978, **17**, 59.
11. Dillon, J. C. In: *Le Fromage*, 1984, Lavoisier, Paris, p. 497.
12. Wortberg, B. and Zieprath, G., *Lebensm. Chem. Ger. Chem.*, 1981, **35**, 89.
13. Feldman, J. M., *Arch. Intern. Med.*, 1983, **143**, 2099.
14. Pechanek, U., Pfannhauser, W. and Woidich, H., *Z. Lebensm. Unters. Forsch.*, 1983, **176**, 335.
15. Taylor, S. L., Keefe, T. J., Windham, E. S. and Howell, J. F., *J. Food Protect.*, 1982, **45**, 455.
16. Binder, E. and Brandl, E., *Oesterr. Milchwirtsch., Wiss. Beilage 1*, 1984, **39**, 1.
17. Terplan, G., Wenzel, S. and Grove, H.-H., *Wien. Tieraerztl. Mschr.*, 1973, **60**, 46.
18. Kaplan, E. R., Sapeika, N. and Moodie, I. M., *Analyst*, 1974, **99**, 565.
19. Blanc, B., *Alimenta*, 1982, **21**, 125.
20. Pahkala, E. and Antila, M., *Finn. Chem. Lett.*, 1976, **1**, 21.
21. Puhan, Z., *Schweiz. Milchw. Forsch.*, 1976, **5**, 55.
22. Krusch, U., *Kieler Milchw. Forsch. Ber.*, 1978, **30**, 341.
23. Barth, C. A. and De Vrese, M., *Kieler Milchw. Forsch. Ber.*, 1984, **36**, 155.
24. Thomas, T. D. and Crow, V. L., *N.Z. J. Dairy Sci. Technol.*, 1983, **18**, 131.
25. Lagrange, V., *Méd. Nutr.*, 1982, **18**, 200.
26. Kansal, V. K. and Chaudhary, S., *Milchwissenschaft*, 1982, **37**, 261.
27. Andlaw, R. J., *J. Human Nutr.*, 1977, **31**, 45.
28. Donovan, S., *Proc. Nutr. Soc.*, 1983, **42**, 375.
29. Kindstedt, P. S. and Kosikowski, F. V., *J. Dairy Sci.*, 1984, **67**, 879.
30. Greenfield, H., Smith, A. M., Maples, J. and Wills, R. B. H., *Human Nutr. appl. Nutr.*, 1984, **38A**, 203.
31. Karahadian, C., Lindsay, R. C., Dillman, L. L. and Deibel, R. H., *J. Food Protect.*, 1985, **48**, 63.
32. Demott, B. J., Hitchcock, J. P. and Sanders, O. G., *J. Dairy Sci.*, 1984, **67**, 1539.
33. Karahadian, C. and Lindsay, R. C., *J. Dairy Sci.*, 1984, **67**, 1892.
34. McCarron, A., Morris, C. D. and Cole, C., *Science*, 1982, **217**, 267.
35. Sadler, A. M., Lacroix, D. E. and Alford, J. A., *J. Dairy Sci.*, 1973, **56**, 1267.
36. Rolls, B. A. and Porter, J. W. G., *Proc. Nutr. Soc.*, 1973, **32**, 9.
37. Reif, G. D., Shahani, K. M., Vakil, J. R. and Crowe, L. K., *J. Dairy Sci.*, 1976, **59**, 410.
38. Zehren, V., *Proc. 21st Intern. Dairy Congr., Moscow*, 1982, Vol. 2, p. 177.
40. Janicki, J., Pedziwilk, F. and Kisza, J., *Nahrung*, 1963, **7**, 406.

41. Puhan, Z. and Flueler, O., *Milchwissenschaft*, 1974, **29**, 148.
42. Renner, E., Karasch, U., Renz-Schauen, A. and Hauber, A., *Deut. Milchwirtsch.*, 1983, **34**, 1410.
43. Thomasow, J. and Hardung, C., *Proc. 20th Intern. Dairy Congress, Paris*, 1978, Vol. E, p. 750.
44. Halden, W., *Milch und Milchprodukte in der Ernaehrung*, 1978, Facultas-Verlag, Vienna.
45. Bijok, F., *Proc. 19th Intern. Dairy Congr.*, *New Delhi*, 1974, Vol. 1E, p. 574.
46. Lee, B. O. and Alais, C., *Lait*, 1981, **61**, 140.
47. Cremer, H.-D. and Buettner, W., *Ernaehr. Umschau*, 1962, **9**, 68.
48. Fingerhut, M., Ruf, F. and Lang, K., *Z. Ernaehrungswiss.*, 1966, **6**, 228.
49. Sen, N. P. and Donaldson, B., *J. Assoc. Off. Analyt. Chem.*, 1978, **61**, 1389.
50. Zerfiridis, G. K. and Manolkidis, K. S., *J. Food Protect.*, 1981, **44**, 576.
51. Kurechi, T. and Kikugawa, K., *J. Food Sci.*, 1979, **44**, 1263.
52. Sieber, R. and Blanc, B., *Deut. Molkerei-Ztg.*, 1978, **99**, 240.
53. Biedermann, R., Leu, D. and Vogelsanger, W., *Deut. Lebensm. Rundschau*, 1980, **76**, 149.
54. Tremp, E., *Mitt. Gebiete Lebensm. Hyg.*, 1980, **71**, 182.
55. Garcia Roche, M. O., Del Pozo, E., Izquierdo, L. and Fontaine, M., *Nahrung*, 1983, **27**, 125.
56. Gray, J. I., Irvine, D. M. and Kakuda, Y., *J. Food Protect.*, 1979, **42**, 261.
57. Antila, P., Antila, V., Mattila, J. and Hakkarainen, H., *Milchwissenschaft*, 1984, **39**, 81.
58. Askar, A., *Ernaehr. Umschau*, 1982, **29**, 143.
59. Fritz, W. and Uhde, W.-J., *Ernaehrungsforsch.*, 1980, **25**, 17.
60. Huynh, C.-H., Huynh, S. and Boivinet, P., *Ann. Nutr. Aliment.*, 1980, **34**, 1069.
61. Gough, T. A., McPhail, M. F., Webb, K. S., Wood, B. J. and Coleman, R. F., *J. Sci. Food Agric.*, 1977, **28**, 345.
62. Stephany, R. W., Elgersma, R. H. C. and Schuller, P. L., *Neth. Milk Dairy J.*, 1978, **32**, 143.
63. Pedersen, E., Thomsen, J. and Werner, H. In: *N-Nitroso Compounds: Analysis, Formation and Occurrence*, E. A. Walker, M. Castegnaro, L. Griciute and M. Boerzsoenyi (eds), IARC Scient. Publ. No. 31, Lyon, 1980, p. 493.
64. Gray, J. I. and Morton, I. D., *J. Human Nutr.*, 1981, **35**, 5.
65. Terplan, G., Bucsis, L. and Heerdegen, C., *Arch. Lebensmittelhyg.*, 1980, **31**, 1.
66. Yamamoto, M., Iwata, R., Ishiwata, H., Yamada, T. and Tanimura, A., *Food Chem. Toxic.*, 1984, **22**, 61.
67. Ware, G. M., Thorpe, C. W. and Pohland, A. E., *J. Assoc. Off. Analyt. Chem.*, 1980, **63**, 637.
68. Engel, G. and Prokopek, D., *Milchwissenschaft*, 1979, **34**, 272.
69. Moreau, C., *Lait*, 1980, **60**, 254.
70. Bullerman, L. B., *J. Dairy Sci.*, 1981, **64**, 2439.
71. Harwig, J., Blanchfield, B. J. and Scott, P. M., *Can. Inst. Food Sci. Technol. J.*, 1978, **11**, 149.
72. Engel, G. and von Milczewski, K. E., *Milchwissenschaft*, 1977, **32**, 517.
73. Krusch, U., Lompe, A., Engel, G. and von Milczewski, K. E., *Milchwissenschaft*, 1977, **32**, 713.

74. Schoch, U., Luethy, J. and Schlatter, C., *Mitt. Gebiete Lebensm. Hyg.*, 1983, **74**, 50.
75. Frank, H. K., Orth, R., Ivankovic, S., Kuhlmann, M. and Schmaehl, D., *Experientia*, 1976, **33**, 515.
76. Schoch, U., Luethy, J. and Schlatter, C., *Z. Lebensm. Unters. Forsch.*, 1984, **178**, 351.
77. Schoch, U., Luethy, J. and Schlatter, C., *Milchwissenschaft*, 1984, **39**, 583.
78. Wallhaeusser, K. H. and Lueck, E., *Z. Lebensm. Unters. Forsch.*, 1978, **167**, 156.
79. Bullerman, L. B., *J. Food Protect.*, 1984, **47**, 312.
80. Corradini, C. and Battistotti, B., *Scienza Tec. Latt.-Casear.*, 1981, **32**, 173.
81. Sofos, J. N. and Busta, F. F., *J. Food Protect.*, 1981, **44**, 614.
82. Kiermeier, F. and Zierer, E., *Z. Lebensm. Unters. Forsch.*, 1975, **157**, 253.
83. De Boer, E. and Stolk-Horsthuis, M., *J. Food Protect.*, 1977, **40**, 533.
84. Cerutti, G. and Battisti, P., *Latte*, 1972, **46**, 1.
85. Elgersma, R. H. C., Sen, N. P., Stephany, R. W., Schuller, P. L., Webb, K. S. and Gough, T. A., *Neth. Milk Dairy J.*, 1978, **32**, 125.

Chapter 10

Proteolysis in Relation to Normal and Accelerated Cheese Ripening

Barry A. Law

AFRC Institute of Food Research (University of Reading),
Shinfield, Reading, UK

1. INTRODUCTION

While lactose metabolism and fat breakdown are seen as fundamental processes in cheese manufacture, their importance in directly influencing the final characteristics and intensity of cheese flavour is in some cases difficult to define. On the other hand, protein breakdown has an obvious role in determining the texture, background flavour intensity and availability of flavour precursors in all matured cheese varieties.[1] Proteolysis has therefore been intensively studied and its progress in most types of cheese is well documented, although its precise role in flavour development remains to be determined. In general terms, the contribution of proteolysis to the maturation of cheeses can be seen in several stages (Fig. 1). A combination of endopeptidases, attributable to secondary coagulant activity, starter bacteria, secondary microflora and indigenous milk proteinase (plasmin), act on cheese proteins to break down structure and bring about changes in body and texture. The enzymes also provide peptide substrates for mainly intracellular enzymes from the cheese microflora, providing for the release of amino acids. The amino acids are thought to contribute to the savoury background flavour in cheese, and to be precursors for flavour volatiles. This chapter describes the sources and perceived roles of the proteolytic enzymes in cheese and also describes how some of these enzymes can be exploited to artificially speed up the maturation process.

365

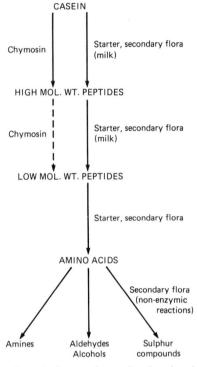

Fig. 1.   Breakdown of casein during cheese ripening: involvement of proteinases from various sources.

2. SOURCES OF PROTEOLYTIC ENZYMES IN CHEESE

2.1 Proteinases in Milk

Cows' milk contains several indigenous proteinases as well as microbial proteinases secreted by its microflora.[2,3] The 'native' enzymes include relatively heat-labile acid and neutral proteinase and aminopeptidases on the one hand and the more heat-stable serine proteinases on the other. The major serine proteinase is identical with blood plasmin[4] and appears to contribute to the breakdown of β-casein in surface-ripened cheeses,[5] and possibly other varieties.

Microbial proteinases in raw milk are mainly derived from its psychrotrophic microflora. Hygienically-produced milk contains only low numbers of these bacteria, which are commonly Gram-negative rods derived from soil, water and teat surfaces. However, it is normal practice in developed countries to transport and store manufacturing milk under refrigeration. At these temperatures (4–7°C), mesophilic bacteria are unable to multiply and psychrotrophs become dominant.[6] As they multiply in milk they produce heat-resistant proteinases and lipases which survive HTST pasteurization and may influence adversely the manufacture and ripening of some cheese varieties. For example, the breakdown of caseins in milk for making soft cheeses (Cottage, Camembert) can reduce yields significantly, though the evidence for similar effects in Cheddar cheese is equivocal.[3,7] A similar division of findings applies to the capacity of psychrotrophic proteinases to induce bitterness in cheese by producing bitter peptides during ripening; the phenomenon has been reported in Camembert but not in Cheddar. Indeed, in most stored cheeses the lipases produced by psychrotrophs are likely to cause spoilage by rancidity before the proteinase action becomes discernible.[3]

Many of the characteristics of psychrotroph proteinases have been reviewed recently by Fairbairn and Law.[8] Most are neutral or alkaline metalloproteinases requiring divalent cations (Zn^{2+}, Co^{2+}, Ca^{2+}) for activity and stability. Molecular weights range from 40 to 50 000 Daltons. Bond specificities are generally assumed to be typical of the proteinase class; neutral proteinases attack bonds having a basic and bulky, or hydrophobic amino acid residue on the amino side, whereas alkaline proteinases have much broader specificities, though also being affected by the residue on the amino side of the bond. Exceptionally, Noreau and Drapeau[9] reported that the alkaline proteinase of *B. fragi* ATCC 4973 cleaved only bonds adjacent to small hydrophobic residues.

2.2 Residual Coagulant Activity

Although the prime function of chymosin and other rennets is to initiate the formation of the milk gel from which cheese curds are produced, a proportion of the coagulant is retained in the curds and continues to act on cheese proteins during ripening. The only known exceptions are Mozzarella and Emmental cheese[10] whose manufacture involves a high temperature cooking stage which denatures the chymosin and most rennet substitutes. In the short term, chymosin is very bond-specific, splitting the Phe–Met bond in κ-casein. However, during the weeks and months of maturation, chymosin makes a significant contribution to the initial stages of casein breakdown by attacking other peptide bonds, particularly in α_{s1}-casein. In general terms, the role of this enzyme is the production of relatively large peptides (>1400 molecular weight) by limited bond cleavage.[11-13] The Phe$_{23}$–Phe$_{24}$ or Phe$_{24}$–Val$_{25}$ bonds of α_{s1}-casein are cleaved early in ripening[14,15] but β-casein degradation by chymosin is slow and only occurs later in the ripening process in the absence of proteolytic secondary micro-organisms. The commonly used microbial coagulants are generally more proteolytic in cheese but their preference for α_{s1}-casein is similar to that of chymosin.[16]

2.3 Proteolytic Enzymes in Cheese Starter Bacteria

The lactic acid bacteria used in starter cultures for the manufacture of cheese are weakly proteolytic compared with many other groups of bacteria (e.g. *Bacillus*, *Proteus*, *Pseudomonas*). However, they possess proteolytic enzymes ranging from endopeptidases to amino-, carboxy- and dipeptidases. Mou *et al.*[17] suggested that the collective specificities of the peptidases in Group N streptococci could account for the complete hydrolysis of casein-derived peptides to amino acids.

A high proportion of the proteolytic activity of Group N streptococci is located in the cell wall.[18] The enzyme(s) itself has not been isolated and purified but studies on crude preparations suggest that the *Str. lactis* proteinase is an EDTA-sensitive metalloenzyme. Exterkate[19] demonstrated that Ca^{2+} are required for the formation of active proteinase in the cell wall of *Str. cremoris* but the involvement of other divalent metal ions has not been investigated. Exterkate[20] suggested that the cell walls of Group N streptococci contain more than one proteinase. This was based on the observations of separate peaks of proteinase activity in whole cells at acid and neutral pH and at 30 and 40°C. Electrophetic zymograms of solubilized cell wall proteinase of *Str. lactis* reveal the presence of four bands of caseinolytic activity[21] but the possibility that these are sub-units of the same enzyme cannot be ruled out. Exterkate[19] distinguished between cell-bound and cell-free extracellular proteinases on the basis of Ca^{2+} dependence, the latter enzyme having no ion requirement for activity. Cell-bound extracellular proteinases almost certainly occur in the thermophilic lactic acid bacteria used as cheese starters but they are poorly documented.[22]

Lactic acid bacteria have intracellular proteinases which may be relevant to proteolysis in cheese when the organisms lyse during cheese maturation. However, controversy remains as to the true localization of the enzymes and they are poorly characterized.[22] Ohmiya and Sato[23] described a high mol.wt. (140 000) proteinase from *Str. cremoris* which hydrolysed α-, β- and κ-caseins, was inhibited by EDTA and activated by Ca^{2+}. The most detailed study was made by Desmazeaud and Zevaco[24] and Zevaco and Desmazeaud[25] on a neutral metalloproteinase (Ca^{2+} and Co^{2+}-activated; 49 500 mol.wt.) from *Str. diacetylactis*. It showed specificity for Pro–Ile, Ala–Phe, Lys–Ala and Lys–Val bonds of β-casein though rapid hydrolysis was demonstrated only on peptides derived from chymosin-degraded β-casein. α_{s1}-Casein was also degraded, though this is of doubtful relevance in cheese against a background of rennet action.

Lactobacilli and thermophilic streptococci contain intracellular neutral proteinases and overall levels of activity are usually higher than those found in the Group N streptococci. The preferred substrate is generally β-casein but detailed characterization of proteinases from these organisms has not been reported. A summary of the available data was prepared by Law and Kolstad[22] and this remains substantially valid.

Peptidases have been detected in, and isolated from, several subcellular fractions of starter lactic acid bacteria. It is probable that the enzymes from most locations have the opportunity to degrade peptides in ripening cheese since the starter bacteria tend to die out during cheese maturation and release their constituent enzymes into the cheese matrix.[26] Although the peptidases function optimally at neutral or alkaline pH, they survive and act for long periods in the acid environment of cheese.[27]

The combined evidence from studies involving cell fractionation, solvent-treatment of whole cells and peptide uptake competition studies[28–30] suggests that the cell envelope of Group N streptococci contains a number of distinct peptidases, ranging from exopeptidases which act on substituted peptides, to di- and tripeptidases. Their true functions are unknown but may be related to peptide transport and/or protein secretion. Many of the 'membrane-bound' peptidases have narrow specificities[30,31] though the latter authors detected broad specificity dipeptidase bands in zymograms of solubilized *Str. lactis* and *Str. cremoris* cell walls. Intracellular peptidases include di- and tripeptidases, aminopeptidase-P, proline iminopeptidase and general aminopeptidase. *Lactobacillus casei* contains similar peptidases and, in addition, a carboxypeptidase.[32,33] El-Soda and Desmazeaud[34] have described the peptidase complements of other species of lactobacilli commonly used in cheesemaking.

2.4 Proteolytic Enzymes in Secondary Cheese Micro-organisms

Secondary microfloras which grow and produce enzymes in cheese include non-starter lactic acid bacteria, *Brevibacterium linens* and the *Penicillium* moulds. Other bacteria and some yeasts are also present but their proteinases are not well defined. The contribution of secondary lactic acid bacteria to proteolysis is qualitatively similar to that of the starter strains, though quantitatively, probably less important.

In Emmental and Gruyère cheese, propionibacteria (*Pr. shermanii*) are added with the starter culture but they grow only after the cheese has been made. They are normally associated with the propionate fermentation but are now thought to contribute also to proteolysis by the production of peptidases which release proline, in particular.[35,36]

Cheeses which develop a bacterial surface smear (e.g. Tellagio, Danbo, Limburg, Compte) are partly dependent on *Brevibacterium linens* and related coryneforms for their flavour development. Although these organisms are recognized for their amino acid catabolic activities (see Section 5), they are also proteolytic[37] and produce a range of peptidases.[38,39] The proteinase activity of *B. linens* is poorly characterized; Friedman *et al.*[37] observed that its action was similar to that of chymosin, producing only large peptides. Recent studies in the author's laboratory (K. Hayashi, personal communication) suggest that the organism produces up to four extracellular proteinases, separable by ion exchange chromatography. The major proteinase is an EDTA-sensitive serine proteinase with an optimum pH of 9·0. However, it remains active at pH 6·0–6·5, the surface pH of surface-smear cheese.

Studies on *B. linens* peptidases show that both intracellular and extracellular enzymes are produced.[38,40,41] A wide range of dipeptide substrates is hydrolysed by both groups of enzymes and an extracellular aminopeptidase has been partly characterized as an EDTA-sensitive alkaline enzyme with a mol.wt. of approximately 48 000.

The white surface mould of Camembert and Brie cheeses (*Penicillium camemberti*) produces two extracellular proteinases (acid aspartyl and neutral metalloproteinase) which have been purified and characterized.[12] Their action on casein produces large peptides; 4 bonds are cleaved in α_{s1}-casein and 3 in β-casein. Extracellular peptidases include two distinct carboxypeptidases and an aminopeptidase.[42] *P. camemberti* also produces peptidases within the mycelium, and these are probably released into the cheese during later stages of ripening. *P. roqueforti* possesses a generally similar array of enzymes. The proteinases of both species are considered in some detail in Chapter 4, Volume 2.

3. MEASUREMENT OF PROTEOLYSIS IN CHEESE

The detection and measurement of the breakdown products of cheese proteins are used as indices of cheese maturation because the extent of the degradation process is linked to the development of typical texture and taste in most cheese varieties.[43] The most commonly used methods for separating intact proteins from the peptide and amino acid breakdown products are fractional precipitation (with acids or solvents), electrophoresis and chromatography.[44]

Fractional precipitation (or solubilization) offers the basis for the simplest and quickest methods for measuring the amount of cheese protein which has been rendered soluble by the action of proteolytic enzymes. These techniques have been both investigated and reviewed by Reville and Fox[45] and Kuchroo and Fox[46-48] and are summarized in Table I.

In Cheddar cheese, most of the proteins quickly become soluble in NaCl; given the fact that the fraction of cheese which is soluble in aqueous solutions is extremely heterogeneous, this and similar methods give little useful information on either the extent or nature of cheese proteolysis. Precipitation of cheese homogenates with trichloroacetic acid (TCA) solutions or with 70% (v/v) aqueous ethanol leaves only peptides and amino acids in solution and although the soluble fraction is heterogeneous, it can be further fractionated by electrophoresis and

TABLE I
Composition of soluble nitrogen fractions used as indices of cheese ripening

Index	Composition
Water-soluble N (water, salt solutions, pH 4·6)	Proteins, peptides, amino acids
Non-protein N (TCA-soluble, alcohol-soluble)	Peptides, amino acids
SSA-soluble N PTA-soluble Picric acid-soluble N	Very small peptides, amino acids

TCA: trichloroacetic acid.
SSA: sulphosalicylic acid.
PTA: phosphotungstic acid.

chromatography.[48] Other acidic precipitants such as picric acid, phosphotungstic acid (PTA) and sulphosalicylic acid (SSA) leave only amino acids and very small peptides in solution, and their use provides a good index of the progress of the late stages of proteolysis in cheese, especially useful when the effect of peptide hydrolases is under investigation.[49] However, the interpretation of cheese ripening indices based on TCA- and PTA- (or SSA-) soluble N must be approached with caution, especially when correlations with flavour are sought. For example, Aston et al.[50] showed that TCA-soluble N was a good index of total flavour intensity in young cheese but correlated poorly as the cheese matured. The PTA-soluble N levels correlated with flavour best in mature cheeses. The authors pointed out that their correlations could not account for flavour defects and this observation reveals a major limitation of such proteolytic indices. The data of Law and Wigmore[51,52] concerning accelerated cheese ripening with exogenous proteinases show how the incidence and extent of bitterness can change the perceived intensity of typical flavour in cheese; the three types of proteinase used in that study produced similar levels of proteolysis according to the indices used, yet different levels of bitterness resulted. These soluble N indices have a general application in the routine assessment of cheese age but organoleptic methods remain essential for the assessment of flavour quality.

A variety of colorimetric and spectrophotometric methods have been employed to measure the amounts of amino N in cheese fractions, as alternatives to the Kjeldahl method. Techniques which measure tryptophan,[53] tyrosine[54,55] and amino acids[51] are most commonly used but greater sensitivity is claimed for more recent methods based on the measurement of free amino groups with trinitrobenzenesulphonic acid[56] and o-phthaldialdehyde.[57] However, these methods have not yet been fully evaluated in the study of cheese.

Further information on the course of proteolysis in cheese can be obtained by fractionating the soluble extracts. Kuchroo and Fox[47] recommended using the 70% ethanol-soluble material as a source of soluble peptides for further separation and described a fractionation scheme involving ion exchange chromatography and gel filtration to separate the constituent peptides. As the authors pointed out, this scheme does not necessarily produce single peptides or amino acids from cheese but its resolution should allow the identification of significant fractions if comparisons are made between cheeses of differing flavour levels and/or profiles. High performance liquid chromatography (HPLC) has been suggested as an alternative and additional fractionation method and this has been applied to a study of bitter peptides in Cheddar cheese.[58] Examples of the application of high resolution fractionation techniques, followed by peptide identification, will be discussed in Section 4.1.

4. THE EFFECTS OF PROTEOLYSIS ON THE MATURATION OF CHEESE

The overall course of proteolysis in cheese was summarized in the Introduction to this chapter and is illustrated in Fig. 1. The relative importance of these stages of proteolysis to the development of the typical characteristics of different cheese varieties depends on the complexity of their microfloras and also on the physico-chemical conditions prevailing in the cheese. These factors are now considered in detail.

4.1 Proteolysis in Soft Cheeses

Early proteolysis by chymosin is recognized as a factor governing texture development in high moisture cheeses; its importance relative to the proteolytic activity of the microflora depends on the presence or absence of a surface mould growth.[59] In Meshanger, cheese which has no surface microflora, the progressive softening of the cheese body during ripening is solely due to the chymosin-mediated degradation of α_{s1}-casein. Chymosin action is favoured near the centre of the cheese and softening occurs from inside to outside.[60-62] Cheeses with a surface flora of *Penicillium camemberti* have a low initial pH which prevents softening, even when α_{s1}-casein is degraded. This is due to the insolubility of caseins near their isoelectric points (ca. 4·5). Softening occurs fron the outside of the cheese, and was previously thought to be caused by *Penicillium* proteinases diffusing inwards from the surface. However, Noomen[59] showed that enzyme diffusion was too slow and limited to account for the progress of softening. He subsequently showed that it was the deacidification of the cheese surface by the mould which, in concert with the chymosin-mediated casein breakdown, caused the textural changes. The increase in surface pH and the creation of a pH gradient is due both to the utilization of lactic acid by the *Penicillium* and the release of ammonia as an end product of its proteolytic and deaminating activities. However, Noomen[59] showed that the softening effect could be simulated by placing experimental cheeses in an atmosphere of ammonia; this effect was observed in cheeses containing only chymosin, with no surface mould growth.

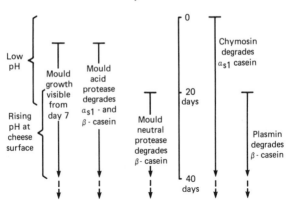

Fig. 2. Sequence of proteolysis in Camembert cheese.

Although the development of texture in Camembert cheese can be explained relatively simply, other proteolytic enzymes are active in the ripening cheese and they contribute to structural and pH changes. Their overall effect is also to release free amino acids as flavour precursors. Trieu-Cuot and Gripon[5] have proposed a proteolytic sequence in Camembert cheese which involves chymosin, plasmin (indigenous milk proteinase) and the extracellular acid and neutral proteinases produced by *P. camemberti* (Fig. 2). In agreement with Noomen,[59] early α_{s1}-casein breakdown is thought to be due to chymosin action, but the similar specificity of the *Penicillium* aspartyl proteinase prevents an assessment of its relative importance beyond the seventh day of maturation, when mould growth and enzyme secretion become significant near the cheese surface. Degradation of β-casein by chymosin is slow so that the action of the mould enzymes on this substrate is more easily seen from the seventh day. Trieu-Cuot *et al.*[63,64] and Trieu-Cuot and Gripon[5] have identified the peptide products of β-casein hydrolysis by both the acid and neutral proteinases of *P. camemberti* and concluded that the acid proteinase is more important throughout the ripening process, despite the changes in pH near the surface of the cheese. On the other hand, Lenoir and Auberger[65] concluded that the acid proteinase acts from the 6th to the 16th days, while the neutral enzyme becomes active from the 13th day and remains so for at least one month.

The action of the alkaline milk proteinase (plasmin) appears to be confined to β-casein during the later stages of ripening (21–35 days) when the cheese pH has risen to near neutral.

P. camemberti produces two distinct extracellular carboxypeptidases and an aminopeptidase which have relatively high optimum pH values. Lack of detailed data on their bond specificities precludes any discussion of their functional relationship with the proteinases in ripening but they probably become significant only when the pH has been raised and peptide substrates have accumulated. Intracellular peptidases are also produced and may be released by dead portions of the mycelium. Proteolytic yeasts are also present on the surface of Camembert cheese and they probably add to the number and type of enzymes present.[66]

4.2 Proteolysis in Blue-veined Cheese

Unlike the white mould, *P. camemberti*, the blue cheese mould, *P. roqueforti*, grows within the cheese matrix after the milk or curds have been inoculated with spores. When air is admitted into the cheese after it has been pressed the spores germinate and mycelial growth is visible within 8–10 days, reaching maximum growth within 1–3 months. *P. roqueforti* produces extracellular acid and neutral proteinases, both of which degrade α_{s1}-casein and β-casein.[67] However, the effect of these proteinases on α_{s1}-casein in cheese is difficult to assess in the presence of chymosin (cf. Camembert cheese) which is the main agent of proteolysis during the first 10–16 weeks of maturation.[68] Also, the action of proteolytic enzymes from the starter culture is superimposed on that of chymosin and the mould enzymes.[69] The rate of protein breakdown increases sharply between the 10th and 16th week of storage, suggesting that the mould mycelium suddenly releases enzymes due to lysis and/or leakage.[68] This observation implies that the intracellular proteinases and peptidases are more important than the extracellular enzymes secreted by the growing mycelium.

The overall effect of proteinase action is that no α_{s1}-casein remains in the lightly-salted regions of the cheese after 16 weeks, whereas β-casein breakdown is slower and some can still be detected after this time. Because blue-veined cheese is surface-salted, there is a NaCl concentration gradient which affects the rate of proteolysis in different regions. Obviously, the surface proteins are least degraded, chiefly because the mould itself is inhibited. Growth occurs optimally in 1–3% salt[70,71] so that a region of the cheese between the surface layer and the centre contains the most proteolytic activity. Samples taken from this area of a mature cheese show that up to 12% of the water-soluble N can be present as free amino acids and 65% as peptides.[68]

4.3 Proteolysis in Cheddar Cheese

The action of chymosin on α_{s1}-casein during the early stages of Cheddar cheese ripening is limited to the cleavage of only a few bonds, yet Creamer and Olson[72] showed that this results in a rapid and large change in the yield force on compression of Cheddar cheese. These authors argued that single α_{s1}-casein molecules interact with several other casein molecules and thus form a network in cheese. This arrangement is easily weakened even by limited proteolytic cleavage. The increase in brittleness (lower compression at yield point) in older cheese was attributed to the negative influence of continued peptide bond cleavage (by endo- and exopeptidases) on the availability of water for solvation of protein chains.

In addition to the rheological effects of protein cleavage during ripening, the decreasing polypeptide size may reduce the binding of flavour compounds by cheese proteins, manifested as an apparent increase in flavour intensity. McGugan *et al.*[73] showed that the soluble, non-volatile N fraction of cheese was the most important determinant of its flavour intensity (though not its quality). They showed that a flavourless, fat-free residue extracted from old cheese had a greater effect on the flavour intensity of reconstituted cheese fractions than did the equivalent extract from young cheese. The conclusion (which requires further testing) is that not only does the non-volatile fraction in the original unfractionated cheese contain vital flavour compounds, but that they become more 'available' as the protein structure is degraded. The idea is not without precedent in relation to fatty acid retention in Swiss cheese[74] and the binding of volatile compounds to soy proteins.[75]

In the absence of the deliberately-added, highly proteolytic secondary microflora of surface mould and blue-veined cheeses, casein breakdown during Cheddar cheese maturation is dependent on residual enzymes from the starter culture and from the adventitious secondary flora. In normal Cheddar cheese this consists mainly of lactobacilli or pediococci, though small numbers (usually $< 10^5$/g) of Gram-negative rods, micrococci and Group D streptococci may be present. Although the proteolytic systems of some lactobacilli have been studied (see Section 2·3), very little is known about their action in the ripening of Cheddar cheese. Most of the available information concerns the starter (Group N) streptococci and it is established that typical Cheddar cheese flavour develops in cheeses made with only the starter present, i.e. when the secondary bacteria are excluded.[76,77] This observation has greatly simplified studies on Cheddar cheese maturation and it can be demonstrated that the proteolytic enzymes of the starter streptococci are responsible for the production of small peptides and amino acids.[77,78] The proteinases of the starters are generally regarded as secondary in importance to chymosin in the early stages of proteolysis and more importance is attached to their peptidases, with which they are well equipped (Section 2.3). Most of the peptidase activity produced by the starter streptococci is cell-bound[29,31] and only released into the cheese matrix as the cells die and lyse or become leaky.[26] The extent of proteolysis in Cheddar cheese is much lower than that in mould-ripened cheese, only approximately 3% of its N being present as free amino acids, even in old cheese.[77]

Most of the discussion concerning proteolysis in Cheddar cheese probably remains valid for other hard and semi-hard varieties made with mesophilic starter cultures. Variations in the rate of proteinase action can be anticipated in washed curd cheeses such as Edam and Gouda, and the gradation of salt concentration within these cheeses must also be taken into account. Also, the effects of proteolysis in cheese are dependent on pH; the higher pH of washed-curd cheese permits the existence of a protein matrix which is likely to become softer as proteolysis progresses, in contrast with the tendency of low pH cheese to become more crumbly as interstitial water is bound by ionic groups.[72]

4.4 Proteolysis in Emmental (and Related) Cheese

This group of hard cheeses is treated separately, firstly because its starter flora differs from that of the Cheddar-like and other semi-hard cheeses in being made up of thermophilic streptococci and lactobacilli. Secondly, the growth of a deliberately-added secondary flora of *Propionibacterium shermanii* is significant in producing the typical pattern of proteolysis in these cheese varieties, mainly through the action of their peptidases (see Section 2.4).

Chymosin action on α_{s1}-casein is assumed to be limited by the high scald temperatures used in Emmental manufacture but plasmin survives and probably contributes significantly to proteolysis. The lactic flora of *Lb. helveticus* and *Str. thermophilus* is proteolytic and capable of releasing small peptides and amino acids, but their relative contribution in this respect has not been studied in detail. The propionibacteria are thought to be the source of proline-releasing peptidases,[35] giving the cheese its characteristic sweet flavour.[79] The sweet component of Emmental flavour resides in the cheese fraction consisting of amino acids and small peptides so that other proteolysis products may also be involved. Biede and

Hammond[80,81] showed that Ca^{2+} and Mg^{2+} were essential for the expression of sweetness in this fraction. 'Brothy' and 'nutty' flavour notes were also present in this amino acid/small peptide fraction, while 'burnt' and bitter flavours resided in the fraction containing tri-to hexapeptides. Biede and Hammond[81] also noted that the non-volatile fraction had a distinct acid flavour note which was not due to the presence of the organic acids.

4.5 Proteolysis and the Bitter Defect in Cheese

The enzymic hydrolysis of all caseins yields a proportion of peptides which have a bitter taste. This taste is correlated with a high degree of hydrophobicity,[82-85] and bitter peptides isolated from cheese satisfy this criterion. Champion and Stanley[58] isolated bitter peptide fractions from Cheddar cheese which were rich in leucine and valine. Bitter fragments of α_{s1}-casein[86,87] and β-casein[88,89] contain many hydrophobic residues (phenylalanyl, isoleucyl, leucyl, valyl, prolyl) and range in length from 2 to 22. There is disagreement as to the source of bitter peptides in maturing cheese but both major casein components probably contribute. The bitter fragments of α_{s1}-casein have been identified as originating from near the chymosin-sensitive Phe 23–Phe 24 bond, suggesting that the secondary action of the coagulant is a cause of bitterness, directly or indirectly. This is consistent with the observation that factors affecting chymosin retention in cheese curd (initial pH of milk, curd washing, scald temperature, amount of chymosin used) also influence the degree of bitterness in maturing cheese.[90,91] Direct evidence that chymosin produces bitter peptides in cheese comes from experiments with artificially acidified cheese containing no micro-organisms.[76,13] The importance of chymosin in producing bitter peptides is likely to vary according to the cheese variety in question. For example, less chymosin is retained in Cheddar than in Gouda cheese,[92] and most investigators believe that the proteinases from the starter culture are relatively more important in Cheddar. Lowrie *et al.*[93] showed that most bitterness is caused by the 'fast' single strain starters which multiply to high numbers (ca. 10^9/g) at the normal scald temperature used for Cheddar cheese. 'Slow' starters, which are inhibited by the scald and only reach numbers of ca. 10^8/g curd, do not produce bitter cheese, unless they were allowed to multiply further by reducing the scald temperature. These authors postulated that large chymosin-produced peptides are not bitter, but that the high starter proteinase levels in cheese made with fast strains release enough smaller, bitter peptides from these chymosin-produced peptides to exceed the flavour threshold for their detection by the consumer. The importance of the cell wall-bound proteinases in producing the bitter defect was confirmed by Mills and Thomas[94] when they showed that proteinase-negative variants (deficient in this enzyme) of bitter starters produced non-bitter cheese. While these are useful observations as aids to the selection of starter strains for defined Cheddar cultures, they do not explain some of the observed effects of starter cultures in non-Cheddar cheeses. In particular, Stadhouders *et al.*[92] pointed out that bitter and non-bitter starters are recognized in Gouda cheese manufacture, in which scald temperatures are 34°C or lower. This is explained in part by strain variations in the capacity of starters to degrade bitter peptides.[95] However, Visser *et al.*[96] suggested that this is an oversimplification; they showed that the cell membranes of both bitter and non-bitter strains hydrolysed bitter peptides. Salt concentration was the most important factor governing the extent of hydrolysis and it was suggested that at high ionic strengths the accessibility of the membrane enzymes to the hydrophobic peptides was reduced. The extent of this phenomenon may be strain-dependent.

Visser *et al.*[89] isolated only fragments of β-casein from bitter peptides extracted from Gouda cheese. They were present in both bitter and non-bitter cheese, suggesting that the concentration of such peptides, rather than their presence or absence, governs whether or not a cheese is bitter. It is not clear at present why some workers only find bitter fragments of α_{s1}-casein, while others find products of β-casein. Recent studies on bitterness in Camembert cheese[97,98] suggest that the rapid growth of *P. camemberti* is the most important factor; they showed that the acid proteinase produced most bitterness and that the defect could be avoided by restricting both the growth of the *Penicillium* and the activity of its acid proteinase. This could be achieved either by placing the cheese in an atmosphere of ammonia, or inoculating the cheese surface with the strongly deaminating mould, *Geotrichium candidum*.

5. AMINO ACID CATABOLISM IN CHEESE

Although the end products of proteolysis are amino acids, the further breakdown of these by decarboxylation, deamination, desulphurylation and demethiolation is considered to be an integral part of the overall process of flavour development in cheese (Fig. 3). The example of ammonia production in Camembert cheese is a case in point; the ammonia

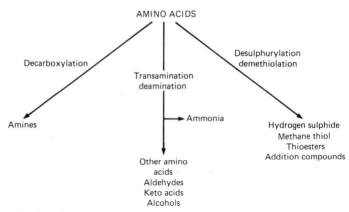

Fig. 3.   General pathways of amino acid catabolism in cheese.

itself contributes to the flavour profile of the cheese and, together with the reduced lactic acid concentration in the presence of lactate-utilizing moulds, it neutralizes the cheese surface. As outlined in Section 4.1, this increase in pH is vital for the softening of Camembert cheese and also encourages the activity of enzymes with neutral or alkaline pH optima.

Cheeses which develop a surface growth of *Brevibacterium linens* usually accumulate a wide variety of deamination and transamination products.[99] Branched chain aldehydes produced in cheese by such reactions (via an additional spontaneous decarboxylation) are probably reduced to their corresponding alcohols which contribute to the general flavour characteristics of surface-ripened cheese. Products in this category include 3-methyl-1-butanol, phenylethanol and 3-methylthiopropanol derived from leucine, phenylalanine and methionine, respectively. Lee and Richard[100] showed that many of the micro-organisms found on the surface of cheese can produce phenylethanol or its derivatives from phenylalanine. They included yeasts, *Moxarella* spp., *B. linens* and *Arthrobacter* sp.

The presence of volatile and non-volatile amines in cheese is explained by simple decarboxylation reactions, though the origin of secondary and tertiary amines is more difficult to explain.[1] Of the primary amines, tyramine is normally the most abundant in cheese.[101]

Volatile sulphur compounds are found in most cheeses and their origin is generally agreed to be the sulphur amino acids. *P. camemberti* was reported to produce H_2S, dimethylsulphide and methanethiol from methionine.[102] Also, *B. linens* is an established producer of methanethiol.[103,104] Methanethiol has no proven direct role in the flavour of the surface-ripened or surface smear cheeses but its increased production in experimental methionine-supplemented cheeses enhances flavour development.[1] Methanethiol probably contributes to flavour in the form of derivatives such as thioesters some of which are known to have cheese-like aromas.[105] *B. linens* is known to produce S-methylthioacetate[106] and micrococci in cheese smear have also been implicated in this type of reaction.[99] The addition of methanethiol to formaldehyde can explain the formation of bis-(methylthio)-methane, a compound thought to be important in Camembert aroma.[107]

Volatile sulphur compounds may contribute to the typical flavour of Cheddar cheese since they are found in Cheddar-like aroma distillates.[108] Manning and Price[109] showed that the selective removal of methanethiol from the head space of Cheddar cheese destroyed its typical aroma and also that its concentration in cheese correlated closely with flavour intensity.[110] Despite more recent evidence casting doubt on the direct involvement of methanethiol in Cheddar aroma[111,112] there remains a strong possibility that it contributes to aroma or flavour via further interactions or reactions with other compounds. However, the mechanism of its production in Cheddar cheese is not certain. Cheddar does not have a surface smear and methanethiol-producing bacteria are only rarely isolated.[113] Manning[114] studied possible chemical mechanisms for methanethiol production in cheese and concluded that it is closely linked to the release of H_2S. The latter compound is usually present in cheese and probably contributes to flavour, though the concentration at which it is present is probably critical only if it is too high, when it can be detected as a flavour defect.[114] Although precise reaction mechanisms were not investigated, it was shown that under reducing conditions (such as exist in cheese), H_2S can release methanethiol from undegraded casein or methionine by an addition or substitution.[114]

6. EXOGENOUS PROTEINASES IN ACCELERATED CHEESE RIPENING

Although milk is the major cost item in commercial cheese manufacture, storage represents a significant proportion of total cost (approximately 6–8% in the UK). For this reason much effort has been expended in the search for methods which shorten the ripening time of cheese without impairing typical flavour and texture. Factors governing the choice of suitable methods, with their advantages and disadvantages, have been reviewed recently.[115] The present discussion will therefore be confined to the acceleration of proteolysis in cheese by the application of exogenous proteinases.

The choice of suitable proteolytic enzymes for aiding ripening presents the investigator with a number of new problems peculiar to their use in cheese. It has to be remembered that although 'faster' ripening is required, the time scale involved remains extremely long in enzymic terms. If the maturation were to be speeded up to match other enzyme-based industrial processes, e.g. brewing or baking, it would be uncontrollable and the inherent stability of cheese, one of its most useful properties, would be lost. The enzyme system required, therefore, is likely to have a pH and temperature optimum well removed from the conditions prevailing in cheese. In addition, it is unlikely that any one enzyme could be added to cheese to accelerate all the stages of proteolysis from initial bond cleavage of the protein, through to peptide breakdown, releasing free amino acids. In normal cheese this involves chymosin, a range of proteinases from starter and non-starter bacteria (many of which remain uncharacterized) and, finally, a number of peptidases from several subcellular organelles, which collectively cover a very wide range of bond specificities. It is hardly surprising, therefore, that early attempts to speed up cheese ripening with uncharacterized commercial proteinases were unsuccessful in providing methods which would give a typical and acceptable flavour and texture to the treated cheese. There is little doubt that some acid and neutral proteinases, when added to cheese, produce a strong flavour in a relatively short time,[116,117] but flavour defects are common. Sood and Kosikowski[118] attempted to overcome the laborious problem of selecting enzymes in long-term cheese experiments by adopting a curd slurry method[119] to screen enzymes in a matter of days rather than months. However, this is a difficult process to control since it involves increasing the water content of the curd and ripening at 30°C. Also, the mechanism by which flavour develops so quickly remains unclear. Used with care, the technique can predict whether or not a particular proteinase is likely to generate flavour defects such as 'meaty' or bitter, but it will not necessarily pinpoint enzymes which can give a good balance of flavour notes in real cheese.

An alternative approach to the choice of cheese ripening enzymes involves a consideration of their theoretically-required characteristics followed by the formulation of an enzyme mixture which fits these requirements. For example, it could be argued that for hard and semi-hard cheeses, the proteinase (endopeptidase) activity should be relatively unstable at low pH. This would be to assume that its function is to lay down a pool of peptide substrates as a source of free amino acids, and to bring about a relatively rapid, but limited change from the elastic texture of the cheese curd to the typical deformable texture of mature cheese. This suggests a neutral or alkaline, rather than an acid, proteinase. Concerning the type of casein degraded by the proteinase, an enzyme which attacks β-casein as well as α_{s1}-casein would be desirable, partly because α_{s1}-casein is normally degraded rapidly in cheese and increased gross proteolysis is more easily achieved with β-casein. An additional advantage lies in the ease with which the progress of accelerated proteolysis can be monitored by observing electrophoretically the disappearance of β-casein.

Law and Wigmore[51,52] carried out cheesemaking trials in which acid, neutral and alkaline proteinases were assessed systematically for their effects on proteolysis, rheological properties and flavour in Cheddar cheeses. The fungal acid proteinase degraded α_{s1}- and β-caseins very quickly in cheese such that its body was soft and weak and its texture was crumbly within two months. The cheeses tasted extremely bitter and reduction of enzyme treatment levels, while decreasing the body/texture defects, had little influence on the incidence of the bitter defect. The cheeses deteriorated rapidly during a further 2 month storage period, suggesting that not only was the proteinase acting too close to its optimum pH for its activity to be attenuated, but also that high levels of activity persisted in the ageing cheese. Unexpectedly, similar flavour results were obtained with a bacterial alkaline proteinase, though body/texture was not so badly affected. This was not investigated further but the high level of bitterness may have been due to the particular bond specificity of the proteinase in terms of bitter peptide production.

A bacterial neutral proteinase (Neutrase, from *Bacillus subtilis*) also produced weak-bodied, bitter cheese when added in relatively large amounts (0·5 Anson units/kg) but an optimum amount was determined (0·02 Anson units/kg) which significantly increased the intensity of cheese flavour without producing bitterness. The cheese treated in this way was more crumbly than untreated cheese and was slightly softer-bodied but its force/compression curve obtained using an Instron tester[51] resembled that of the 'old' cheese tested by Creamer and Olson,[72] rather than the curve obtained with the young cheese in both investigations.

The flavour level reached with the commercial food-grade neutral proteinase could be easily controlled by manipulating the cheese storage temperature and it was apparent that the enzyme was unstable in cheese.

This provides the potential for controlled accelerated ripening, provided that body/texture problems can be overcome. Ridha *et al.*[120] also noted similar adverse effects on cheese treated with the same proteinase, though these authors also claimed that bitterness could not be eliminated even at low addition levels. Since they noted marked mottling of the treated cheese it is possible that there may have been high localized concentrations of enzyme which produced excessive proteolysis.

Although *B. subtilis* neutral proteinase produced an acceptable acceleration of flavour production without marked defects, its use is limited by its tendency to produce body/texture defects at the levels required for flavour enhancement. Observations of the progress of ripening in normal cheese suggest that the inclusion of peptide-degrading enzymes with a proteinase would produce a synergistic effect such that a relatively low concentration of the proteinase could, in concert with the peptidases, release sufficient free amino acids to significantly influence flavour intensity. This would not only obviate the need for proteinase levels detrimental to texture, but also ensure that there could be no build-up of bitter peptide. There are at present no broad-specificity food grade peptidase preparations available commercially in sufficient quantities for the conduct of cheesemaking trials on a scale suitable for organoleptic assessment. Law and Wigmore[49] used intracellular cell-free extracts prepared from lysozyme lysates of *Str. lactis* as a crude source of peptidases and added them to cheese curd together with *B. subtilis* neutral proteinase. The level of added peptidase extract was based arbitrarily on the equivalent of twice the viable population of milled curd. This treatment not only improved the quality of the cheese flavour over that obtained with Neutrase alone but also increased the intensity of flavour in 2 month old cheese to that normally expected in 5–6 month old cheese (Table II). The peptidase extract alone had only a minor effect on flavour intensity, presumably because no additional proteolysis had been achieved to provide more peptide substrates. It is significant that the level of TCA-soluble N reached in the cheese treated with the enzyme combination would have produced bitterness in the absence of the peptidase (cf. Ref. 51) but the ratio of amino acid (SSA-soluble) N to TCA-soluble N indicates that the peptidase had maintained a high degree of peptide breakdown in the cheese, preventing the onset of bitterness even at high rates of proteolysis.

Other claims of accelerated cheese ripening with combinations of proteolytic enzymes have been reported briefly, but definitive chemical and organoleptic data are not available. For example, Kalinowski *et al.*[121,122]

TABLE II

Accelerated ripening of Cheddar cheese with proteolytic enzymes (2 months) (based on data from Ref. 49)

Treatment	Cheddar intensity (0–8)	Proteolysis (TCA-sol N)	AA:Peptide ratio
None	2·8	100	2·3
Peptidase	3·2	100	4·0
Neutrase	[a]3·5	140	2·9
Peptidase + Neutrase	4·0	200	4·4

[a] Defect score ranges from 0·2 to 0·4, meaty and/or bitter.
AA = Amino acid.

used the intracellular proteinases of *P. candidum* and *P. roqueforti* with extracts of *Str. lactis* or *Lb. casei* to speed up the maturation of semi-hard cheeses. The synergistic action of these enzymes in normal cheesemaking had already been demonstrated by Gripon *et al.*[69]

El-Soda *et al.*[123,124] added cell-free extracts of lactobacilli to Cheddar cheese curds to speed up protein breakdown but the curds became very bitter. This is surprising in view of the multiplicity of peptidases in these organisms[33,34] but may reflect the more proteolytic, rather than peptidolytic collective action of the enzymes. Despite these difficulties, the development of ripening systems based on proteinase/peptidase combinations looks promising and it is to be expected that commercially-applicable preparations will emerge within the foreseeable future.

Although proteolytic enzymes can be used to accelerate cheese ripening, their use does present some new technological and economic problems, stemming chiefly from their interactions with milk proteins during cheesemaking and their distribution between curds and whey at separation (Table III). Proteinases added to the cheese milk are likely to

TABLE III

Alternative modes of proteinase addition to cheese

	Direct in milk	Encapsulated in milk	Direct in curd
Distribution	Good	Good	Poor
Curd texture	Poor	Normal	Normal
Yield	Reduced	Normal	Normal
Whey contamination	Complete	None(?)	Press only

decrease cheese yields by producing soluble N from casein. There is also a strong possibility of the proteolytic action weakening the structure of the curds, affecting both yield (fat retention) and cheese body/texture. Unless the proteinase(s) has a particularly high affinity for casein or fat globule membranes, most of it will be lost in the whey when the curds are recovered. This not only leaves little residual enzyme for cheese ripening but also necessitates further whey processing to ensure that the same enzyme does not interfere with the use of the by-product in other applications (Table III). Estimates of the retention of exogenous proteinases in cheese curd vary but Law and King[125] showed that it can be as low as 2–4%, the theoretical figure achieved if the protein partitioned simply between the water of curds and whey.

These problems can be overcome by adding the enzymes to the finished cheese curd using salt as a vehicle and diluent. Using this method, the cheese industry can rapidly exploit proven enzyme systems for varieties like Cheddar which are internally salted. Enzyme distribution is not perfect, however, and brine or surface-salted cheeses are not amenable to such treatment. Ideally, the enzyme should be added via the milk to give even distribution and provide a universal delivery system, irrespective of the manufacturing technique. This can be achieved using microencapsulation to separate the proteinase from its substrate until the cheese has been made (Table III). Examples of fat capsules as carriers and protectors of labile enzymes and multienzyme complexes have been reported by Olson and collaborators,[126–129] and Rippe *et al.*[130] This technology has important potential in controlling the activity of flavour-producing enzymes in cheese. Law and King[125] used liposomes to add *B. subtilis* neutral proteinase to Cheddar cheese via the milk. The principle of this technique is summarized in Fig. 4. Liposomes are micro-vesicles formed by hydrating dried phospholipids.[131] If an enzyme is present during hydration, a proportion of it is trapped between the vesicle membranes. Liposomes formed from phosphatidylcholine are stable in milk long enough for the entrapped enzyme to be included in the curd and for the curd to be cheddared. Enzyme release in the pressed cheese is inferred from the similar rate of protein breakdown in cheese treated with proteinase either directly via the salt, or with liposome-entrapped proteinase via the milk.[125] The multilamellar vesicles used in this initial study were retained to the extent of approximately 17% in the curd, but subsequent work (Kirby and Law, unpublished) with dehydration-rehydration vesicles[132] has shown that up to 90% of encapsulated enzyme can be held in the curd to the end of Cheddaring.

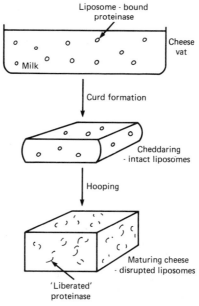

Fig. 4. Proteinase incorporation into cheese via liposomes.

7. CONCLUSIONS

The contribution of proteolysis to the maturation of cheeses can be seen in several stages. For example, a combination of endopeptidases due to secondary coagulant action, indigenous milk proteinase(s), starter bacteria and secondary microflora act on cheese proteins to break down structure and bring about changes to cheese body and texture. These enzymes also provide peptide substrates for intracellular enzymes from the cheese flora, providing for the release of amino acids. The amino acids are thought to contribute to savoury background flavour in cheese, and also act as precursors for flavour volatiles.

The need to accelerate cheese ripening arises from the high cost of storing the product until it has reached a suitable state of maturity. The benefits of potential enzyme treatments are relatively easy to calculate.

Although there are many claims in the literature for successful accelerated ripening with commercial proteinases, it is unlikely that any single enzyme can speed up cheese maturation while maintaining natural texture and flavour balance. Enzyme mixtures are more likely to be successful, and this theme has been pursued by combining bacterial and fungal endopeptidases with exopeptidases which degrade small peptides. The advantages of such mixtures are discussed. Problems of incorporating proteinases into cheese arise from the need to achieve homogeneous mixing, yet avoid premature proteolysis in the cheese vat. At present the best mode of enzyme addition is to the cheese curd, but advances in encapsulation technology may lead to a universally applicable route of addition via the milk.

REFERENCES

1. Adda, J., Gripon, J.-C. and Vassal, L., *Food Chem.*, 1982, **9**, 115.
2. Humbert, G. and Alais, C., *J. Dairy Res.*, 1979, **46**, 559.
3. Law, B. A., *J. Dairy Res.*, 1979, **46**, 573.
4. Reimerdes, E. H., *J. Dairy Sci.*, 1983, **66**, 1591.
5. Trieu-Cuot, P. and Gripon, J.-C., *J. Dairy Res.*, 1982, **49**, 501.
6. Law, B. A. and Mabbitt, L. A. In: *Food Microbiology: Advances and Prospects*, 1983, JAB Symposium Series No. 11, T. A. Roberts and F. A. Skinner (eds), Academic Press, London, p. 131.
7. Cousin, M. A., *J. Food Protect.*, 1982, **45**, 172.
8. Fairbairn, D. J. and Law, B. A., *J. Dairy Res.*, 1986, **53**, 139.
9. Noreau, J. and Drapeau, G. R., *J. Bacteriol.*, 1979, **140**, 911.
10. Matheson, A. R., *N.Z. J. Dairy Sci. Technol.*, 1981, **16**, 33.
11. O'Keeffe, R. B., Fox, P. F. and Daly, C., *J. Dairy Res.*, 1976, **43**, 97.
12. Desmazeaud, M. J. and Gripon, J.-C., *Milchwissenschaft*, 1977, **32**, 731.
13. Visser, F. M. W., *Neth. Milk Dairy J.*, 1977, **31**, 210.
14. Hill, R. D., Lehav, E. and Givol, D., *J. Dairy Res.*, 1974, **41**, 147.
15. Creamer, L. K. and Richardson, B. C., *N.Z. J. Dairy Sci. Technol.*, 1974, **9**, 9.
16. Pelissier, J.-P., *Science Aliment*, 1984, **4**, 1.
17. Mou, L., Sullivan, J. T. and Jago, G. R., *J. Dairy Res.*, 1975, **42**, 147.
18. Thomas, T. D., Jarvis, B. D. W. and Skipper, N. A., *J. Bacteriol.*, 1974, **118**, 329.
19. Exterkate, F. A., *Arch. Microbiol.*, 1979, **120**, 247.
20. Exterkate, F. A., *Neth. Milk Dairy J.*, 1976, **30**, 95.
21. Cliffe, A. J. and Law, B. A., *J. appl. Bacteriol.*, 1985, **58**, 245.
22. Law, B. A. and Kolstad, J., *Antonie van Leeuwenhoek J. Microbiol.*, 1983, **49**, 225.
23. Ohmiya, K. and Sato, Y., *Appl. Microbiol.*, 1975, **30**, 738.
24. Desmazeaud, M. J. and Zevaco, C., *Ann. Biol. Anim. Biochem. Biophys.*, 1976, **16**, 851.
25. Zevaco, C. and Desmazeaud, M. J., *J. Dairy Sci.*, 1980, **63**, 15.
26. Law, B. A., Sharpe, M. E. and Reiter, B., *J. Dairy Res.*, 1974, **41**, 137.
27. Cliffe, A. J. and Law, B. A., *J. appl. Bacteriol.*, 1979, **47**, 65.
28. Law, B. A., *J. gen. Microbiol.*, 1978, **105**, 113.

29. Law, B. A., *J. appl. Bacteriol.*, 1979, **46**, 455.
30. Exterkate, F. A., *Appl. Environ. Microbiol.*, 1984, **47**, 177.
31. Kolstad, J. and Law, B. A., *J. appl. Bacteriol.*, 1985, **58**, 449.
32. El-Soda, M., Desmazeaud, M. J. and Bergere, J.-L., *J. Dairy Res.*, 1978, **45**, 445.
33. El-Soda, M., Bergere, J.-L. and Desmazeaud, M. J., *J. Dairy Res.*, 1978, **45**, 519.
34. El-Soda, M. and Desmazeaud, M. J., *Can. J. Microbiol.*, 1982, **28**, 1181.
35. Langsrud, T.,|Reinbold, G. W. and Hammond, E. G., *J. Dairy Sci.*, 1977, **60**, 16.
36. Langsrud, T.,Reinbold, G. W. and Hammond, E. G., *J. Dairy Sci.*, 1978, **61**, 303.
37. Friedman, M. E., Nelson, W. O. and Wood, W. A., *J. Dairy Sci.*, 1953, **36**, 1124.
38. Torgensen, H. and Sorhaug, T., *FEMS Microbiol. Lett.*, 1978, **4**, 151.
39. Sorhaug, T., *Milchwissenschaft*, 1981, **36**, 137.
40. Foissy, H., *J. gen. Microbiol.*, 1974, **80**, 197.
41. Foissy, H., *Milchwissenschaft*, 1978, **33**, 221.
42. Gripon, J.-C. and Debest, B., *Le Lait*, 1976, **56**, 423.
43. Law, B. A. In: *Advances in the Microbiology and Biochemistry of Cheese and Fermented Milk*, F. L. Davies and B. A. Law (eds), 1984, Elsevier Applied Science Publishers, London, p. 187.
44. Rank, T. C., Grappin, R. and Olson, N. F., *J. Dairy Sci.*, 1985, **68**, 801.
45. Reville, W. J. and Fox, P. F., *Ir. J. Food Sci. Technol.*, 1978, **2**, 67.
46. Kuchroo, C. N. and Fox, P. F., *Milchwissenschaft*, 1982, **37**, 331.
47. Kuchroo, C. N. and Fox, P. F., *Milchwissenschaft*, 1982, **37**, 561.
48. Kuchroo, C. N. and Fox, P. F., *Milchwissenschaft*, 1983, **38**, 76.
49. Law, B. A. and Wigmore, A. S., *J. Dairy Res.*, 1983, **50**, 519.
50. Aston, J. W., Durwood, I. G. and Dulley, J. R., *Aust. J. Dairy Technol.*, 1983, **38**, 55.
51. Law, B. A. and Wigmore, A. S., *J. Dairy Res.*, 1982, **49**, 137.
52. Law, B. A. and Wigmore, A. S., *J. Soc. Dairy Technol.*, 1982, **35**, 75.
53. Vakaleris, D. G. and Price, W. V., *J. Dairy Sci.*, 1959, **42**, 264.
54. Hull, M. E., *J. Dairy Sci.*, 1947, **30**, 881.
55. Dulley, J. R., *Aust. J. Dairy Technol.*, 1976, **31**, 143.
56. Church, F. C., Catignani, G. L. and Swaisgood, H. E., *J. Dairy Sci.*, 1981, **64**, 724.
57. Church, F. C., Swaisgood, H. E., Porter, D. H. and Catignani, G. L., *J. Dairy Sci.*, 1983, **66**, 1219.
58. Champion, H. M. and Stanley, D. W., *Can. Inst. Food Sci. Technol. J.*, 1982, **15**, 283.
59. Noomen, A., *Neth. Milk Dairy J.*, 1983, **37**, 229.
60. Noomen, A., *Neth. Milk Dairy J.*, 1977, **31**, 75.
61. Noomen, A., *Neth. Milk Dairy J.*, 1978, **32**, 49.
62. De Jong, L., *Neth. Milk Dairy J.*, 1976, **30**, 242.
63. Trieu-Cuot, P., Archieri-Haze, M.-J. and Gripon, J.-C., *J. Dairy Res.*, 1982, **49**, 487.
64. Trieu-Cuot, P., Archieri-Haze, M.-J. and Gripon, J.-C., *Le Lait*, 1982, **62**, 234.

65. Lenoir, J. and Auberger, B., *Proc. XXI Int. Dairy Congr.*, *Moscow*, 1982, Vol. 1, Book 1, p. 336.
66. Schmidt, J. L., *Proc. XXI Int. Dairy Congr.*, *Moscow*, 1982, Vol. 1, Book 1, 1982, p. 365.
67. Le Bars, D. and Gripon, J.-C., *J. Dairy Res.*, 1981, **48**, 479.
68. Hewedi, M. M. and Fox, P. F., *Milchwissenschaft*, 1984, **39**, 198.
69. Gripon, J.-C., Desmazeaud, M. J., Le Bars, D. and Bergere, J.-L., *J. Dairy Sci.*, 1977, **60**, 1532.
70. Godinho, M. and Fox, P. F., *Milchwissenschaft*, 1981, **36**, 205.
71. Godinho, M. and Fox, P. F., *Milchwissenschaft*, 1981, **36**, 329.
72. Creamer, L. K. and Olson, N. F., *J. Food Sci.*, 1982, **47**, 631.
73. McGugan, W. A., Emmons, D. B. and Larmond, E., *J. Dairy Sci.*, 1979, **62**, 398.
74. Biede, S. L., *Diss. Abstr.*, 1978, **38**, 3110-B.
75. Fujimaki, M. S., Arai, S. and Yamashita, M., *Proc. Int. Symp. Conversion & Manufacturing of Foodstuffs by Microorganisms, Kyoto*, 1971, Saikon Publishing Co., Tokyo, p. 19.
76. Reiter, B., Fryer, T. F., Pickering, A., Chapman, H. R., Lawrence, R. C. and Sharpe, M. E., *J. Dairy Res.*, 1967, **34**, 257.
77. Law, B. A., Castanon, M. J. and Sharpe, M. E., *J. Dairy Res.*, 1976, **43**, 117.
78. Reiter, B., Sorokin, Y., Pickering, A. and Hall, A. J., *J. Dairy Res.*, 1969, **36**, 65.
79. Langler, J. E., Lisbey, L. M. and Day, E. A., *J. Agric. Food Chem.*, 1967, **15**, 386.
80. Biede, S. L. and Hammond, E. G., *J. Dairy Sci.*, 1979, **62**, 227.
81. Biede, S. L. and Hammond, E. G., *J. Dairy Sci.*, 1979, **62**, 238.
82. Ney, K. H., *Z. Lebensm. Unters. Forsch.*, 1971, **147**, 64.
83. Ney, K. H., *Z. Lebensm. Unters. Forsch.*, 1972, **149**, 321.
84. Matoba, T. and Hata, T., *Agric. Biol. Chem.*, 1972, **36**, 1423.
85. Guigoz, Y. and Solms, J., *Chem. Senses Flavor*, 1976, **2**, 71.
86. Hodges, R., Kent, S. B. H. and Richardson, B. C., *Biochim. Biophys. Acta*, 1972, **257**, 54.
87. Richardson, B. C. and Creamer, L. K., *N.Z. J. Dairy Sci. Technol.*, 1973, **8**, 46.
88. Hamilton, J. S., Hill, R. D. and van Leeuwen, H., *Agric. Biol. Chem.*, 1974, **38**, 375.
89. Visser, S., Slangen, K. J., Hup, G. and Stadhouders, J., *Neth. Milk Dairy J.*, 1983, **37**, 181.
90. Stadhouders, J. and Hup, G., *Neth. Milk Dairy J.*, 1975, **29**, 335.
91. Stadhouders, J., Hup, G. and van der Waals, C. B., *Neth. Milk Dairy J.*, 1977, **31**, 3.
92. Stadhouders, J., Hup, G., Exterkate, F. A. and Visser, S., *Neth. Milk Dairy J.*, 1983, **37**, 157.
93. Lowrie, R. J., Lawrence, R. C. and Beberdy, H. F., *N.Z. J. Dairy Sci. Technol.*, 1974, **9**, 116.
94. Mills, O. E. and Thomas, T. D., *N.Z. J. Dairy Sci. Technol.*, 1980, **15**, 131.
95. Sullivan, J. J., Mou, L., Rood, J. I. and Jago, G. R., *Aust. J. Dairy Tech.*, 1973, **28**, 20.

96. Visser, S., Hup, G., Exterkate, F. A. and Stadhouders, J., *Neth. Milk Dairy J.*, 1983, **37**, 169.
97. Mourgues, R., Bergere, J. L. and Vassal, L., *Tech. Lait.*, B, 1983, **978**, 11.
98. Vassal, L. and Gripon, J. C., *Le Lait*, 1984, **64**, 397.
99. Hemme, D., Bouillanne, C., Metro, I. and Desmazeaud, M. J., *Sciences Aliment*, 1982, **2**, 113.
100. Lee, C. W. and Richard, J., *J. Dairy Res.*, 1984, **51**, 461.
101. Smith, T. A., *Food Chem.*, 1981, **6**, 169.
102. Tsugo, T. and Matsuoko, H. *Proc. XVI Int. Dairy Congr.*, Copenhagen, 1962, Vol. B, p. 385.
103. Law, B. A. and Sharpe, M. E., *Dairy Ind. Inter.*, 1977, **42**(12), 10.
104. Sharpe, M. E., Law, B. A., Phillips, B. A. and Pitcher, D. G., *J. gen. Microbiol.*, 1977, **101**, 345.
105. Bosch, S., van den Land, E. V. and Stoffelsma, J., *U.S. Patent*, 1982, **4**, 332, 829.
106. Cuer, A., Dauphin, G., Kergomard, A., Dumont, J.-P. and Adda, J., *Agric. Biol. Chem.*, 1979, **43**, 1783.
107. Dumont, J.-P., Pradel, G., Roger, S. and Adda, J., *Le Lait*, 1976, **56**, 18.
108. Manning, D. J. and Robinson, H. M., *J. Dairy Res.*, 1973, **40**, 63.
109. Manning, D. J. and Price, J. C., *J. Dairy Res.*, 1977, **44**, 357.
110. Manning, D. J., Chapman, H. R. and Hosking, Z. D., *J. Dairy Res.*, 1976, **43**, 313.
111. Lamparsky, D. and Klimes, I. *Proc. Weurman. Symp.*, 1981, Vol. 3, P. Schreiar (ed.), Walter de Gruyter & Co., Berlin, p. 557.
112. Aston, J. W. and Douglas, K., *Aust. J. Dairy Technol.*, 1983, **38**, 66.
113. Law, B. A. and Sharpe, M. E., *J. Dairy Res.*, 1978, **45**, 267.
114. Manning, D. J., *J. Dairy Res.*, 1979, **46**, 523.
115. Law, B. A. In: *Advances in the Microbiology and Biochemistry of Cheese and Fermented Milk*, F. L. Davies and B. A. Law (eds), 1984, Elsevier Applied Science Publishers, London, p. 209.
116. Kosikowski, F. V. and Iwasaki, T., *J. Dairy Sci.*, 1975, **58**, 963.
117. Sood, V. K. and Kosikowski, F. V., *J. Dairy Sci.*, 1979, **62**, 1865.
118. Sood, V. K. and Kosikowski, F. V., *J. Food Sci.*, 1979, **44**, 1690.
119. Kristoffersen, T., Mikolajcik, E. M. and Gould, I. A., *J. Dairy Sci.*, 1967, **50**, 292.
120. Ridha, S. H., Crawford, R. J. M. and Tamime, A. Y., *Egypt J. Dairy Sci.*, 1984, **12**, 63.
121. Kalinowski, L., Frackiewicz, E., Janiszewska, L., Pawlik, A. and Kikolska, D., *U.S. Patent*, 1979, **4**, 158, 607.
122. Kalinowski, L., Frackiewicz, E. and Janiszewska, L. *Proc. XXI Int. Dairy Congr.*, Moscow, 1982, Vol. 1, Book 1, p. 500.
123. El-Soda, M., Desmazeaud, M. J., Aboudonia, S. and Kamal, N., *Milchwissenschaft*, 1981, **36**, 140.
124. El-Sida, M., Desmazeaud, M. J., Aboudonia, S. and Badran, A., *Milchwissenschaft*, 1982, **37**, 325.
125. Law, B. A. and King, J. S., *J. Dairy Res.*, 1985, **52**, 183.
126. Magee, E. L. and Olson, N. F., *J. Dairy Sci.*, 1981, **64**, 600.
127. Magee, E. L. and Olson, N. F., *J. Dairy Sci.*, 1981, **64**, 616.

128. Braun, S. D. and Olson, N. F., *J. Dairy Sci.*, 1983, **66** (Suppl. 1), 77.
129. Braun, S. D., Olson, N. F. and Lindsay, R. C., *J. Food Sci.*, 1982, **47**, 1803.
130. Rippe, J. K., Lindsay, R. C. and Olson, N. F., *J. Dairy Sci.*, 1983, **66** (Suppl. 1), 77.
131. Bangham, A. D., Standish, M. M. and Watkins, J. C., *J. Molec. Biol.*, 1965, **13**, 238.
132. Kirby, C. J. and Gregoriadis, G., *J. Microencapsulation*, 1984, **1**, 33.

Index

400 *Index*